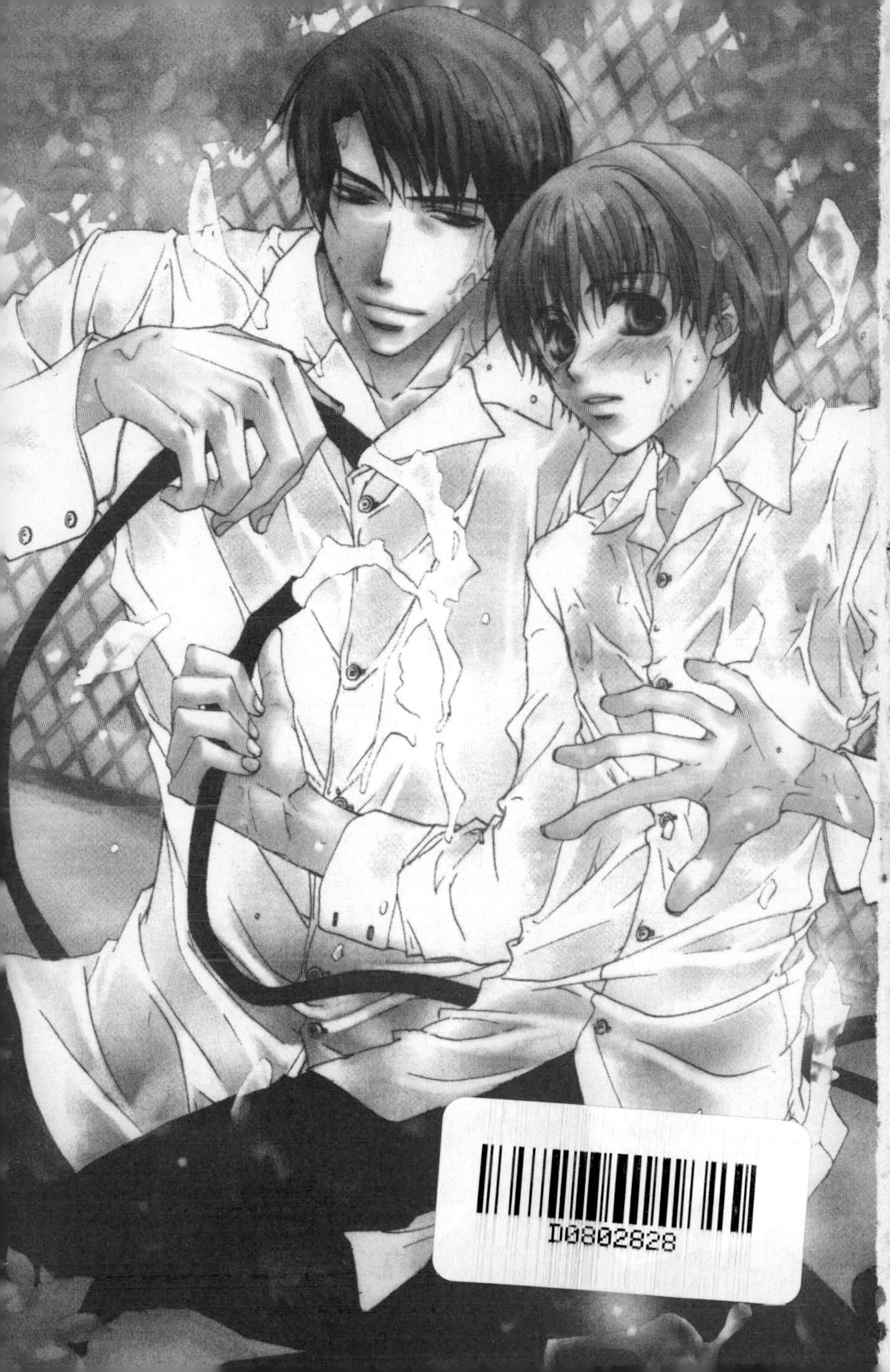

CONTENTS

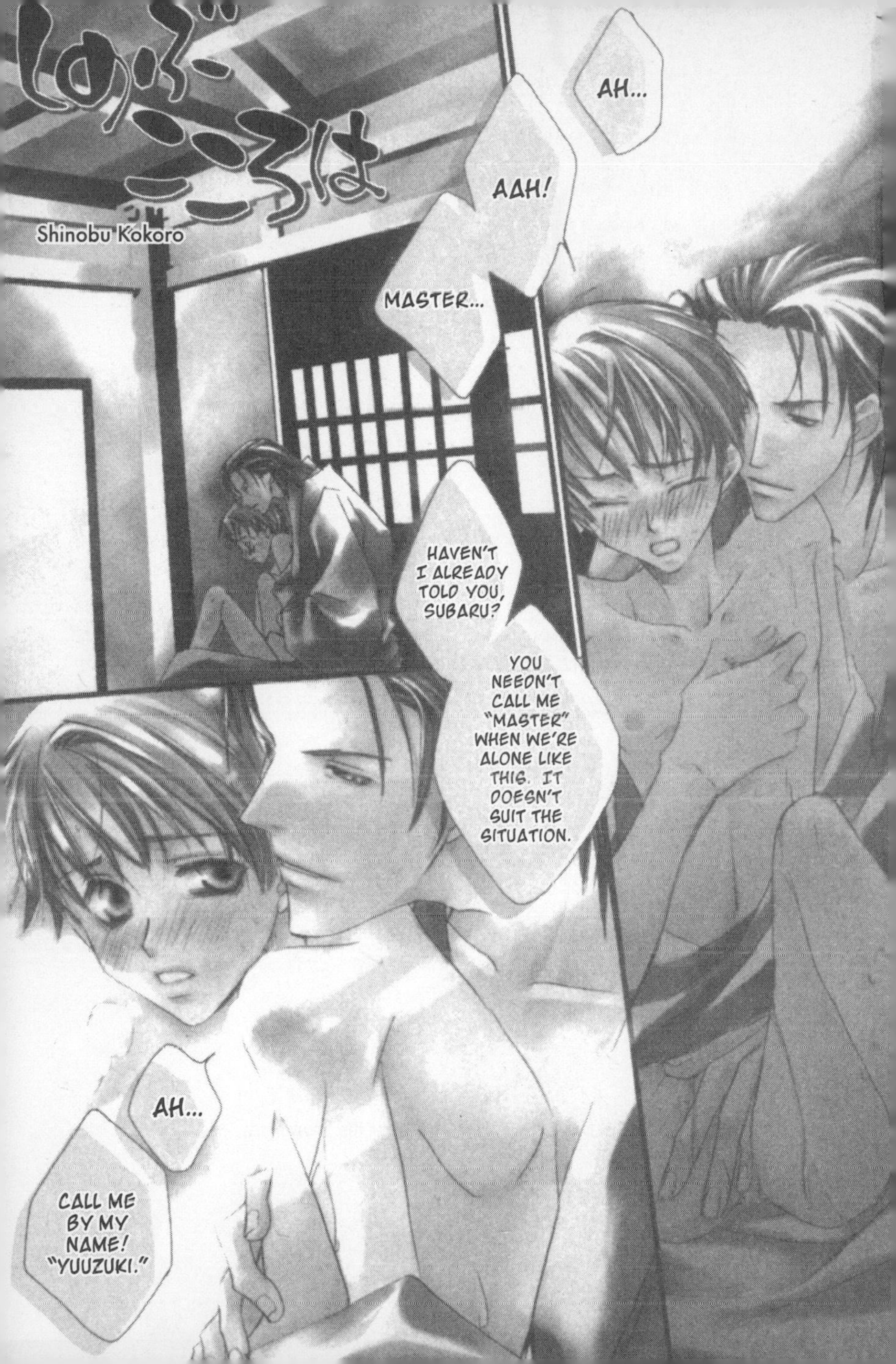

AH...
AAH!
MASTER...
Shinobu Kokoro
HAVEN'T I ALREADY TOLD YOU, SUBARU?
YOU NEEDN'T CALL ME "MASTER" WHEN WE'RE ALONE LIKE THIS. IT DOESN'T SUIT THE SITUATION.
AH...
CALL ME BY MY NAME! "YUUZUKI."

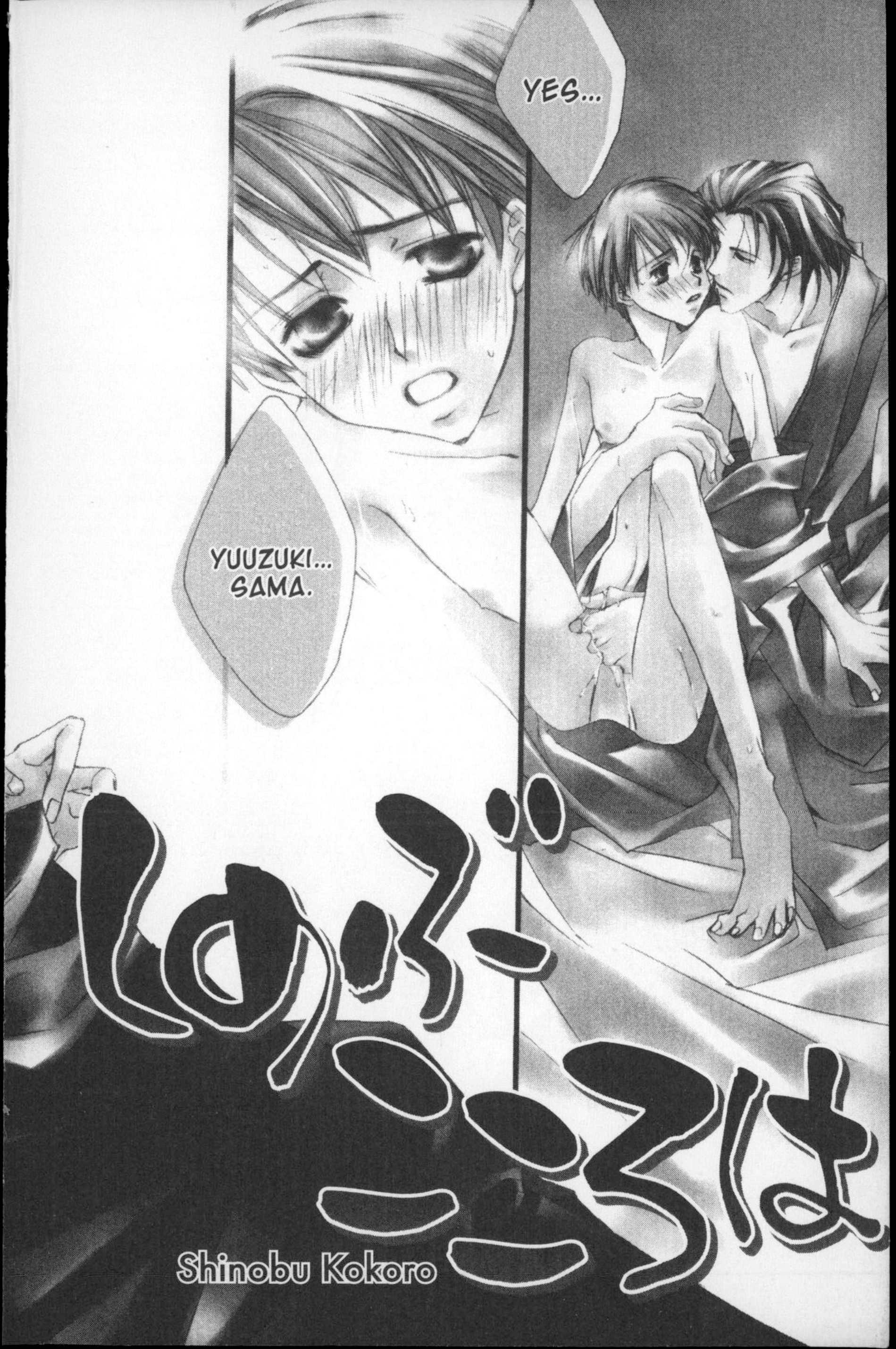
YES...
YUUZUKI... SAMA.
しのぶこころは
Shinobu Kokoro

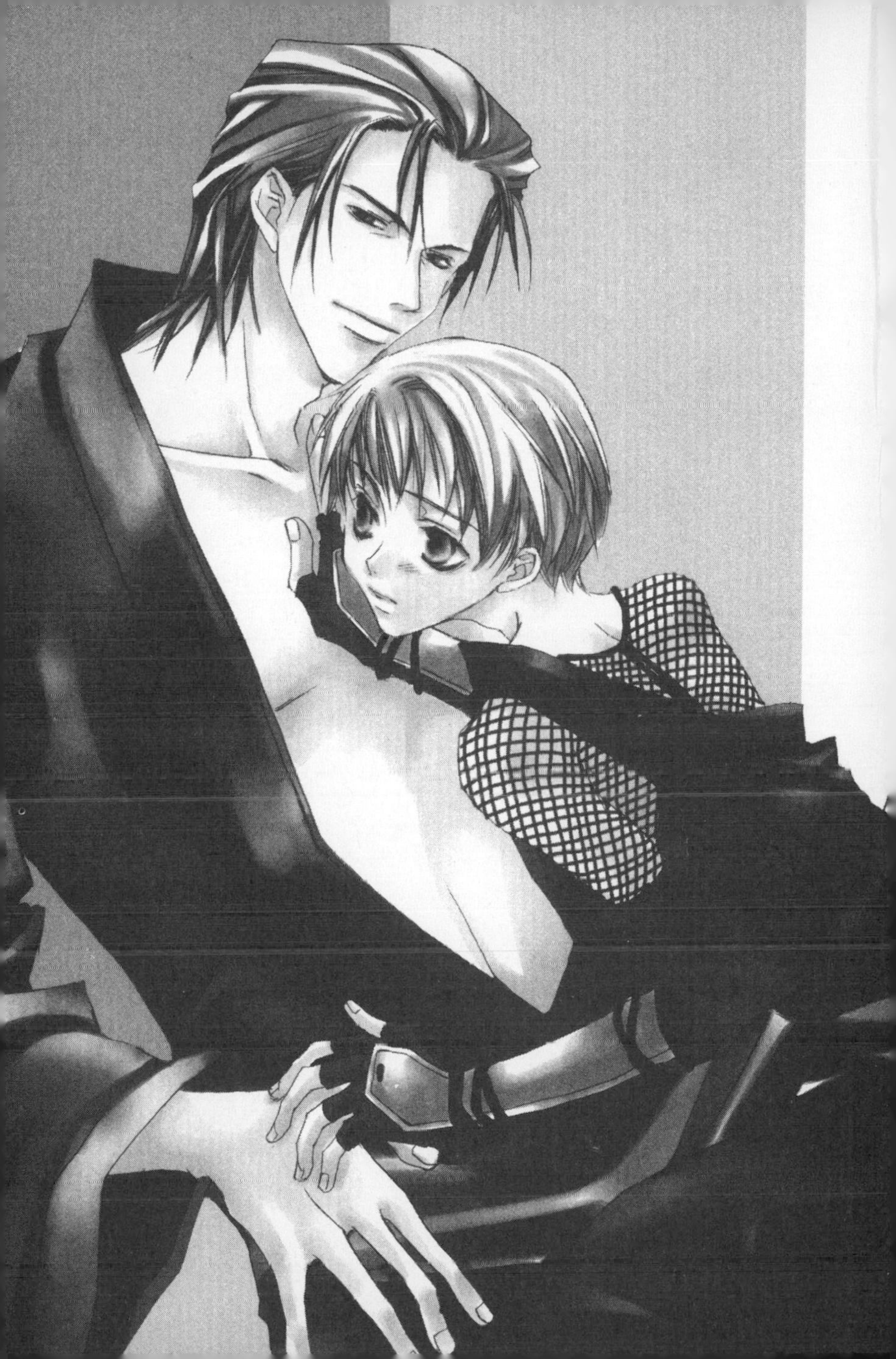

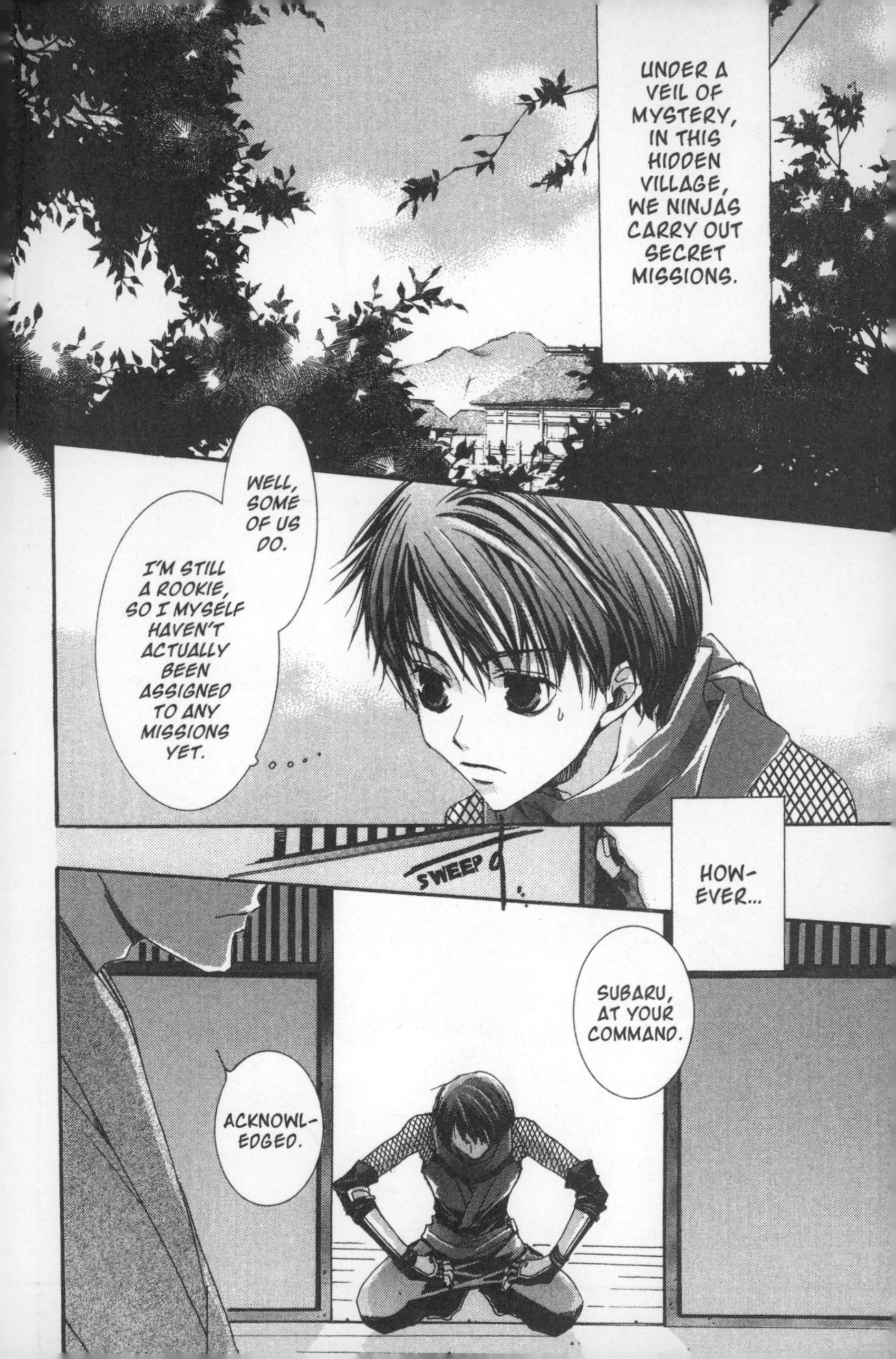
UNDER A VEIL OF MYSTERY, IN THIS HIDDEN VILLAGE, WE NINJAS CARRY OUT SECRET MISSIONS.
WELL, SOME OF US DO.
I'M STILL A ROOKIE, SO I MYSELF HAVEN'T ACTUALLY BEEN ASSIGNED TO ANY MISSIONS YET.
SWEEP
HOW-EVER...
SUBARU, AT YOUR COMMAND.
ACKNOWL-EDGED.

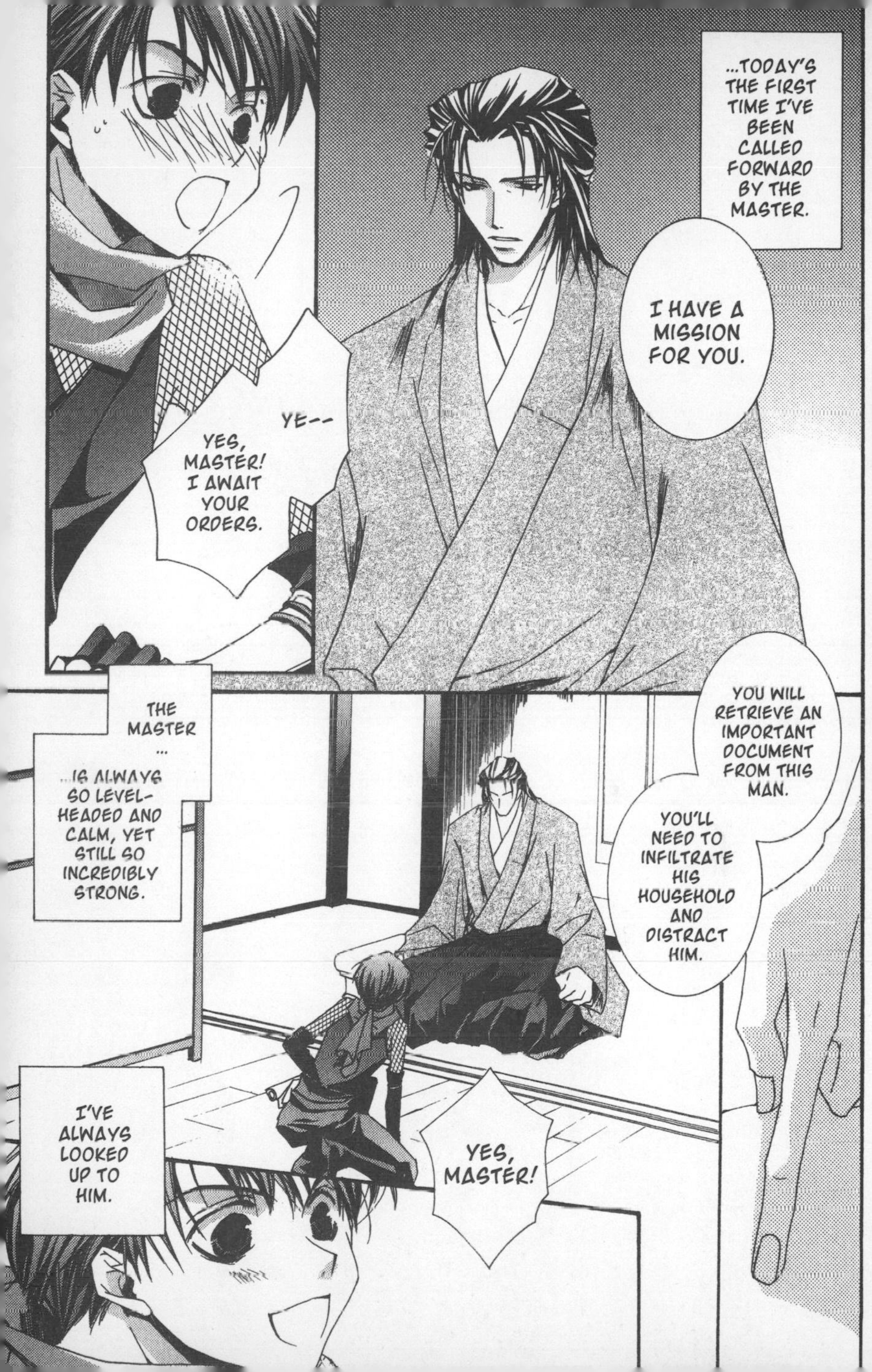
...TODAY'S THE FIRST TIME I'VE BEEN CALLED FORWARD BY THE MASTER.
I HAVE A MISSION FOR YOU.
YE--
YES, MASTER! I AWAIT YOUR ORDERS.
YOU WILL RETRIEVE AN IMPORTANT DOCUMENT FROM THIS MAN.
YOU'LL NEED TO INFILTRATE HIS HOUSEHOLD AND DISTRACT HIM.
THE MASTER ...
...IS ALWAYS SO LEVEL-HEADED AND CALM, YET STILL SO INCREDIBLY STRONG.
YES, MASTER!
I'VE ALWAYS LOOKED UP TO HIM.

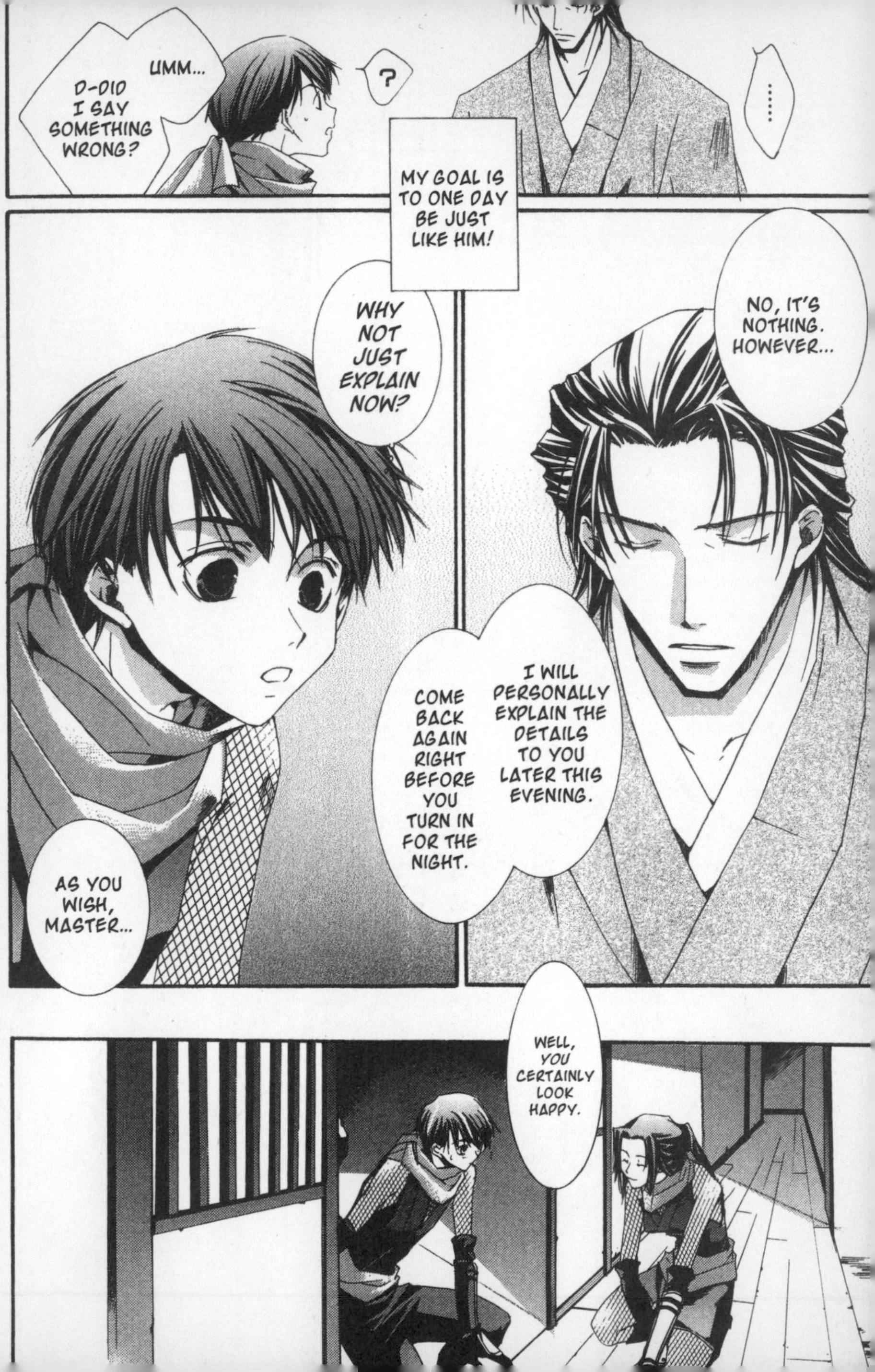
......
?
UMM... D-DID I SAY SOMETHING WRONG?
MY GOAL IS TO ONE DAY BE JUST LIKE HIM!
NO, IT'S NOTHING. HOWEVER...
I WILL PERSONALLY EXPLAIN THE DETAILS TO YOU LATER THIS EVENING.
COME BACK AGAIN RIGHT BEFORE YOU TURN IN FOR THE NIGHT.
WHY NOT JUST EXPLAIN NOW?
AS YOU WISH, MASTER...
WELL, YOU CERTAINLY LOOK HAPPY.

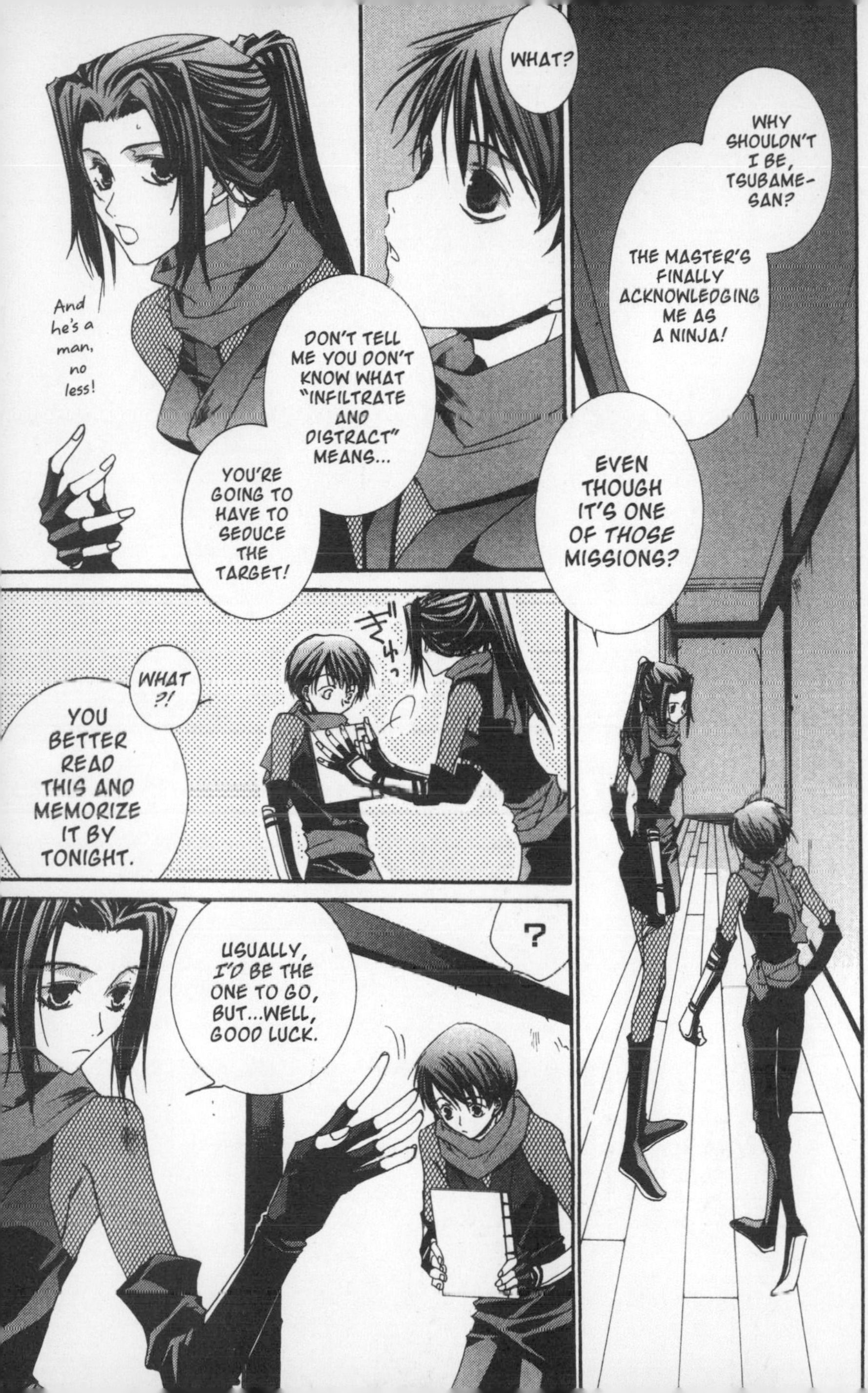
WHY SHOULDN'T I BE, TSUBAME-SAN?
THE MASTER'S FINALLY ACKNOWLEDGING ME AS A NINJA!
EVEN THOUGH IT'S ONE OF THOSE MISSIONS?
WHAT?
DON'T TELL ME YOU DON'T KNOW WHAT "INFILTRATE AND DISTRACT" MEANS...
YOU'RE GOING TO HAVE TO SEDUCE THE TARGET!
And he's a man, no less!
WHAT?!
YOU BETTER READ THIS AND MEMORIZE IT BY TONIGHT.
?
USUALLY, I'D BE THE ONE TO GO, BUT...WELL, GOOD LUCK.

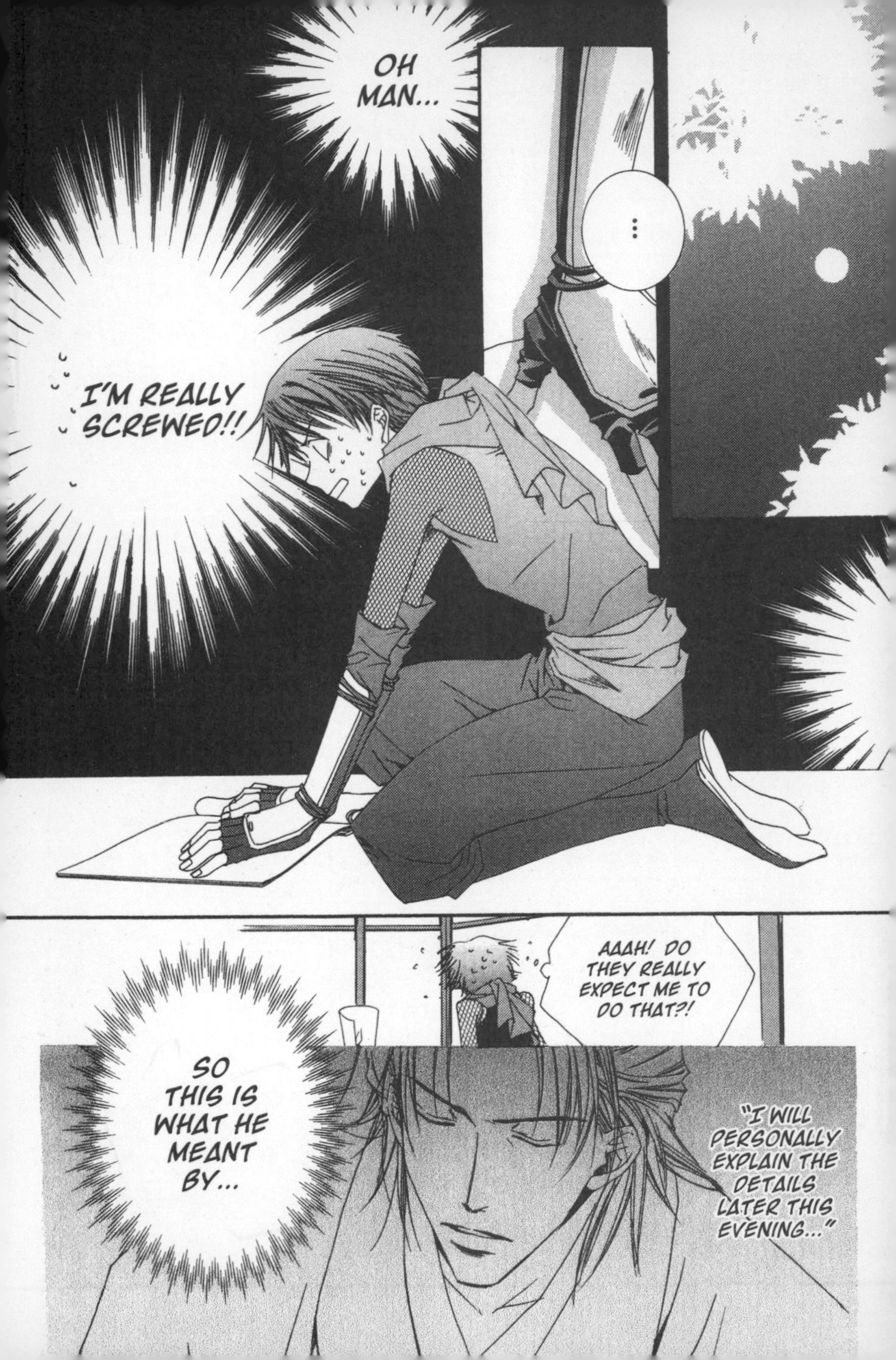
...
OH MAN...
I'M REALLY SCREWED!!
AAAH! DO THEY REALLY EXPECT ME TO DO THAT?!
SO THIS IS WHAT HE MEANT BY...
"I WILL PERSONALLY EXPLAIN THE DETAILS LATER THIS EVENING..."

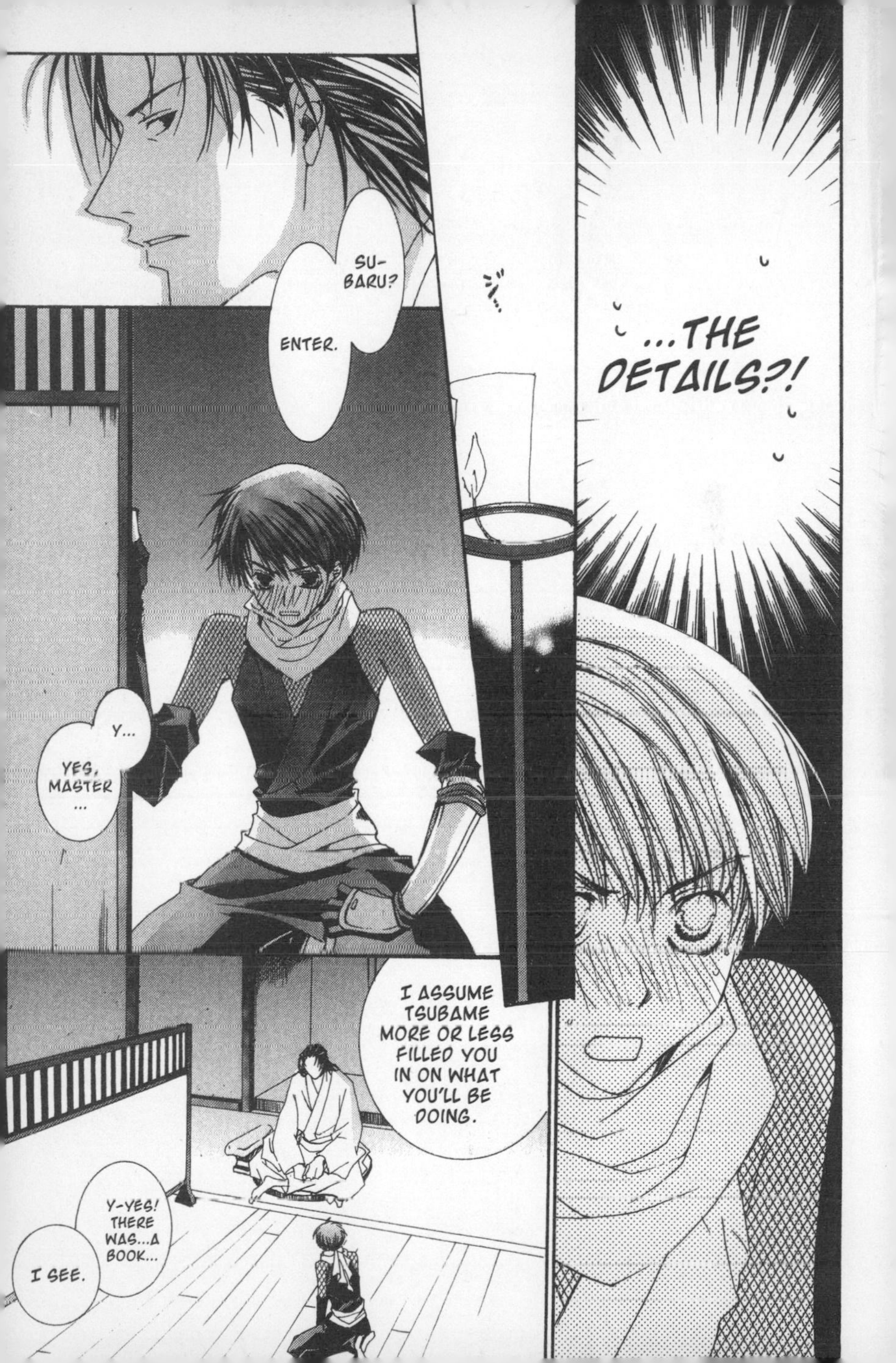
...THE DETAILS?!
SU-BARU?
ENTER.
Y...
YES, MASTER ...
I ASSUME TSUBAME MORE OR LESS FILLED YOU IN ON WHAT YOU'LL BE DOING.
Y-YES! THERE WAS...A BOOK...
I SEE.

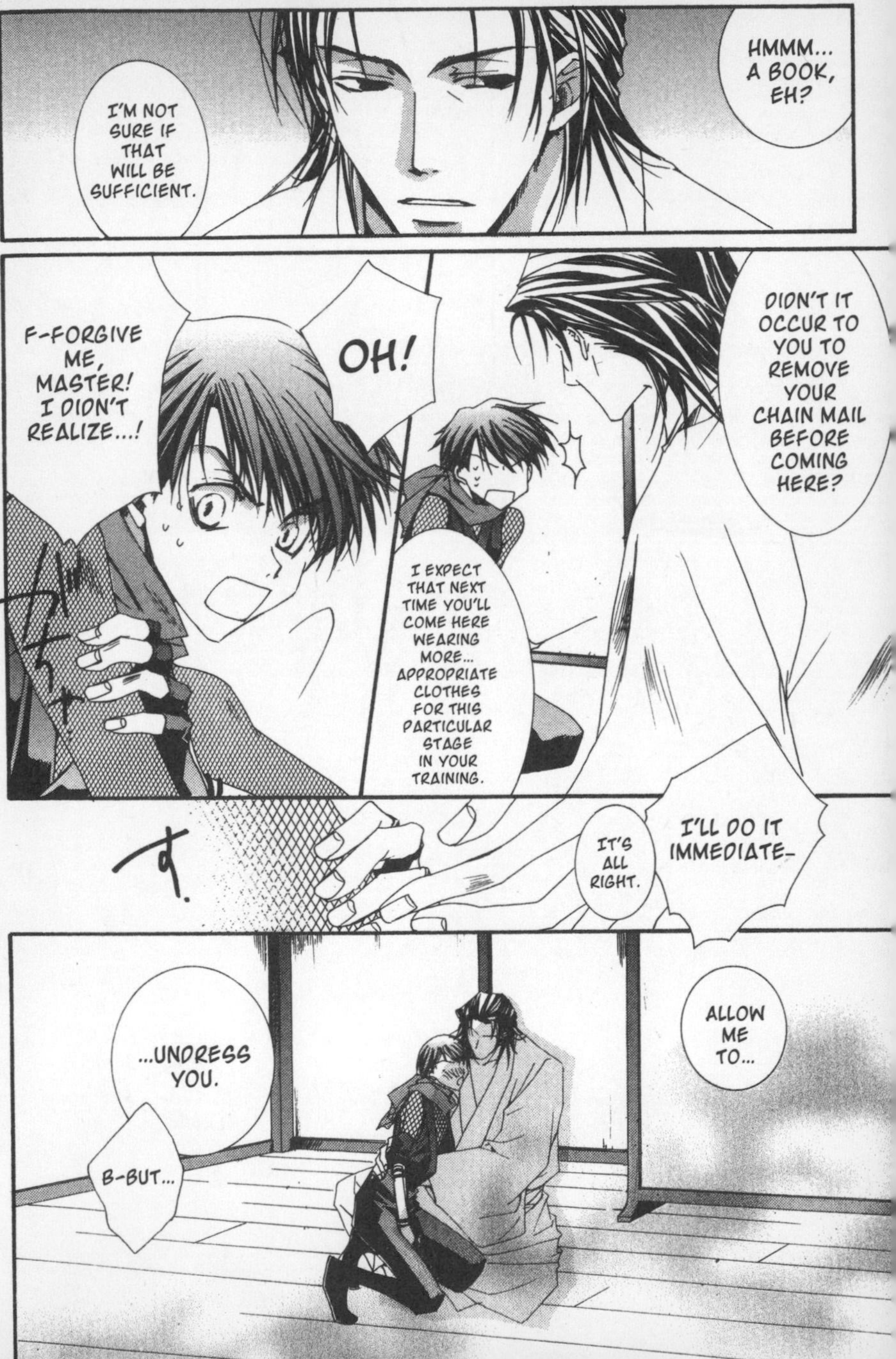
HMMM... A BOOK, EH?
I'M NOT SURE IF THAT WILL BE SUFFICIENT.
DIDN'T IT OCCUR TO YOU TO REMOVE YOUR CHAIN MAIL BEFORE COMING HERE?
I EXPECT THAT NEXT TIME YOU'LL COME HERE WEARING MORE... APPROPRIATE CLOTHES FOR THIS PARTICULAR STAGE IN YOUR TRAINING.
OH!
F-FORGIVE ME, MASTER! I DIDN'T REALIZE...!
I'LL DO IT IMMEDIATE-
IT'S ALL RIGHT.
す
ALLOW ME TO...
...UNDRESS YOU.
B-BUT...

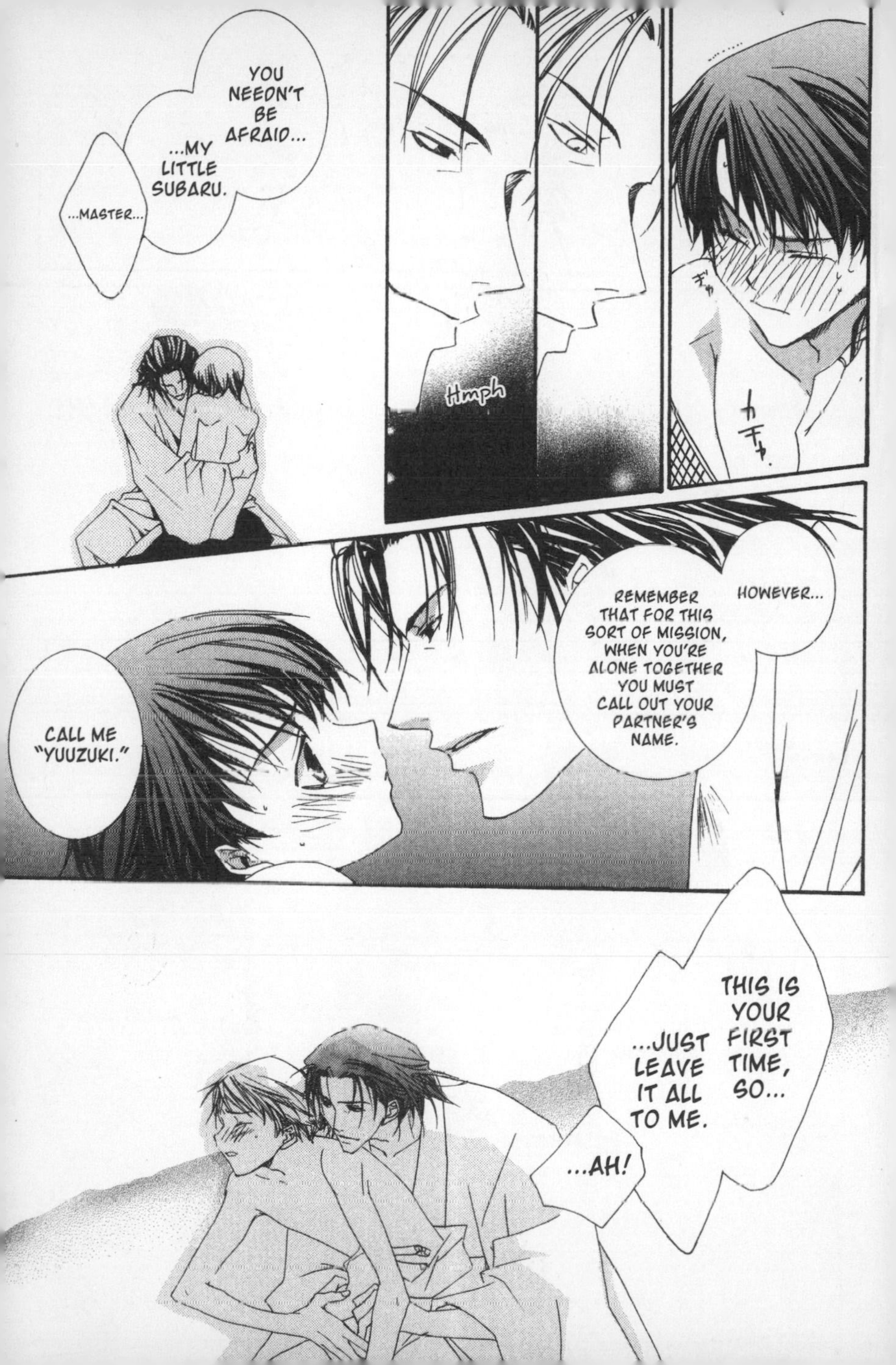
Hmph
YOU NEEDN'T BE AFRAID...
...MY LITTLE SUBARU.
...MASTER...
HOWEVER...
REMEMBER THAT FOR THIS SORT OF MISSION, WHEN YOU'RE ALONE TOGETHER YOU MUST CALL OUT YOUR PARTNER'S NAME.
CALL ME "YUUZUKI."
THIS IS YOUR FIRST TIME, SO...
...JUST LEAVE IT ALL TO ME.
...AH!

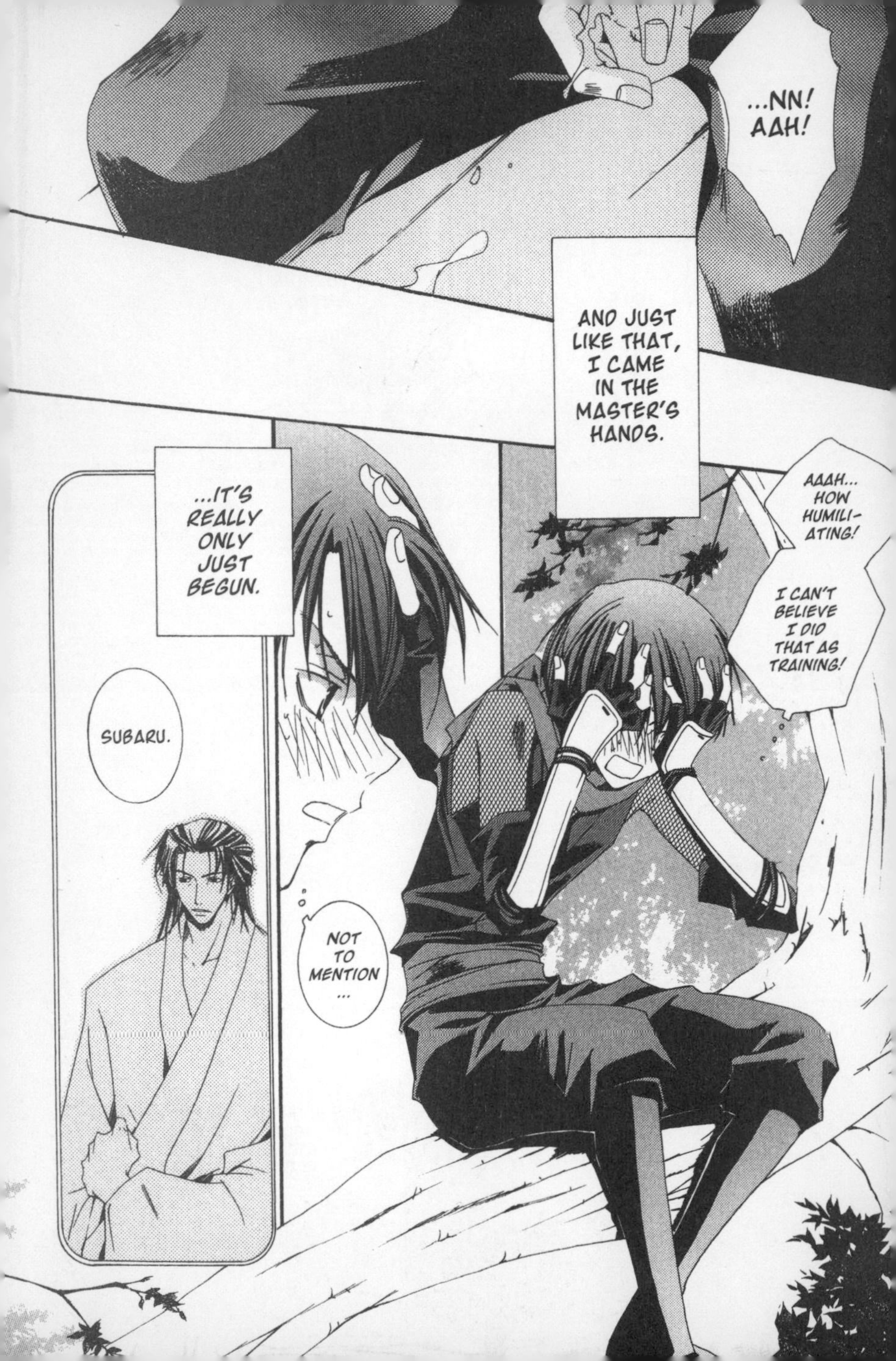

...NN! AAH!
AND JUST LIKE THAT, I CAME IN THE MASTER'S HANDS.
AAAH... HOW HUMILI-ATING!
I CAN'T BELIEVE I DID THAT AS TRAINING!
NOT TO MENTION ...
...IT'S REALLY ONLY JUST BEGUN.
SUBARU.

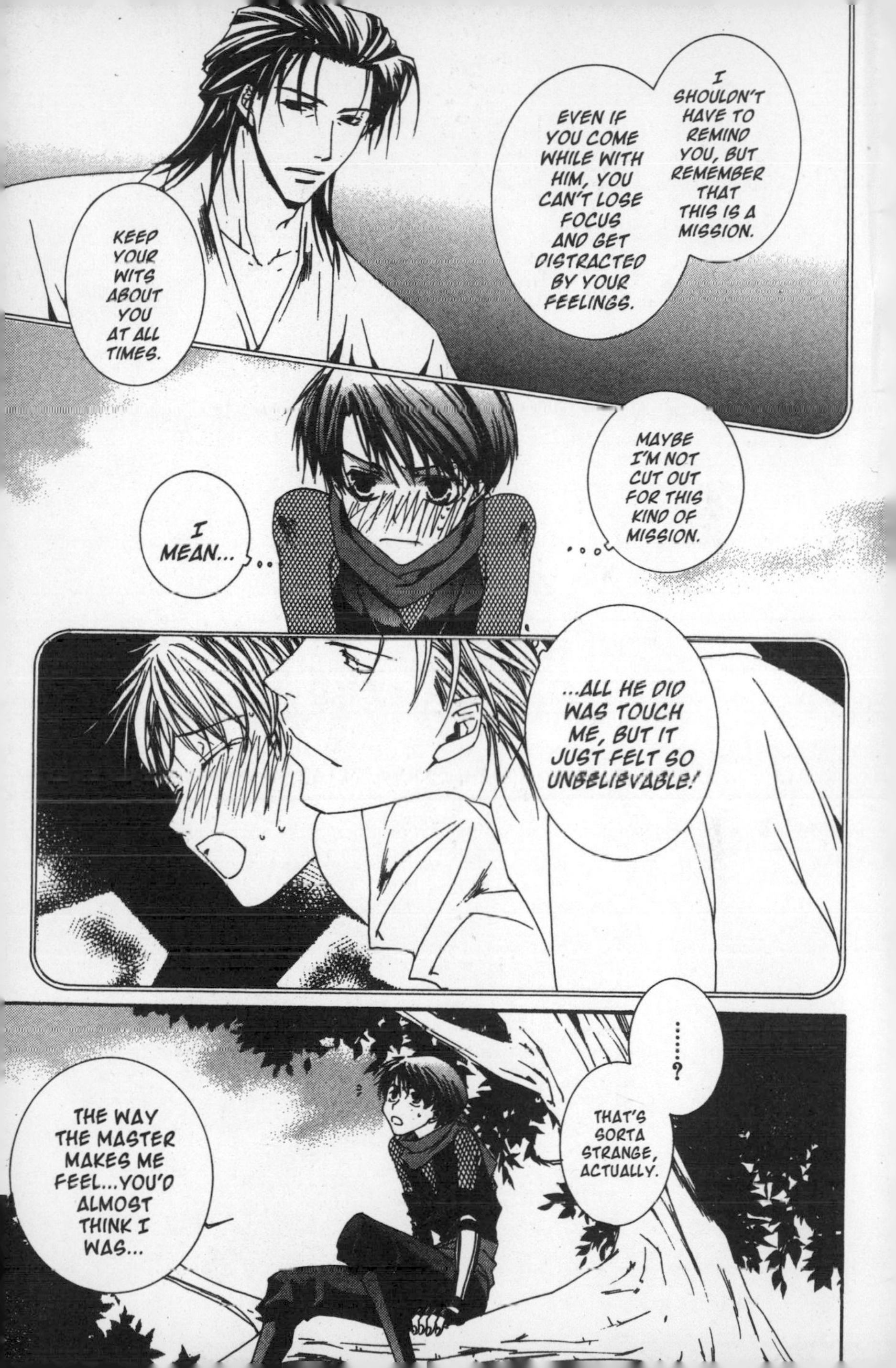

I SHOULDN'T HAVE TO REMIND YOU, BUT REMEMBER THAT THIS IS A MISSION.
EVEN IF YOU COME WHILE WITH HIM, YOU CAN'T LOSE FOCUS AND GET DISTRACTED BY YOUR FEELINGS.
KEEP YOUR WITS ABOUT YOU AT ALL TIMES.
MAYBE I'M NOT CUT OUT FOR THIS KIND OF MISSION.
I MEAN...
...ALL HE DID WAS TOUCH ME, BUT IT JUST FELT SO UNBELIVABLE!
......?
THAT'S SORTA STRANGE, ACTUALLY.
THE WAY THE MASTER MAKES ME FEEL...YOU'D ALMOST THINK I WAS...

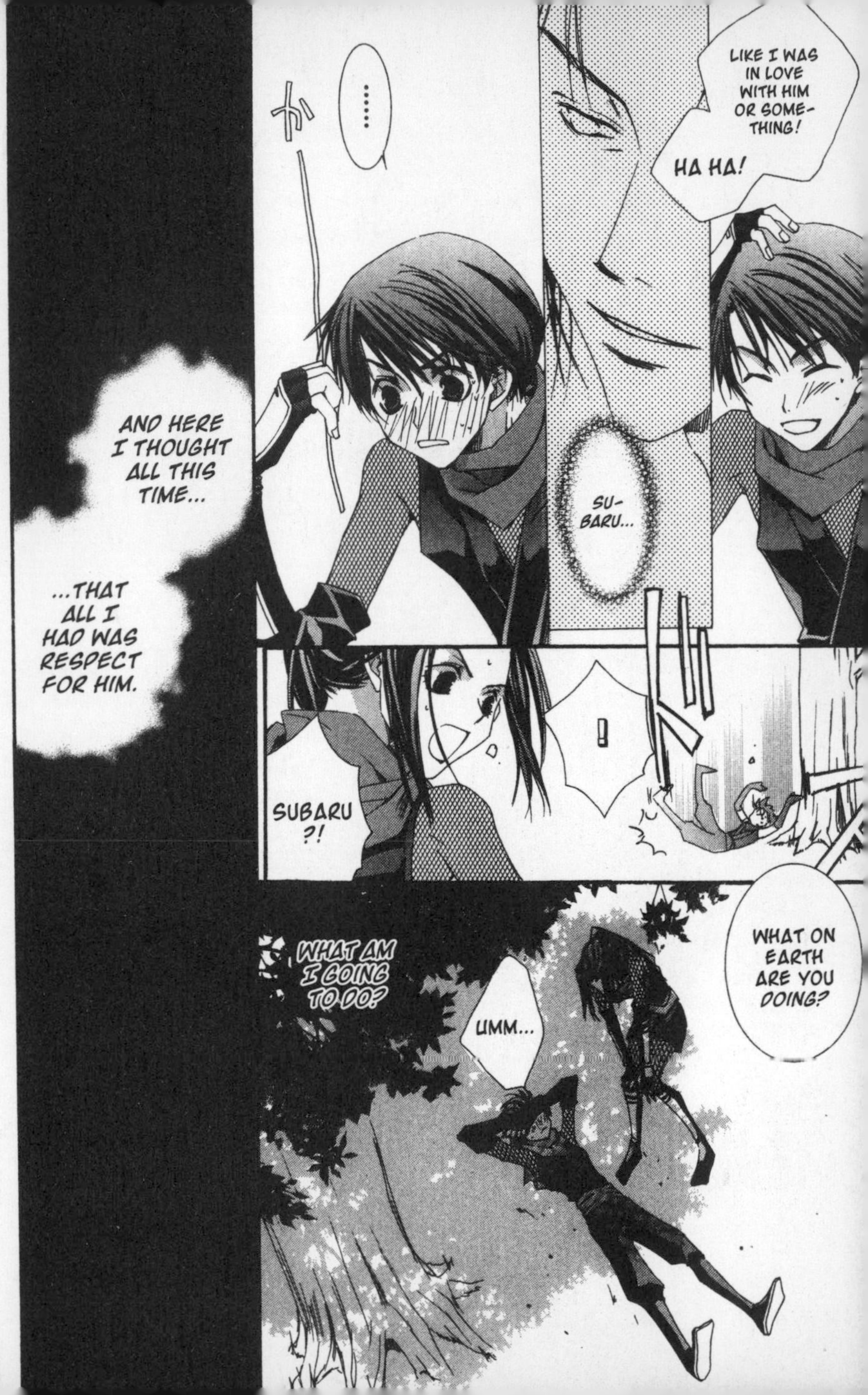
LIKE I WAS IN LOVE WITH HIM OR SOMETHING!
HA HA!
SU-BARU...
......
か
!
SUBARU ?!
WHAT ON EARTH ARE YOU DOING?
UMM...
WHAT AM I GOING TO DO?
AND HERE I THOUGHT ALL THIS TIME...
...THAT ALL I HAD WAS RESPECT FOR HIM.

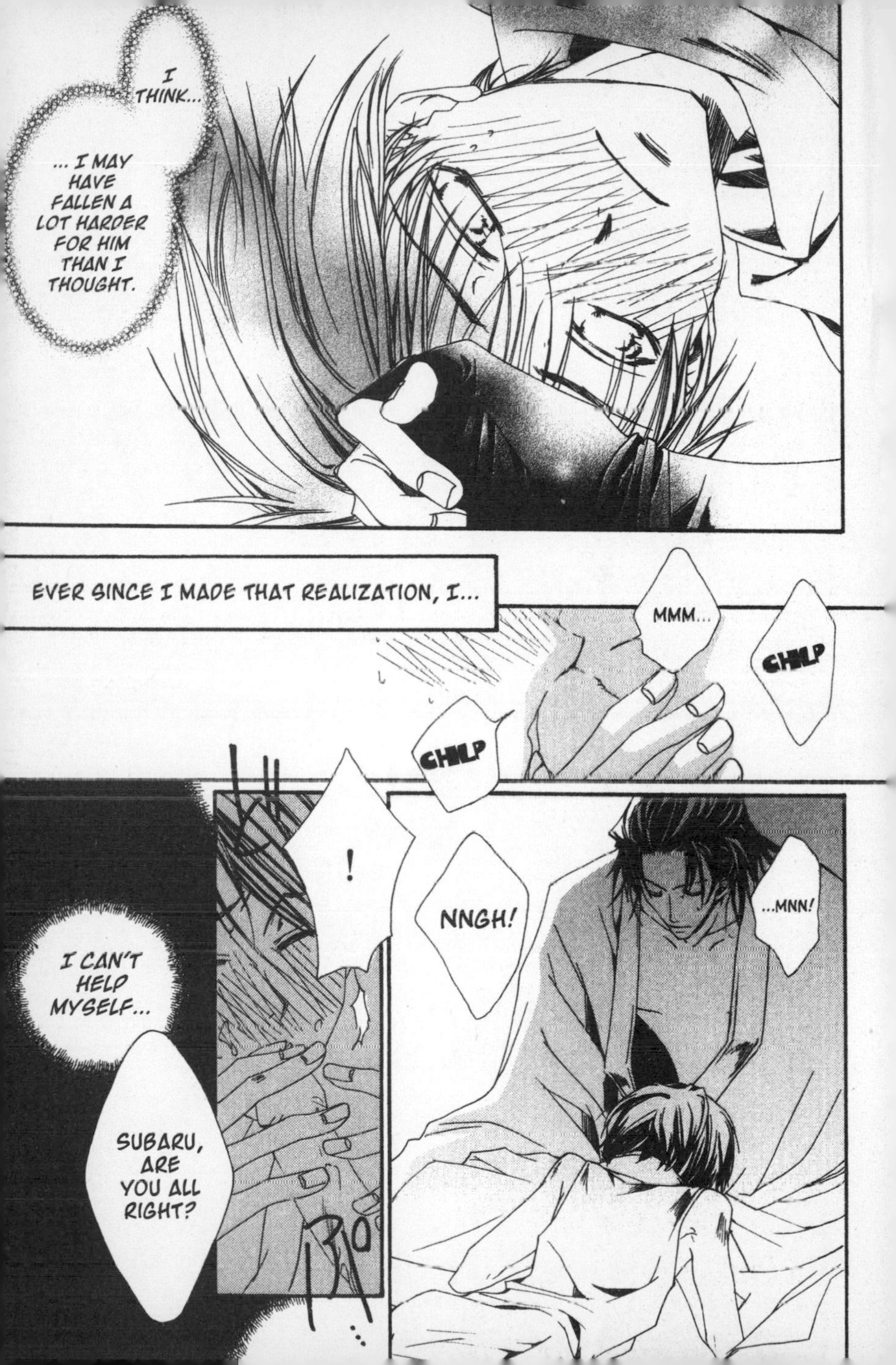
I THINK...
... I MAY HAVE FALLEN A LOT HARDER FOR HIM THAN I THOUGHT.
MMM...
CHILP
EVER SINCE I MADE THAT REALIZATION, I...
CHILP
...MNN!
NNGH!
!
I CAN'T HELP MYSELF...
SUBARU, ARE YOU ALL RIGHT?

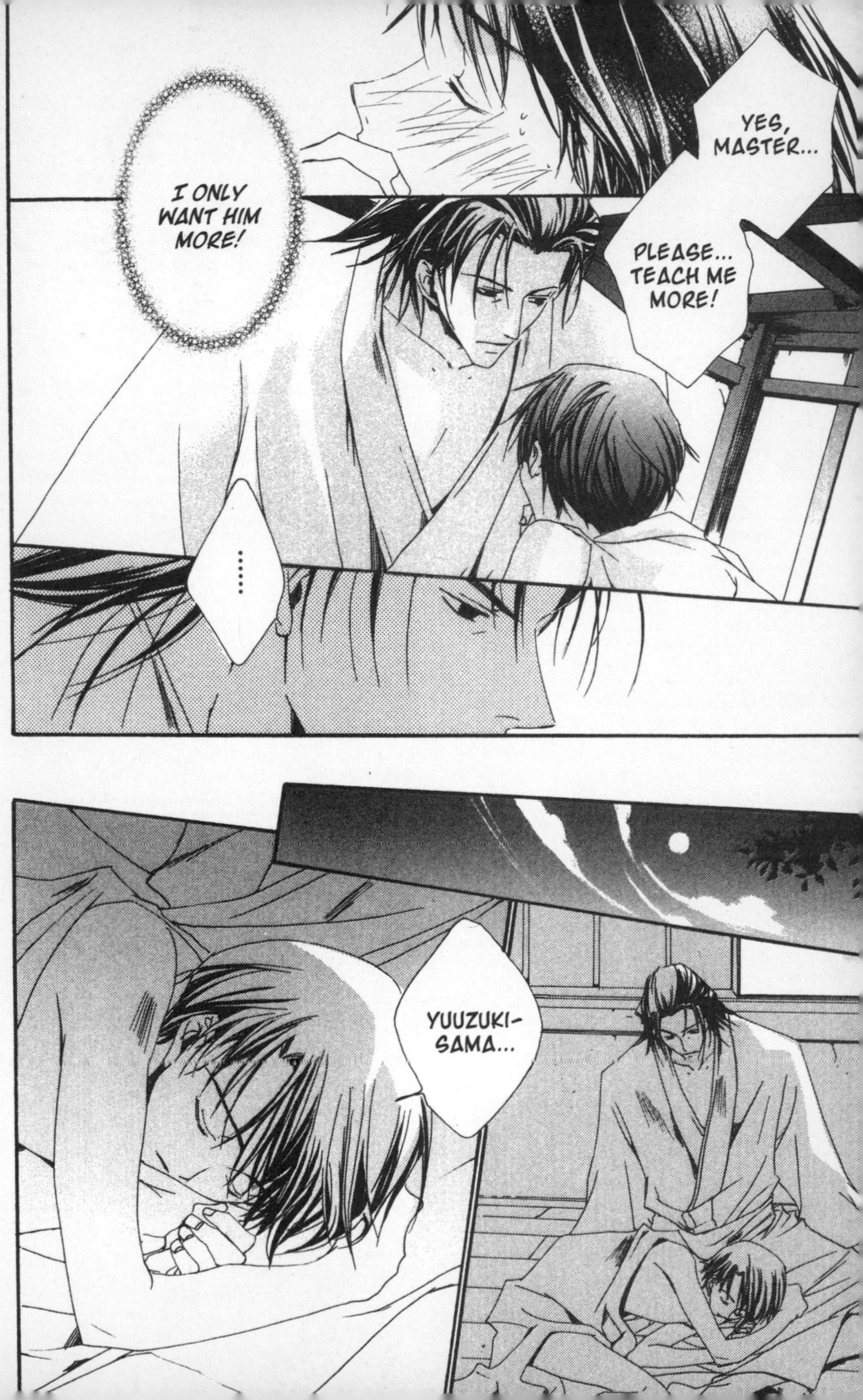
YES, MASTER...
PLEASE... TEACH ME MORE!
I ONLY WANT HIM MORE!
......
YUUZUKI-SAMA...

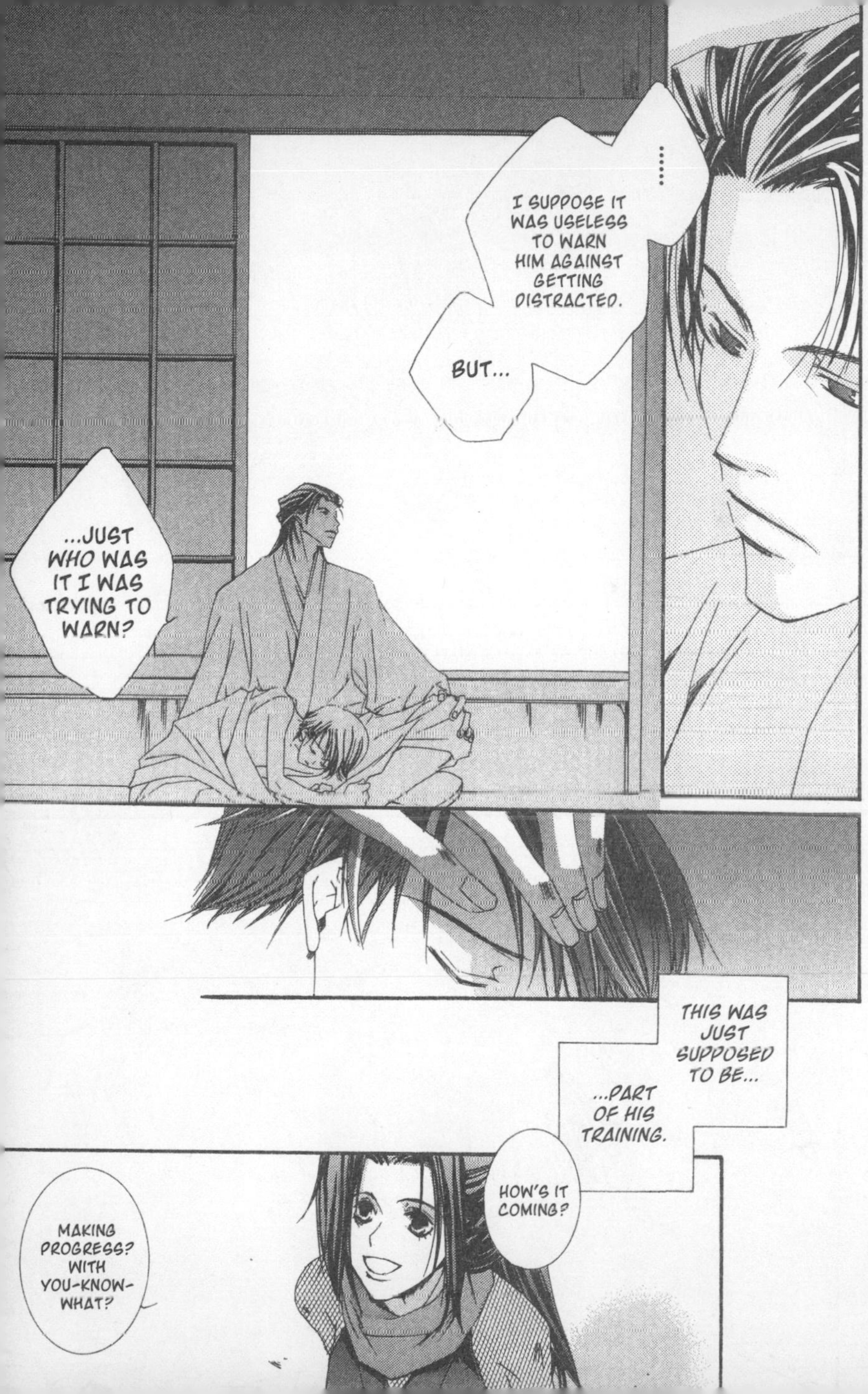
......
I SUPPOSE IT WAS USELESS TO WARN HIM AGAINST GETTING DISTRACTED.
BUT...
...JUST WHO WAS IT I WAS TRYING TO WARN?
THIS WAS JUST SUPPOSED TO BE...
...PART OF HIS TRAINING.
HOW'S IT COMING?
MAKING PROGRESS? WITH YOU-KNOW-WHAT?

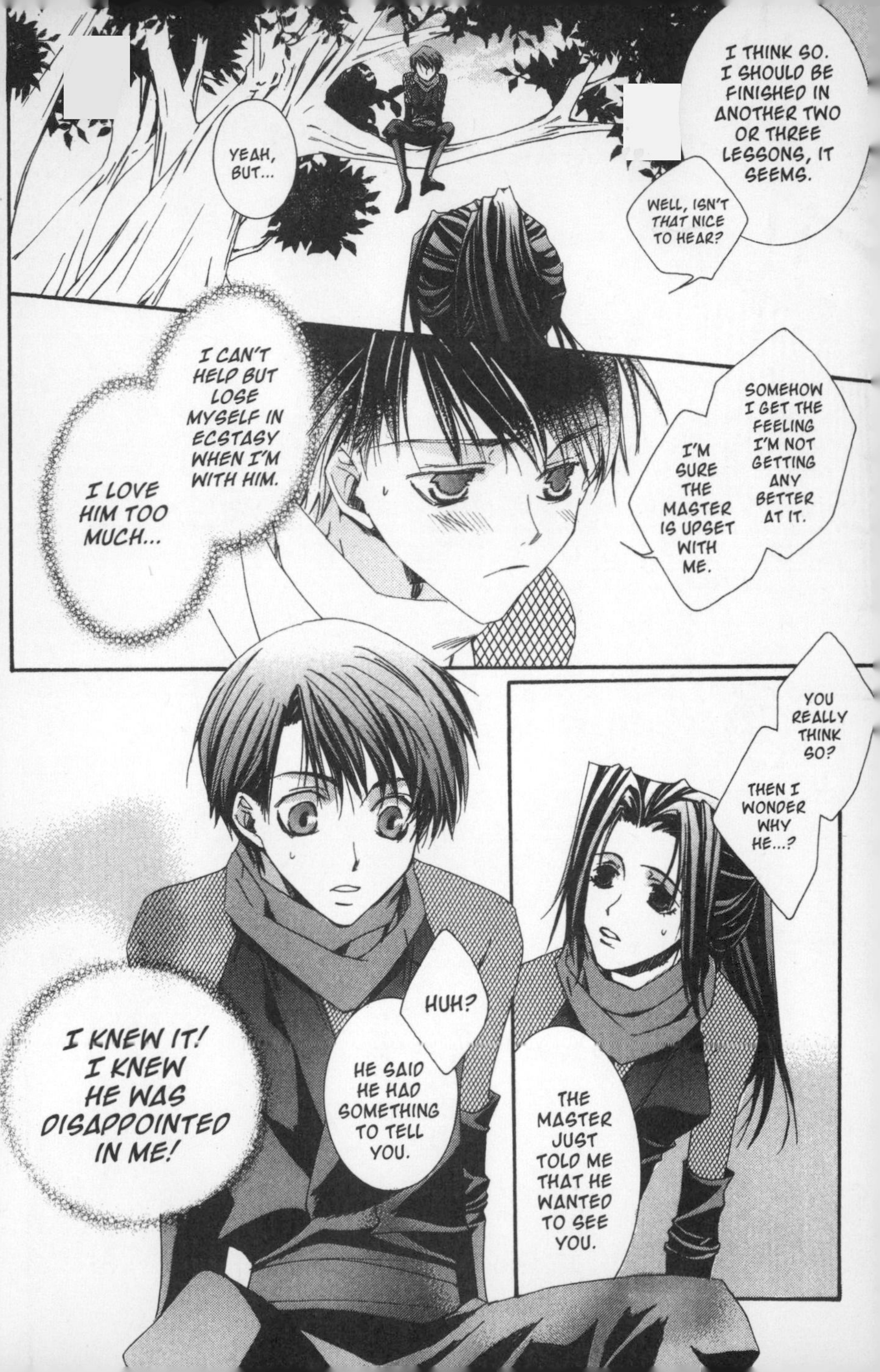
I THINK SO. I SHOULD BE FINISHED IN ANOTHER TWO OR THREE LESSONS, IT SEEMS.
WELL, ISN'T THAT NICE TO HEAR?
YEAH, BUT...
SOMEHOW I GET THE FEELING I'M NOT GETTING ANY BETTER AT IT.
I'M SURE THE MASTER IS UPSET WITH ME.
I CAN'T HELP BUT LOSE MYSELF IN ECSTASY WHEN I'M WITH HIM.
I LOVE HIM TOO MUCH...
YOU REALLY THINK SO?
THEN I WONDER WHY HE...?
THE MASTER JUST TOLD ME THAT HE WANTED TO SEE YOU.
HUH?
HE SAID HE HAD SOMETHING TO TELL YOU.
I KNEW IT! I KNEW HE WAS DISAPPOINTED IN ME!

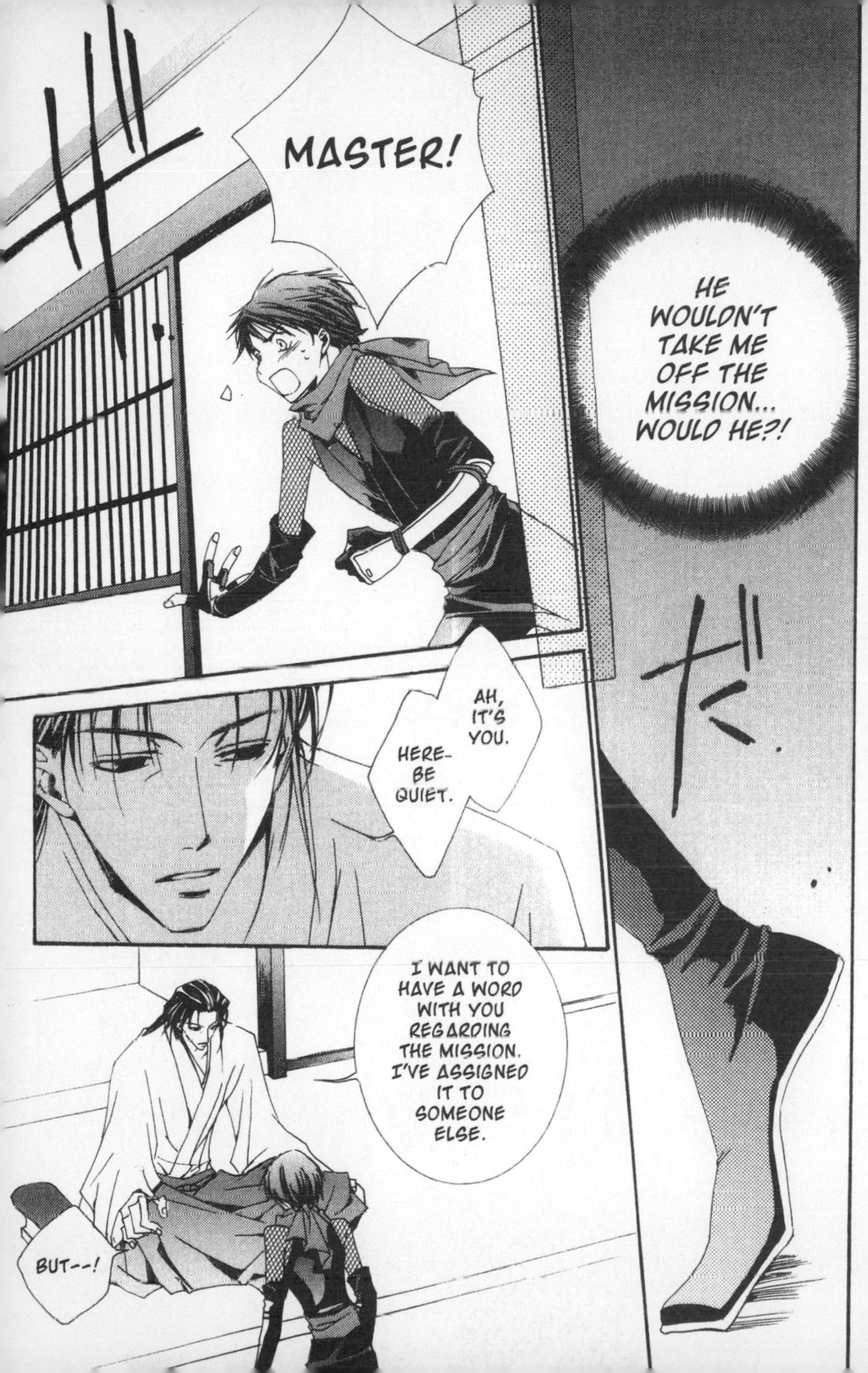
HE WOULDN'T TAKE ME OFF THE MISSION... WOULD HE?!
MASTER!
AH, IT'S YOU.
HERE- BE QUIET.
I WANT TO HAVE A WORD WITH YOU REGARDING THE MISSION. I'VE ASSIGNED IT TO SOMEONE ELSE.
BUT--!

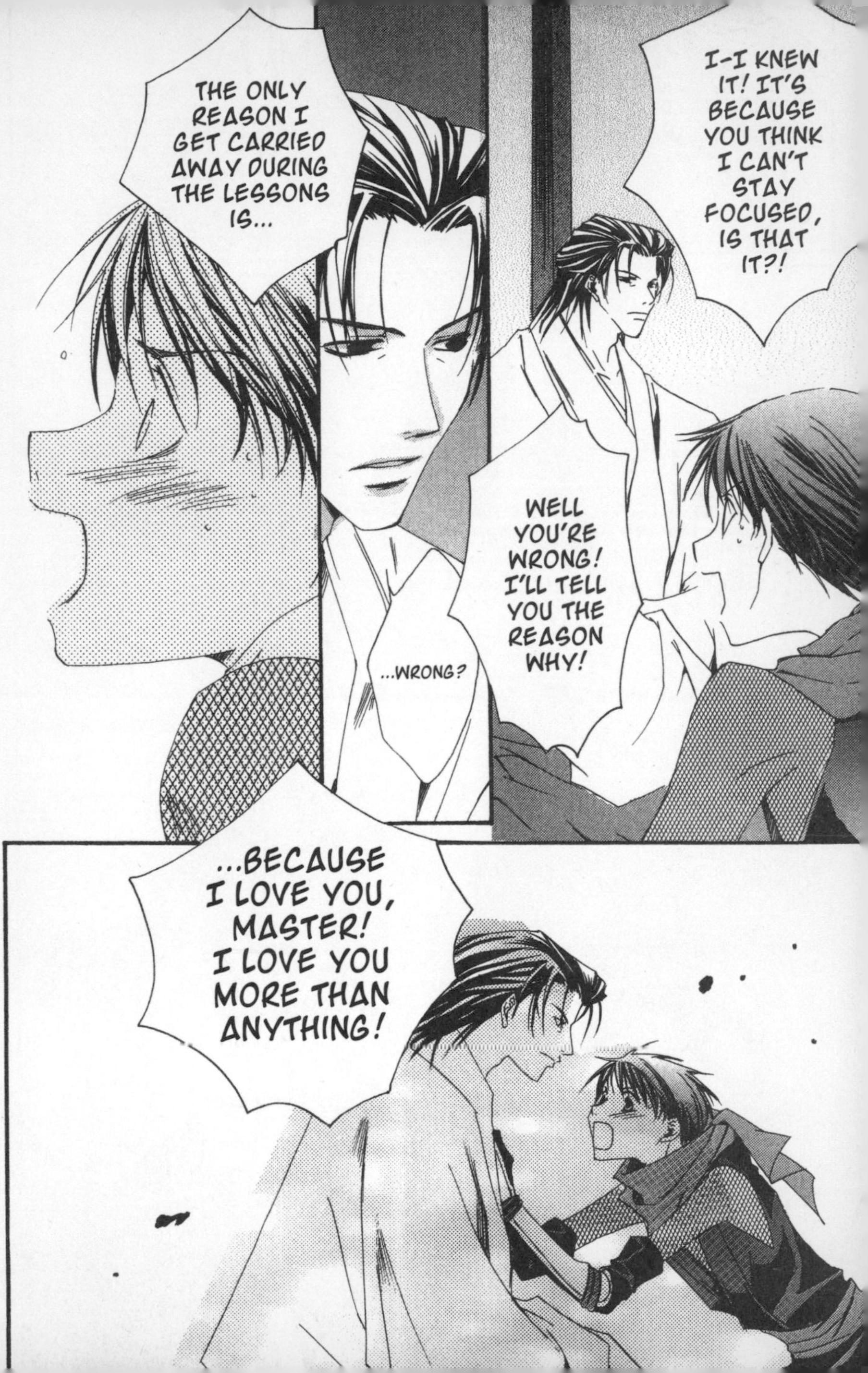
I-I KNEW IT! IT'S BECAUSE YOU THINK I CAN'T STAY FOCUSED, IS THAT IT?!
WELL YOU'RE WRONG! I'LL TELL YOU THE REASON WHY!
...WRONG?
THE ONLY REASON I GET CARRIED AWAY DURING THE LESSONS IS...
...BECAUSE I LOVE YOU, MASTER! I LOVE YOU MORE THAN ANYTHING!

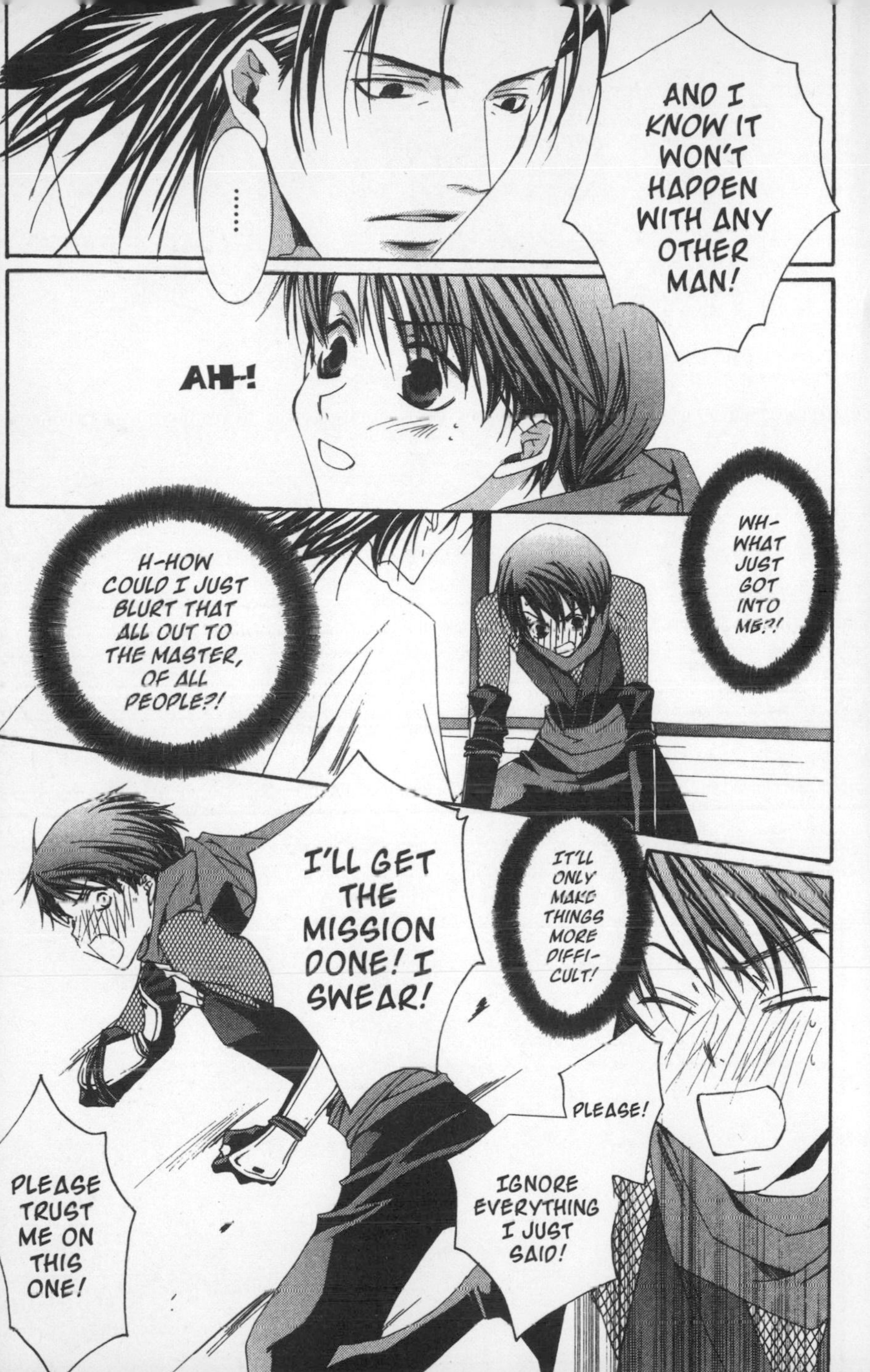
AND I KNOW IT WON'T HAPPEN WITH ANY OTHER MAN!
......
AHH-!
WH-WHAT JUST GOT INTO ME?!
H-HOW COULD I JUST BLURT THAT ALL OUT TO THE MASTER, OF ALL PEOPLE?!
IT'LL ONLY MAKE THINGS MORE DIFFI-CULT!
PLEASE!
IGNORE EVERYTHING I JUST SAID!
I'LL GET THE MISSION DONE! I SWEAR!
PLEASE TRUST ME ON THIS ONE!

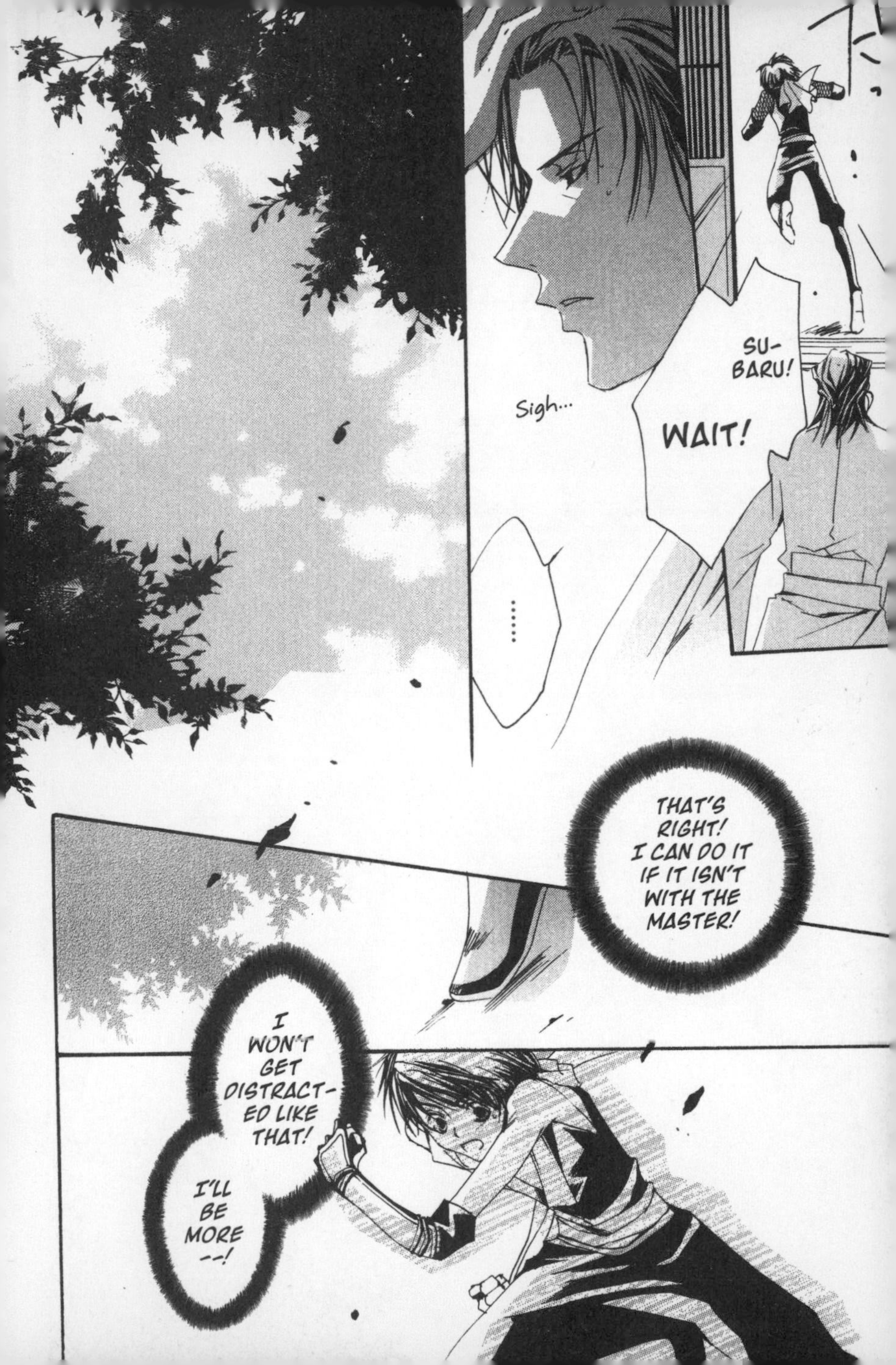
SU-BARU!
WAIT!
Sigh...
......
THAT'S RIGHT! I CAN DO IT IF IT ISN'T WITH THE MASTER!
I WON'T GET DISTRACTED LIKE THAT!
I'LL BE MORE--!

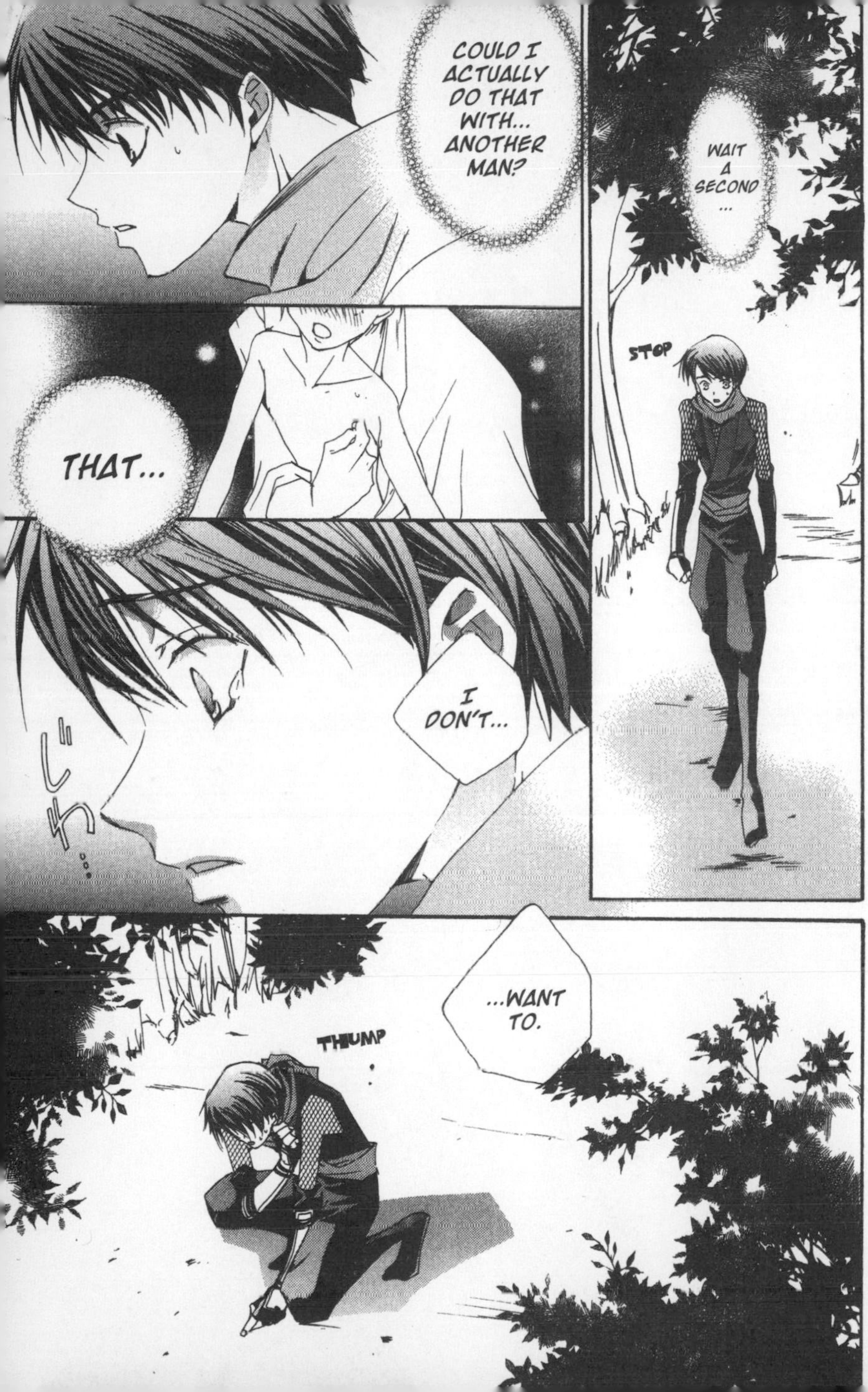
WAIT A SECOND ...
STOP
COULD I ACTUALLY DO THAT WITH... ANOTHER MAN?
THAT...
I DON'T...
...WANT TO.
THUMP

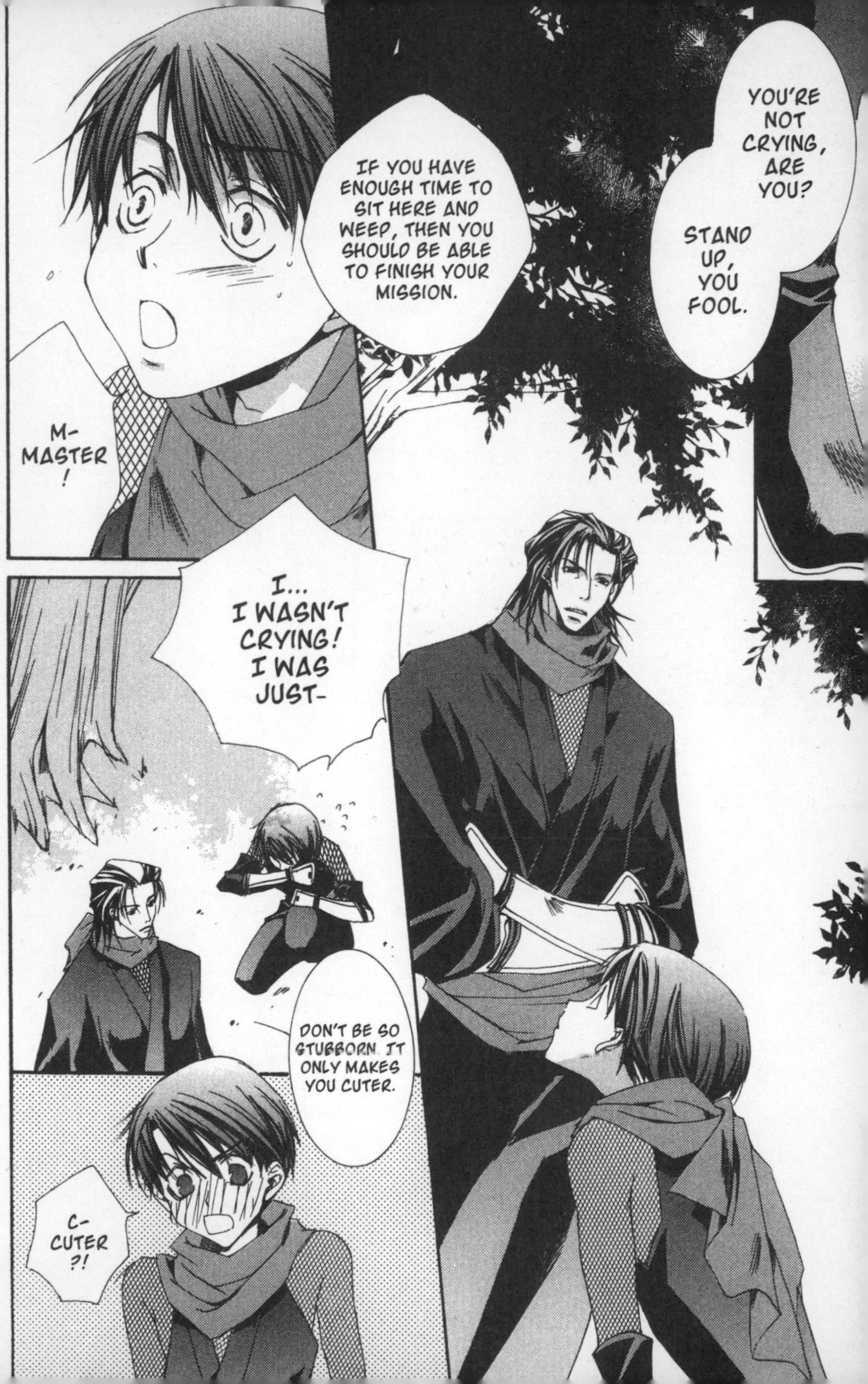
YOU'RE NOT CRYING, ARE YOU?
STAND UP, YOU FOOL.
M-MASTER!
IF YOU HAVE ENOUGH TIME TO SIT HERE AND WEEP, THEN YOU SHOULD BE ABLE TO FINISH YOUR MISSION.
I... I WASN'T CRYING! I WAS JUST-
DON'T BE SO STUBBORN. IT ONLY MAKES YOU CUTER.
C-CUTER?!

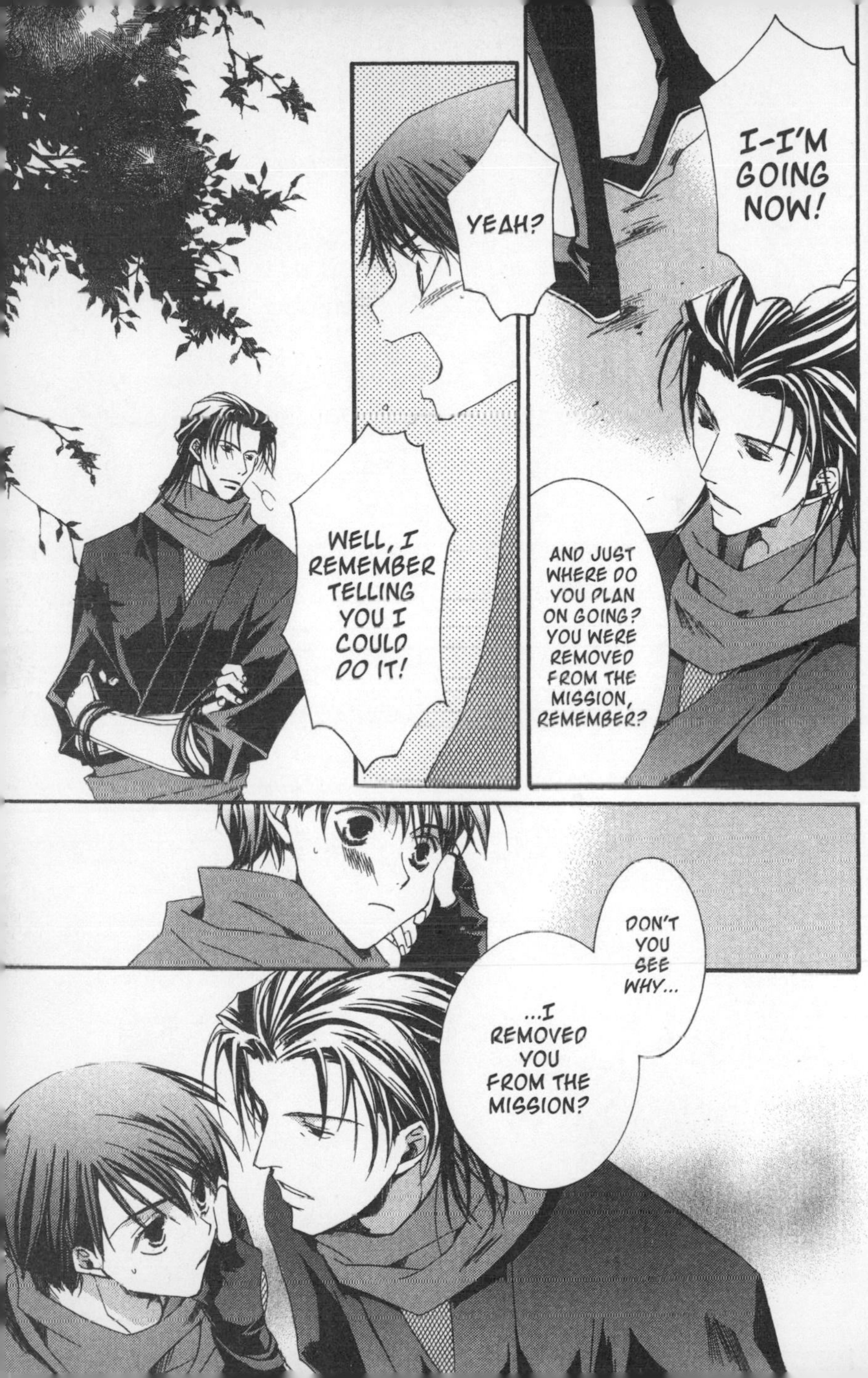

I-I'M GOING NOW!
AND JUST WHERE DO YOU PLAN ON GOING? YOU WERE REMOVED FROM THE MISSION, REMEMBER?
YEAH?
WELL, I REMEMBER TELLING YOU I COULD DO IT!
DON'T YOU SEE WHY...
...I REMOVED YOU FROM THE MISSION?

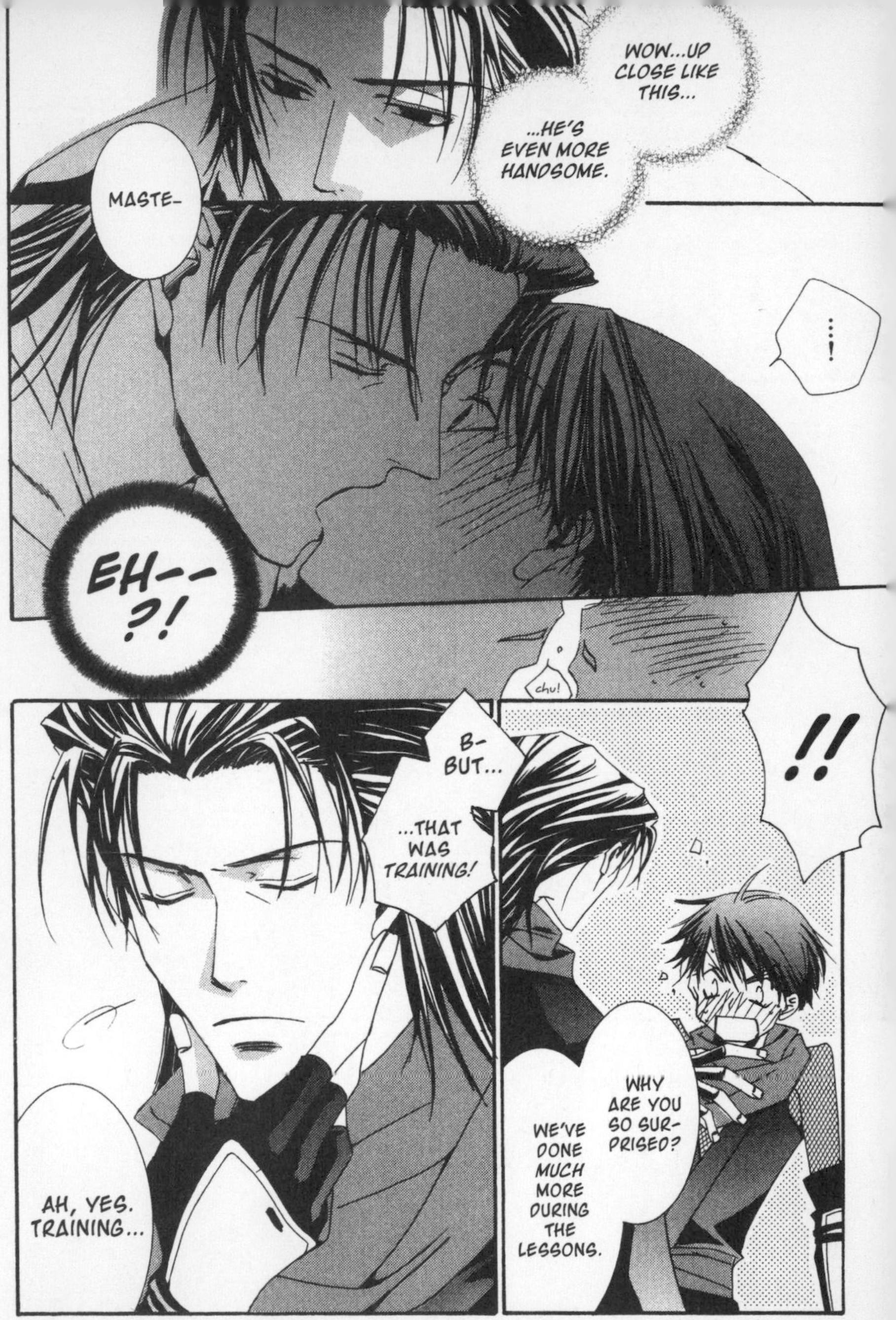
WOW...UP CLOSE LIKE THIS...
...HE'S EVEN MORE HANDSOME.
MASTE-
...!
EH--?!
chu!
!!
WHY ARE YOU SO SUR-PRISED?
WE'VE DONE MUCH MORE DURING THE LESSONS.
B-BUT...
...THAT WAS TRAINING!
AH, YES. TRAINING...

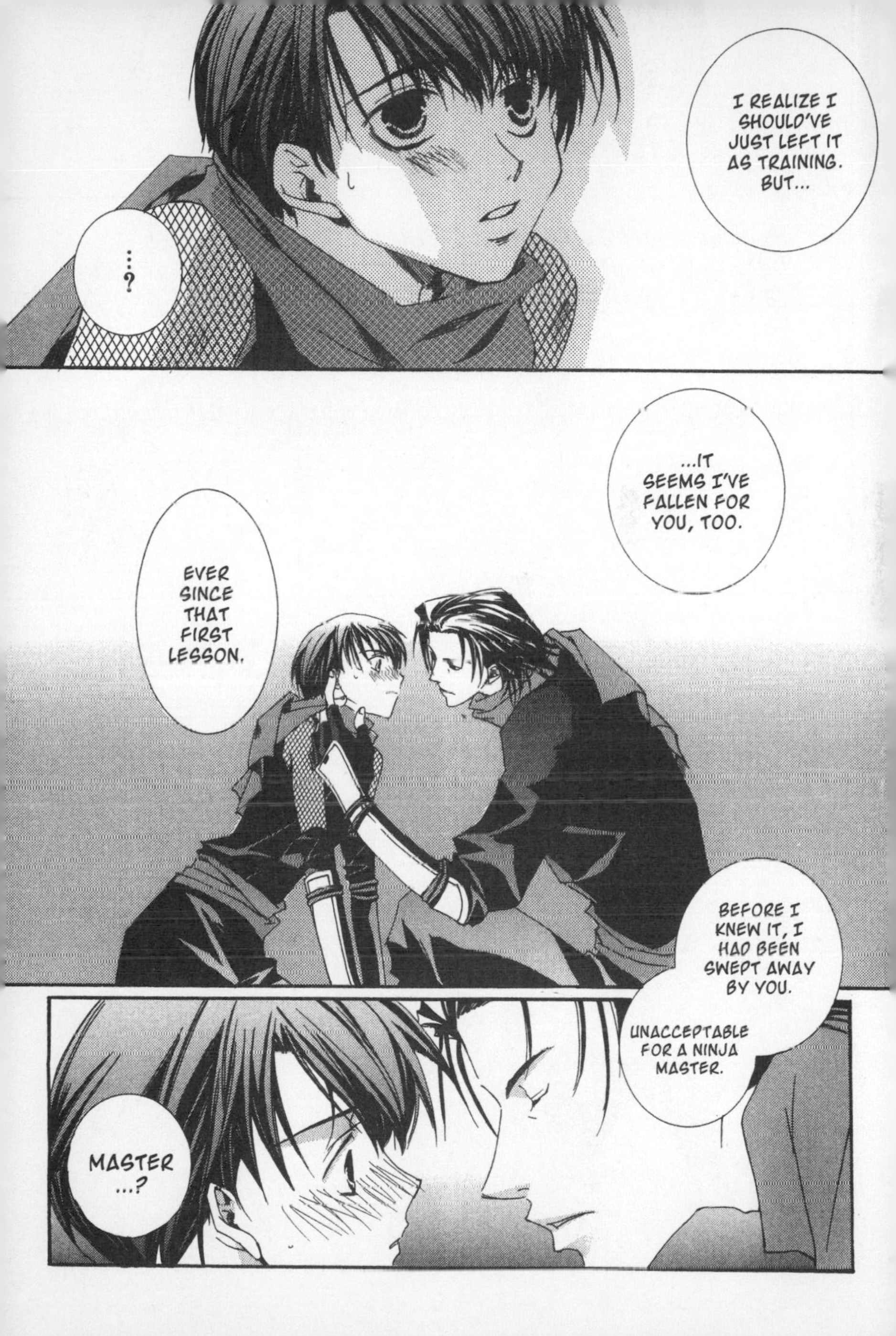
I REALIZE I SHOULD'VE JUST LEFT IT AS TRAINING. BUT...
...?
...IT SEEMS I'VE FALLEN FOR YOU, TOO.
EVER SINCE THAT FIRST LESSON.
BEFORE I KNEW IT, I HAD BEEN SWEPT AWAY BY YOU.
UNACCEPTABLE FOR A NINJA MASTER.
MASTER ...?

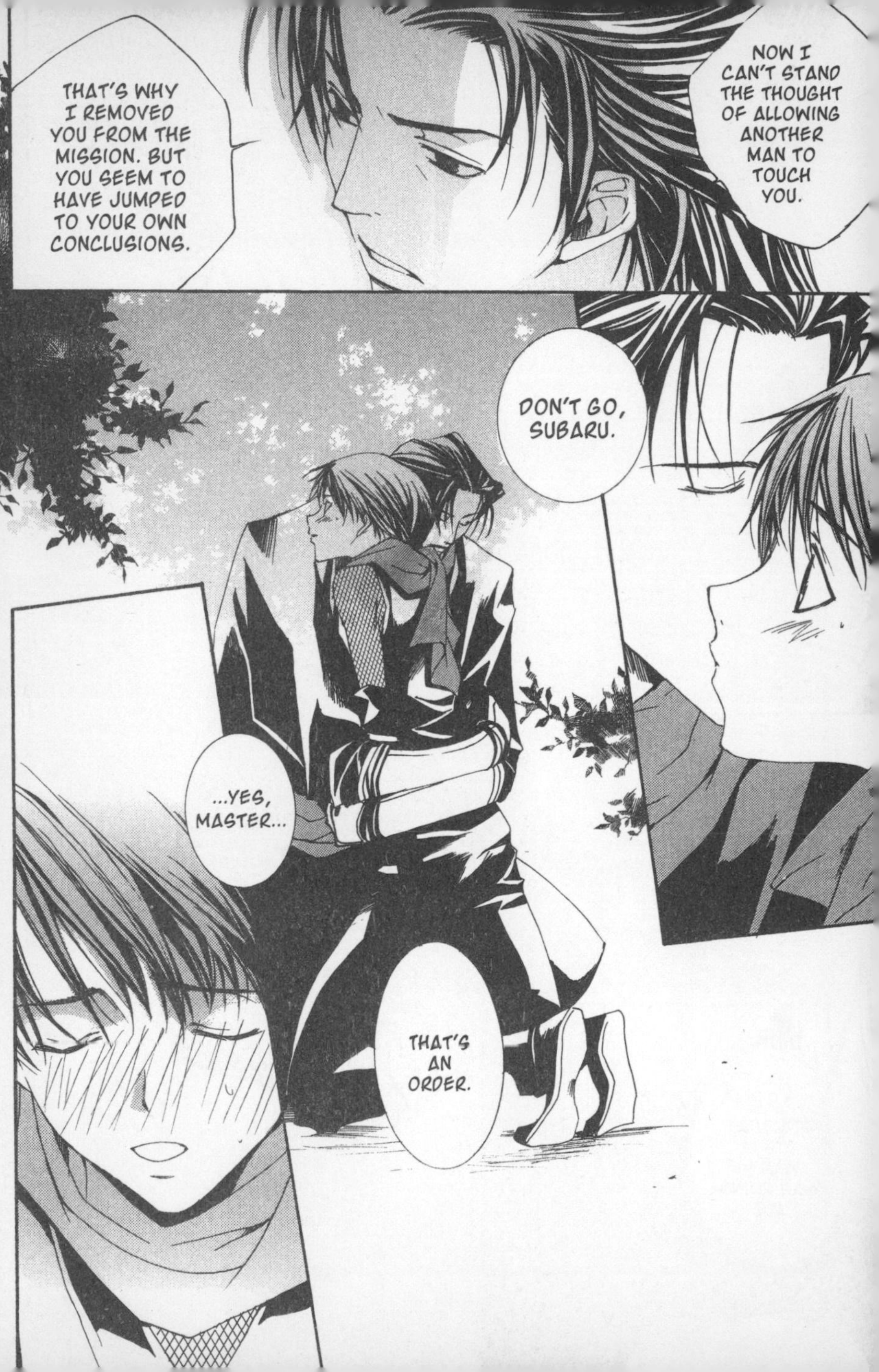
NOW I CAN'T STAND THE THOUGHT OF ALLOWING ANOTHER MAN TO TOUCH YOU.
THAT'S WHY I REMOVED YOU FROM THE MISSION. BUT YOU SEEM TO HAVE JUMPED TO YOUR OWN CONCLUSIONS.
DON'T GO, SUBARU.
THAT'S AN ORDER.
...YES, MASTER...

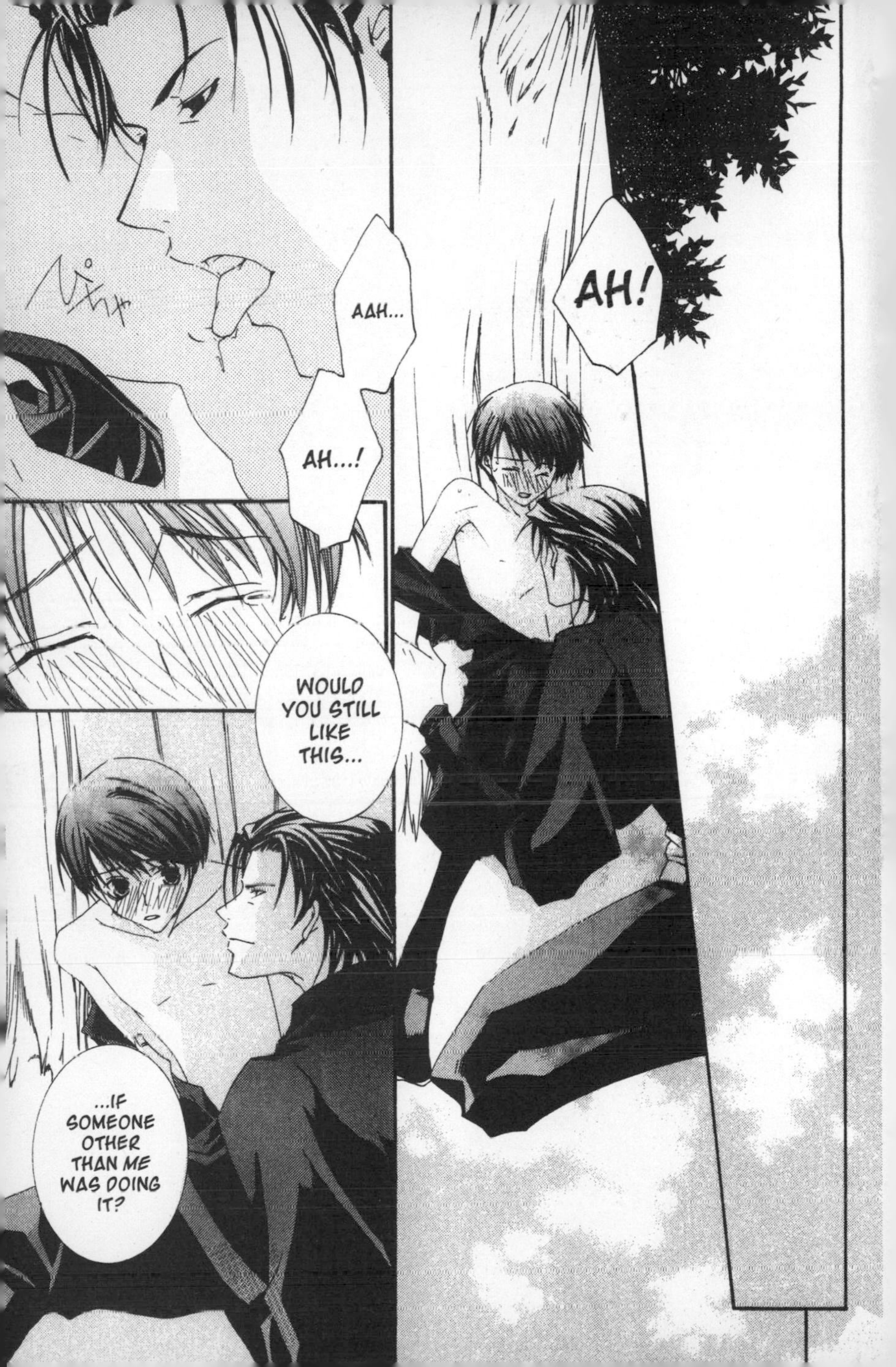
AH!
AAH...
AH...!
WOULD YOU STILL LIKE THIS...
...IF SOMEONE OTHER THAN ME WAS DOING IT?

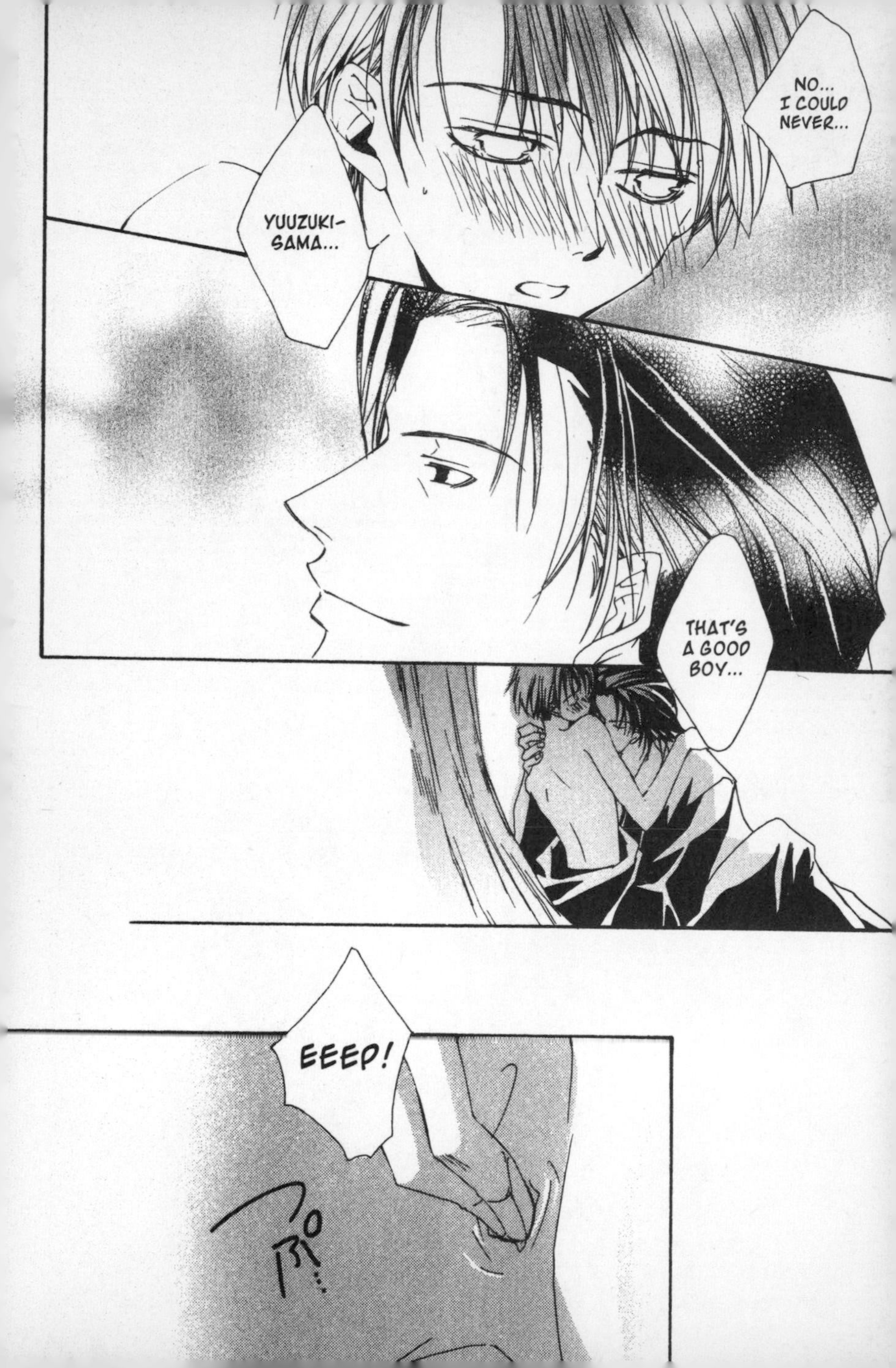
NO... I COULD NEVER...
YUUZUKI-SAMA...
THAT'S A GOOD BOY...
EEEP!

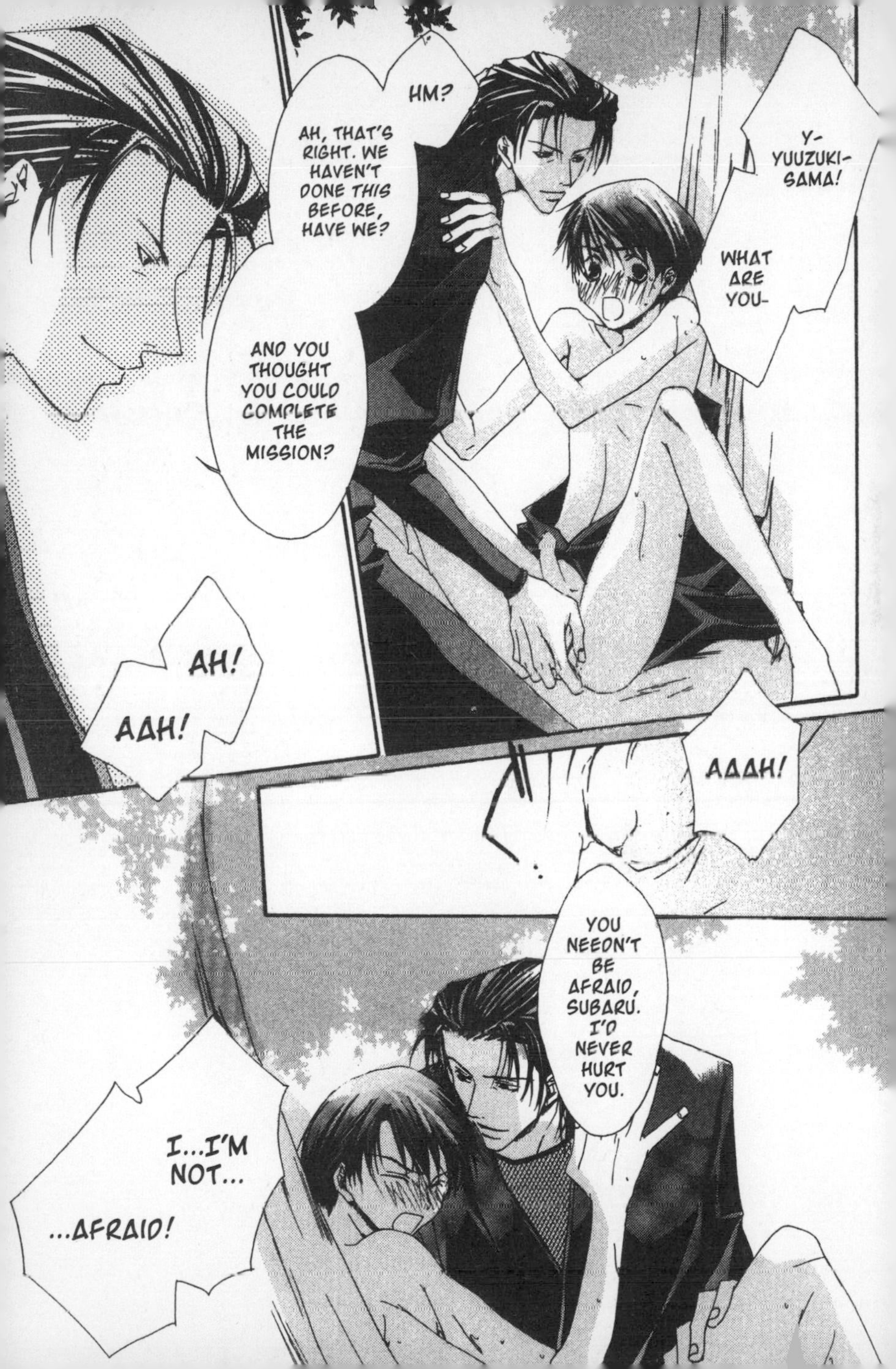
Y-YUUZUKI-SAMA!
WHAT ARE YOU-
HM?
AH, THAT'S RIGHT. WE HAVEN'T DONE THIS BEFORE, HAVE WE?
AND YOU THOUGHT YOU COULD COMPLETE THE MISSION?
AH!
AAH!
AAAH!
YOU NEEDN'T BE AFRAID, SUBARU. I'D NEVER HURT YOU.
I...I'M NOT...
...AFRAID!

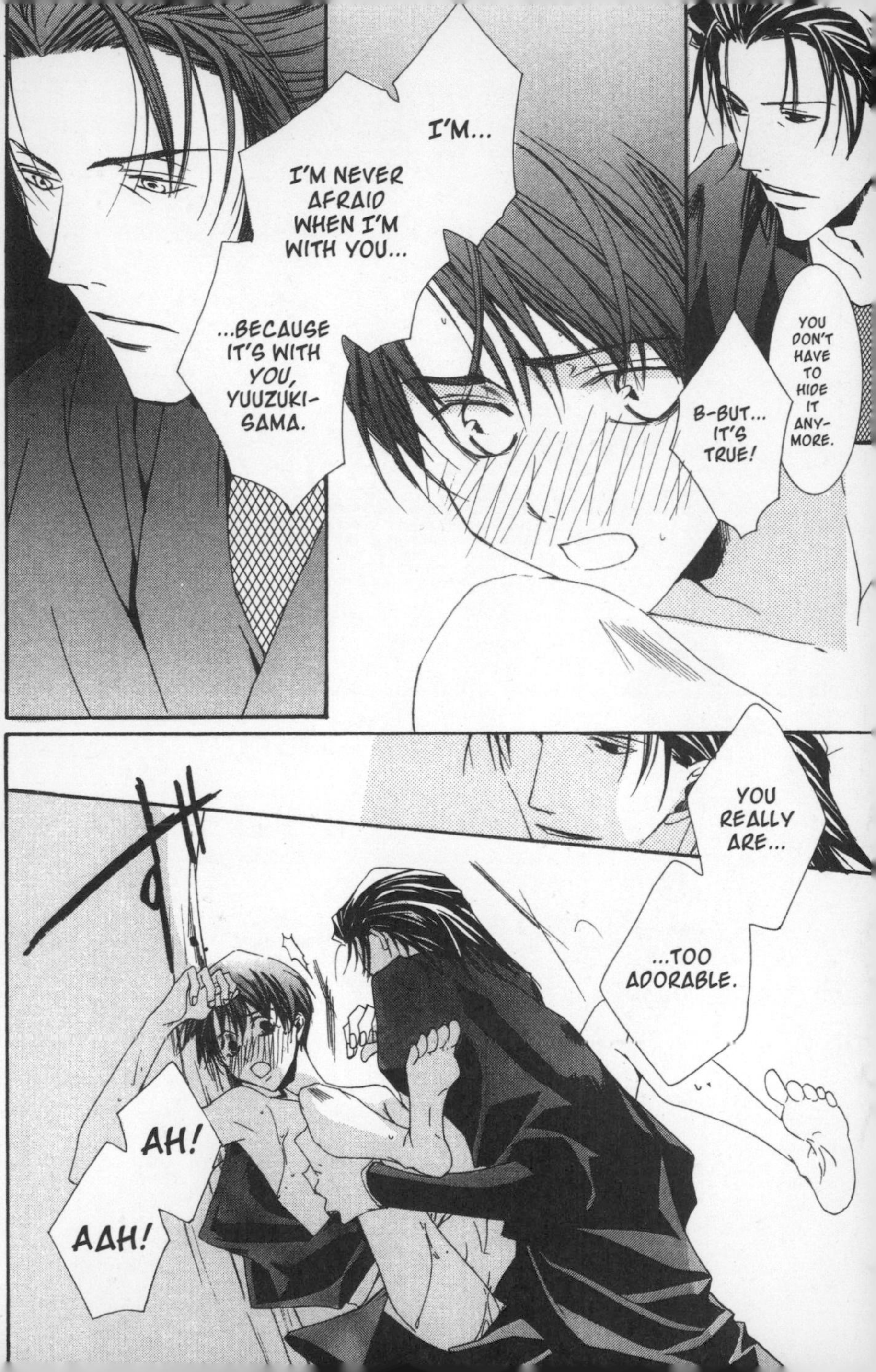
YOU DON'T HAVE TO HIDE IT ANYMORE.
B-BUT... IT'S TRUE!
I'M...
I'M NEVER AFRAID WHEN I'M WITH YOU...
...BECAUSE IT'S WITH YOU, YUUZUKI-SAMA.
YOU REALLY ARE...
...TOO ADORABLE.
AH!
AAH!

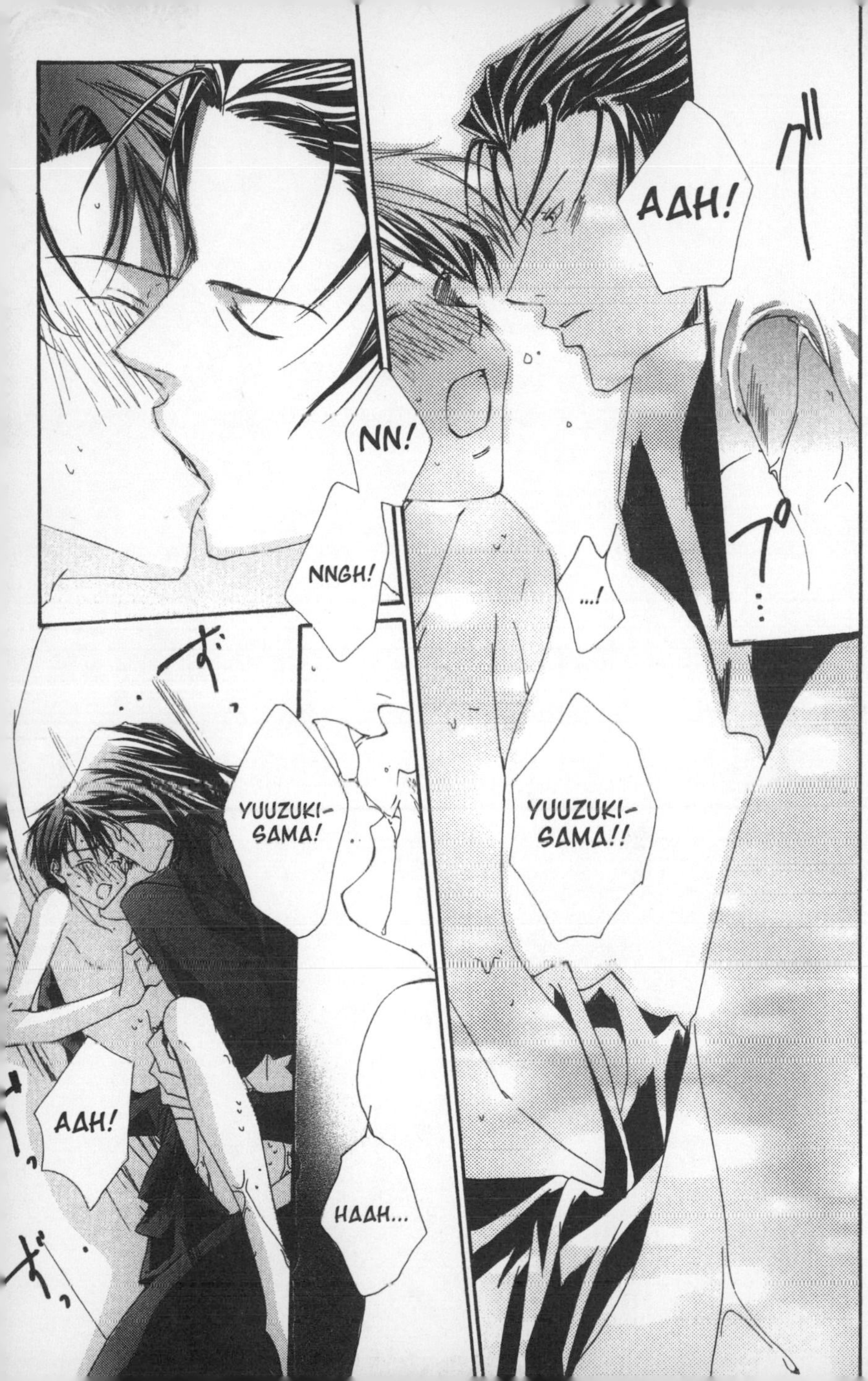
AAH!
NN!
...!
YUUZUKI-SAMA!!
NNGH!
YUUZUKI-SAMA!
HAAH...
AAH!

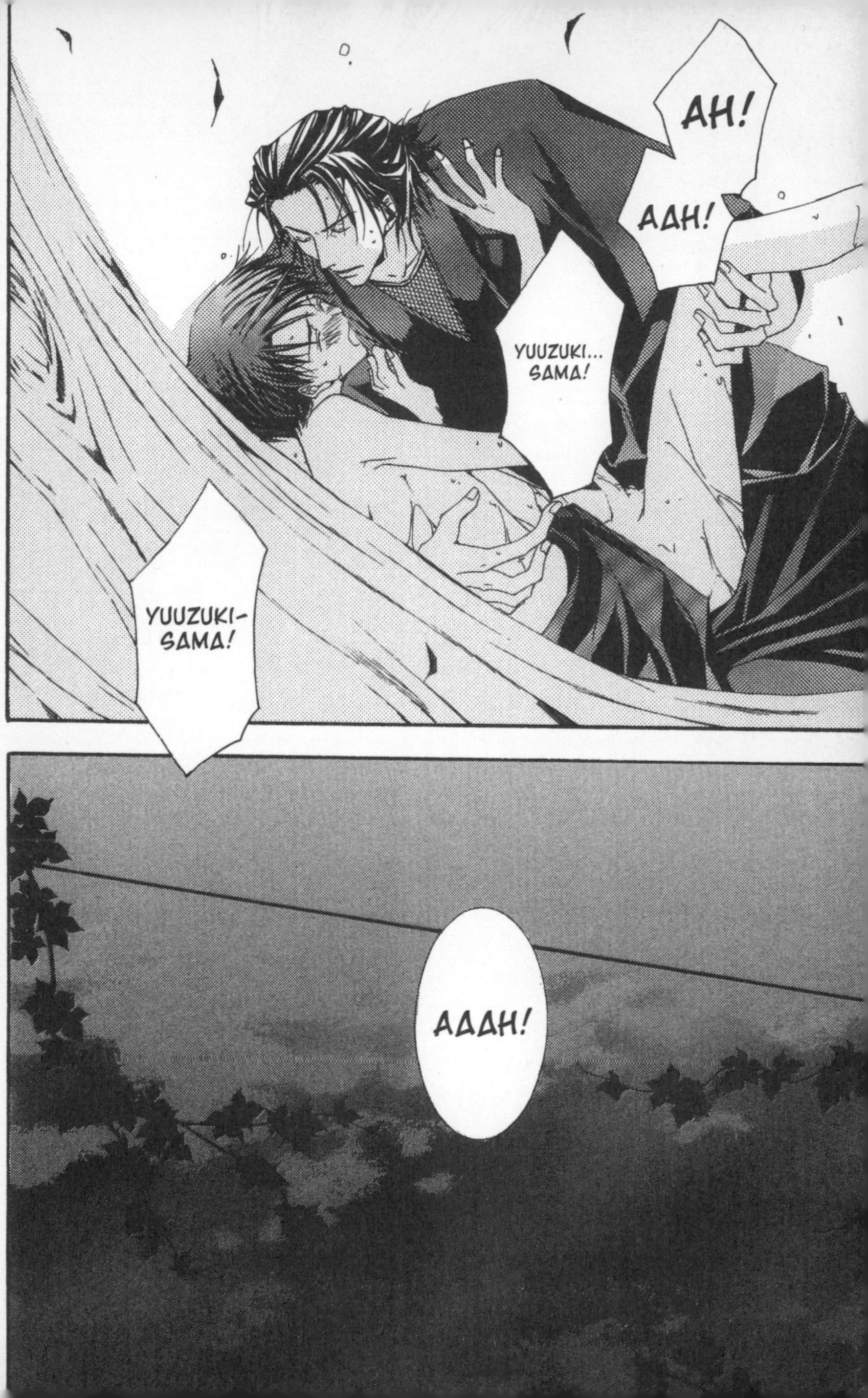
AH!
AAH!
YUUZUKI... SAMA!
YUUZUKI-SAMA!
AAAH!

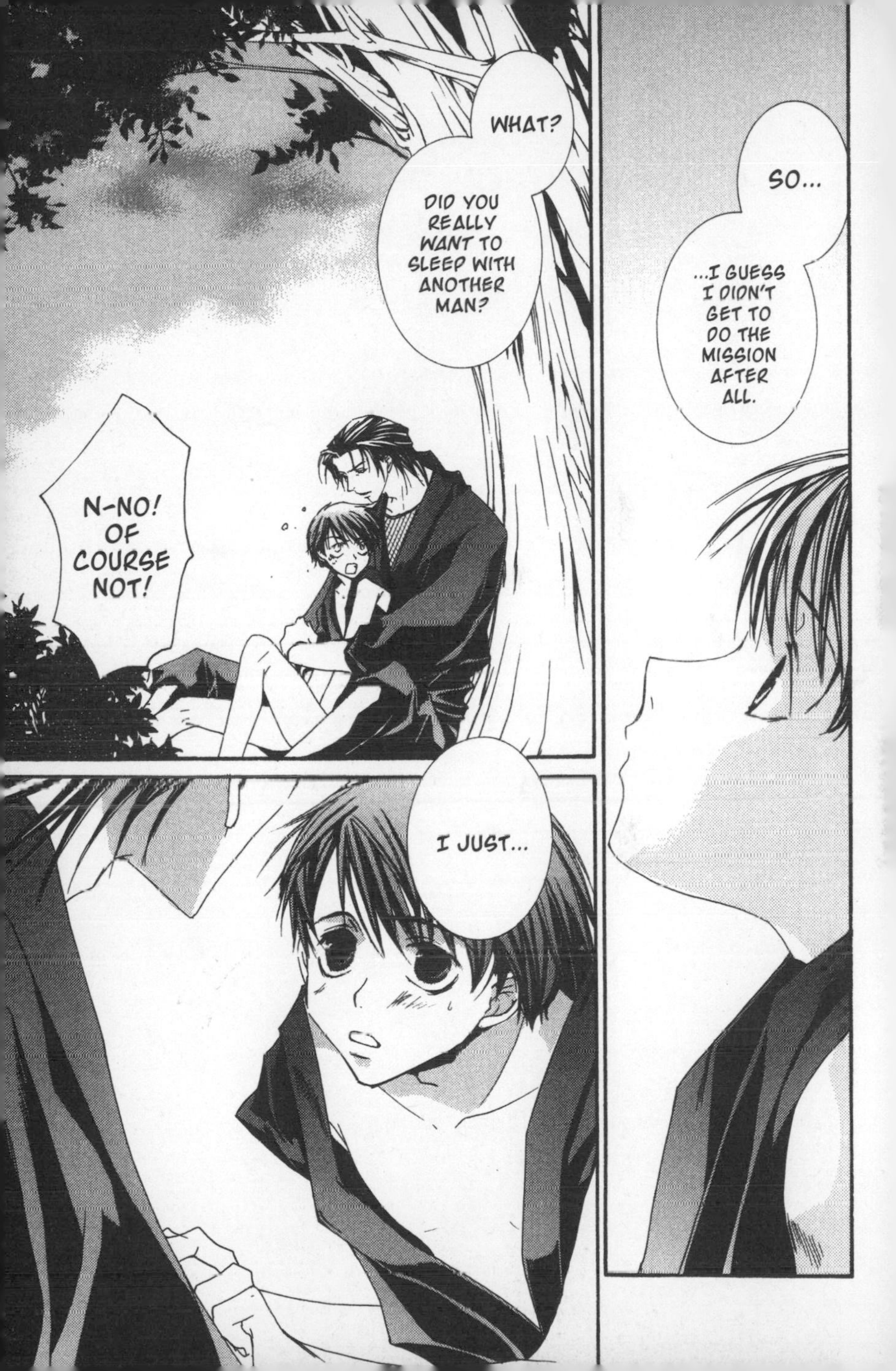
SO...
...I GUESS I DIDN'T GET TO DO THE MISSION AFTER ALL.
WHAT?
DID YOU REALLY WANT TO SLEEP WITH ANOTHER MAN?
N-NO! OF COURSE NOT!
I JUST...

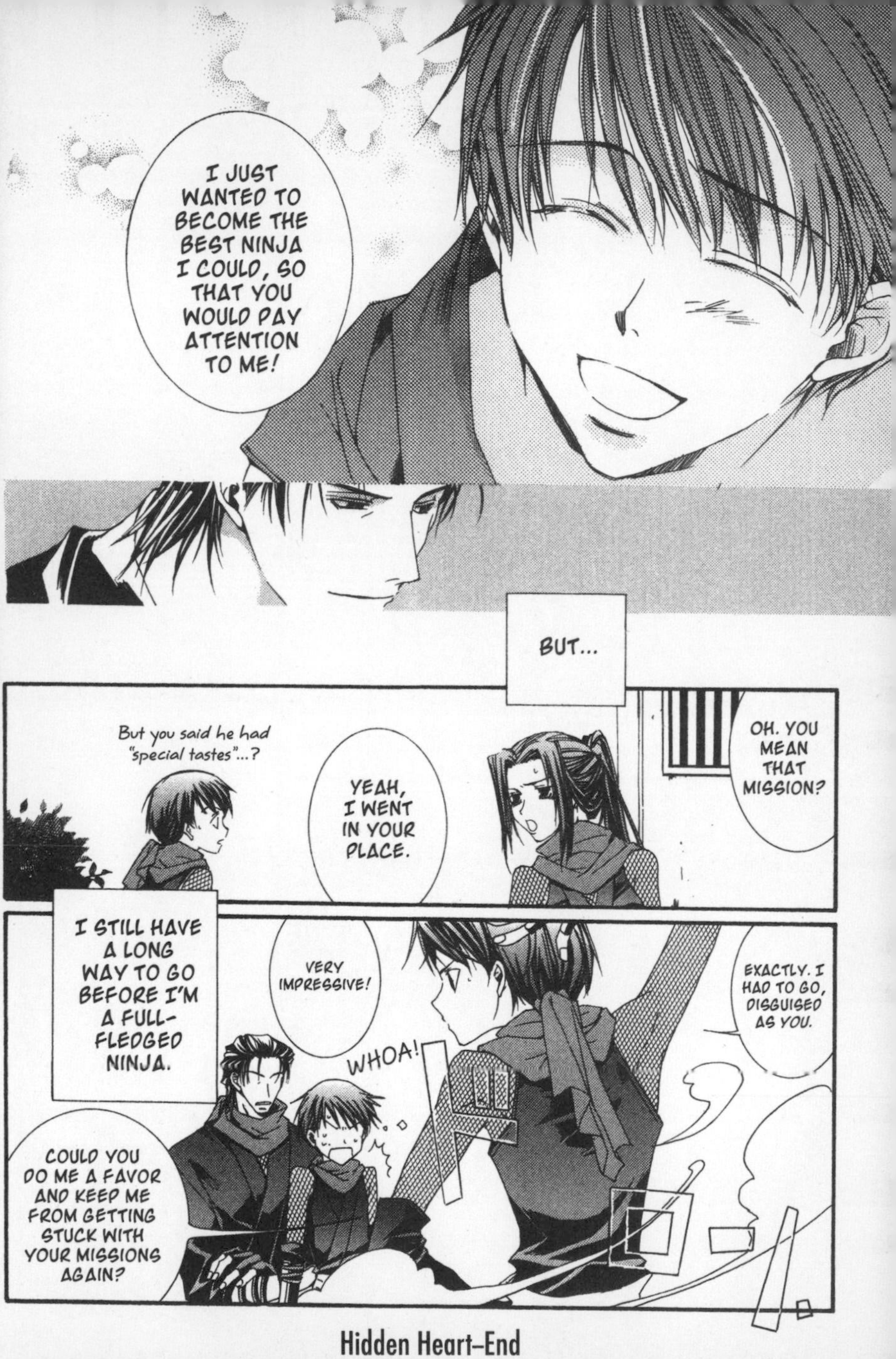
I JUST WANTED TO BECOME THE BEST NINJA I COULD, SO THAT YOU WOULD PAY ATTENTION TO ME!
BUT...
OH. YOU MEAN THAT MISSION?
YEAH, I WENT IN YOUR PLACE.
But you said he had "special tastes"...?
EXACTLY. I HAD TO GO, DISGUISED AS YOU.
VERY IMPRESSIVE!
I STILL HAVE A LONG WAY TO GO BEFORE I'M A FULL-FLEDGED NINJA.
WHOA!
COULD YOU DO ME A FAVOR AND KEEP ME FROM GETTING STUCK WITH YOUR MISSIONS AGAIN?

Hidden Heart–End

しのぶこころは

Shinobu Kokoro...

TEMARI MATSUMOTO

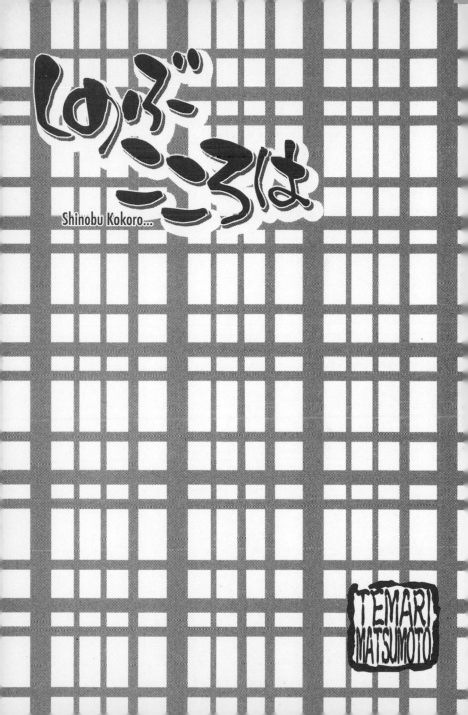

SUBARU

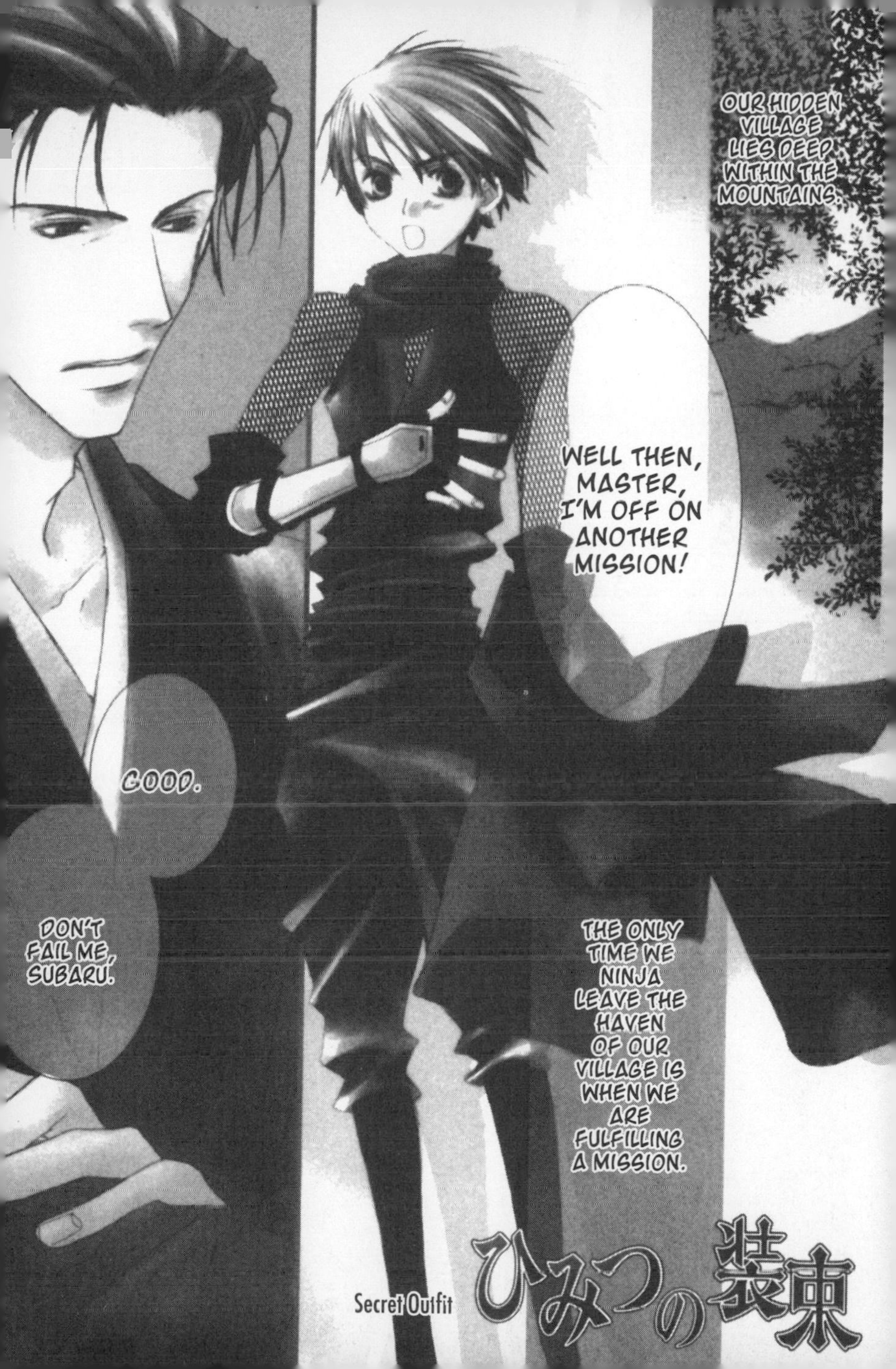
OUR HIDDEN VILLAGE LIES DEEP WITHIN THE MOUNTAINS.
WELL THEN, MASTER, I'M OFF ON ANOTHER MISSION!
GOOD.
DON'T FAIL ME, SUBARU.
THE ONLY TIME WE NINJA LEAVE THE HAVEN OF OUR VILLAGE IS WHEN WE ARE FULFILLING A MISSION.
ひみつの装束
Secret Outfit

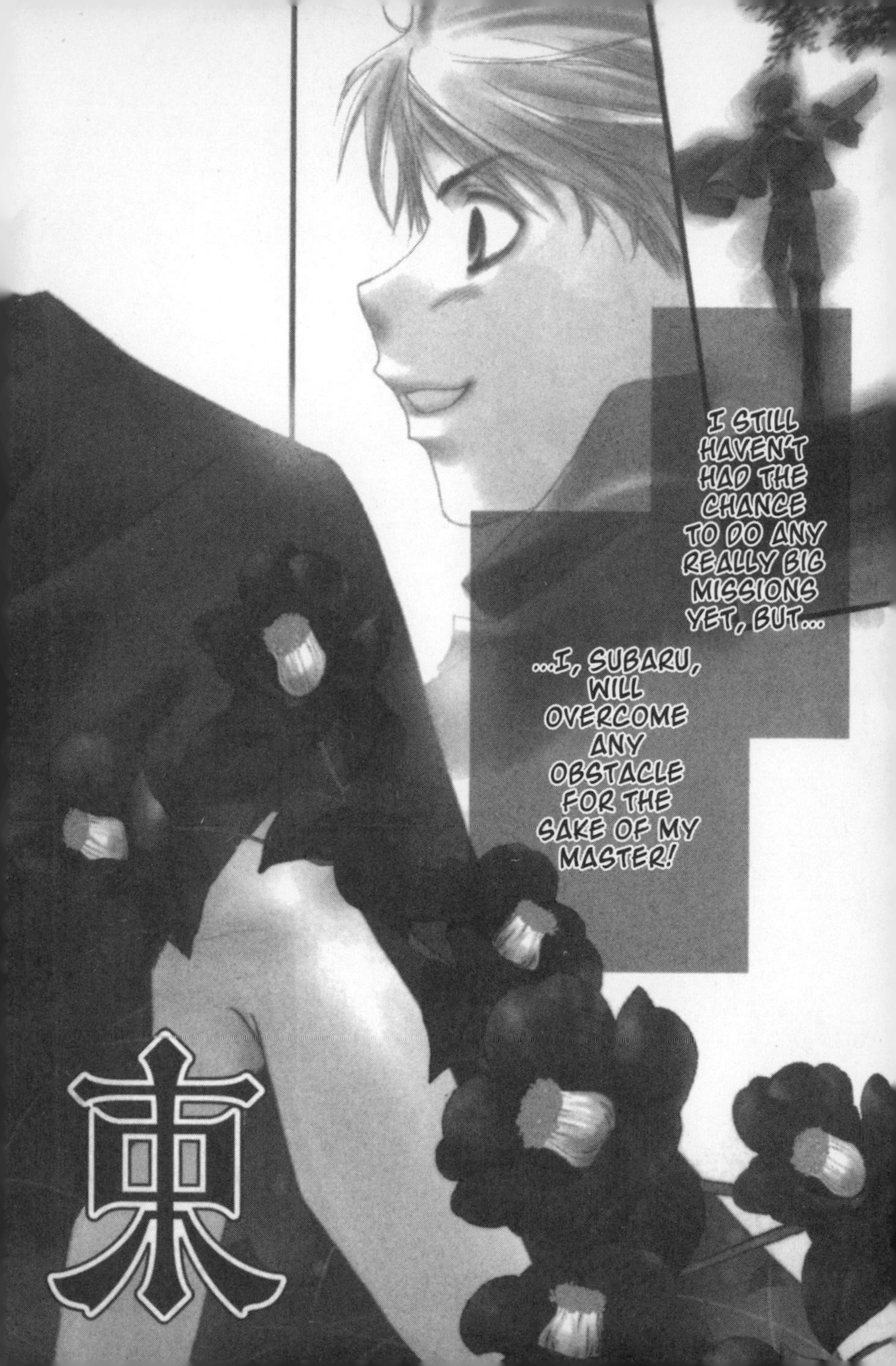
I STILL HAVEN'T HAD THE CHANCE TO DO ANY REALLY BIG MISSIONS YET, BUT...
...I, SUBARU, WILL OVERCOME ANY OBSTACLE FOR THE SAKE OF MY MASTER!
東

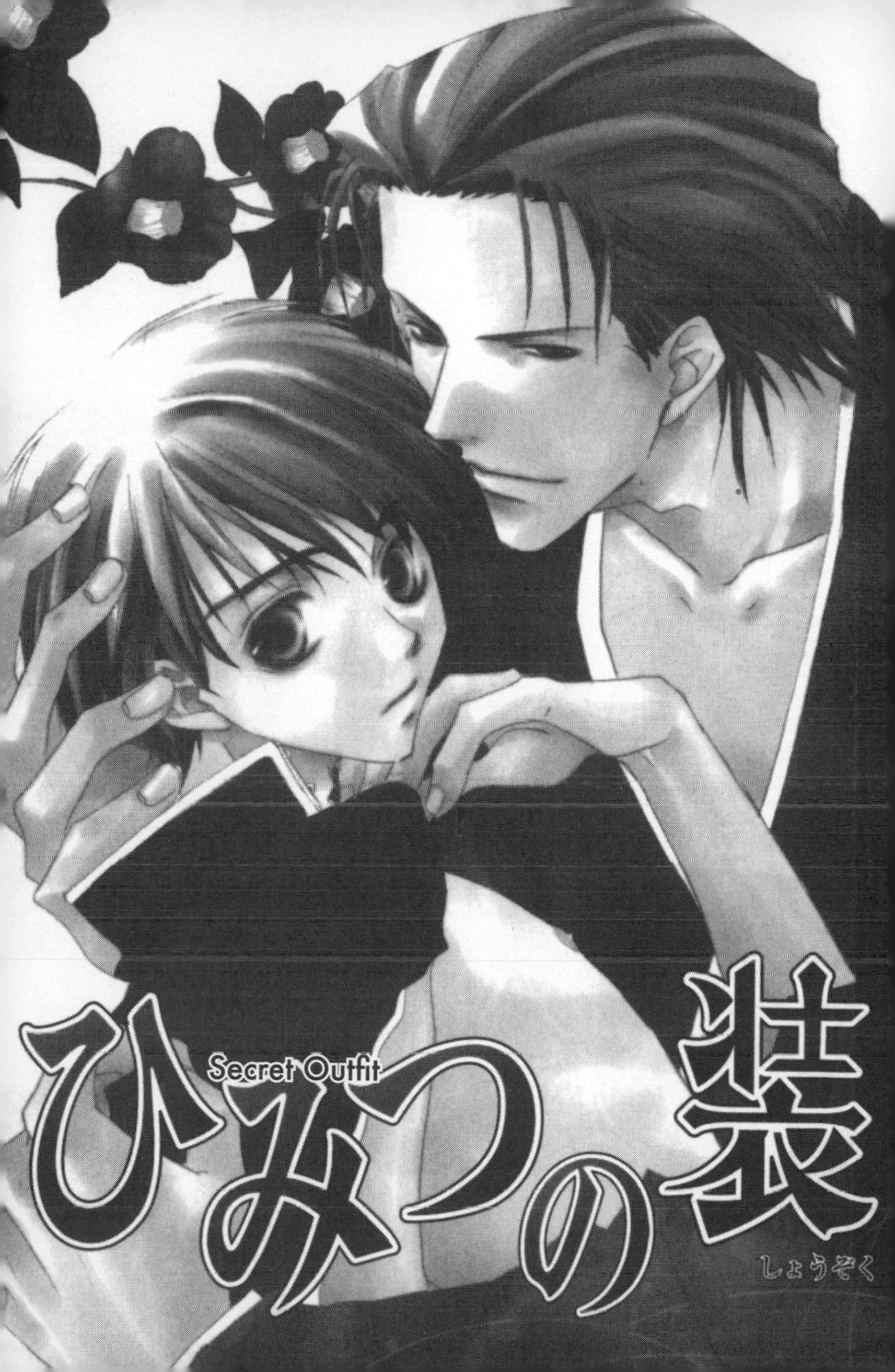
ひみつの装
しょうぞく
Secret Outfit

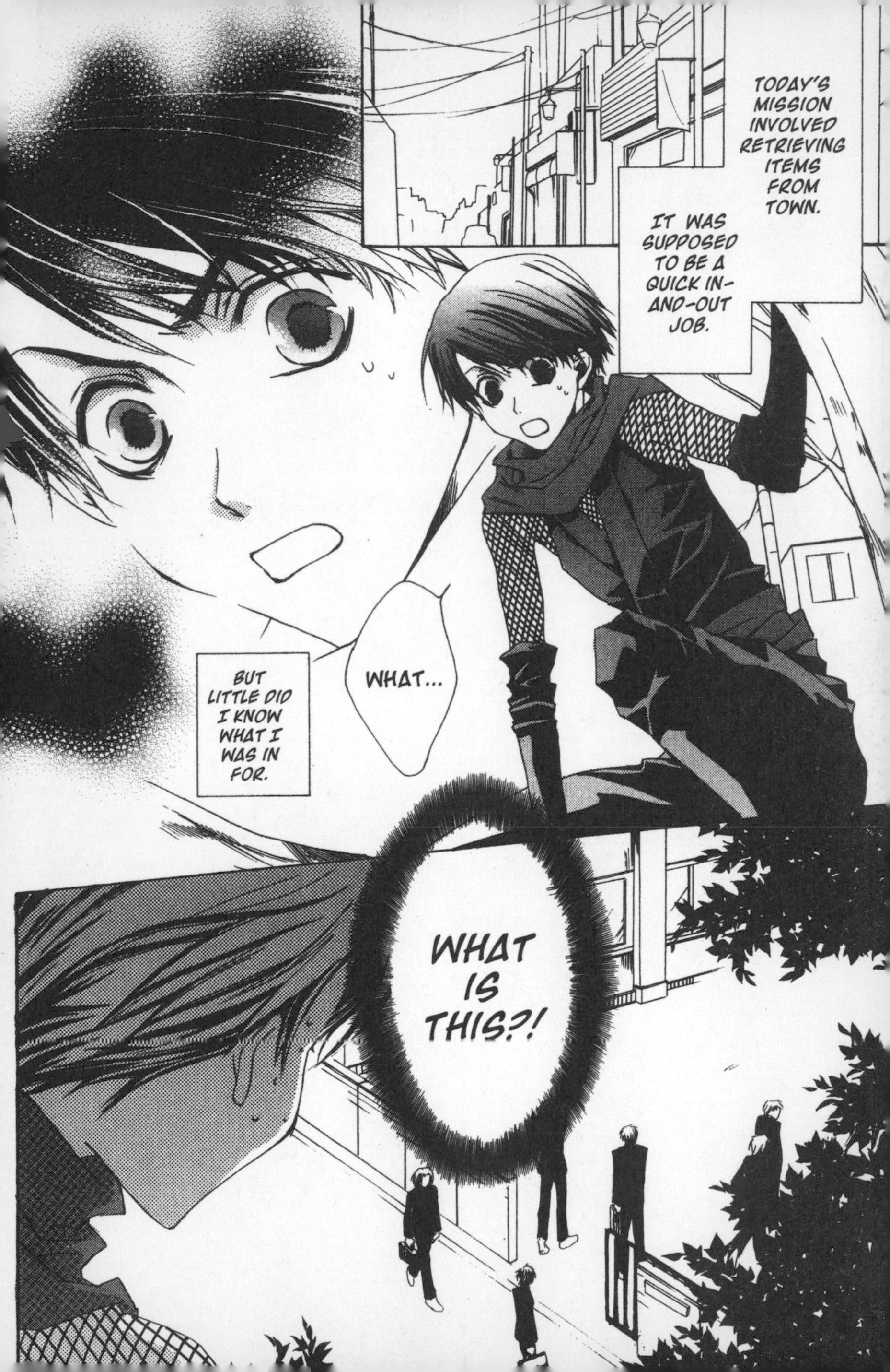
TODAY'S MISSION INVOLVED RETRIEVING ITEMS FROM TOWN.
IT WAS SUPPOSED TO BE A QUICK IN-AND-OUT JOB.
WHAT...
BUT LITTLE DID I KNOW WHAT I WAS IN FOR.
WHAT IS THIS?!

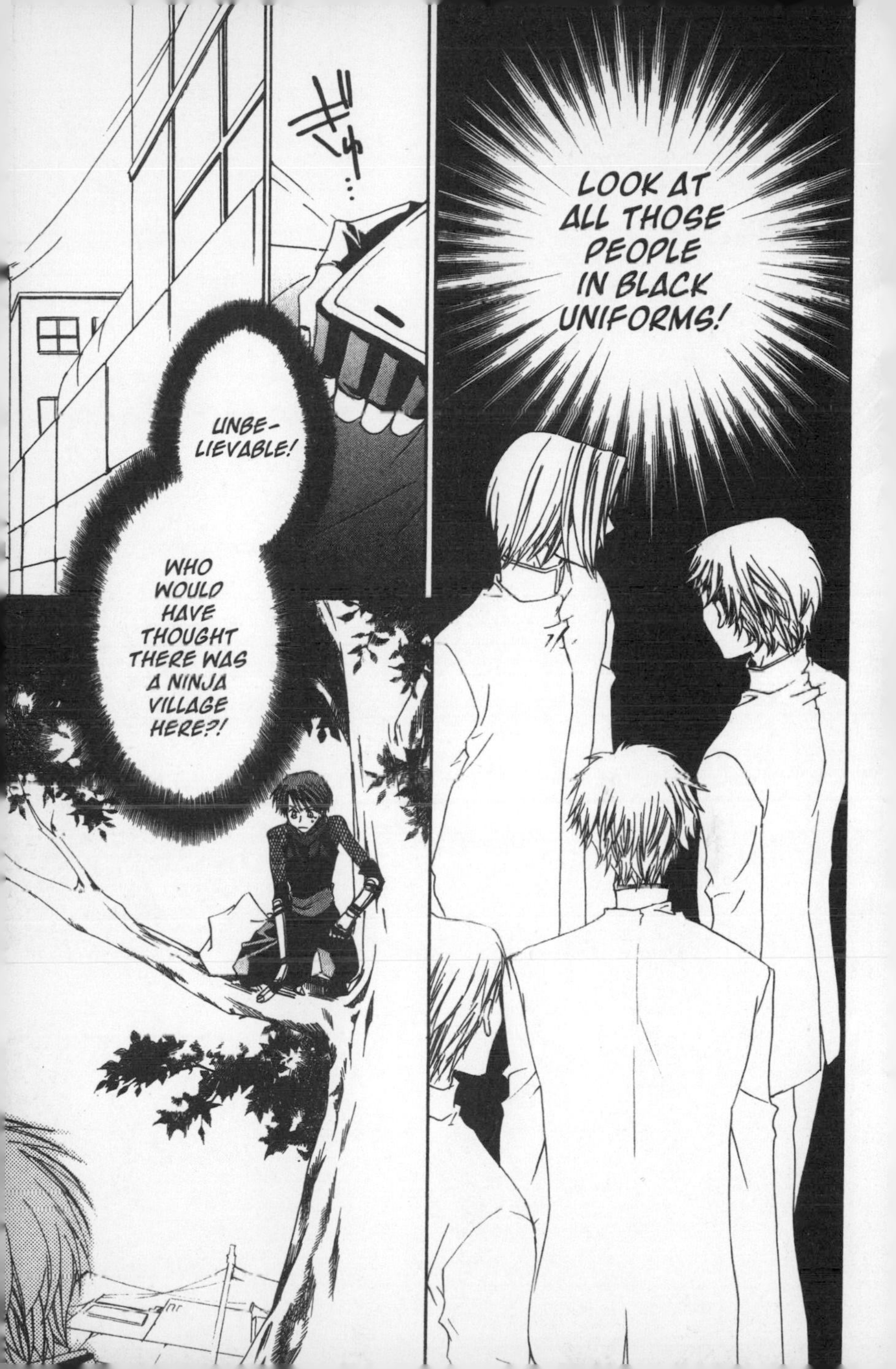
LOOK AT ALL THOSE PEOPLE IN BLACK UNIFORMS!
ぎゅ…
UNBE- LIEVABLE!
WHO WOULD HAVE THOUGHT THERE WAS A NINJA VILLAGE HERE?!

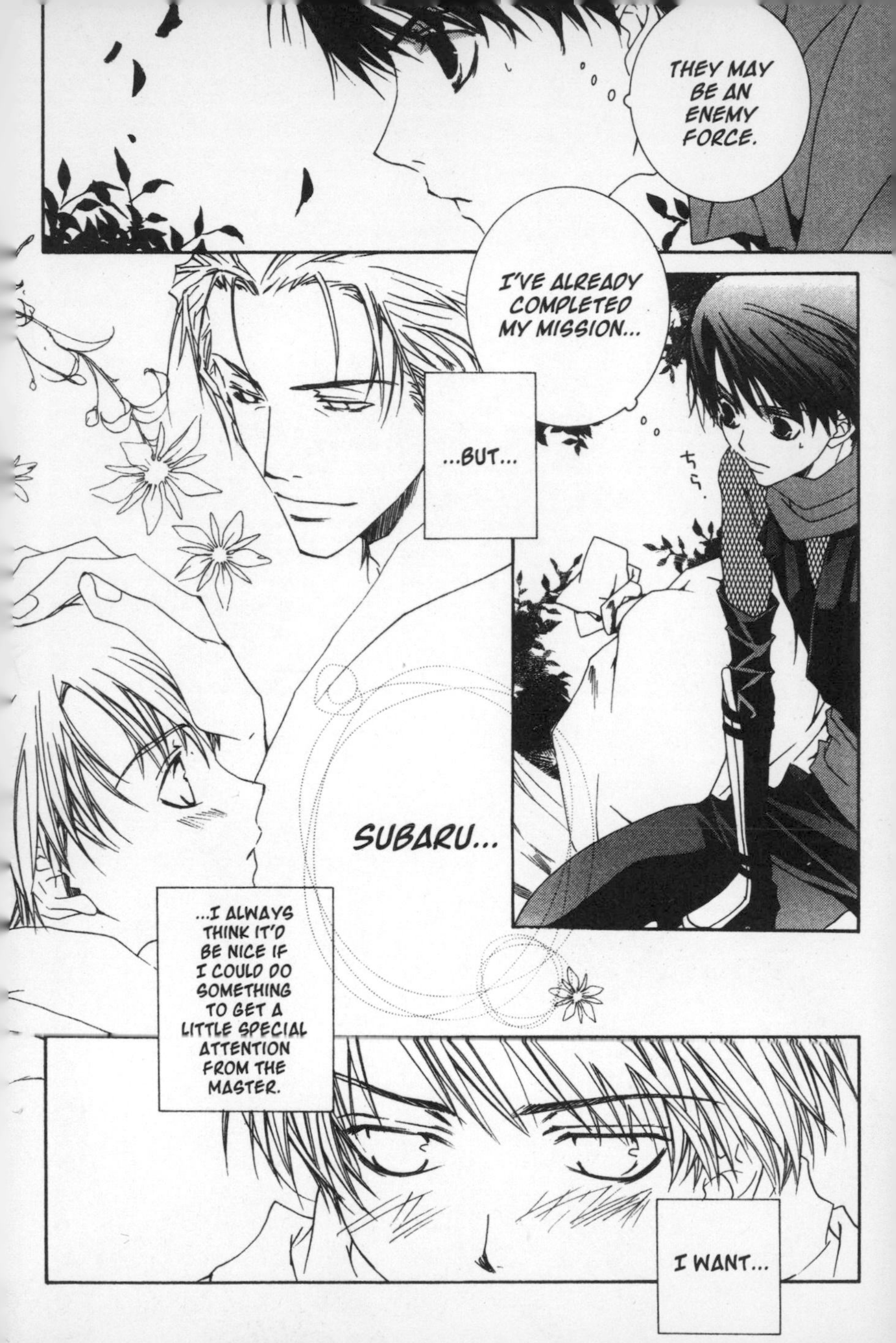
THEY MAY BE AN ENEMY FORCE.
I'VE ALREADY COMPLETED MY MISSION...
ちら
...BUT...
SUBARU...
...I ALWAYS THINK IT'D BE NICE IF I COULD DO SOMETHING TO GET A LITTLE SPECIAL ATTENTION FROM THE MASTER.
I WANT...

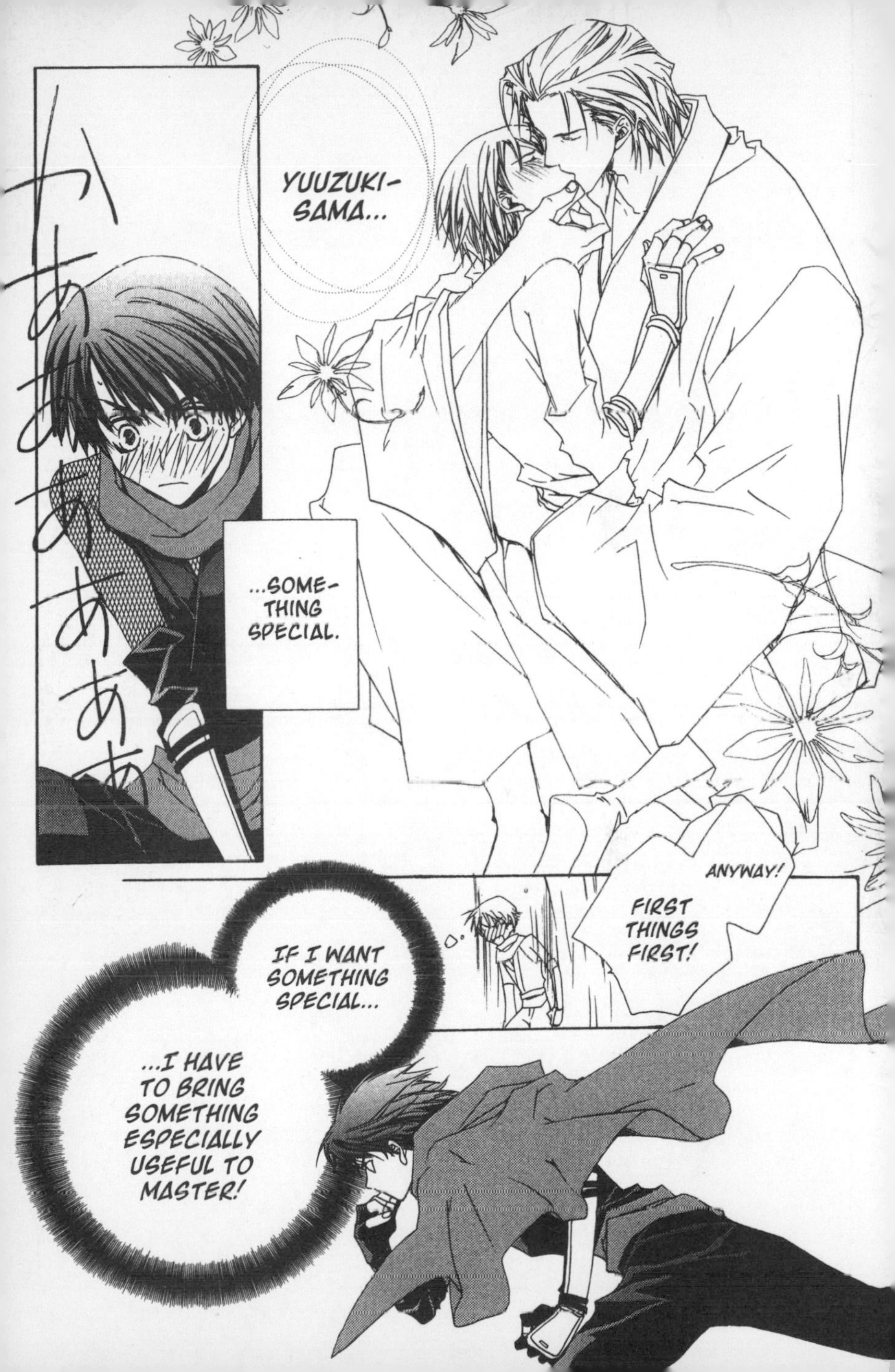
YUUZUKI-SAMA...
...SOME-THING SPECIAL.
かああああああ
ANYWAY!
FIRST THINGS FIRST!
IF I WANT SOMETHING SPECIAL...
...I HAVE TO BRING SOMETHING ESPECIALLY USEFUL TO MASTER!

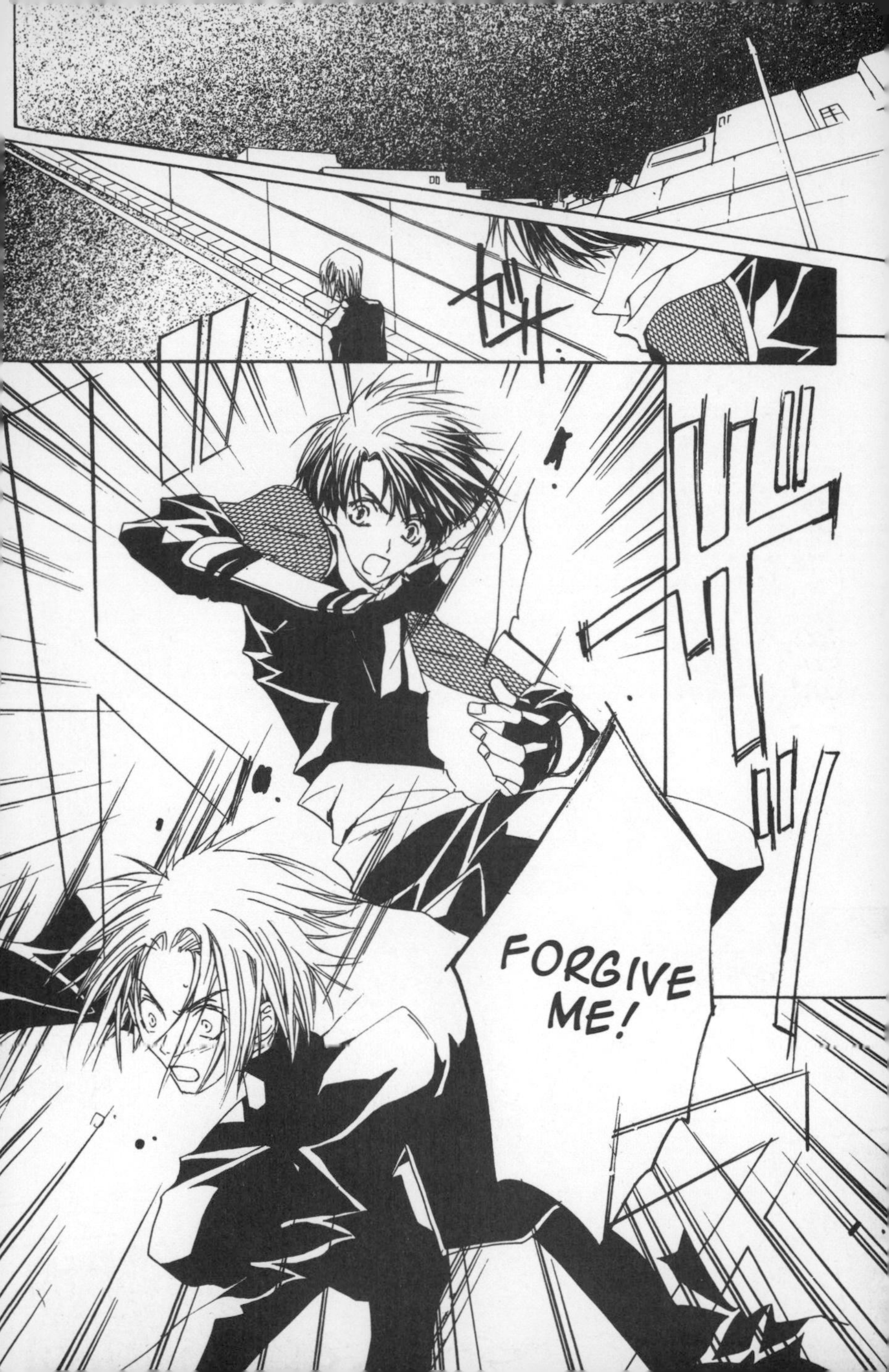
FORGIVE ME!

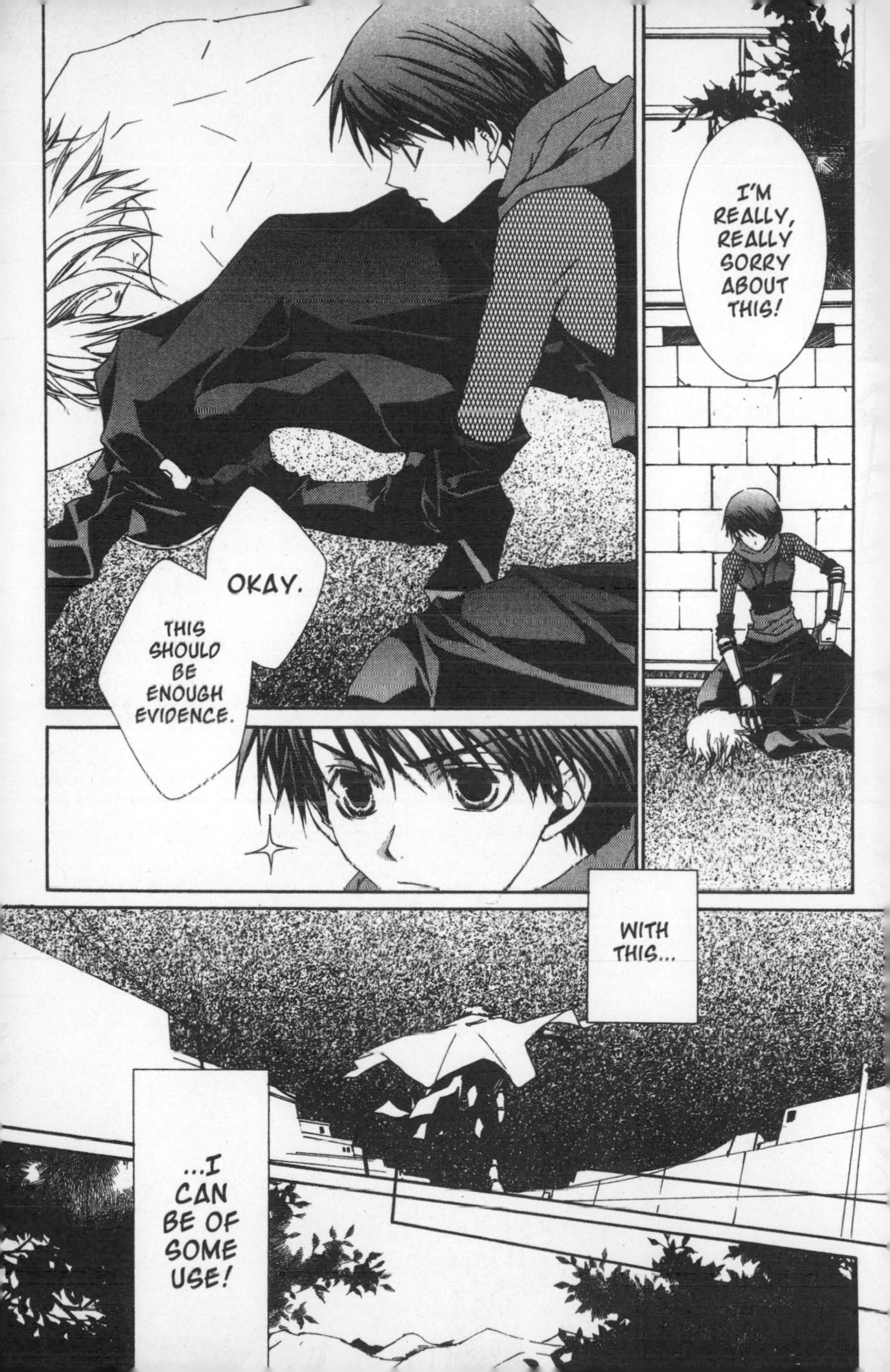
I'M REALLY, REALLY SORRY ABOUT THIS!
OKAY.
THIS SHOULD BE ENOUGH EVIDENCE.
WITH THIS...
...I CAN BE OF SOME USE!

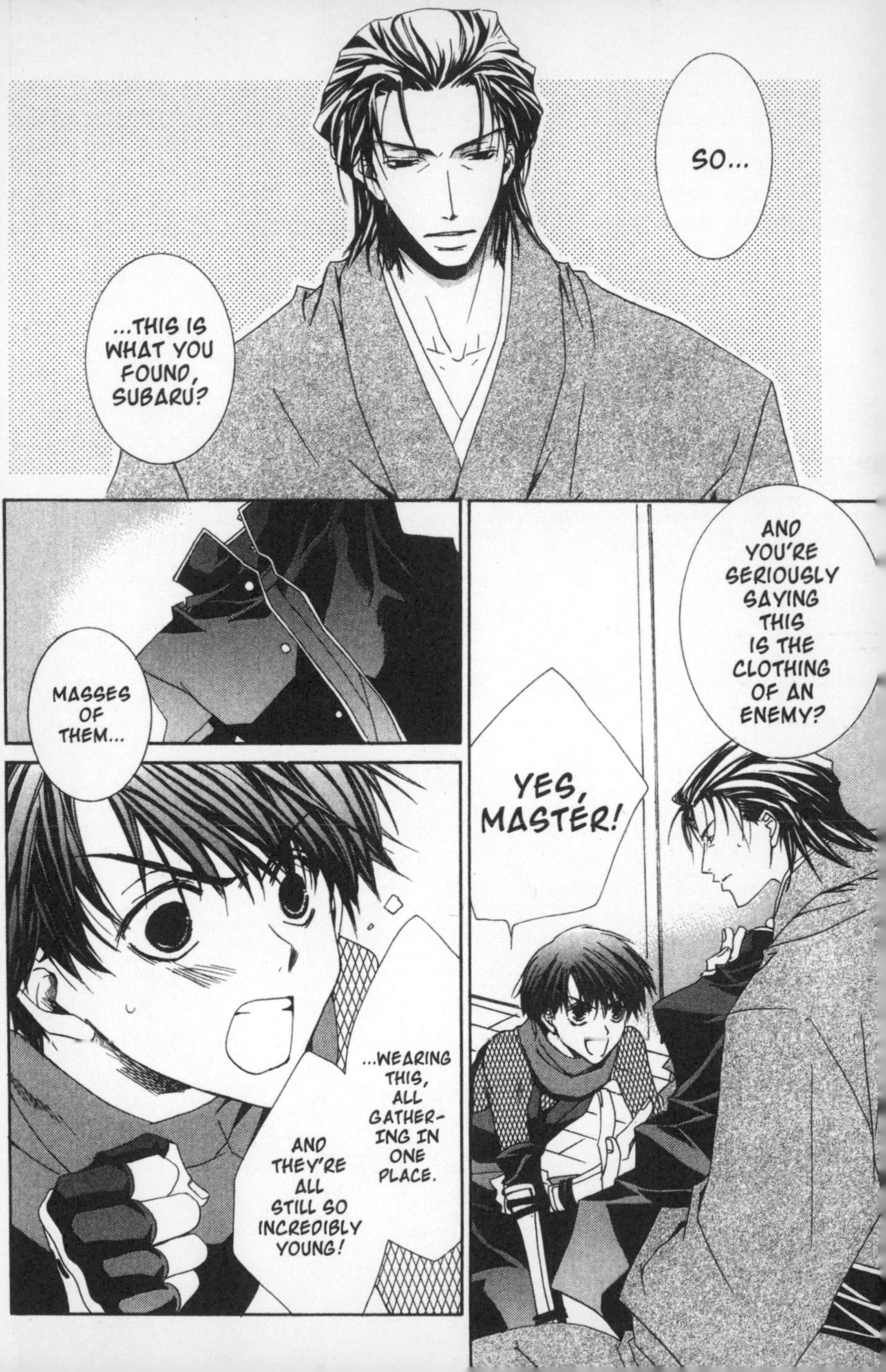
SO...
...THIS IS WHAT YOU FOUND, SUBARU?
AND YOU'RE SERIOUSLY SAYING THIS IS THE CLOTHING OF AN ENEMY?
YES, MASTER!
MASSES OF THEM...
...WEARING THIS, ALL GATHERING IN ONE PLACE.
AND THEY'RE ALL STILL SO INCREDIBLY YOUNG!

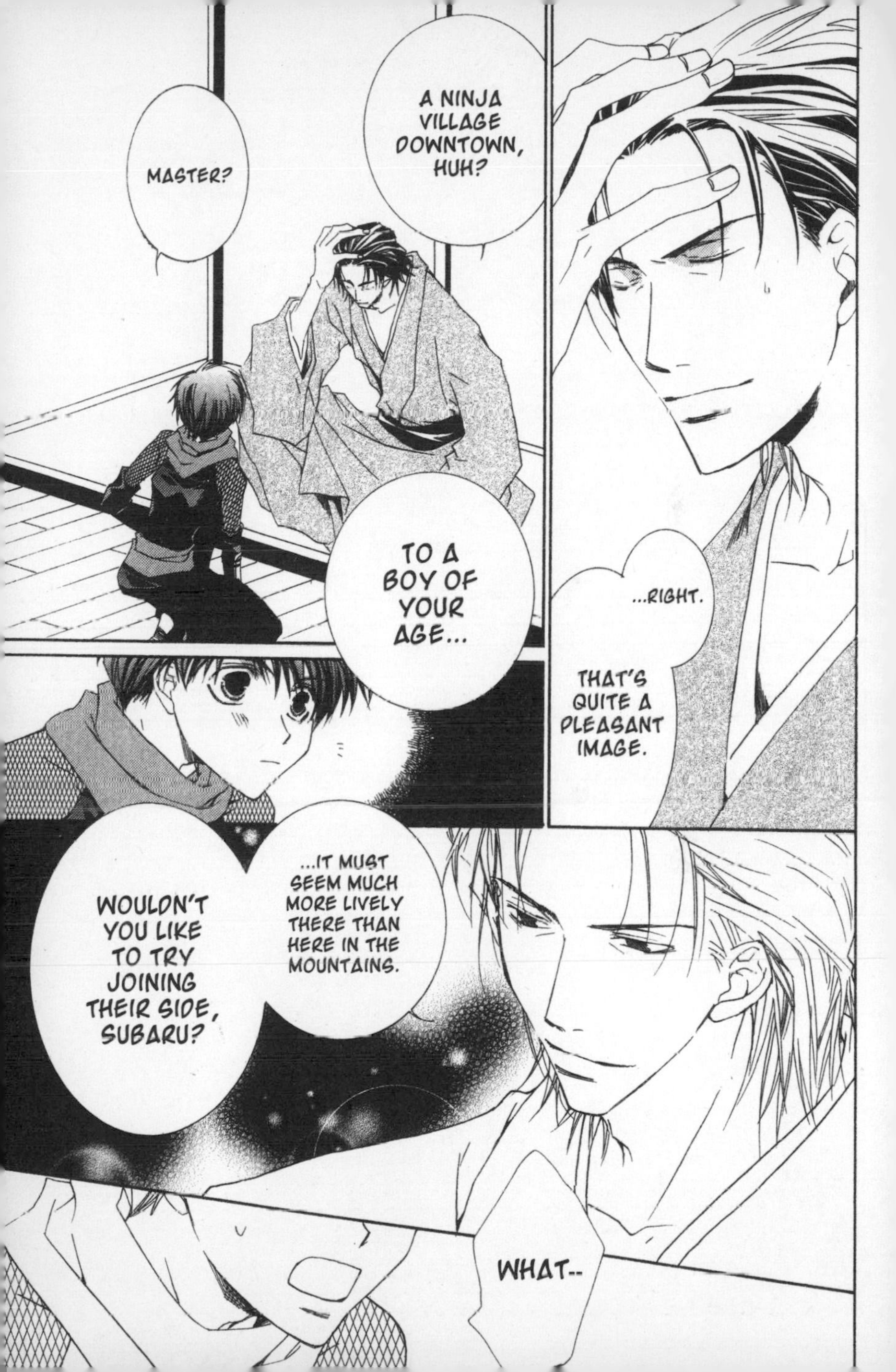
...RIGHT.
THAT'S QUITE A PLEASANT IMAGE.
A NINJA VILLAGE DOWNTOWN, HUH?
MASTER?
TO A BOY OF YOUR AGE...
...IT MUST SEEM MUCH MORE LIVELY THERE THAN HERE IN THE MOUNTAINS.
WOULDN'T YOU LIKE TO TRY JOINING THEIR SIDE, SUBARU?
WHAT--

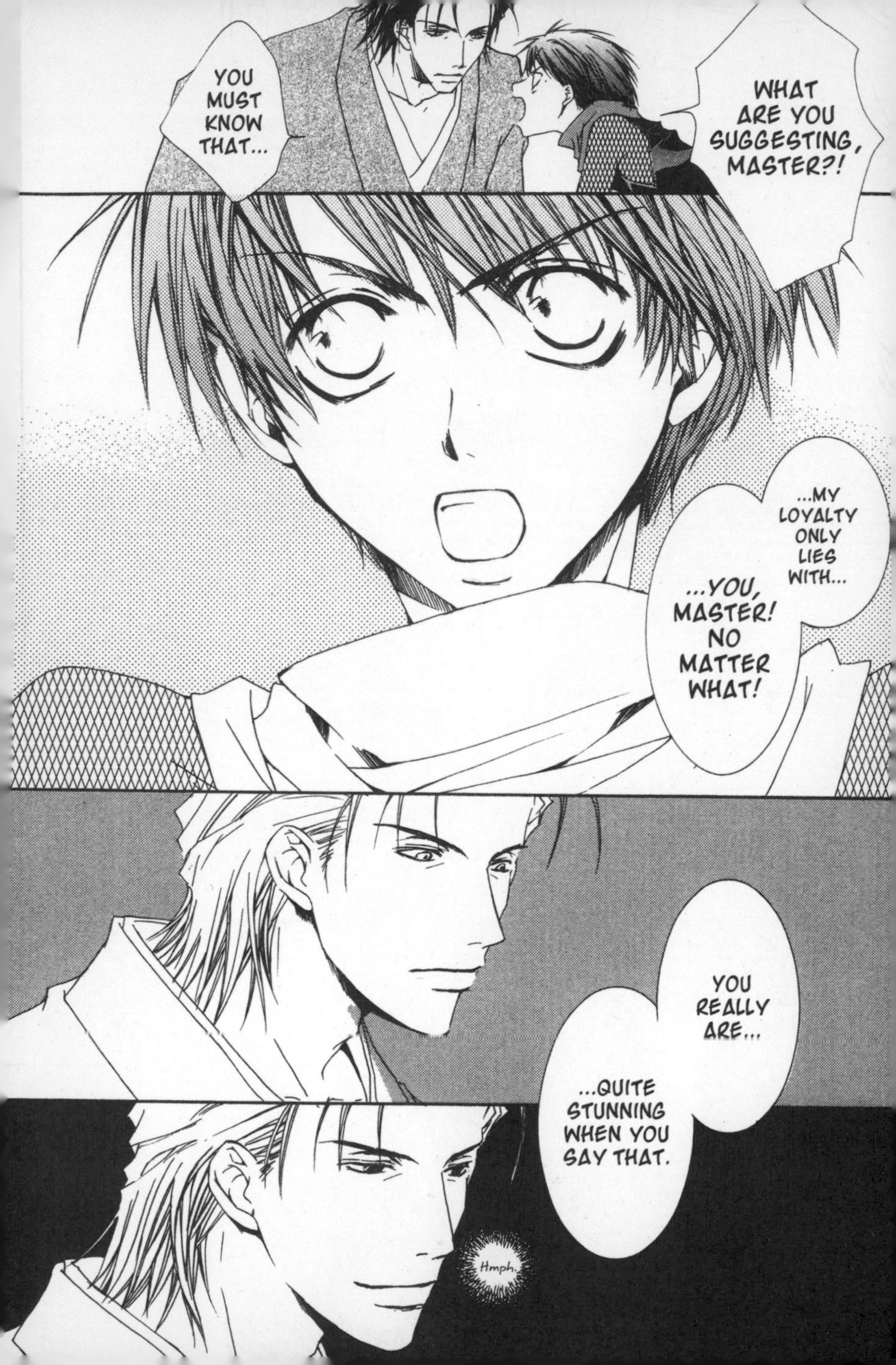
WHAT ARE YOU SUGGESTING, MASTER?!
YOU MUST KNOW THAT...
...MY LOYALTY ONLY LIES WITH...
...YOU, MASTER! NO MATTER WHAT!
YOU REALLY ARE...
...QUITE STUNNING WHEN YOU SAY THAT.
Hmph.

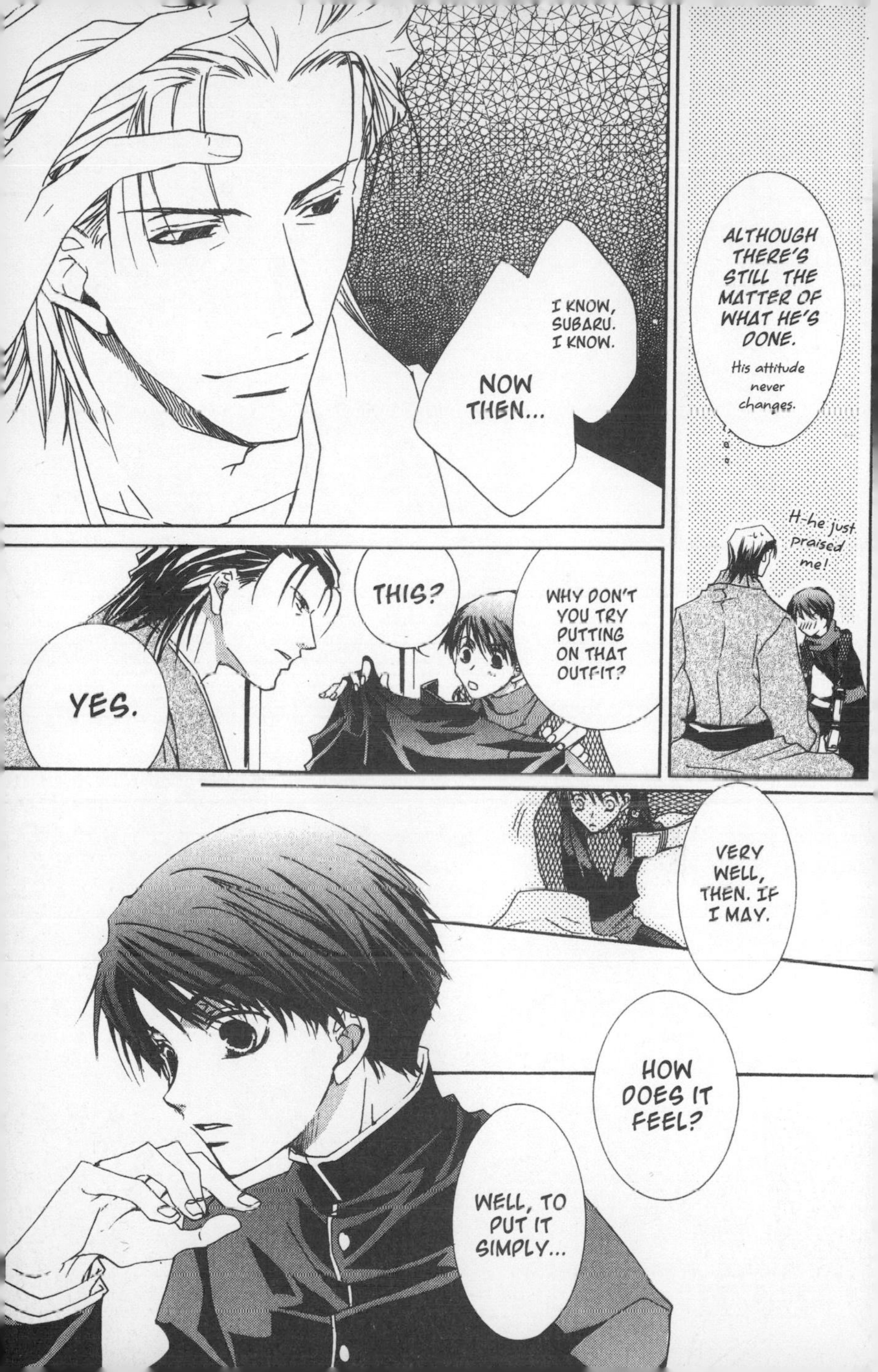
ALTHOUGH THERE'S STILL THE MATTER OF WHAT HE'S DONE.
His attitude never changes.
H-he just praised me!
I KNOW, SUBARU. I KNOW.
NOW THEN...
WHY DON'T YOU TRY PUTTING ON THAT OUTFIT?
THIS?
YES.
VERY WELL, THEN. IF I MAY.
HOW DOES IT FEEL?
WELL, TO PUT IT SIMPLY...

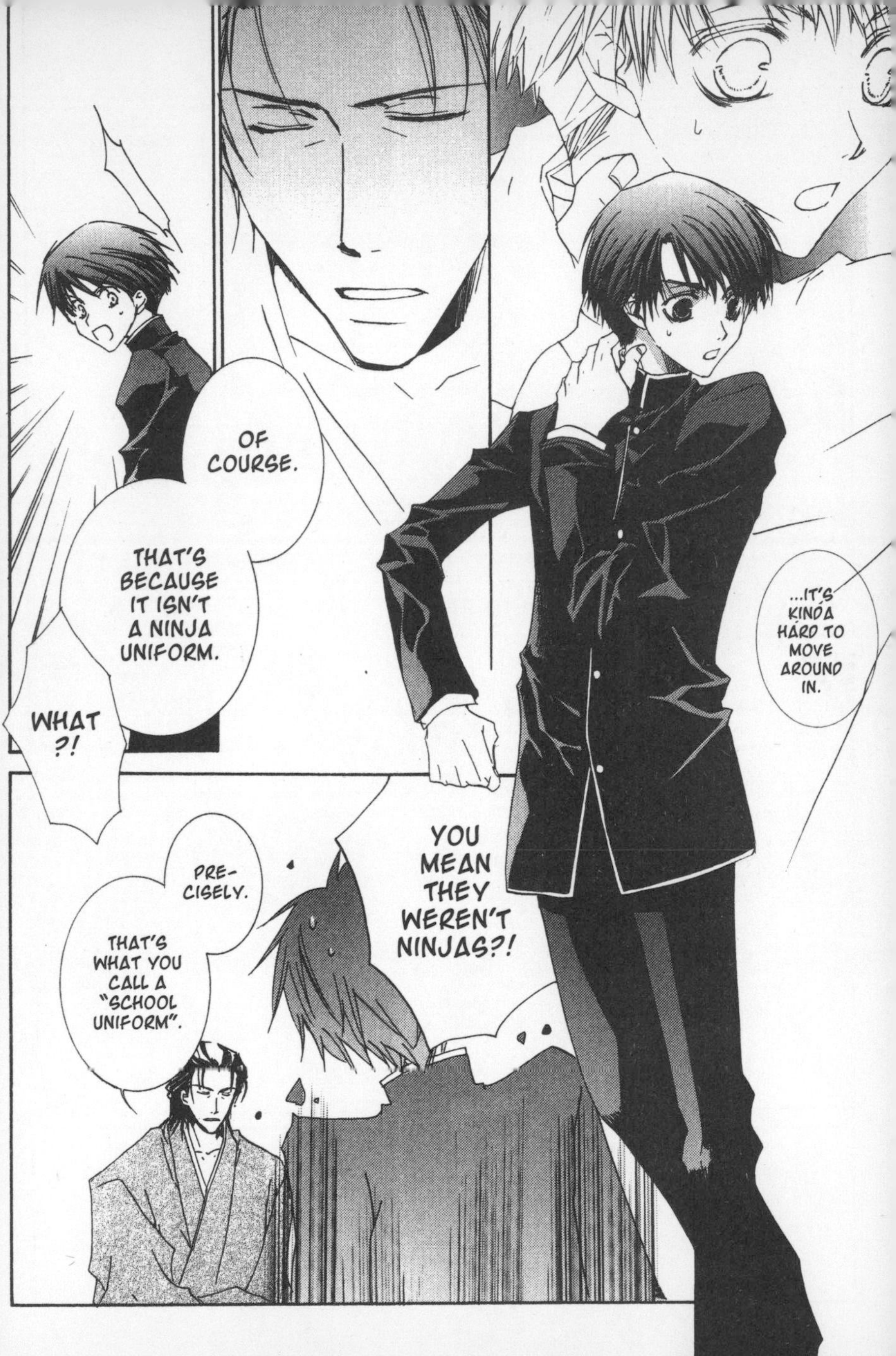
...IT'S KINDA HARD TO MOVE AROUND IN.
OF COURSE.
THAT'S BECAUSE IT ISN'T A NINJA UNIFORM.
WHAT?!
YOU MEAN THEY WEREN'T NINJAS?!
PRE-CISELY.
THAT'S WHAT YOU CALL A "SCHOOL UNIFORM".

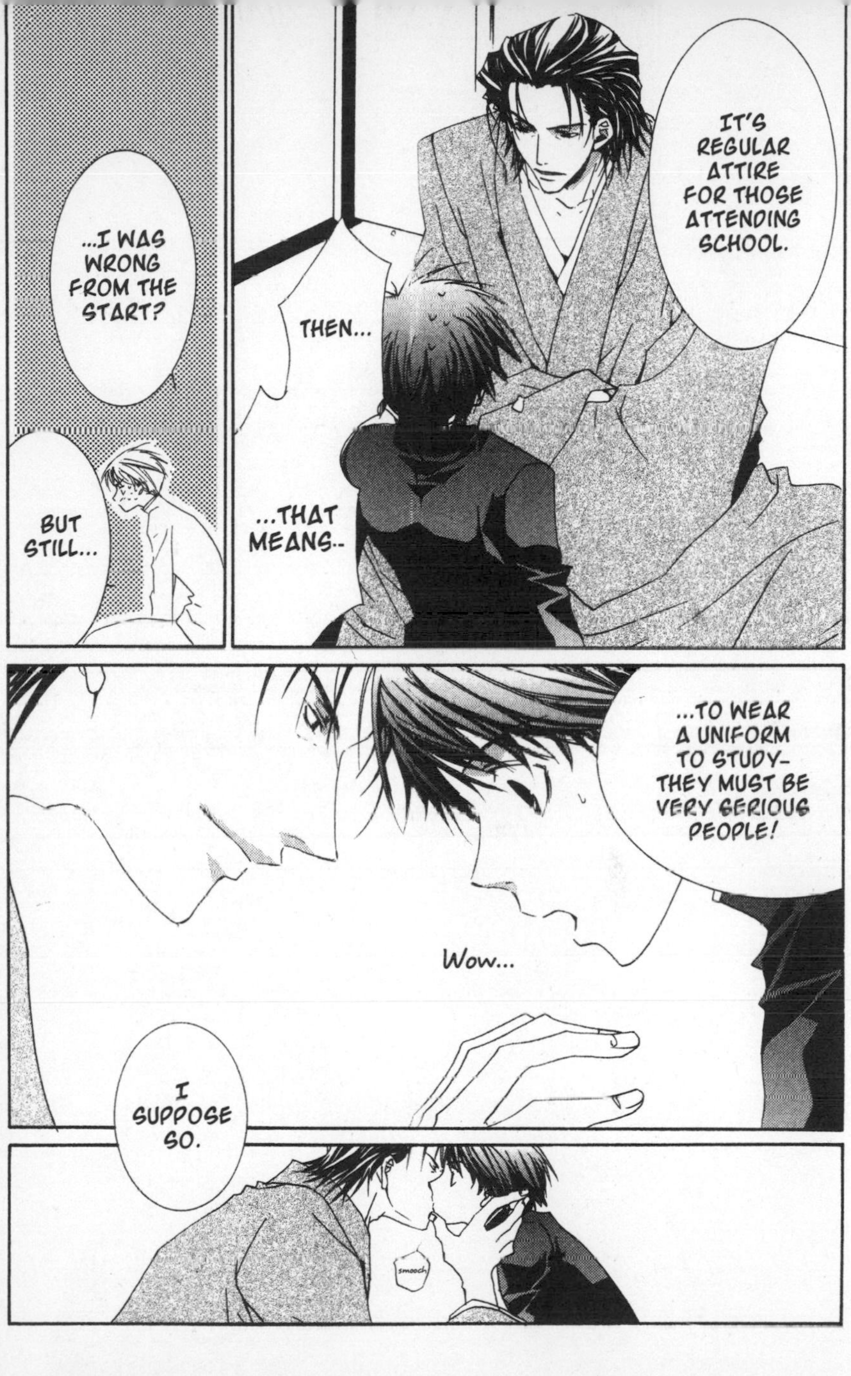
IT'S REGULAR ATTIRE FOR THOSE ATTENDING SCHOOL.
THEN...
...THAT MEANS..
...I WAS WRONG FROM THE START?
BUT STILL...
...TO WEAR A UNIFORM TO STUDY- THEY MUST BE VERY SERIOUS PEOPLE!
Wow...
I SUPPOSE SO.
smooch

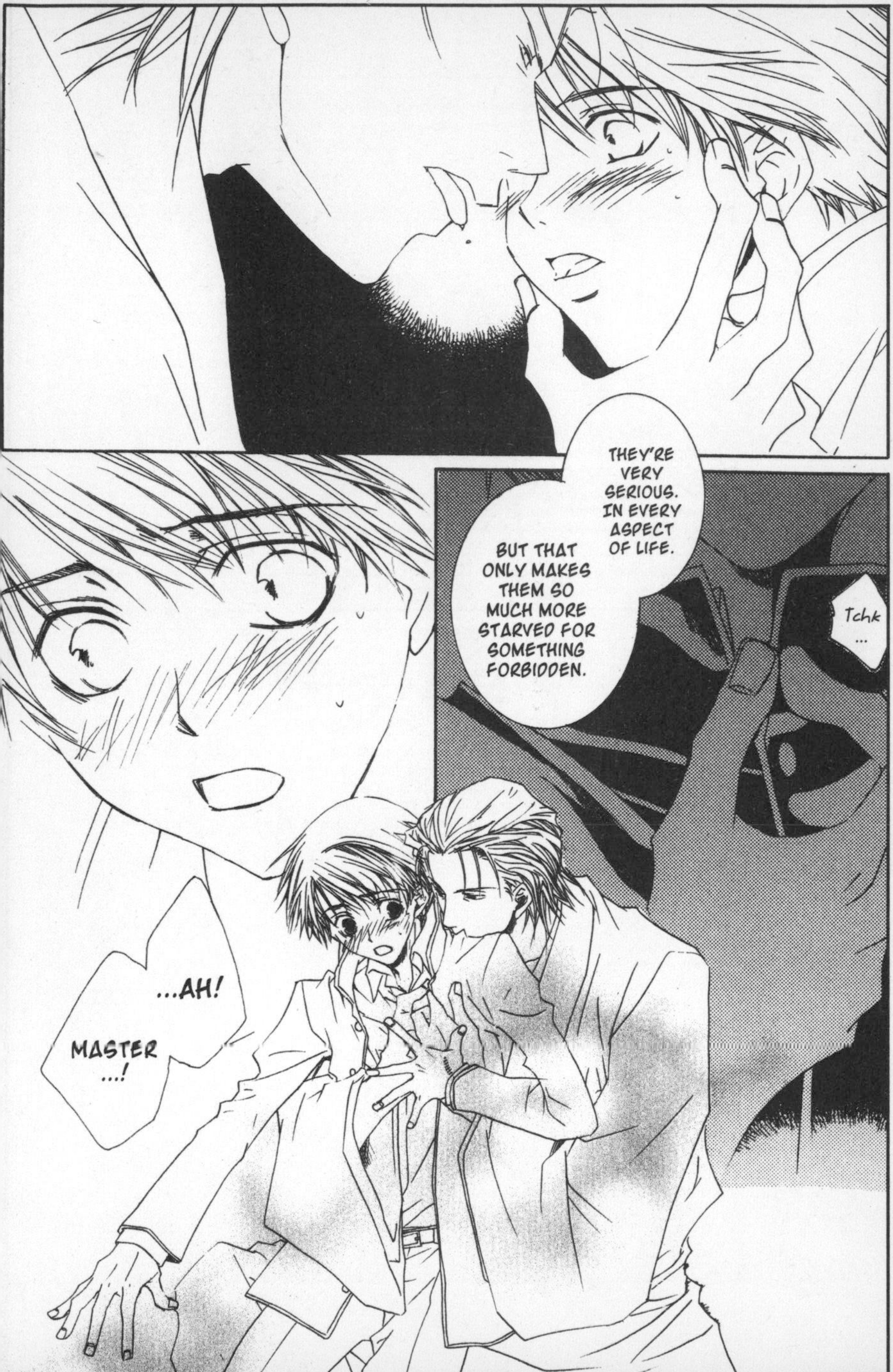
THEY'RE VERY SERIOUS. IN EVERY ASPECT OF LIFE.
BUT THAT ONLY MAKES THEM SO MUCH MORE STARVED FOR SOMETHING FORBIDDEN.
Tchk ...
...AH!
MASTER ...!

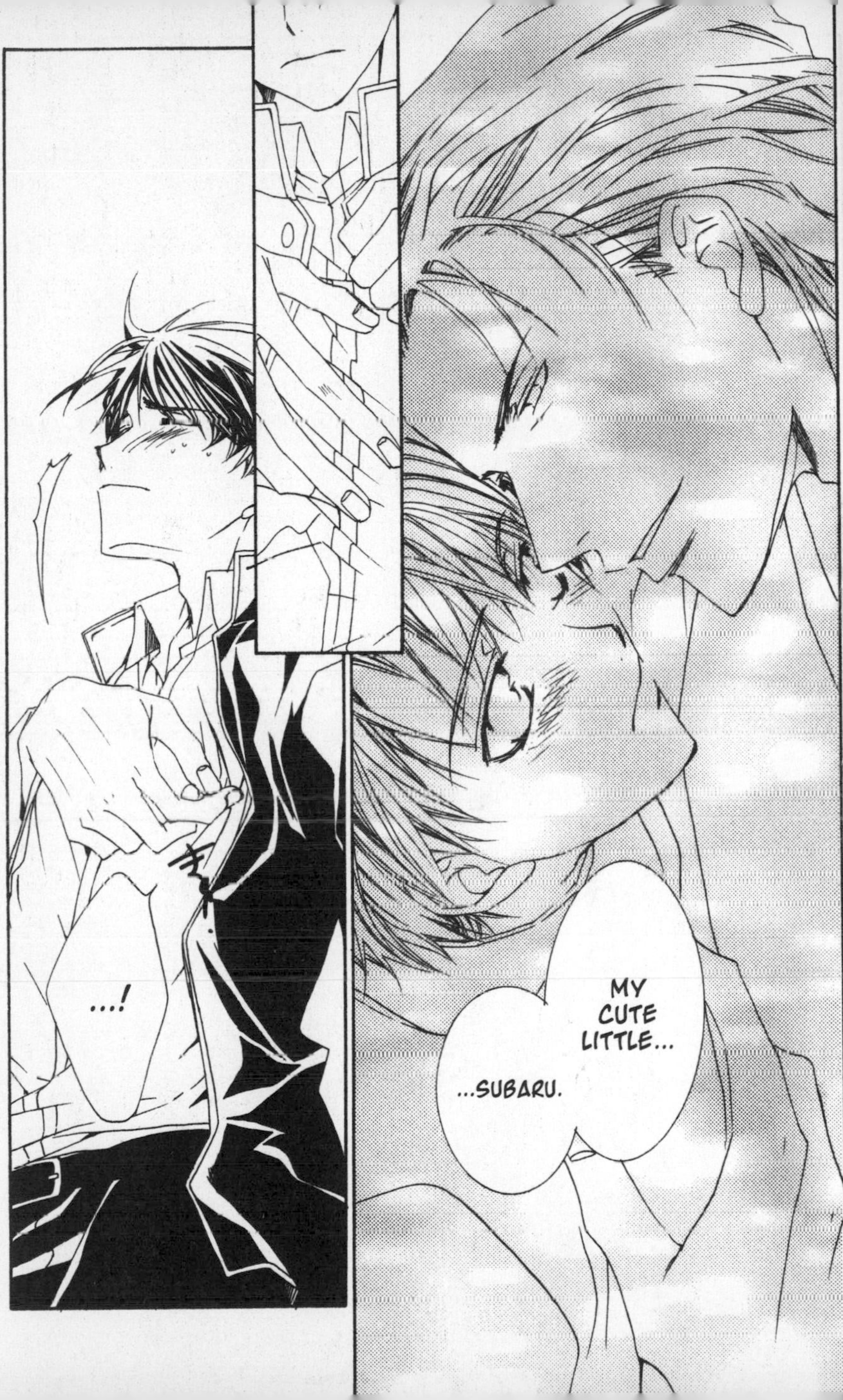
MY CUTE LITTLE...
...SUBARU.
...!

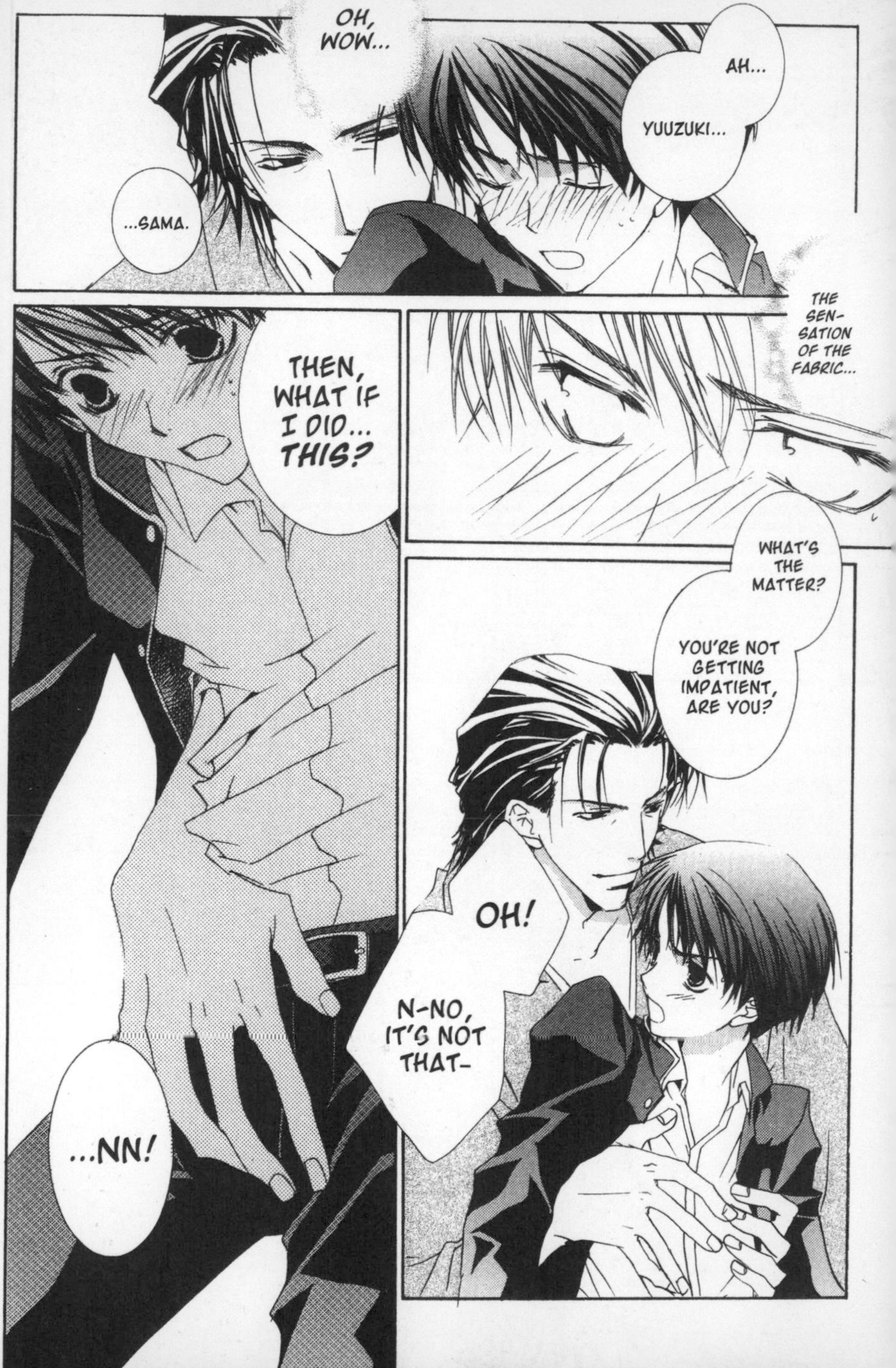
AH...
YUUZUKI...
OH, WOW...
...SAMA.
THE SEN-SATION OF THE FABRIC...
WHAT'S THE MATTER?
YOU'RE NOT GETTING IMPATIENT, ARE YOU?
OH!
N-NO, IT'S NOT THAT-
THEN, WHAT IF I DID... THIS?
...NN!

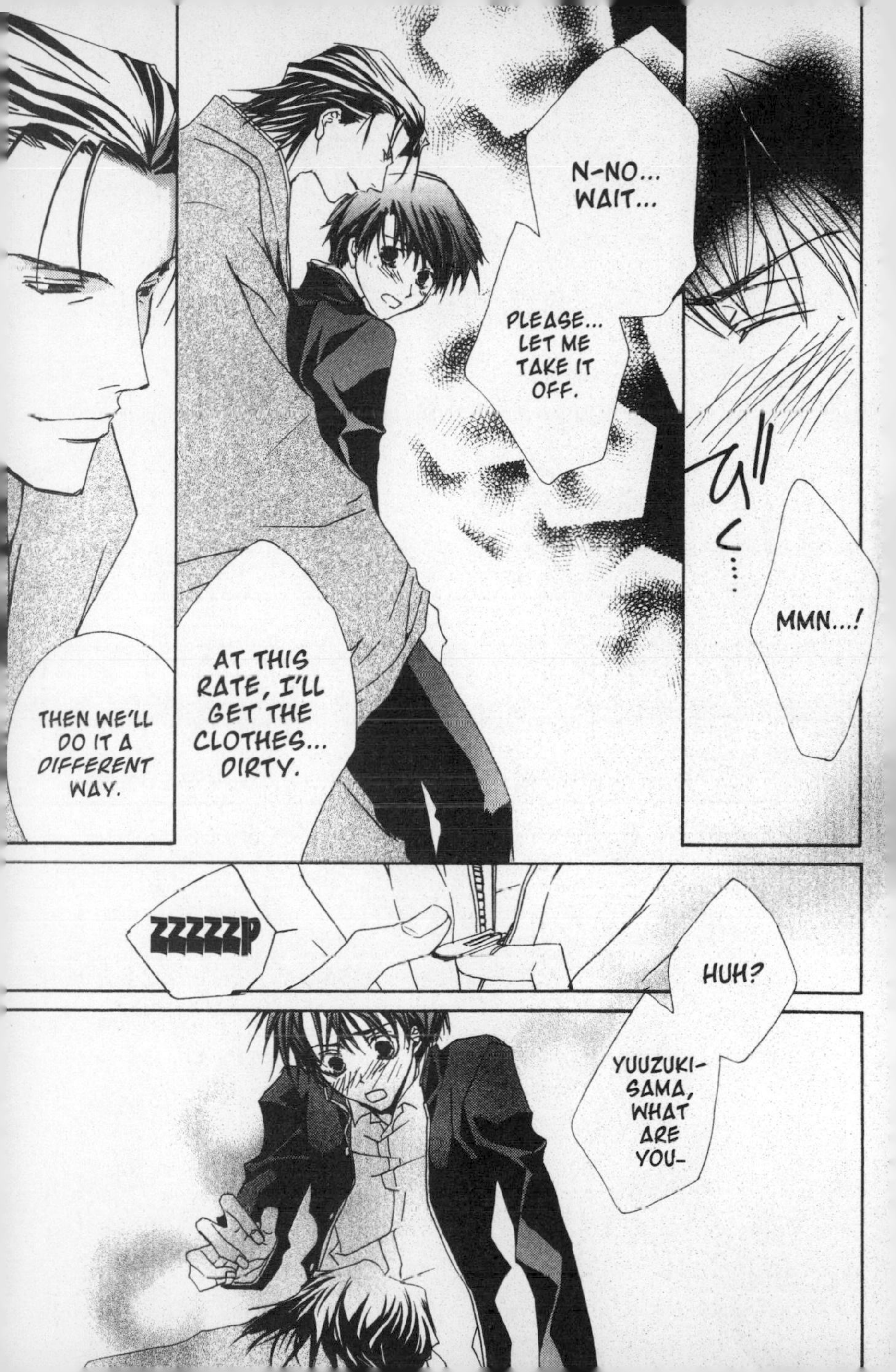
MMN...!
N-NO... WAIT...
PLEASE... LET ME TAKE IT OFF.
AT THIS RATE, I'LL GET THE CLOTHES... DIRTY.
THEN WE'LL DO IT A DIFFERENT WAY.
ZZZZZP
HUH?
YUUZUKI-SAMA, WHAT ARE YOU-

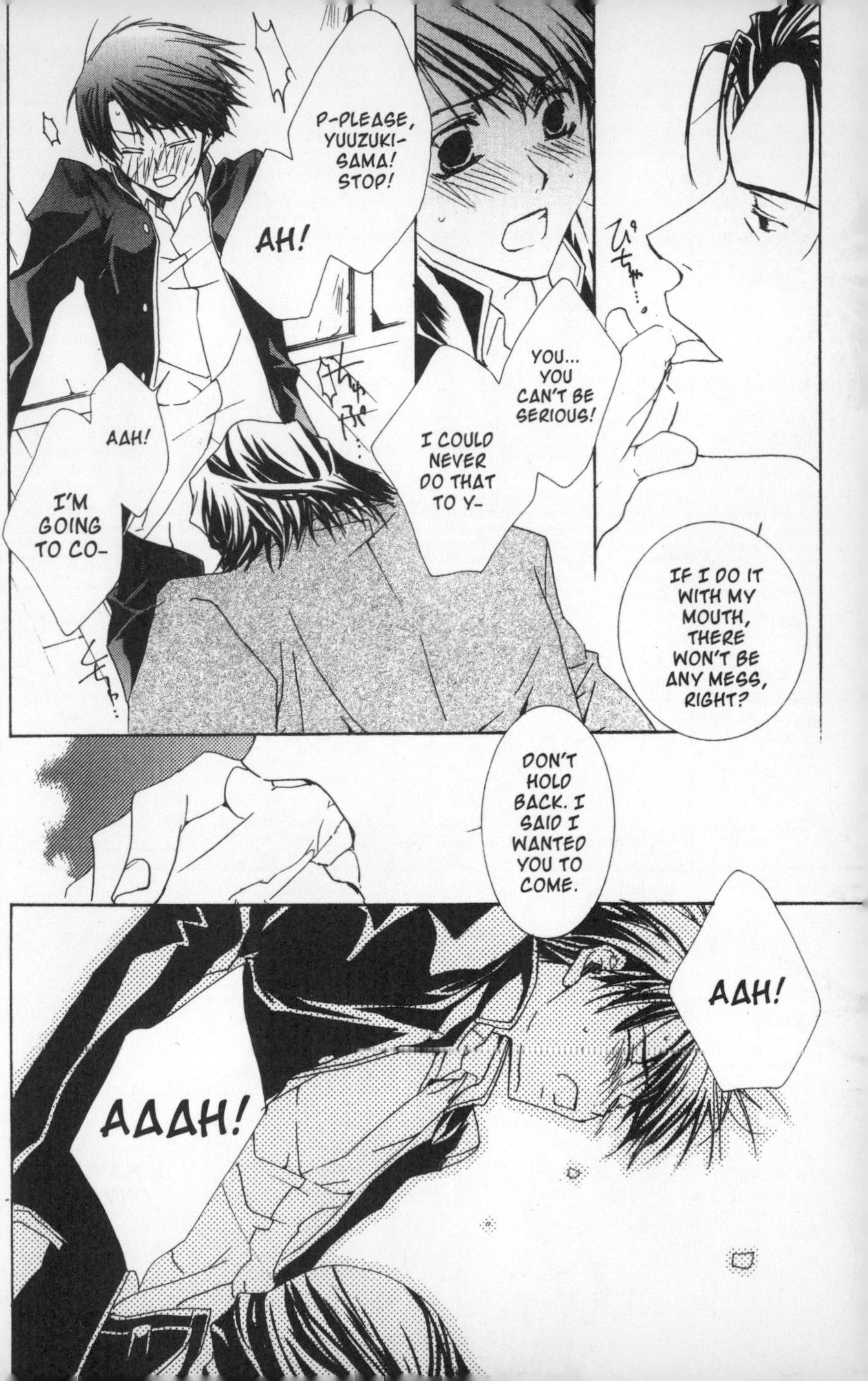
YOU... YOU CAN'T BE SERIOUS!
I COULD NEVER DO THAT TO Y-
IF I DO IT WITH MY MOUTH, THERE WON'T BE ANY MESS, RIGHT?
P-PLEASE, YUUZUKI-SAMA! STOP!
AH!
AAH!
I'M GOING TO CO-
DON'T HOLD BACK. I SAID I WANTED YOU TO COME.
AAH!
AAAH!

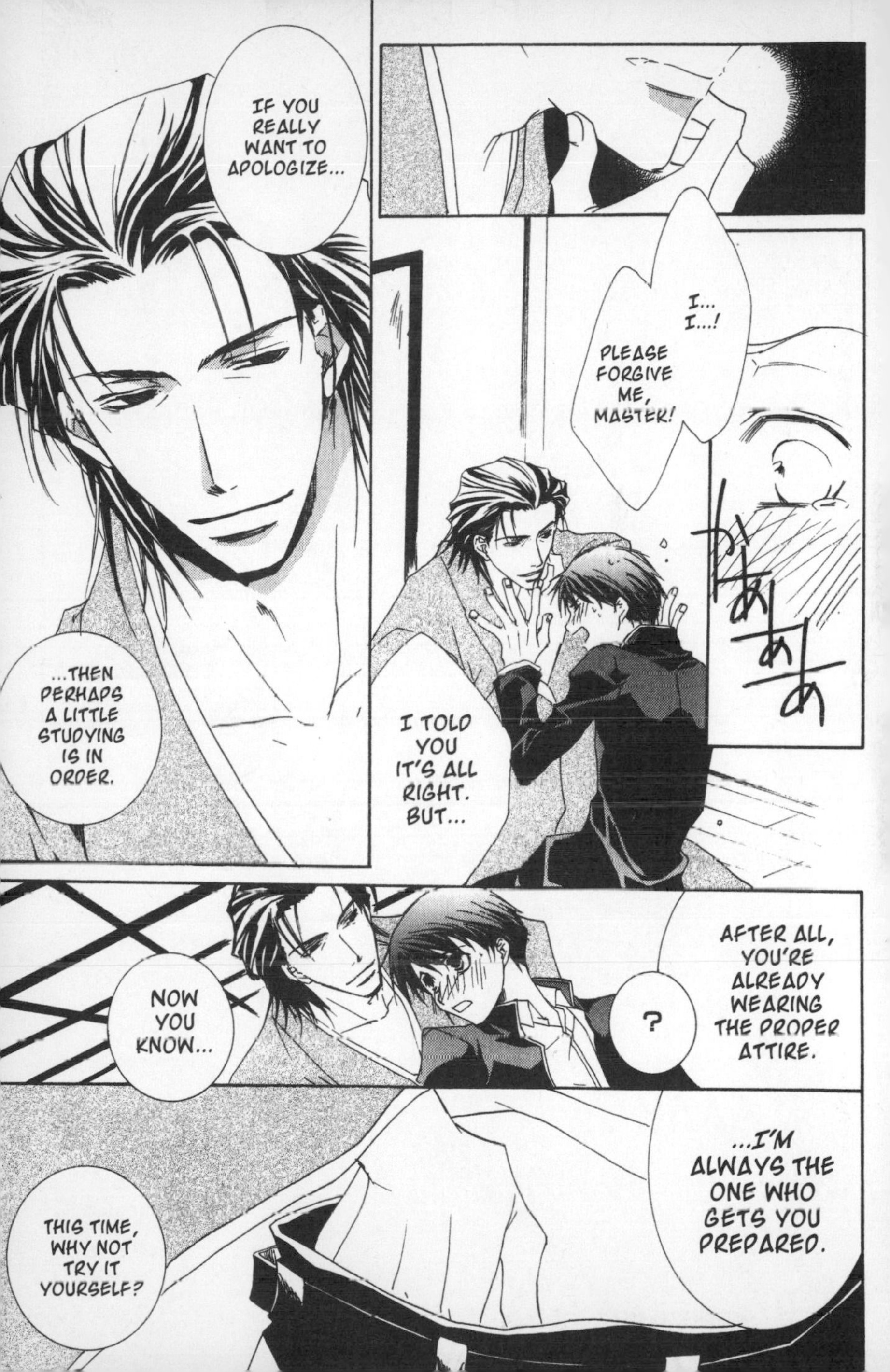
I... I...!
PLEASE FORGIVE ME, MASTER!
I TOLD YOU IT'S ALL RIGHT. BUT...
IF YOU REALLY WANT TO APOLOGIZE...
...THEN PERHAPS A LITTLE STUDYING IS IN ORDER.
AFTER ALL, YOU'RE ALREADY WEARING THE PROPER ATTIRE.
?
NOW YOU KNOW...
...I'M ALWAYS THE ONE WHO GETS YOU PREPARED.
THIS TIME, WHY NOT TRY IT YOURSELF?

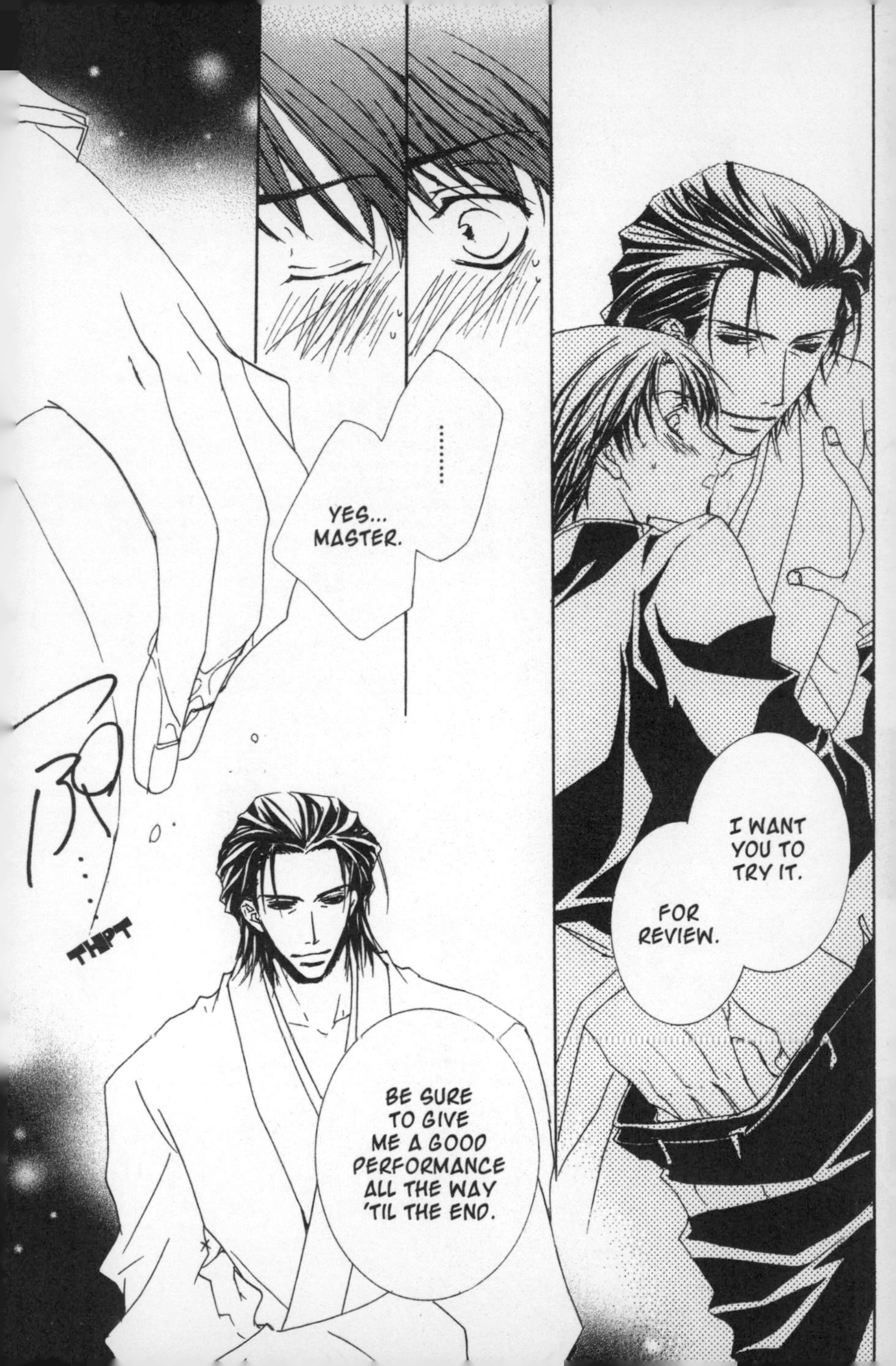
I WANT YOU TO TRY IT.
FOR REVIEW.
......
YES... MASTER.
THPT
BE SURE TO GIVE ME A GOOD PERFORMANCE ALL THE WAY 'TIL THE END.

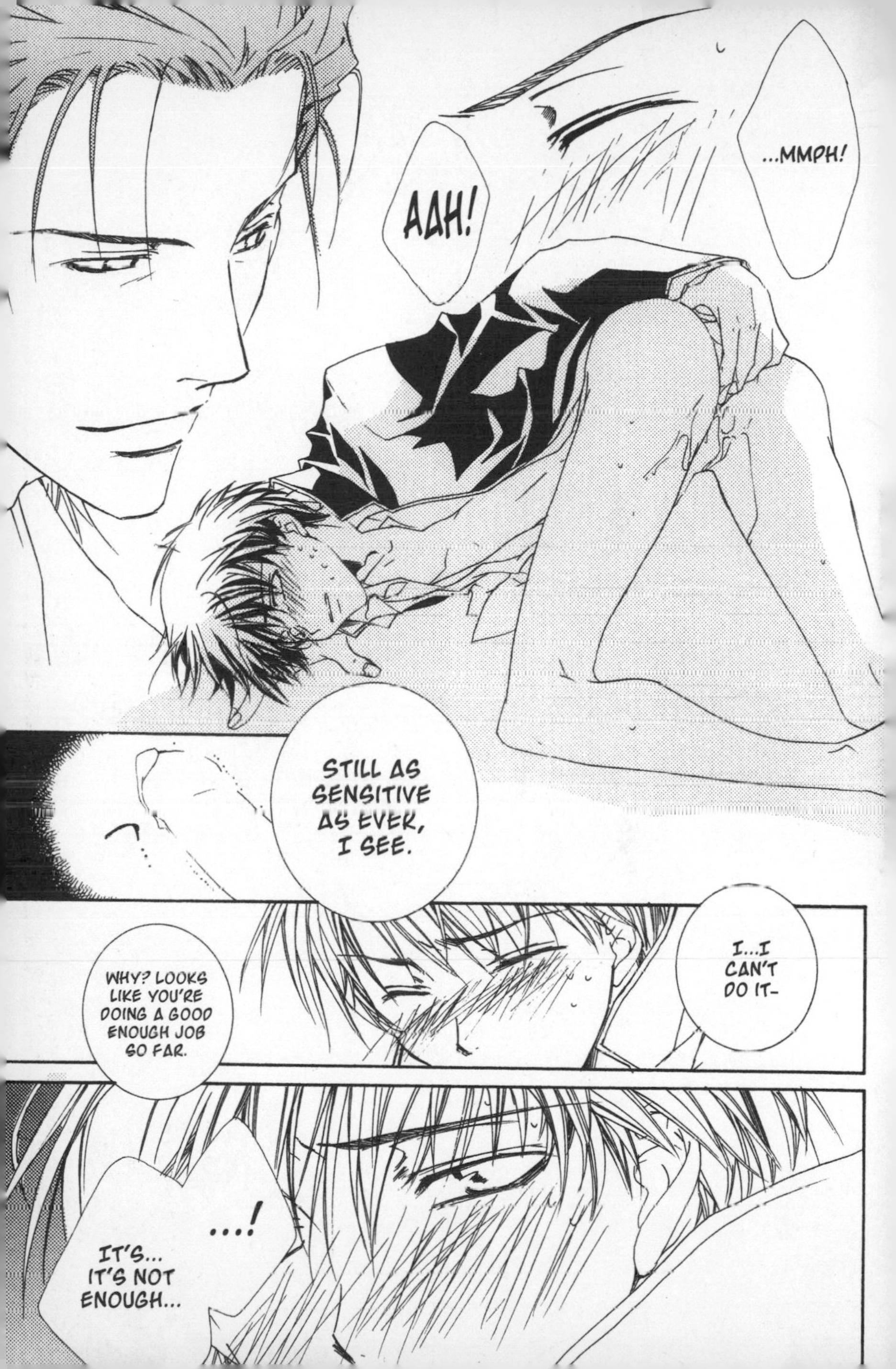
...MMPH!
AAH!
STILL AS SENSITIVE AS EVER, I SEE.
I...I CAN'T DO IT-
WHY? LOOKS LIKE YOU'RE DOING A GOOD ENOUGH JOB SO FAR.
...!
IT'S... IT'S NOT ENOUGH...

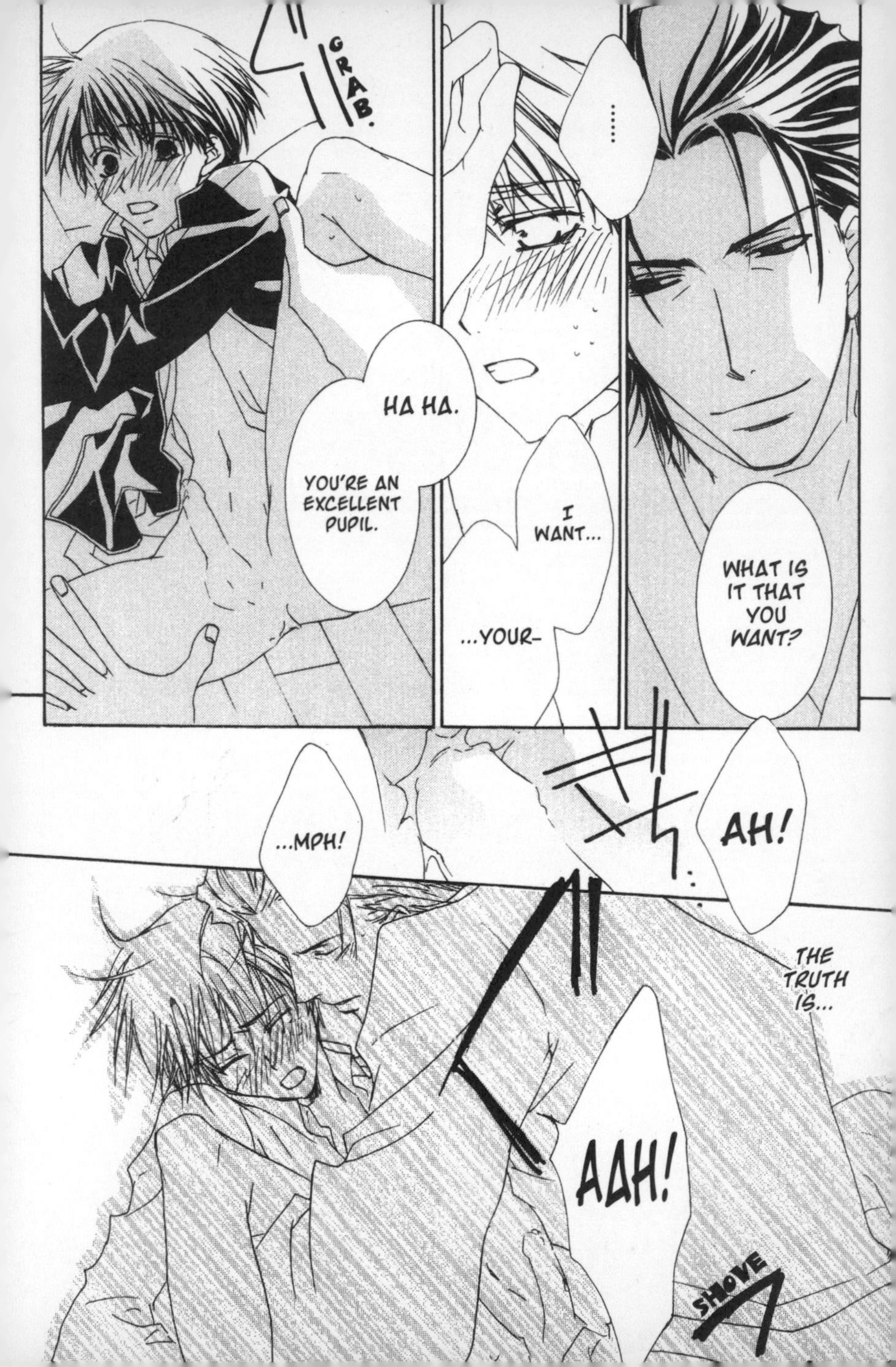
......
WHAT IS IT THAT YOU WANT?
I WANT...
...YOUR-
GRAB.
HA HA.
YOU'RE AN EXCELLENT PUPIL.
AH!
...MPH!
THE TRUTH IS...
AAH!
SHOVE

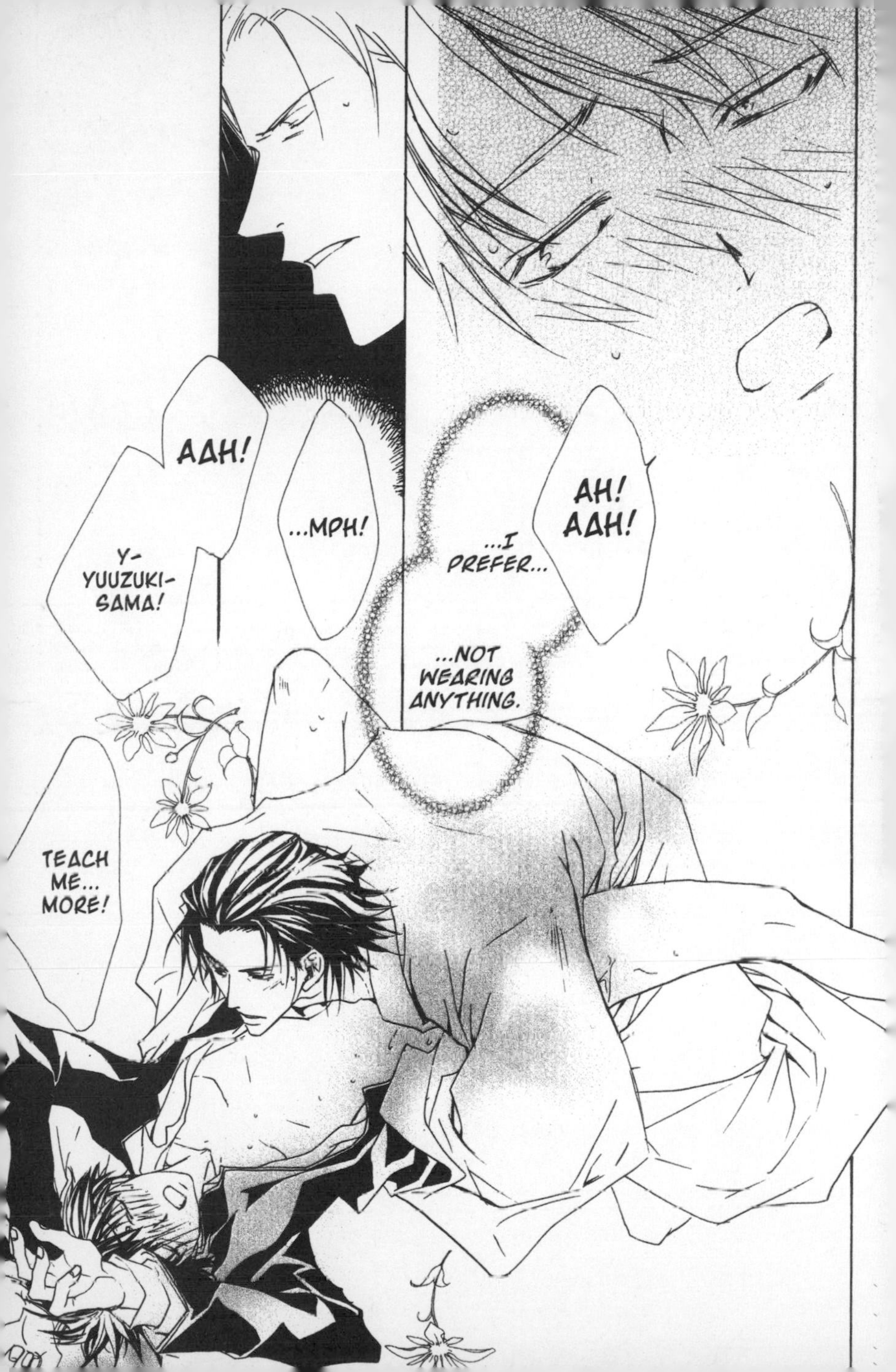
AH! AAH!
AAH!
...MPH!
Y-YUUZUKI-SAMA!
...I PREFER...
...NOT WEARING ANYTHING.
TEACH ME... MORE!

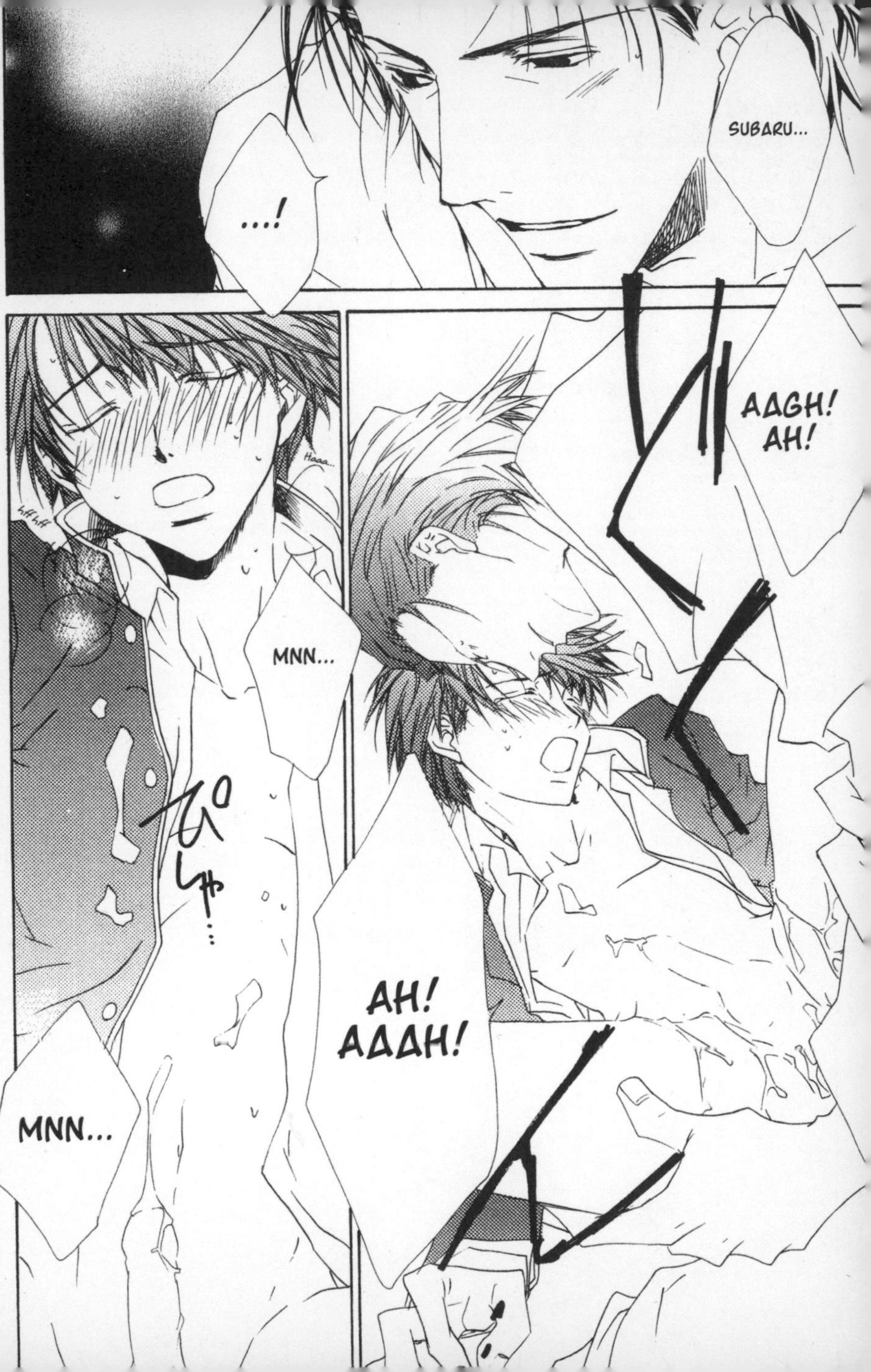
SUBARU...
...!
AAGH! AH!
AH! AAAH!
Haaa...
hff hff
MNN...
ぴしゃ...
MNN...

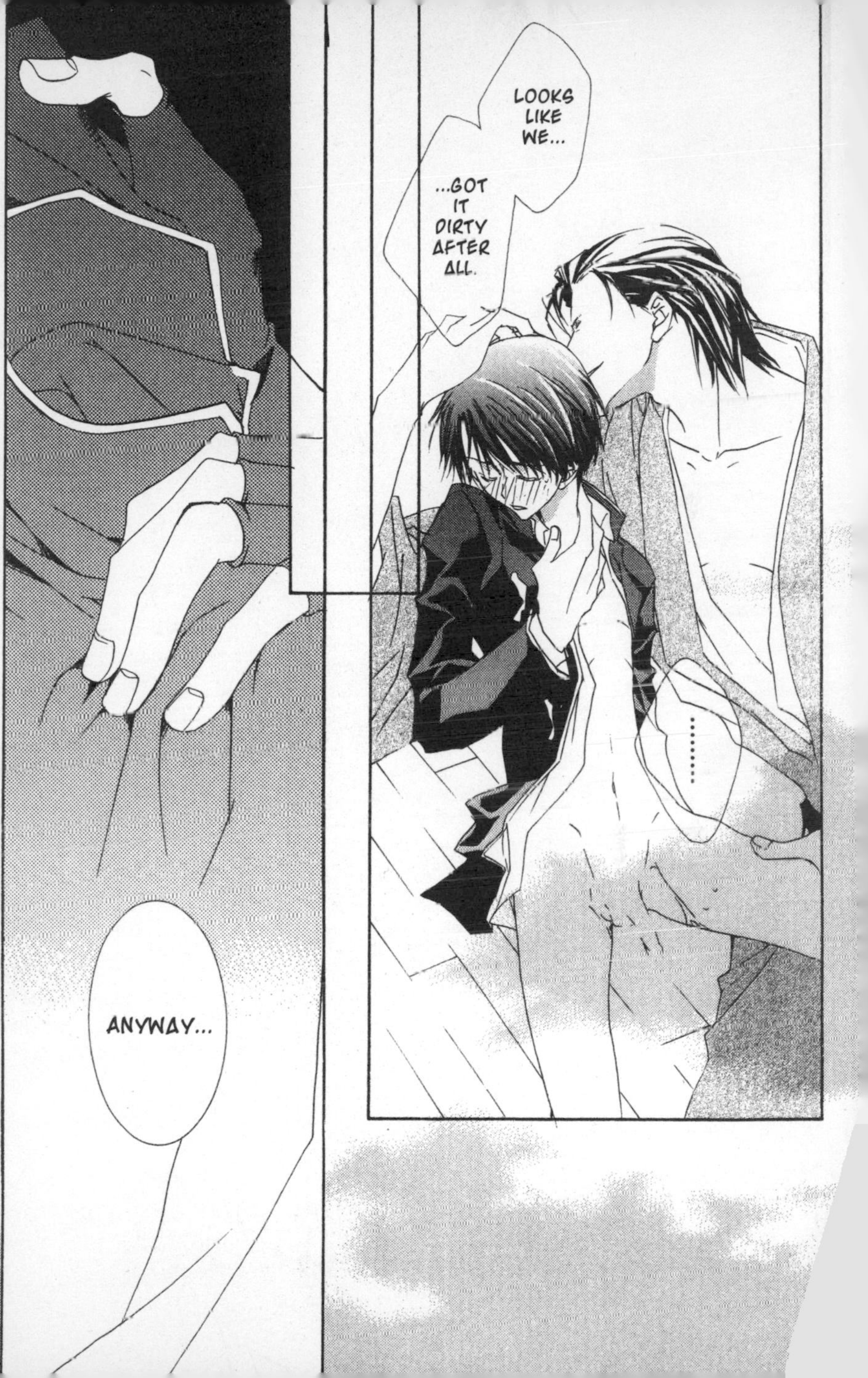
LOOKS LIKE WE...
...GOT IT DIRTY AFTER ALL.
......
ANYWAY...

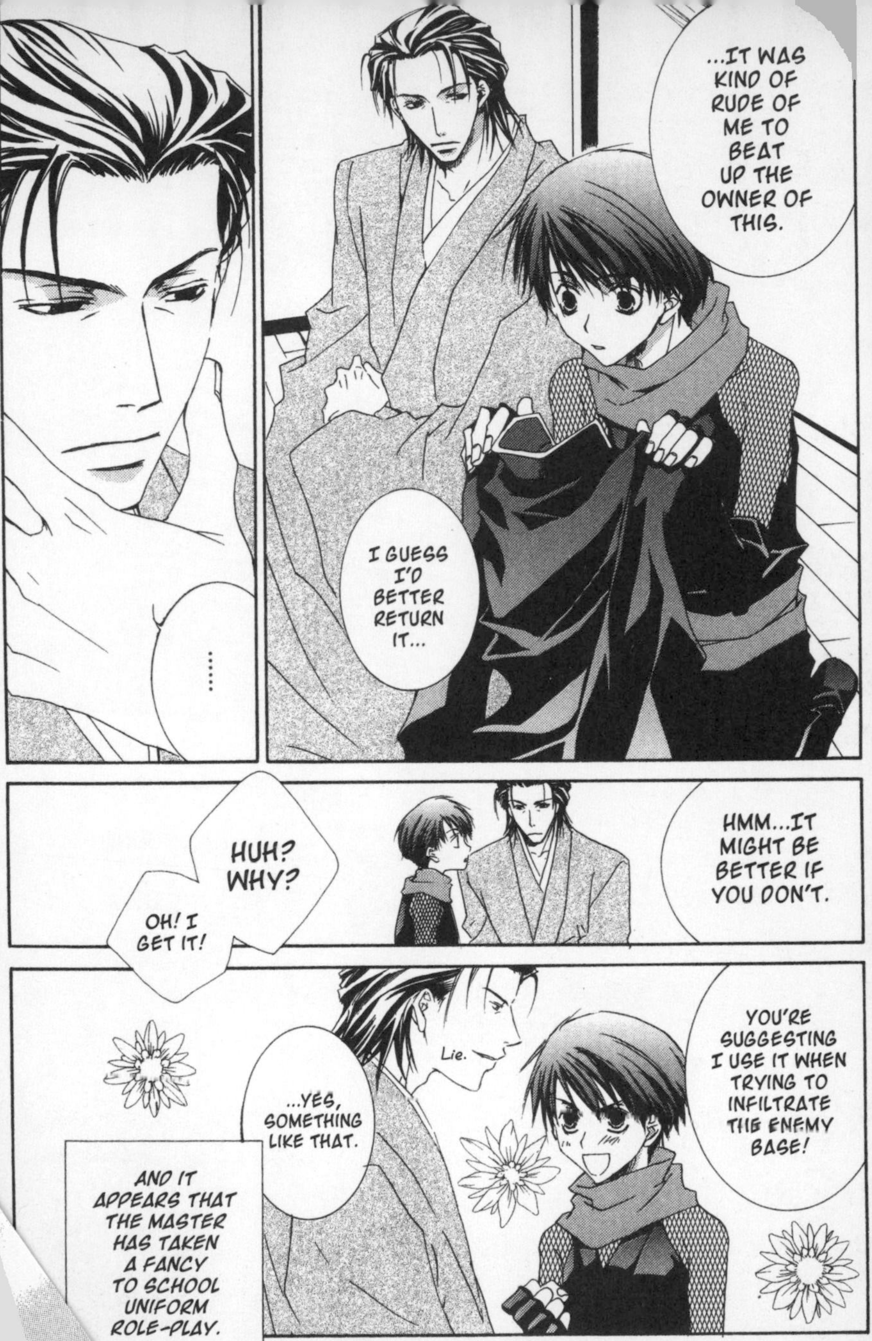
...IT WAS KIND OF RUDE OF ME TO BEAT UP THE OWNER OF THIS.
I GUESS I'D BETTER RETURN IT...
......
HMM...IT MIGHT BE BETTER IF YOU DON'T.
HUH? WHY?
OH! I GET IT!
YOU'RE SUGGESTING I USE IT WHEN TRYING TO INFILTRATE THE ENEMY BASE!
Lie.
...YES, SOMETHING LIKE THAT.
AND IT APPEARS THAT THE MASTER HAS TAKEN A FANCY TO SCHOOL UNIFORM ROLE-PLAY.

Secret Outfit / End

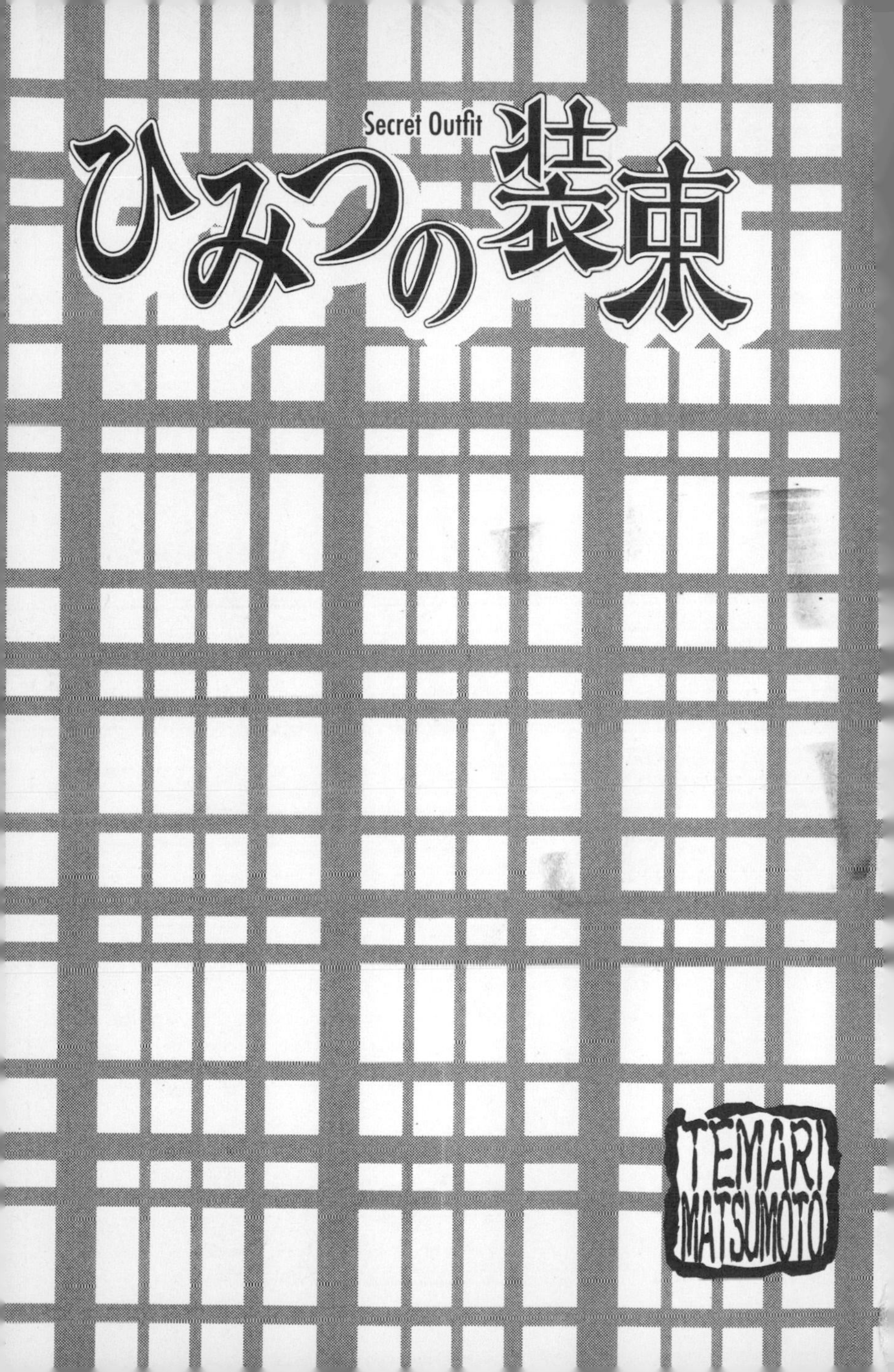
Secret Outfit
ひみつの装束
TEMARI MATSUMOTO

YÛDUKI

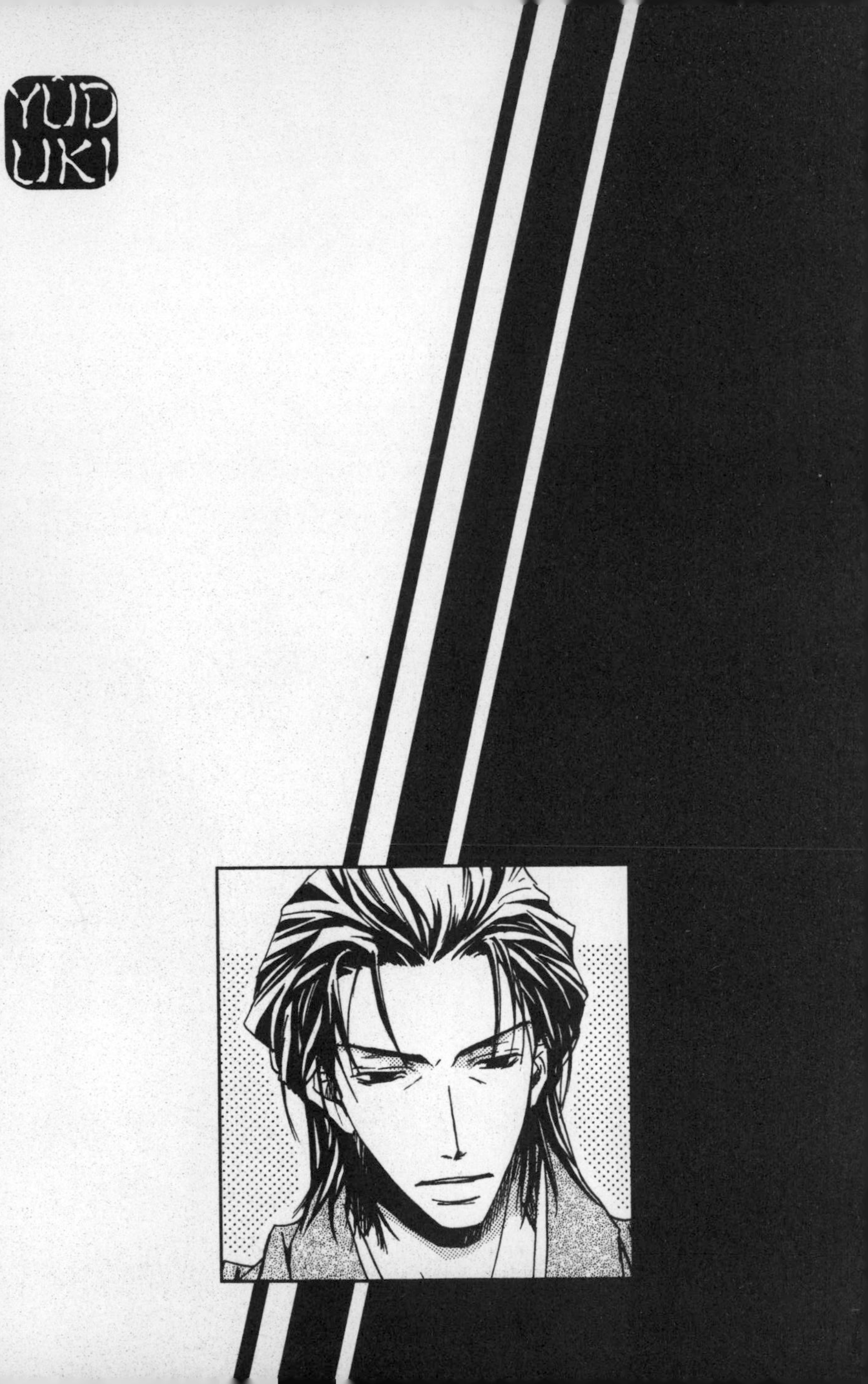

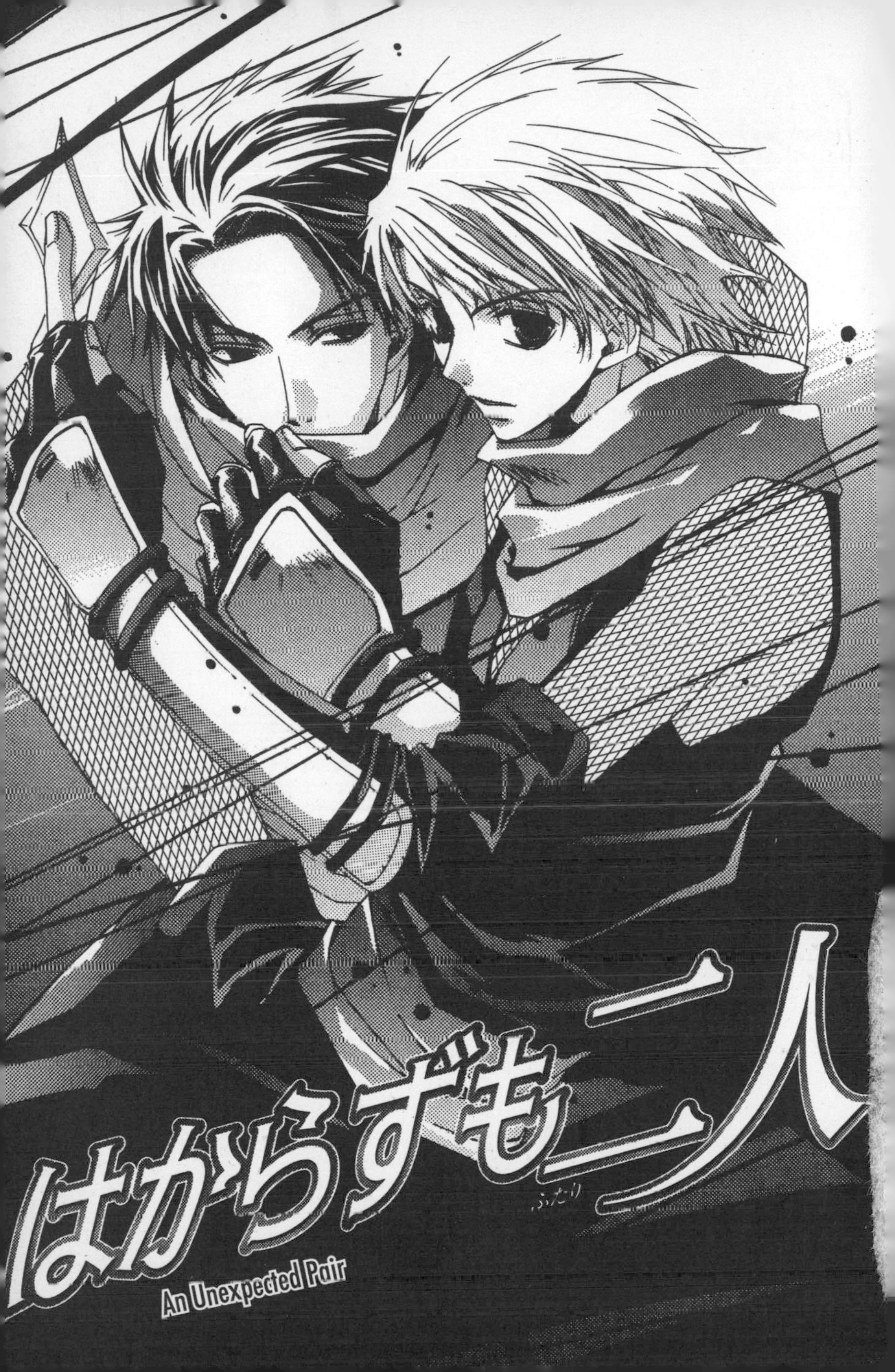
はからずも二人
ふたり
An Unexpected Pair

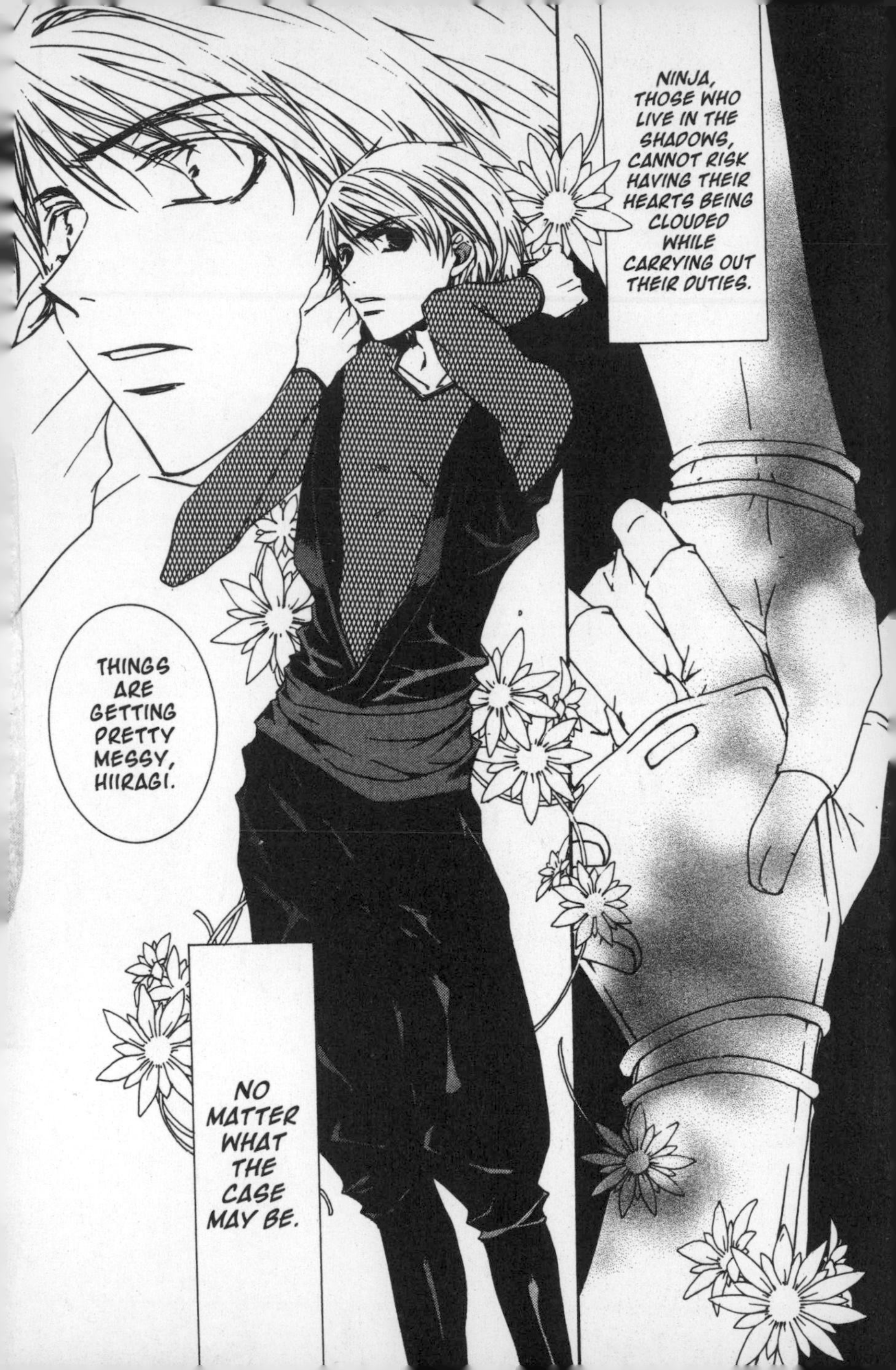
NINJA, THOSE WHO LIVE IN THE SHADOWS, CANNOT RISK HAVING THEIR HEARTS BEING CLOUDED WHILE CARRYING OUT THEIR DUTIES.
THINGS ARE GETTING PRETTY MESSY, HIIRAGI.
NO MATTER WHAT THE CASE MAY BE.

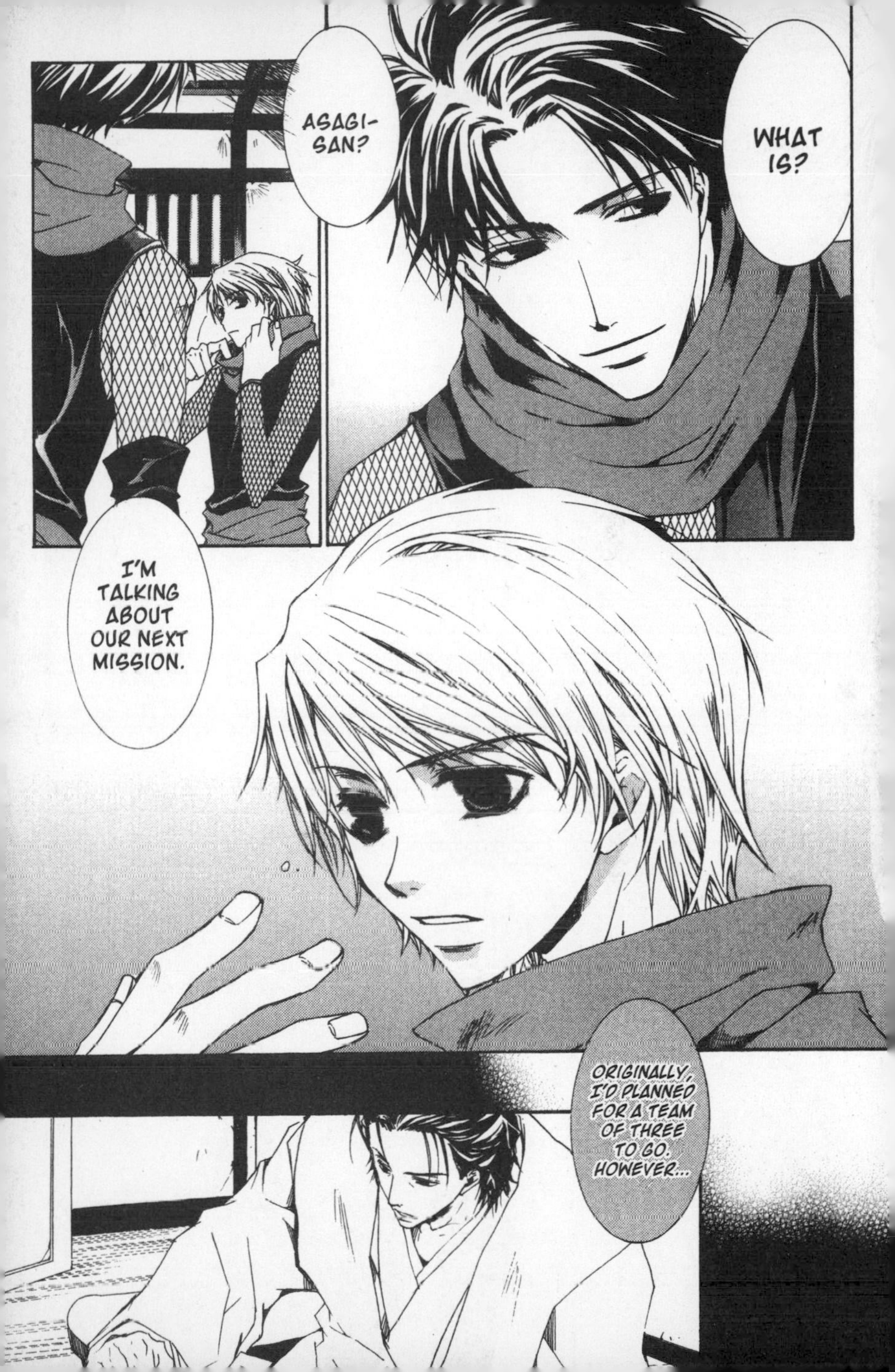
WHAT IS?
ASAGI-SAN?
I'M TALKING ABOUT OUR NEXT MISSION.
ORIGINALLY, I'D PLANNED FOR A TEAM OF THREE TO GO. HOWEVER...

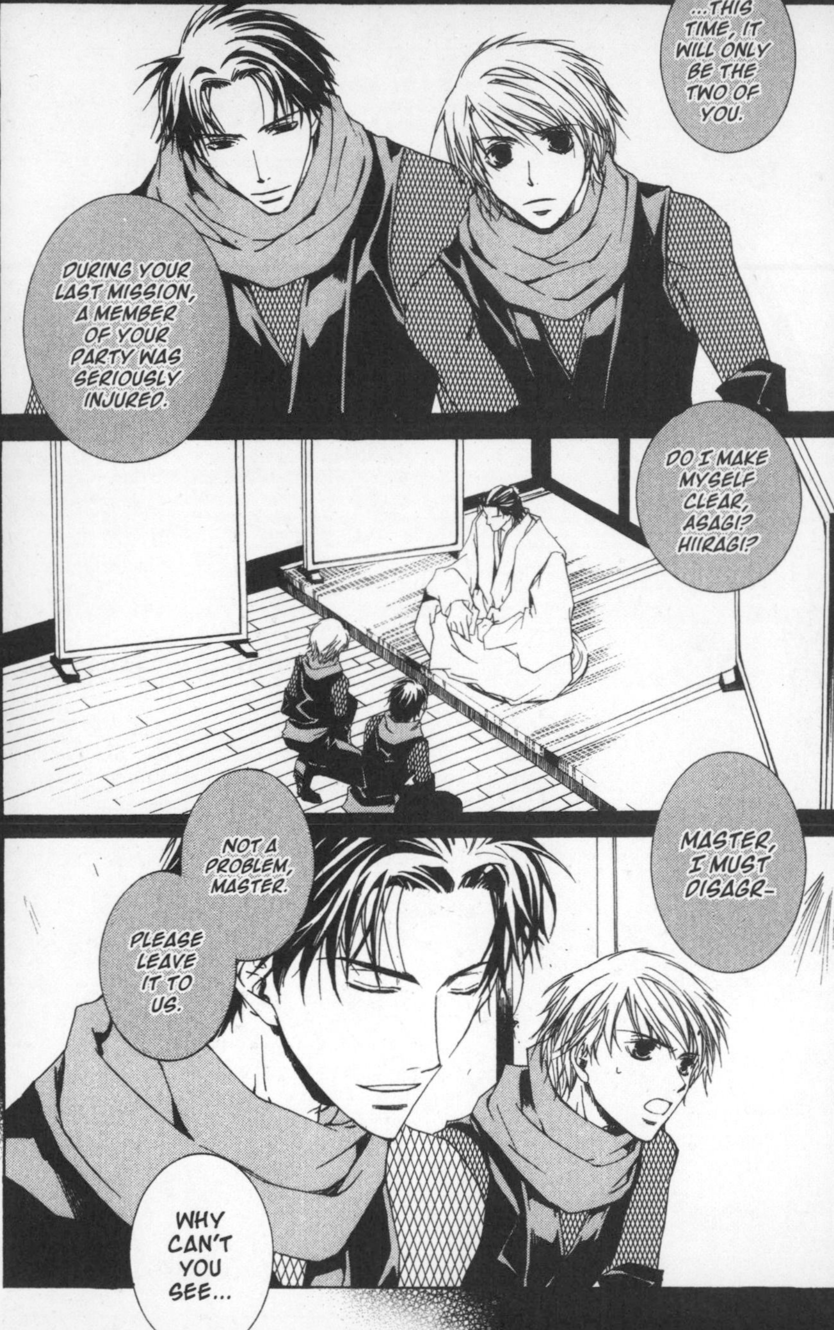
...THIS TIME, IT WILL ONLY BE THE TWO OF YOU.
DURING YOUR LAST MISSION, A MEMBER OF YOUR PARTY WAS SERIOUSLY INJURED.
DO I MAKE MYSELF CLEAR, ASAGI? HIIRAGI?
MASTER, I MUST DISAGR-
NOT A PROBLEM, MASTER.
PLEASE LEAVE IT TO US.
WHY CAN'T YOU SEE...

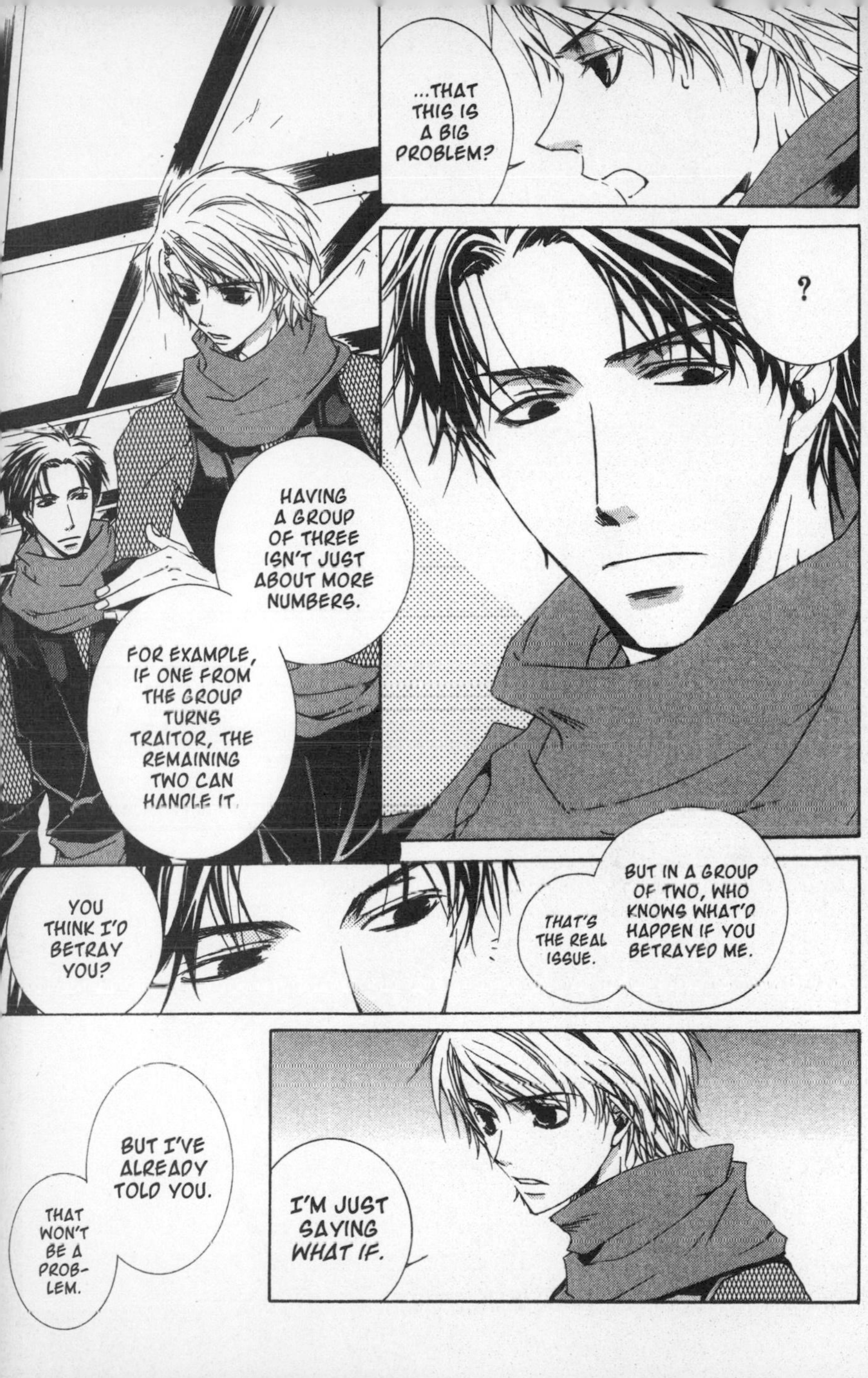

...THAT THIS IS A BIG PROBLEM?
?
HAVING A GROUP OF THREE ISN'T JUST ABOUT MORE NUMBERS.
FOR EXAMPLE, IF ONE FROM THE GROUP TURNS TRAITOR, THE REMAINING TWO CAN HANDLE IT.
BUT IN A GROUP OF TWO, WHO KNOWS WHAT'D HAPPEN IF YOU BETRAYED ME.
THAT'S THE REAL ISSUE.
YOU THINK I'D BETRAY YOU?
I'M JUST SAYING WHAT IF.
BUT I'VE ALREADY TOLD YOU.
THAT WON'T BE A PROB-LEM.

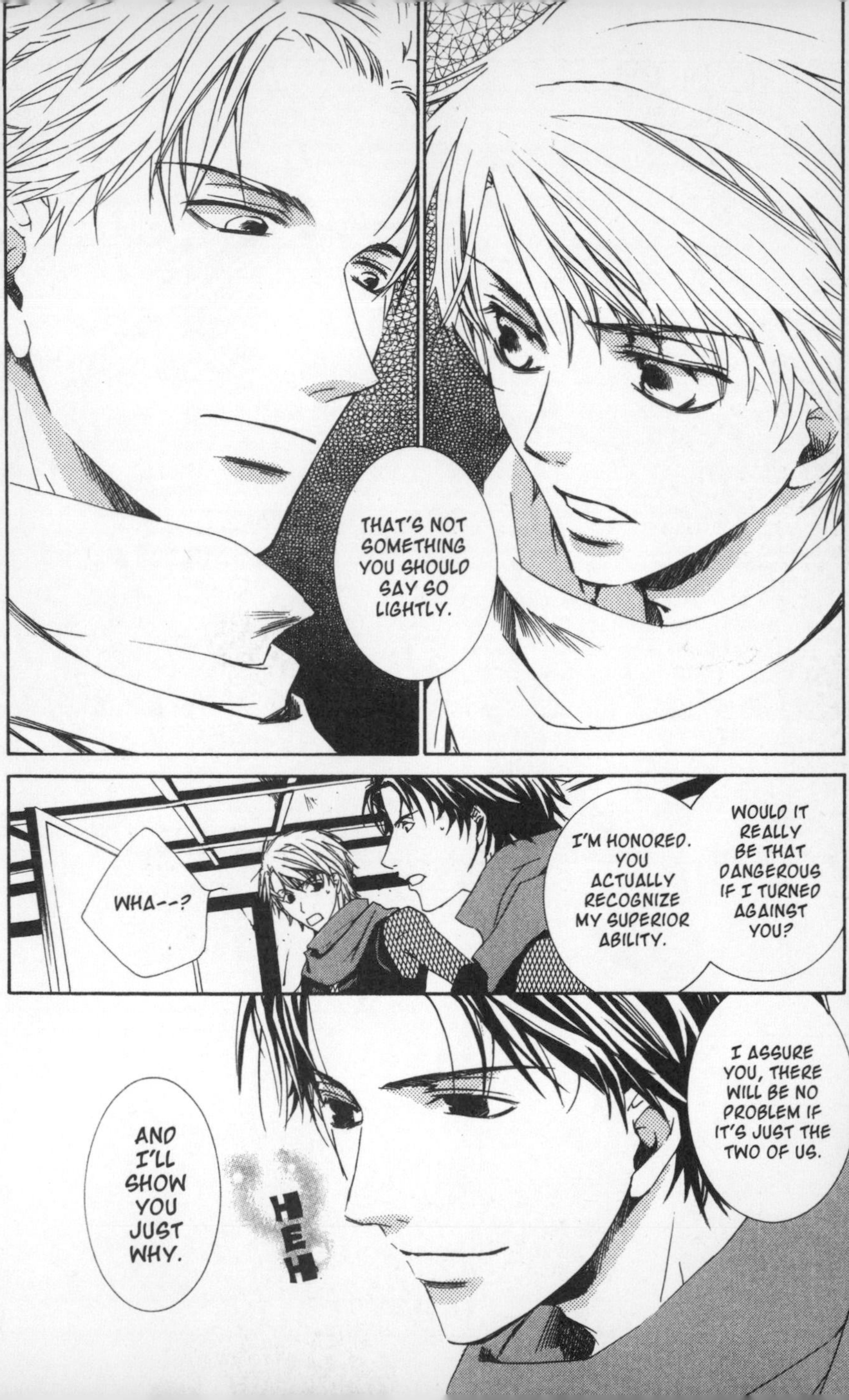
THAT'S NOT SOMETHING YOU SHOULD SAY SO LIGHTLY.
WOULD IT REALLY BE THAT DANGEROUS IF I TURNED AGAINST YOU?
I'M HONORED. YOU ACTUALLY RECOGNIZE MY SUPERIOR ABILITY.
WHA--?
I ASSURE YOU, THERE WILL BE NO PROBLEM IF IT'S JUST THE TWO OF US.
HEH
AND I'LL SHOW YOU JUST WHY.

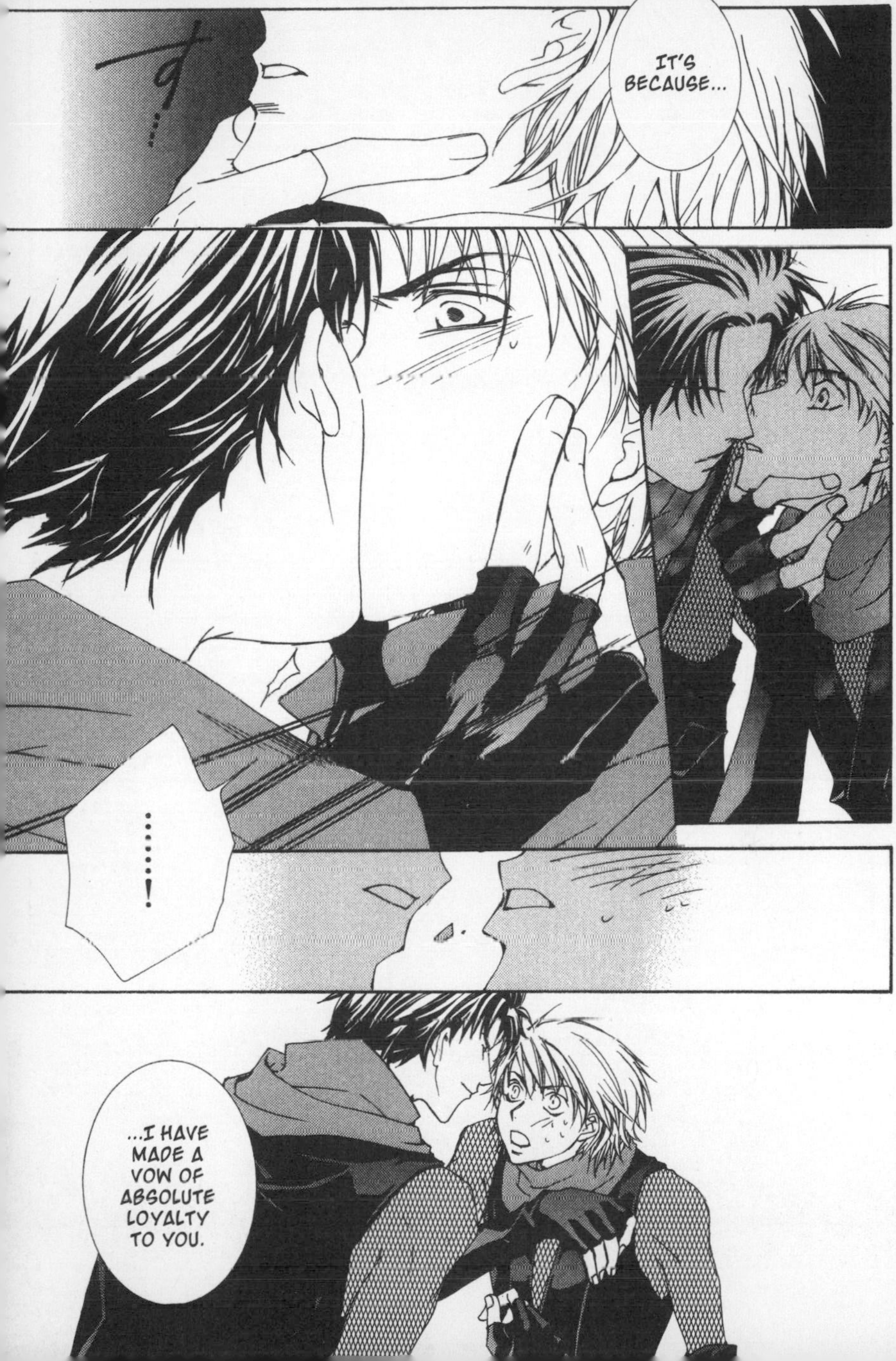
IT'S BECAUSE...
す…
......!
...I HAVE MADE A VOW OF ABSOLUTE LOYALTY TO YOU.

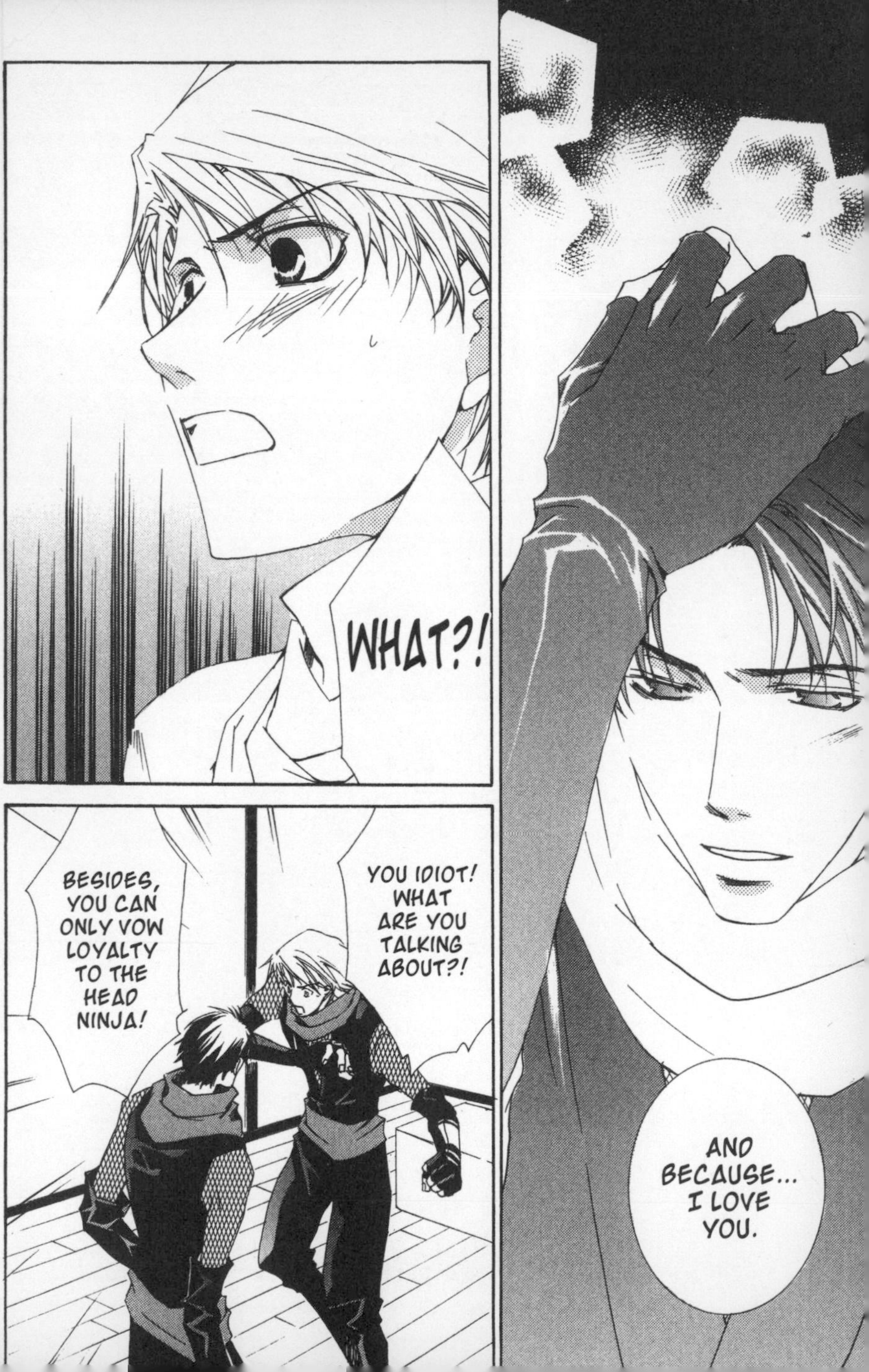
AND BECAUSE... I LOVE YOU.
WHAT?!
YOU IDIOT! WHAT ARE YOU TALKING ABOUT?!
BESIDES, YOU CAN ONLY VOW LOYALTY TO THE HEAD NINJA!

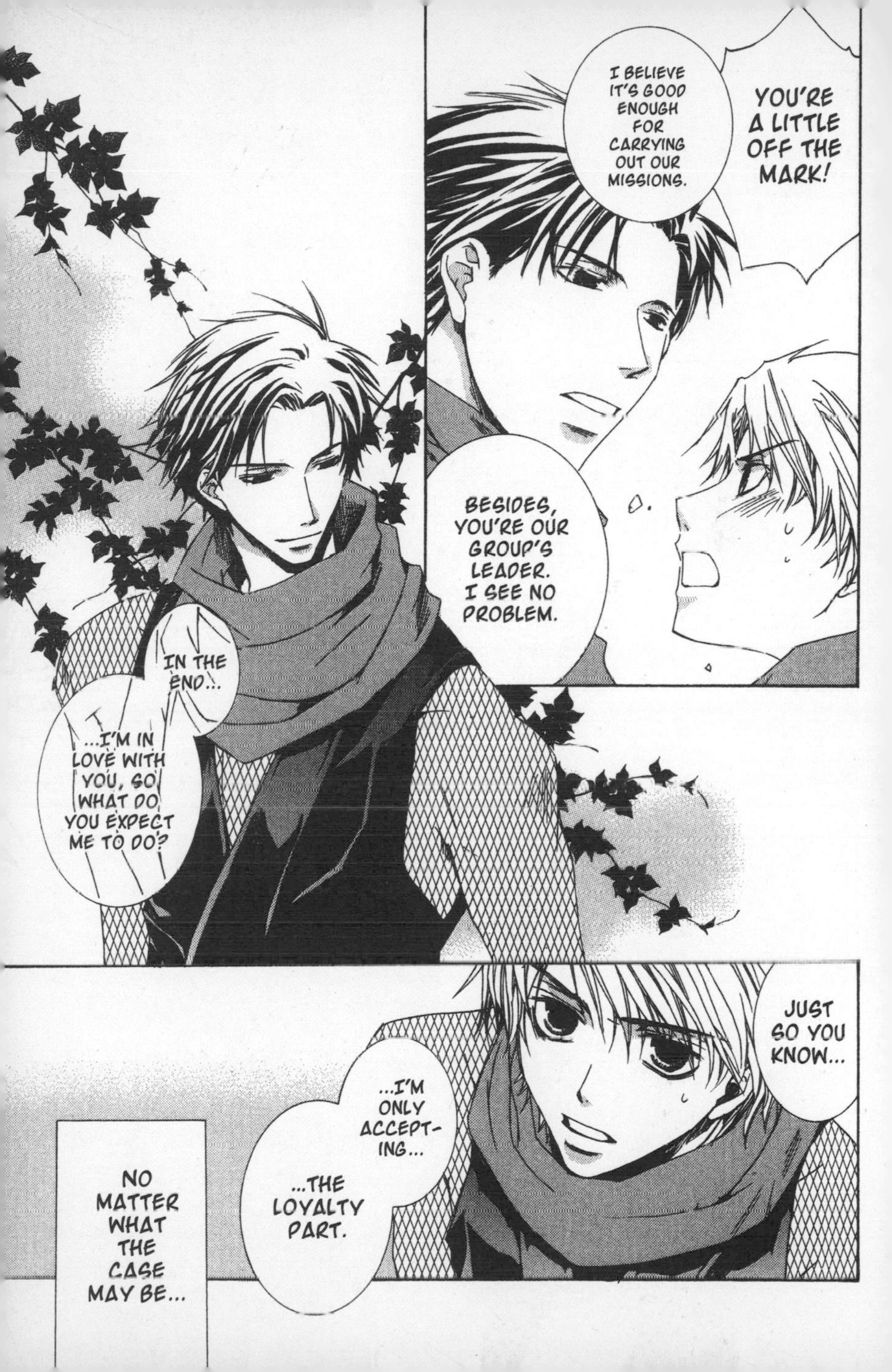
YOU'RE A LITTLE OFF THE MARK!
I BELIEVE IT'S GOOD ENOUGH FOR CARRYING OUT OUR MISSIONS.
BESIDES, YOU'RE OUR GROUP'S LEADER. I SEE NO PROBLEM.
IN THE END...
...I'M IN LOVE WITH YOU, SO WHAT DO YOU EXPECT ME TO DO?
JUST SO YOU KNOW...
...I'M ONLY ACCEPTING...
...THE LOYALTY PART.
NO MATTER WHAT THE CASE MAY BE...

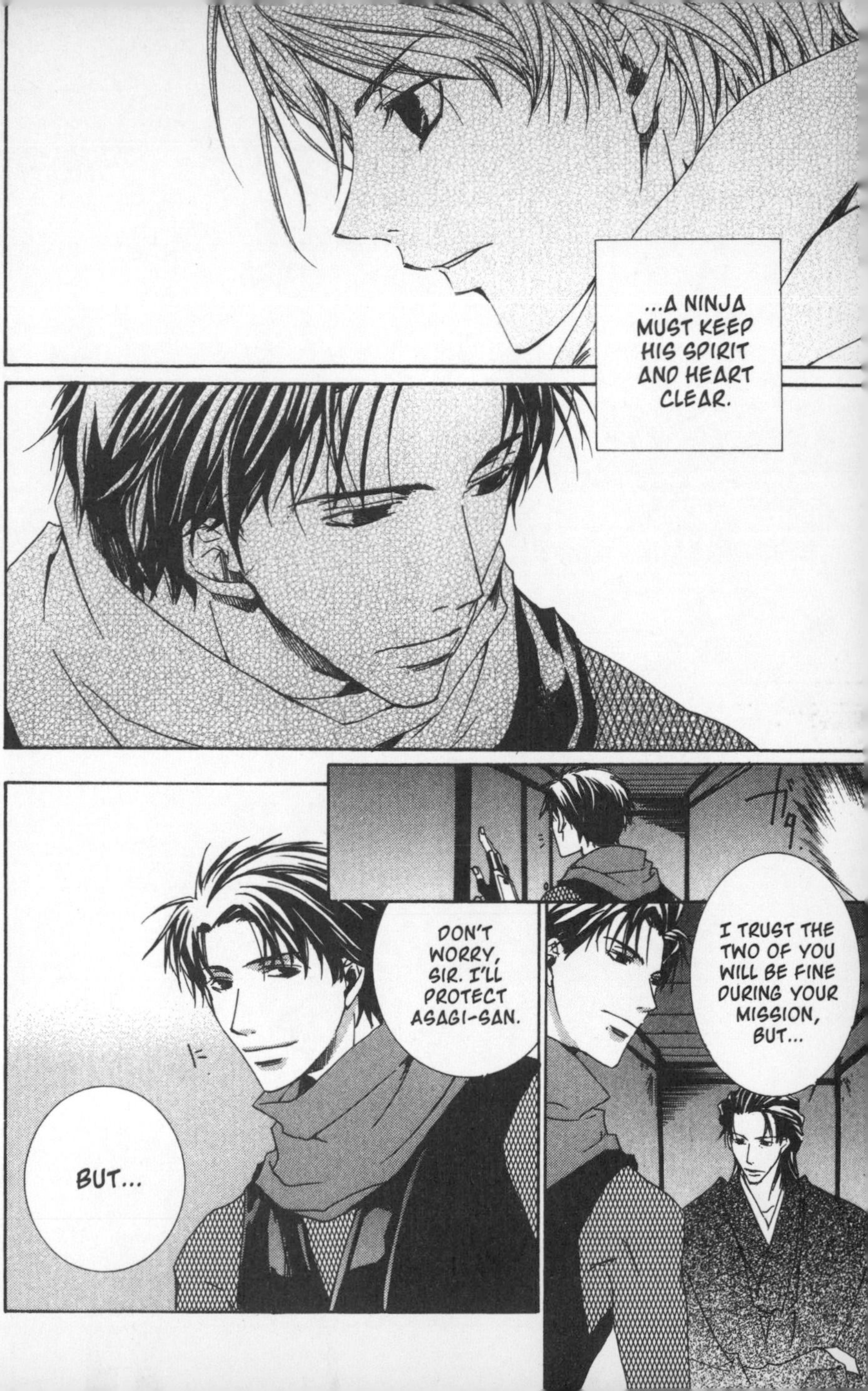
...A NINJA MUST KEEP HIS SPIRIT AND HEART CLEAR.
I TRUST THE TWO OF YOU WILL BE FINE DURING YOUR MISSION, BUT...
DON'T WORRY, SIR. I'LL PROTECT ASAGI-SAN.
BUT...

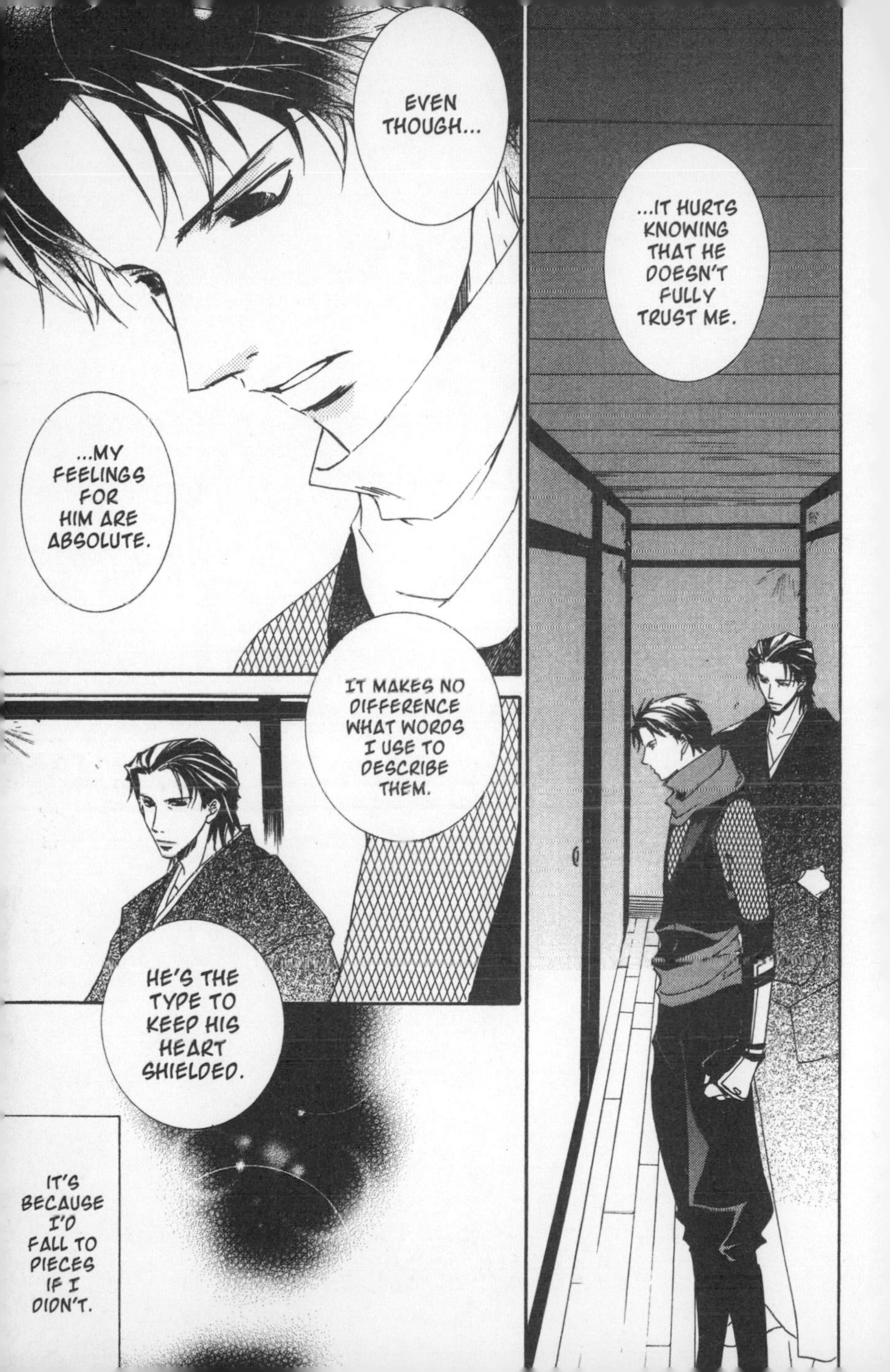
...IT HURTS KNOWING THAT HE DOESN'T FULLY TRUST ME.
EVEN THOUGH...
...MY FEELINGS FOR HIM ARE ABSOLUTE.
IT MAKES NO DIFFERENCE WHAT WORDS I USE TO DESCRIBE THEM.
HE'S THE TYPE TO KEEP HIS HEART SHIELDED.
IT'S BECAUSE I'D FALL TO PIECES IF I DIDN'T.

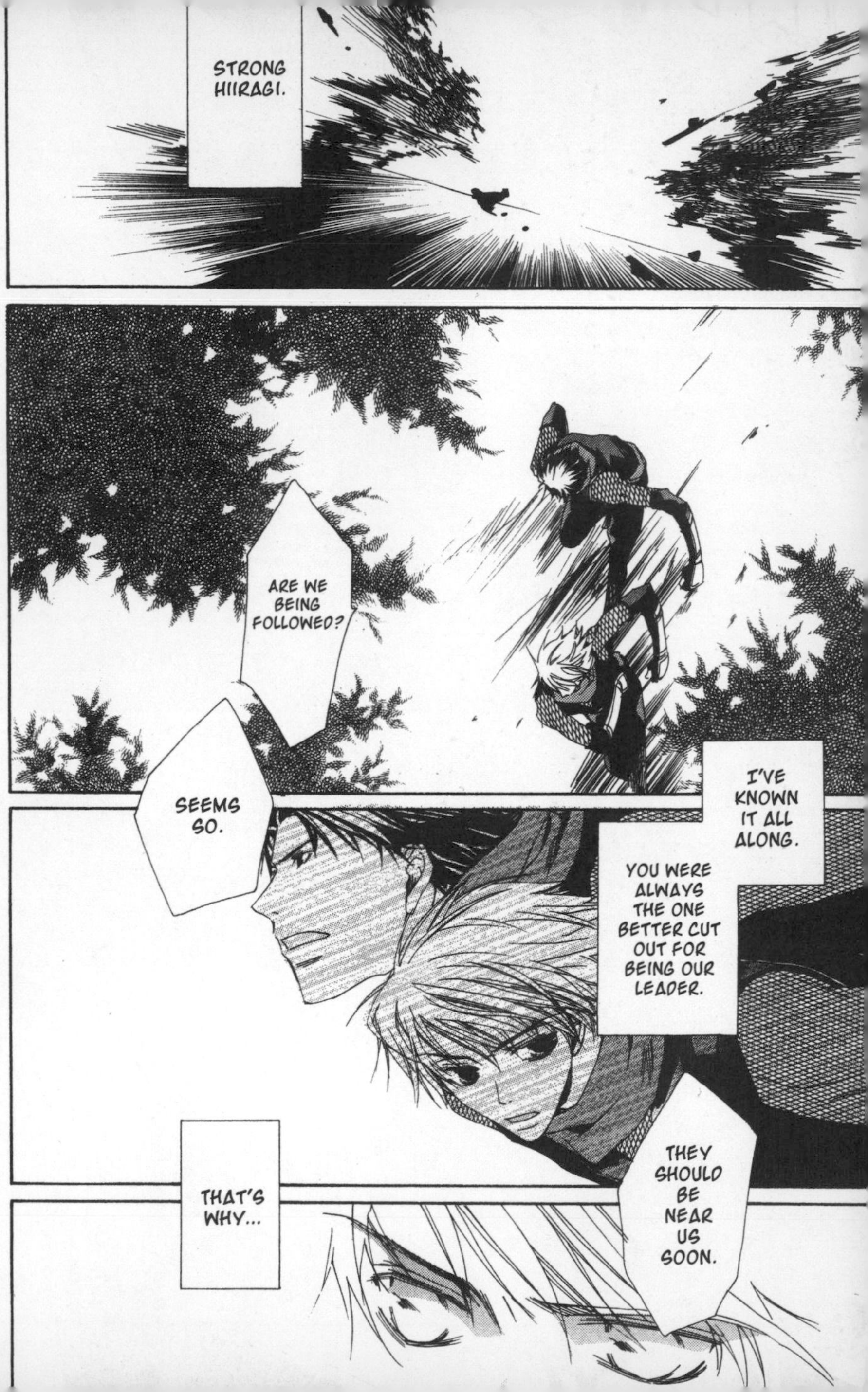
STRONG HIIRAGI.
ARE WE BEING FOLLOWED?
SEEMS SO.
I'VE KNOWN IT ALL ALONG.
YOU WERE ALWAYS THE ONE BETTER CUT OUT FOR BEING OUR LEADER.
THEY SHOULD BE NEAR US SOON.
THAT'S WHY...

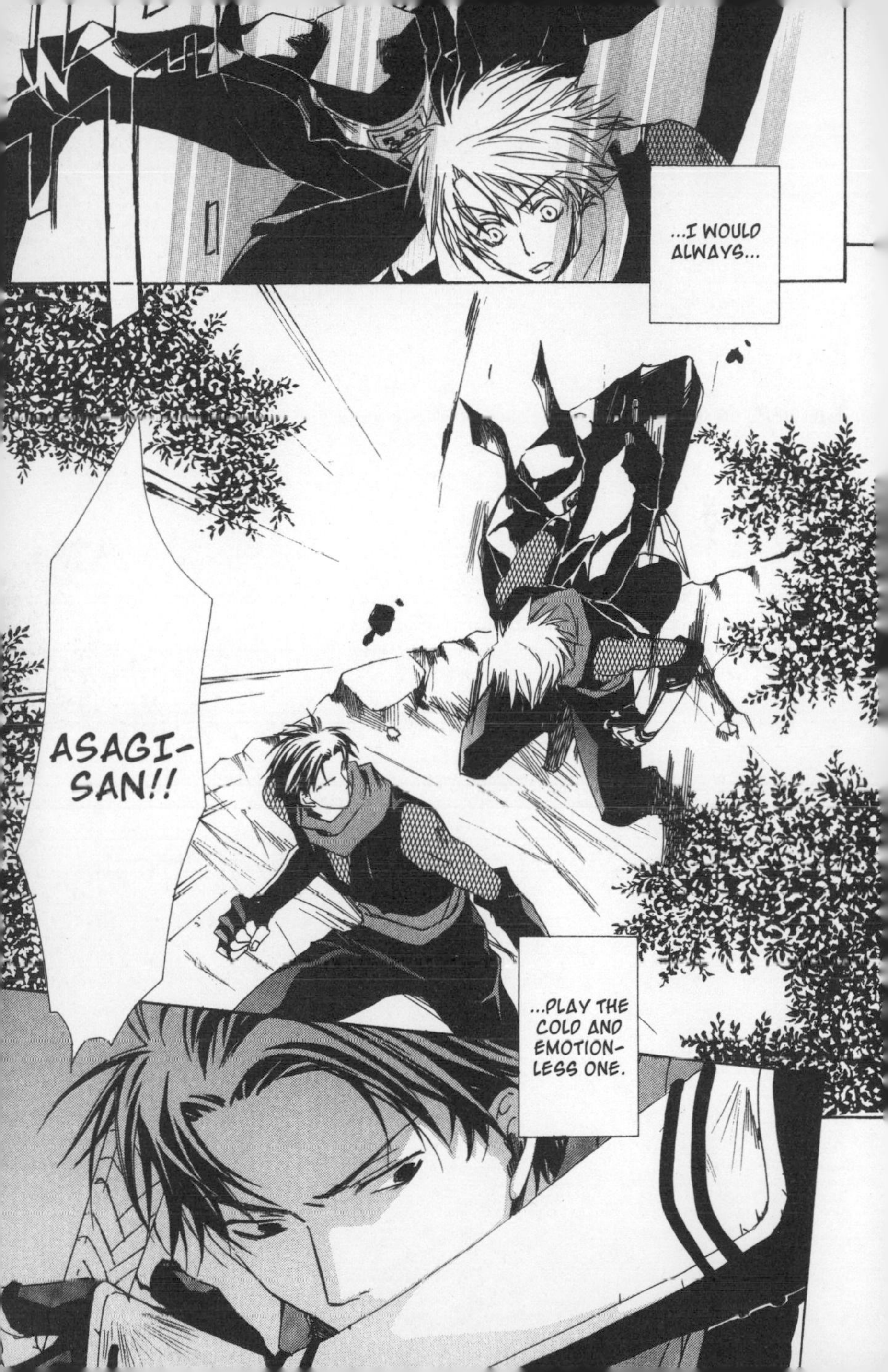
...I WOULD ALWAYS...
ASAGI-SAN!!
...PLAY THE COLD AND EMOTION-LESS ONE.

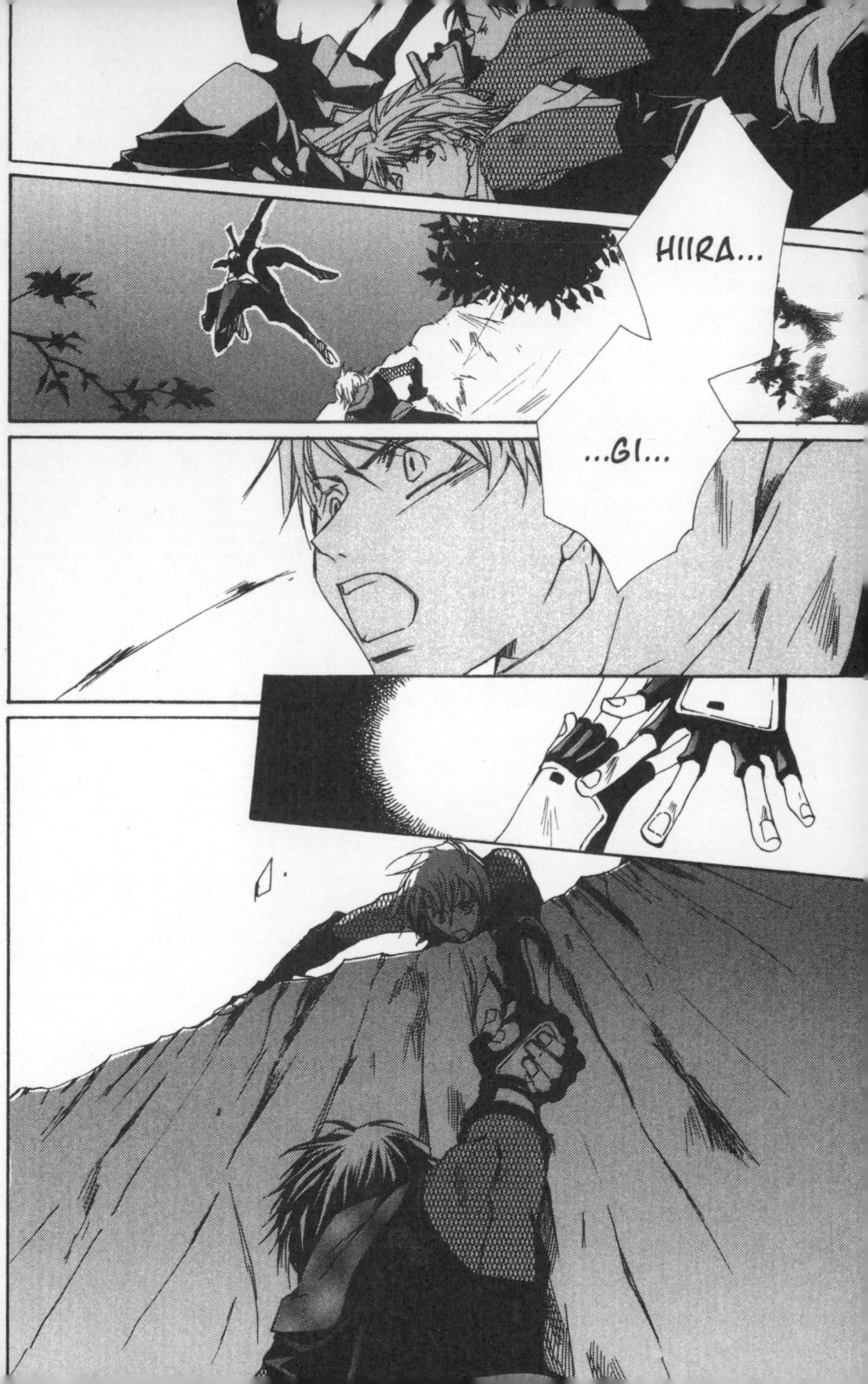
HIIRA...
...GI...

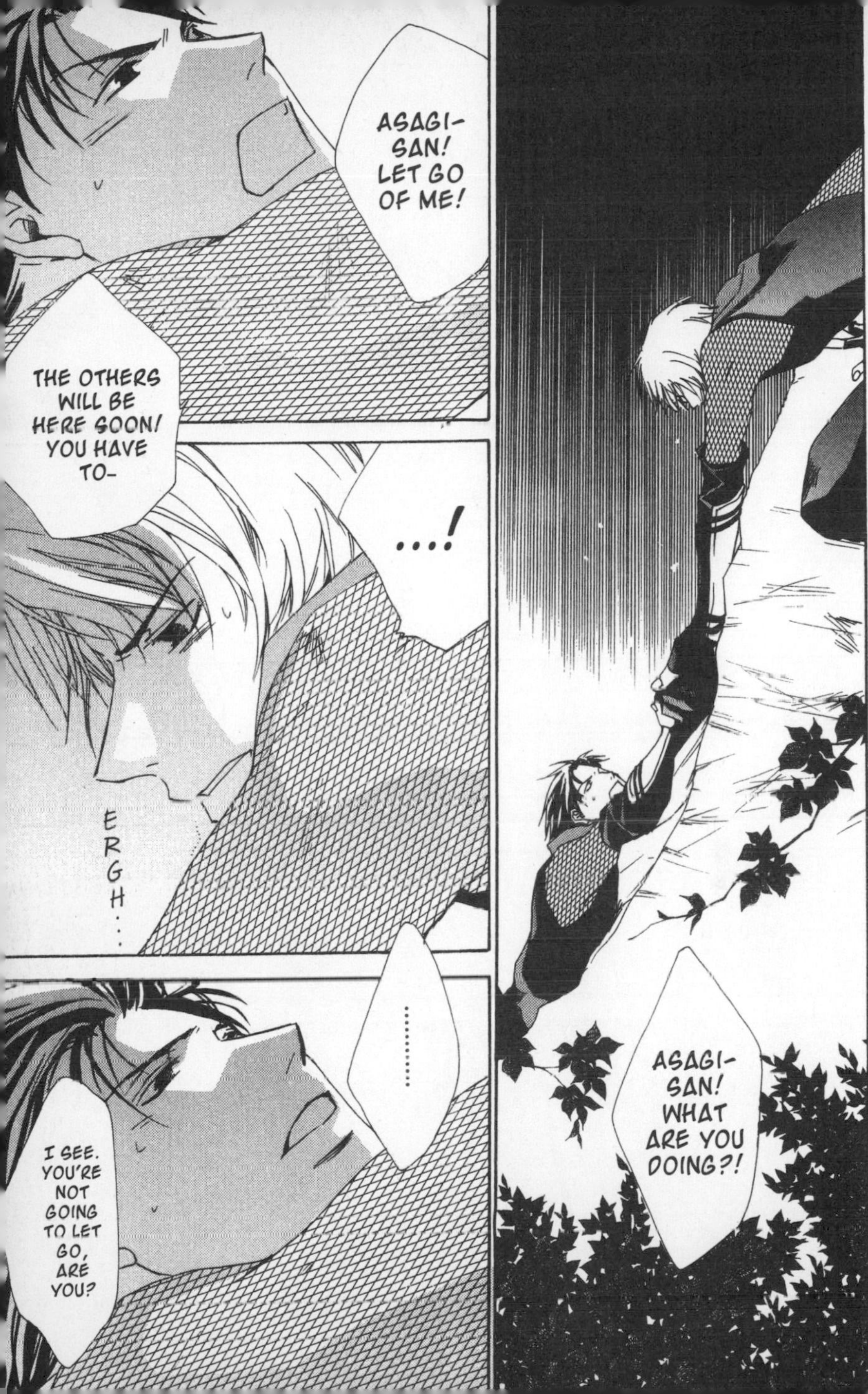
ASAGI-SAN! WHAT ARE YOU DOING?!
ASAGI-SAN! LET GO OF ME!
THE OTHERS WILL BE HERE SOON! YOU HAVE TO-
...!
ERGH...
......
I SEE. YOU'RE NOT GOING TO LET GO, ARE YOU?

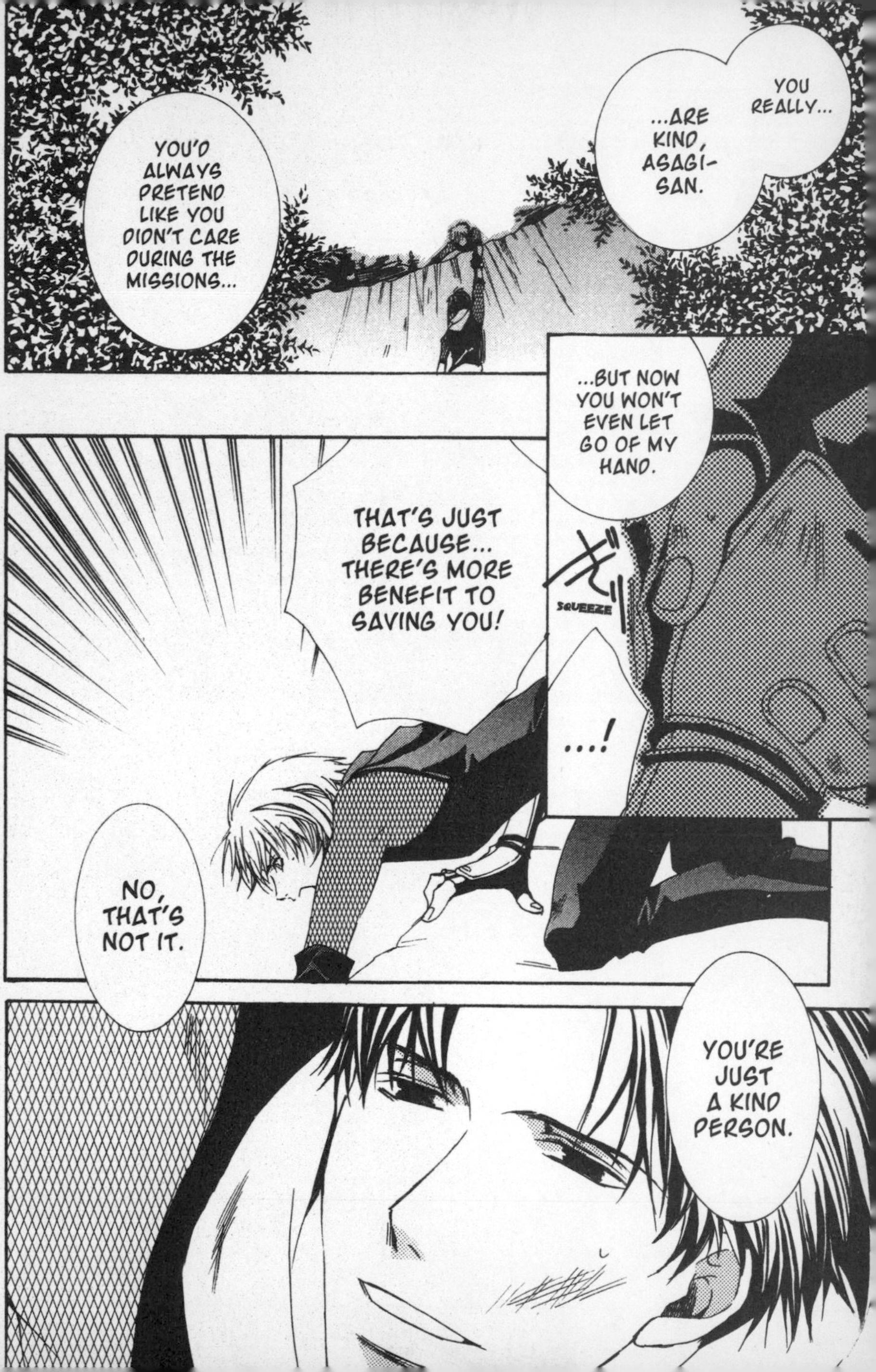
YOU REALLY...
...ARE KIND, ASAGI-SAN.
YOU'D ALWAYS PRETEND LIKE YOU DIDN'T CARE DURING THE MISSIONS...
...BUT NOW YOU WON'T EVEN LET GO OF MY HAND.
SQUEEZE
...!
THAT'S JUST BECAUSE... THERE'S MORE BENEFIT TO SAVING YOU!
NO, THAT'S NOT IT.
YOU'RE JUST A KIND PERSON.

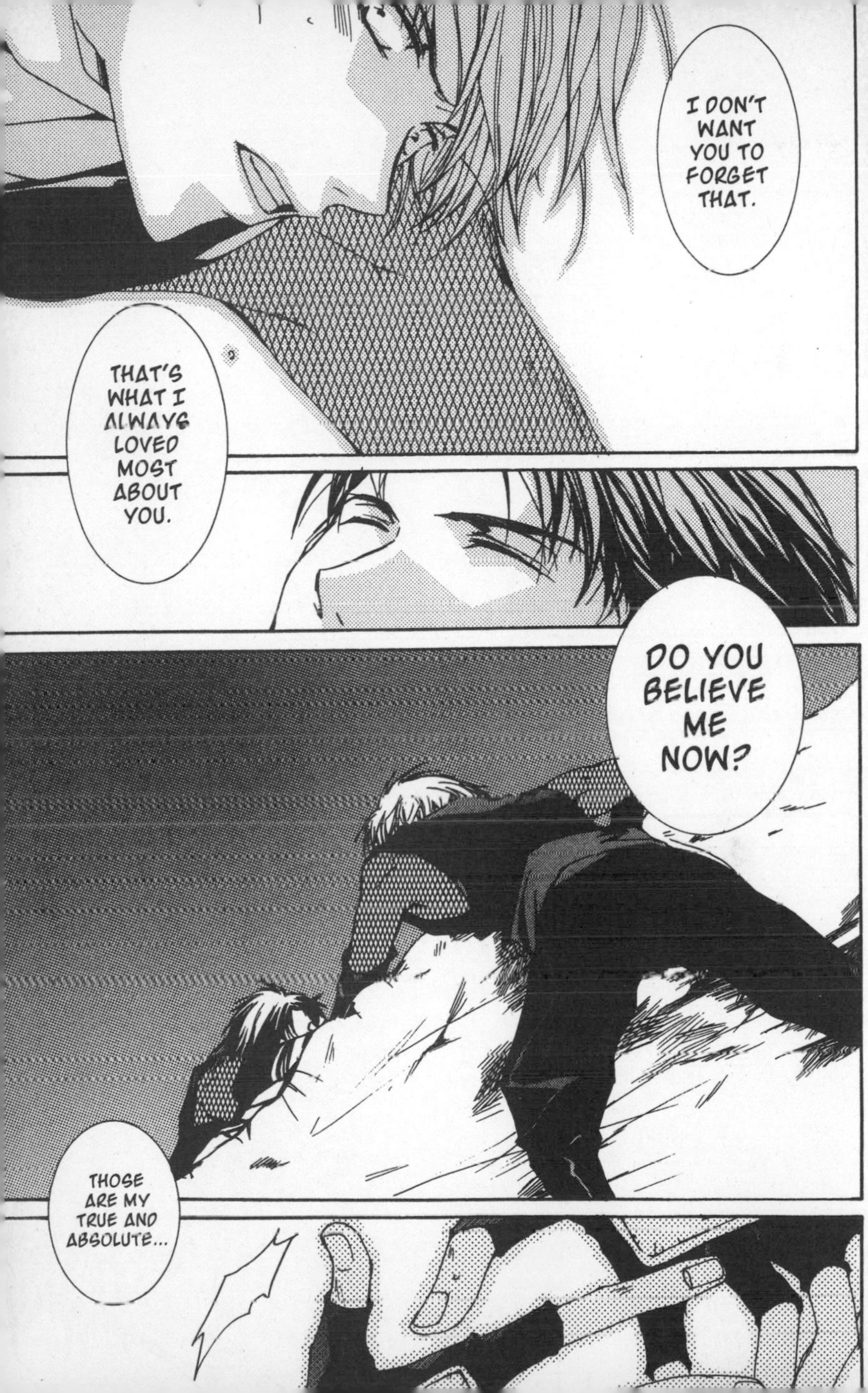
I DON'T WANT YOU TO FORGET THAT.
THAT'S WHAT I ALWAYS LOVED MOST ABOUT YOU.
DO YOU BELIEVE ME NOW?
THOSE ARE MY TRUE AND ABSOLUTE...

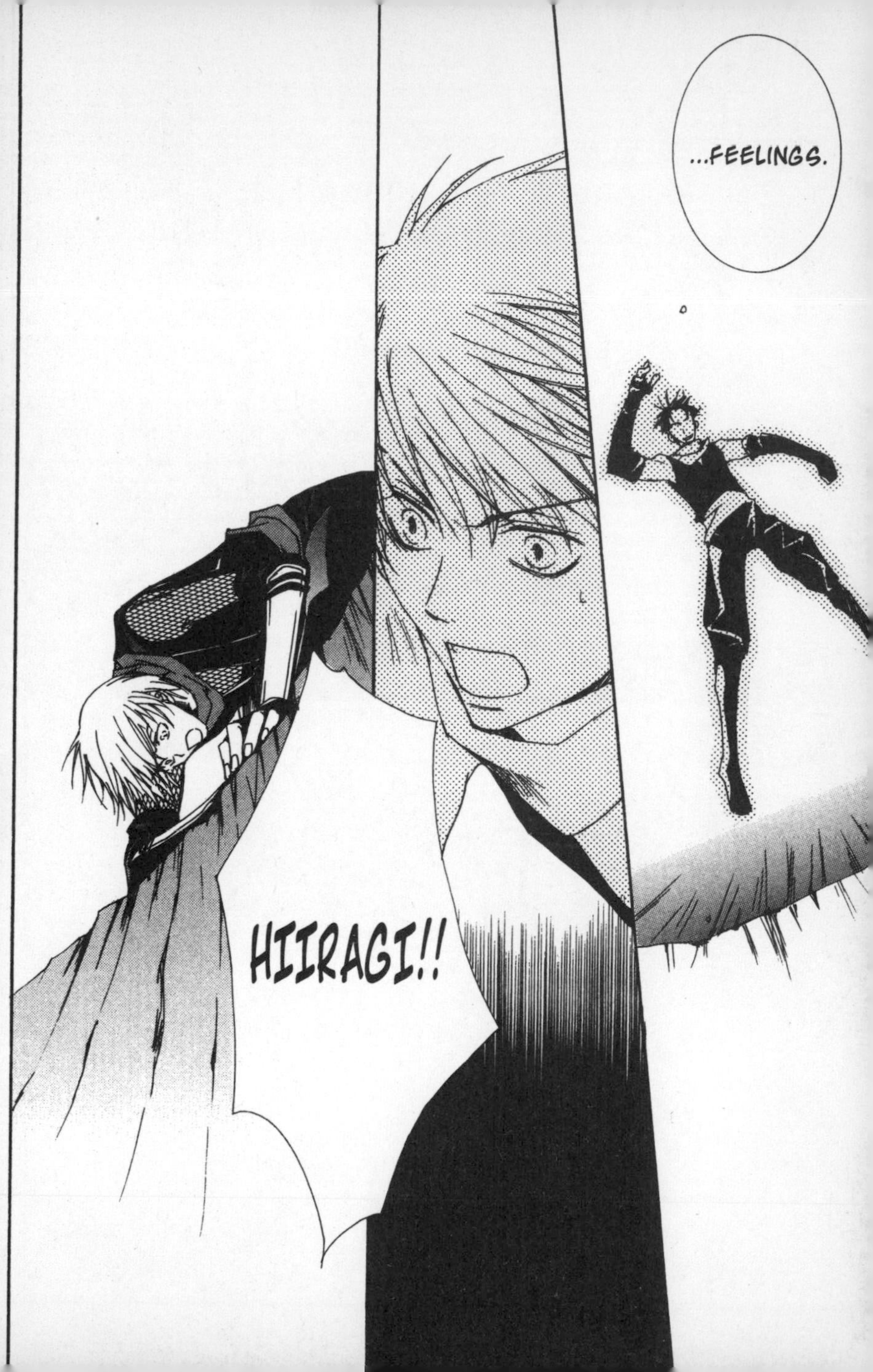
...FEELINGS.
HIIRAGI!!

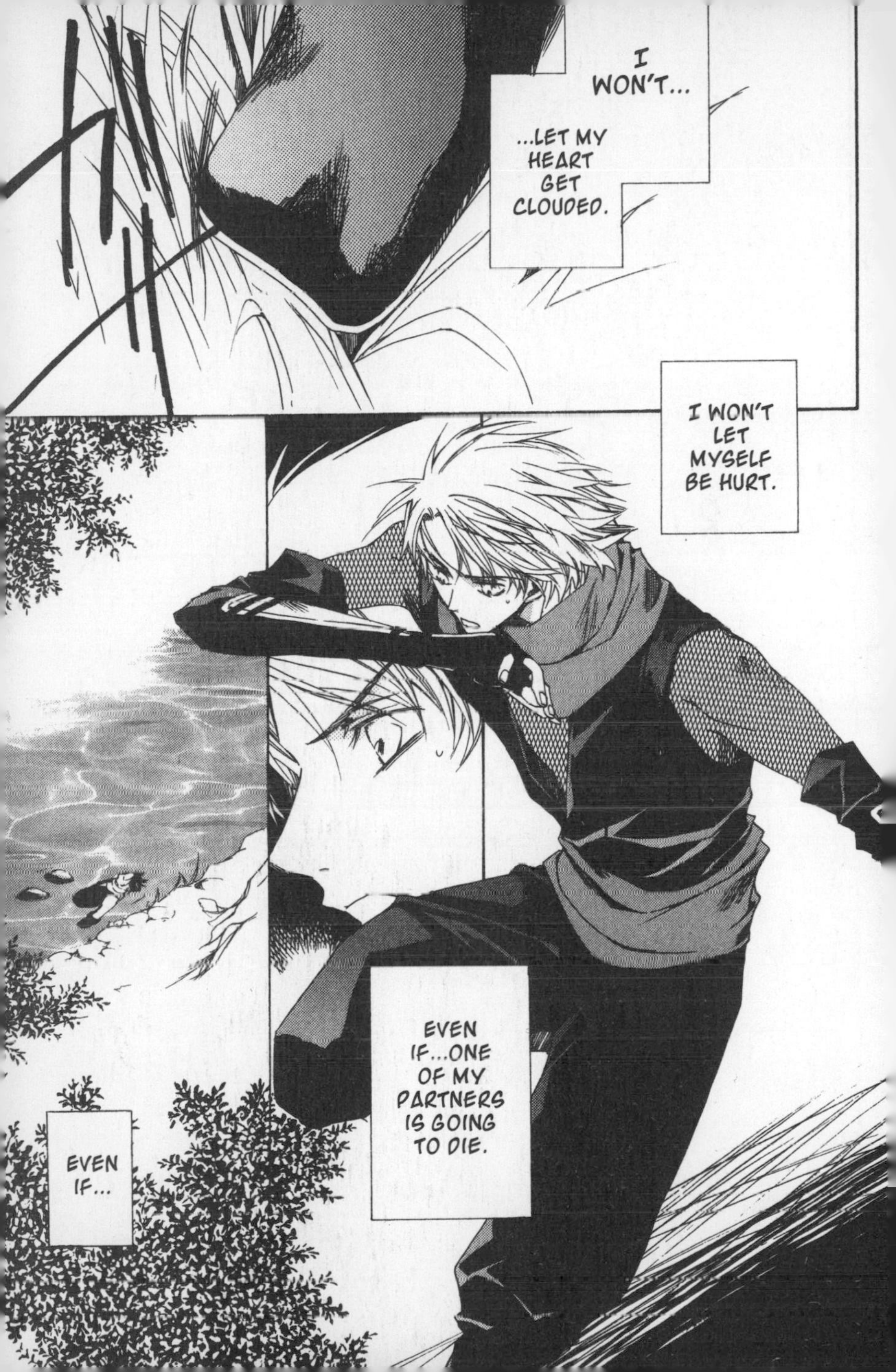
I WON'T...
...LET MY HEART GET CLOUDED.
I WON'T LET MYSELF BE HURT.
EVEN IF...ONE OF MY PARTNERS IS GOING TO DIE.
EVEN IF...

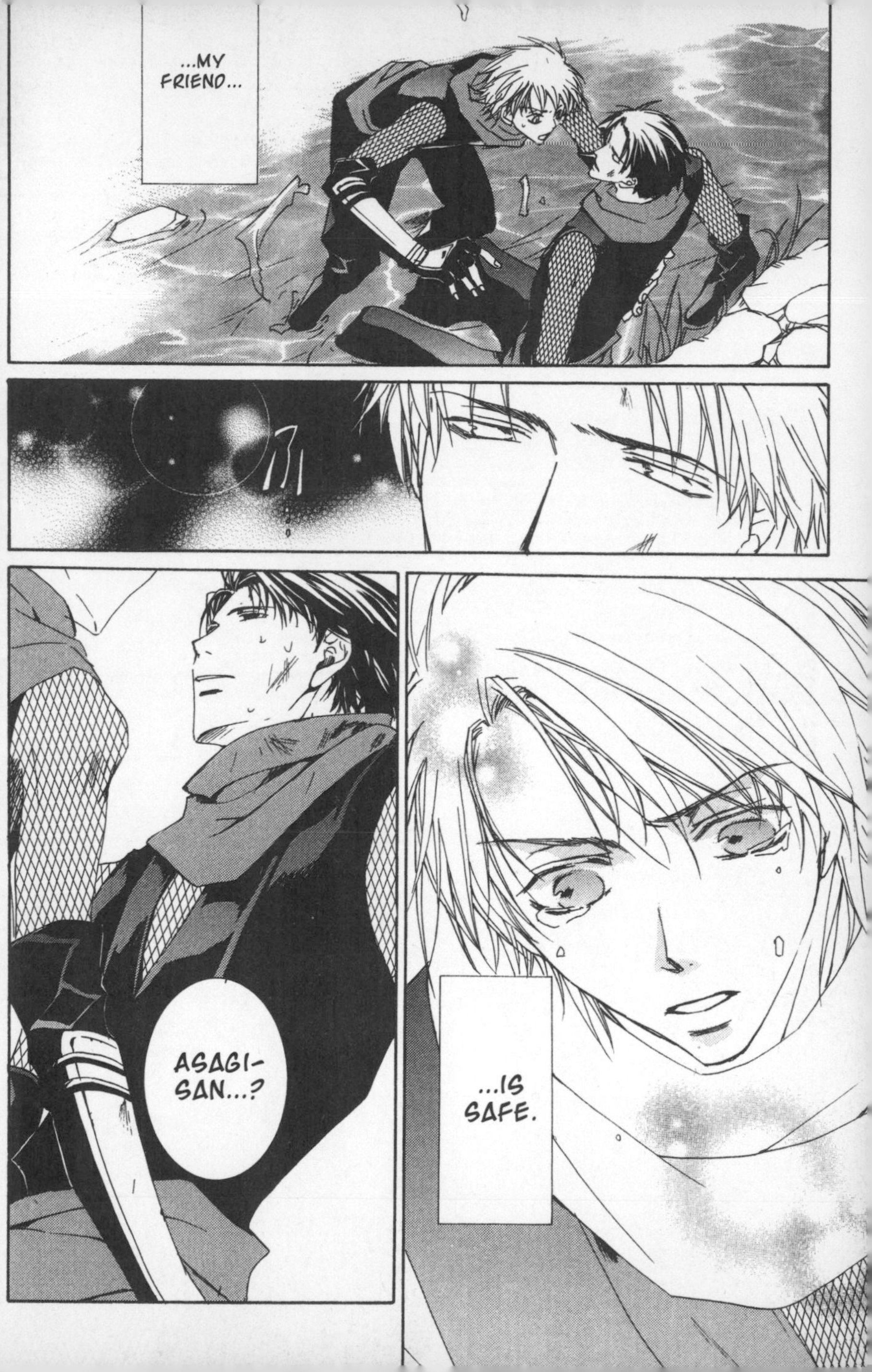
...MY FRIEND...
...IS SAFE.
ASAGI-SAN...?

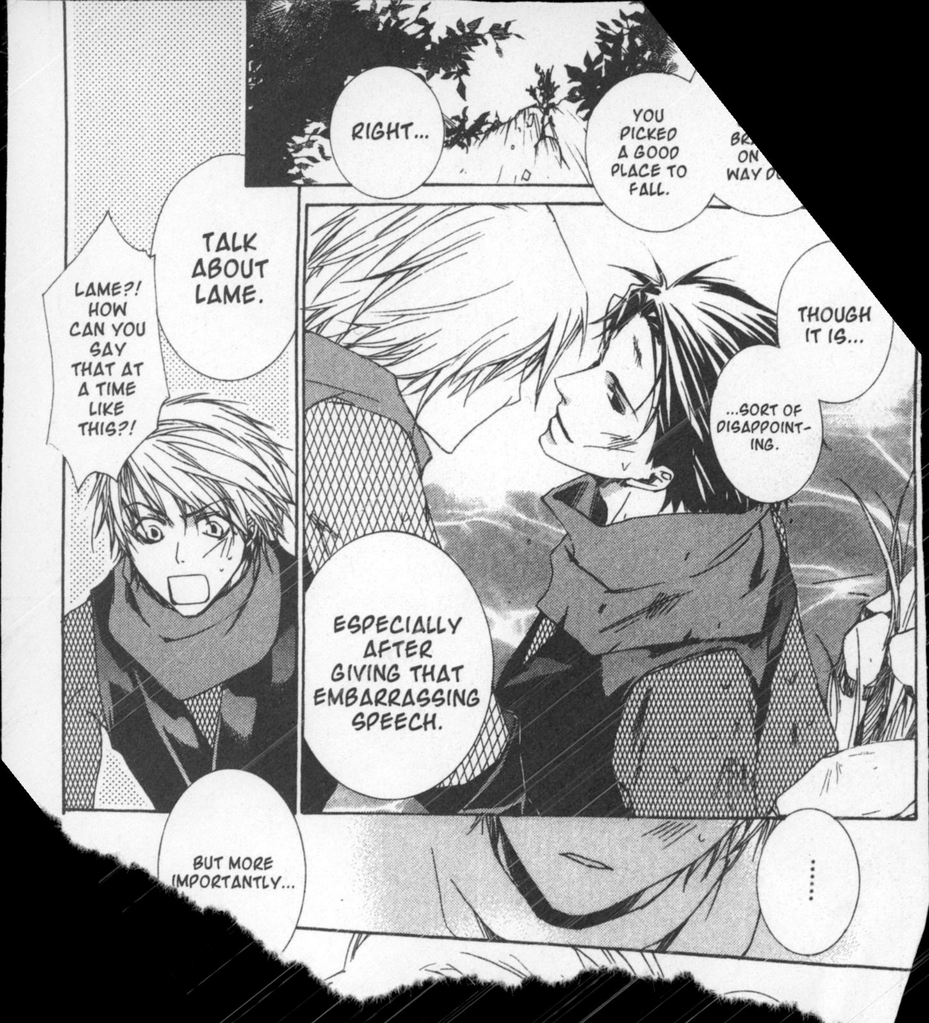
YOU PICKED A GOOD PLACE TO FALL.
RIGHT...
THOUGH IT IS...
...SORT OF DISAPPOINT-ING.
ESPECIALLY AFTER GIVING THAT EMBARRASSING SPEECH.
TALK ABOUT LAME.
LAME?! HOW CAN YOU SAY THAT AT A TIME LIKE THIS?!
......
BUT MORE IMPORTANTLY...

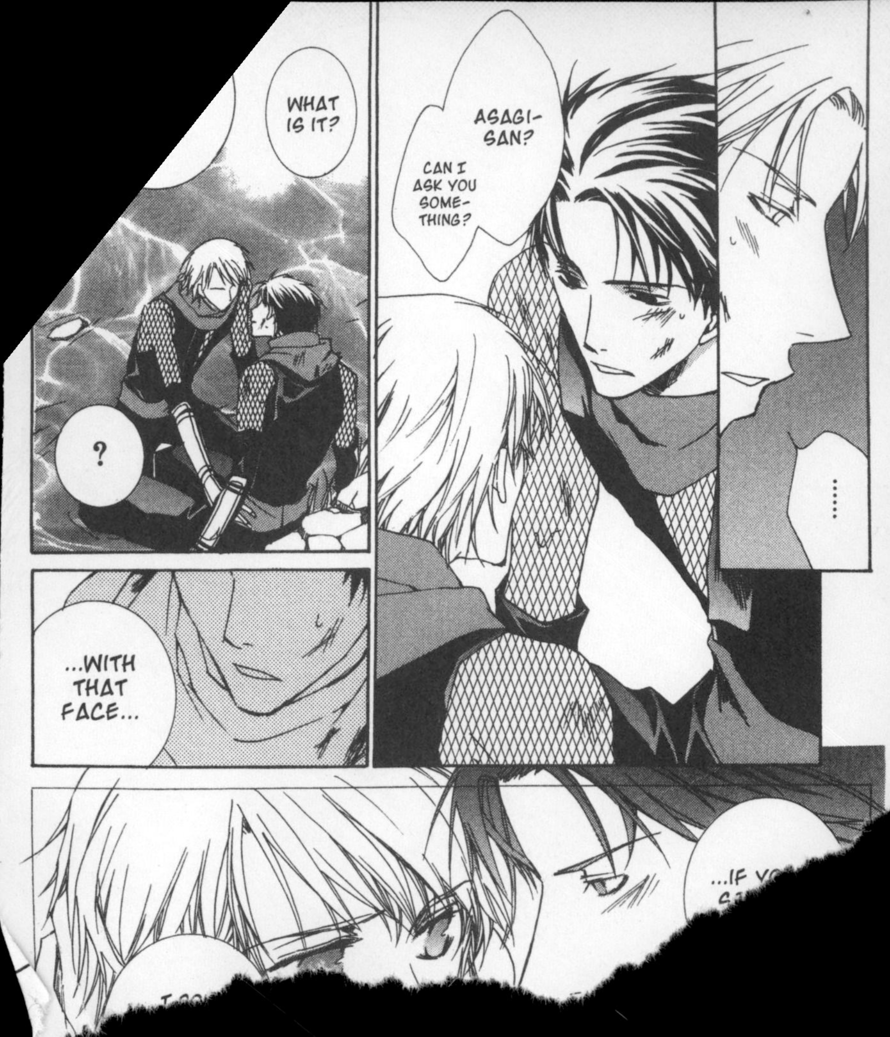
......
ASAGI-SAN?
CAN I ASK YOU SOMETHING?
WHAT IS IT?
?
...WITH THAT FACE...
...IF

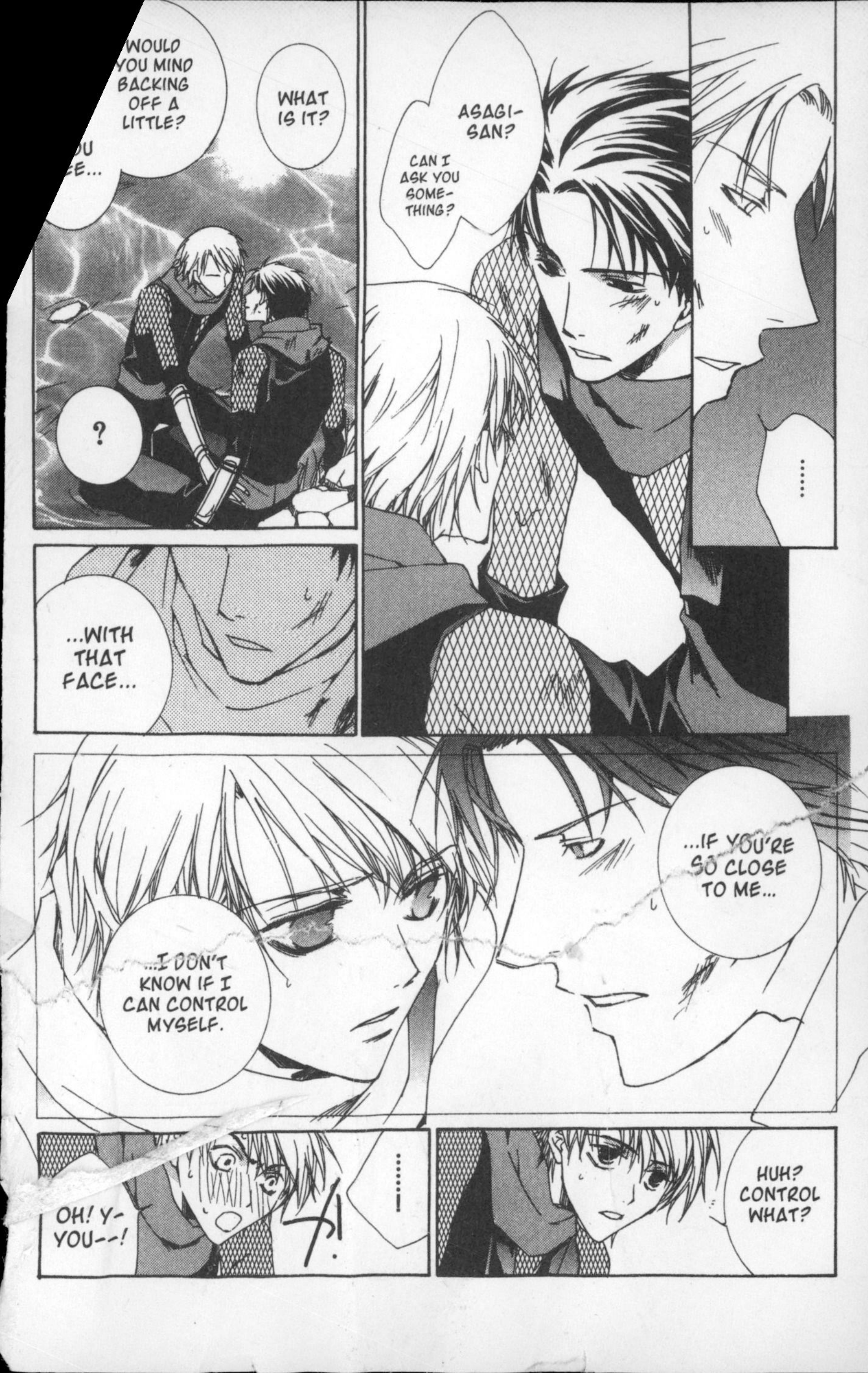
......
ASAGI-SAN?
CAN I ASK YOU SOMETHING?
WHAT IS IT?
WOULD YOU MIND BACKING OFF A LITTLE?
OU EE...
?
...WITH THAT FACE...
...IF YOU'RE SO CLOSE TO ME...
...I DON'T KNOW IF I CAN CONTROL MYSELF.
HUH? CONTROL WHAT?
......!
OH! Y-YOU--!

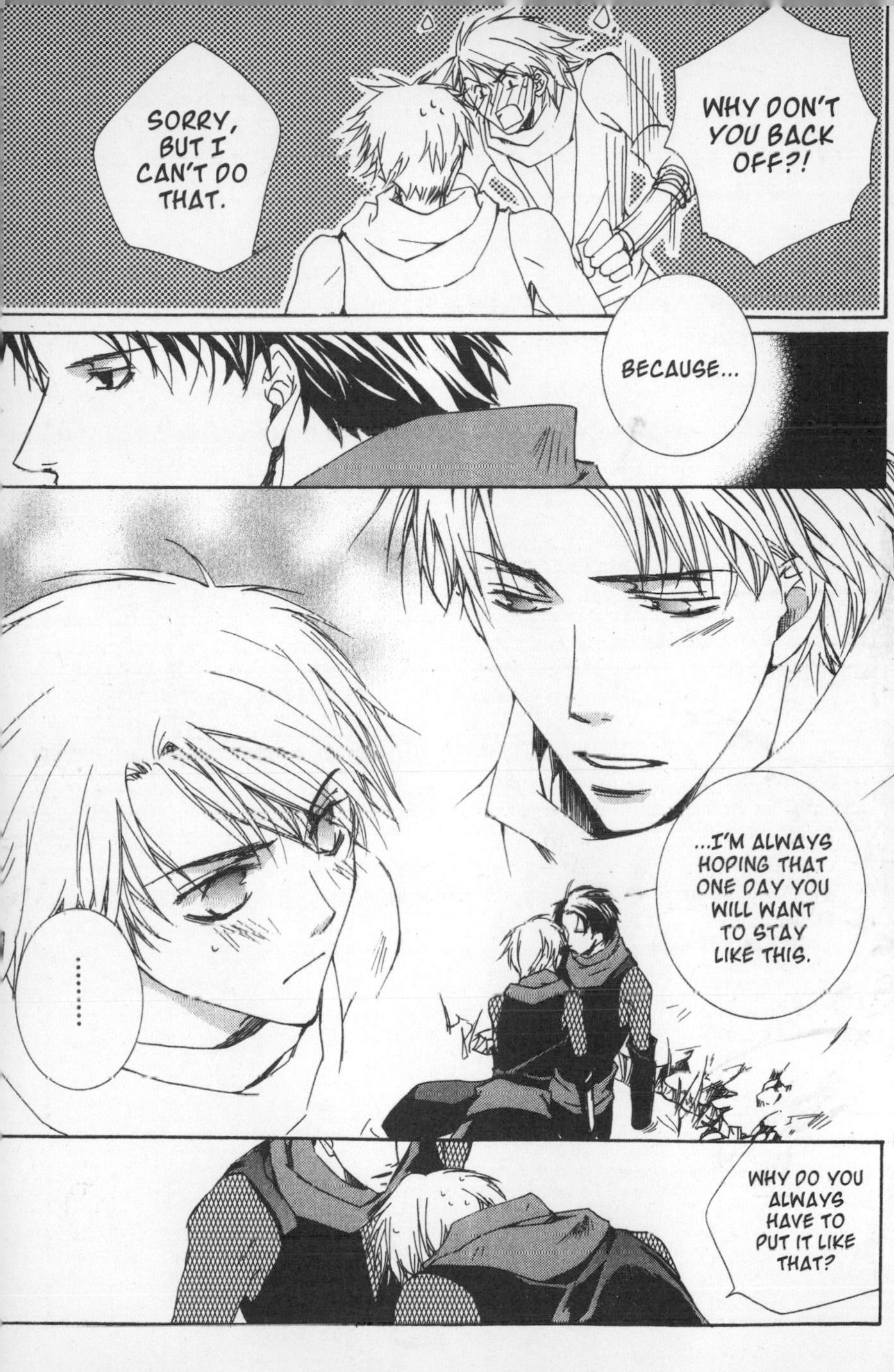
WHY DON'T YOU BACK OFF?!
SORRY, BUT I CAN'T DO THAT.
BECAUSE...
...I'M ALWAYS HOPING THAT ONE DAY YOU WILL WANT TO STAY LIKE THIS.
......
WHY DO YOU ALWAYS HAVE TO PUT IT LIKE THAT?

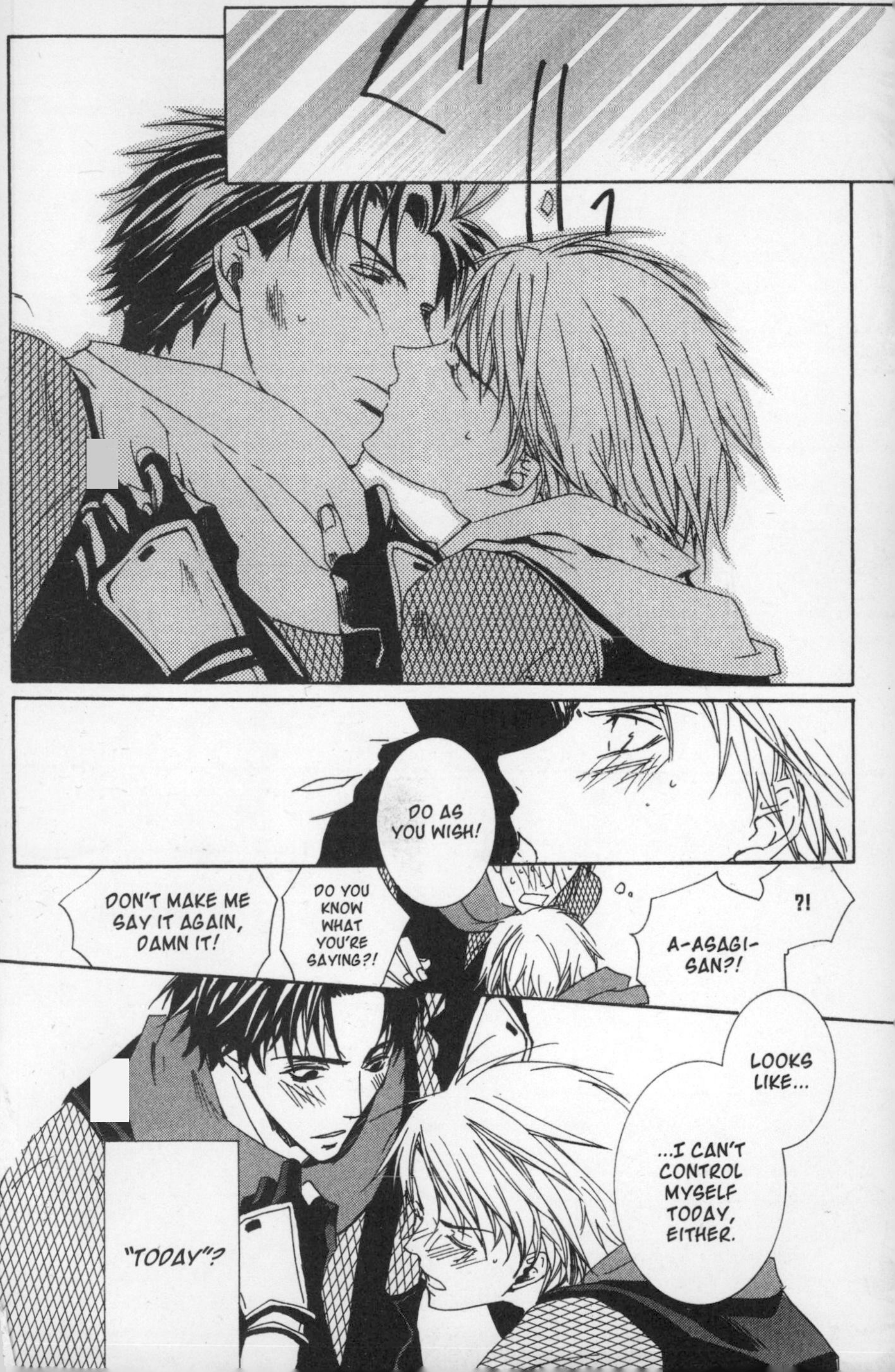
DO AS YOU WISH!
?!
A-ASAGI-SAN?!
DO YOU KNOW WHAT YOU'RE SAYING?!
DON'T MAKE ME SAY IT AGAIN, DAMN IT!
LOOKS LIKE...
...I CAN'T CONTROL MYSELF TODAY, EITHER.
"TODAY"?

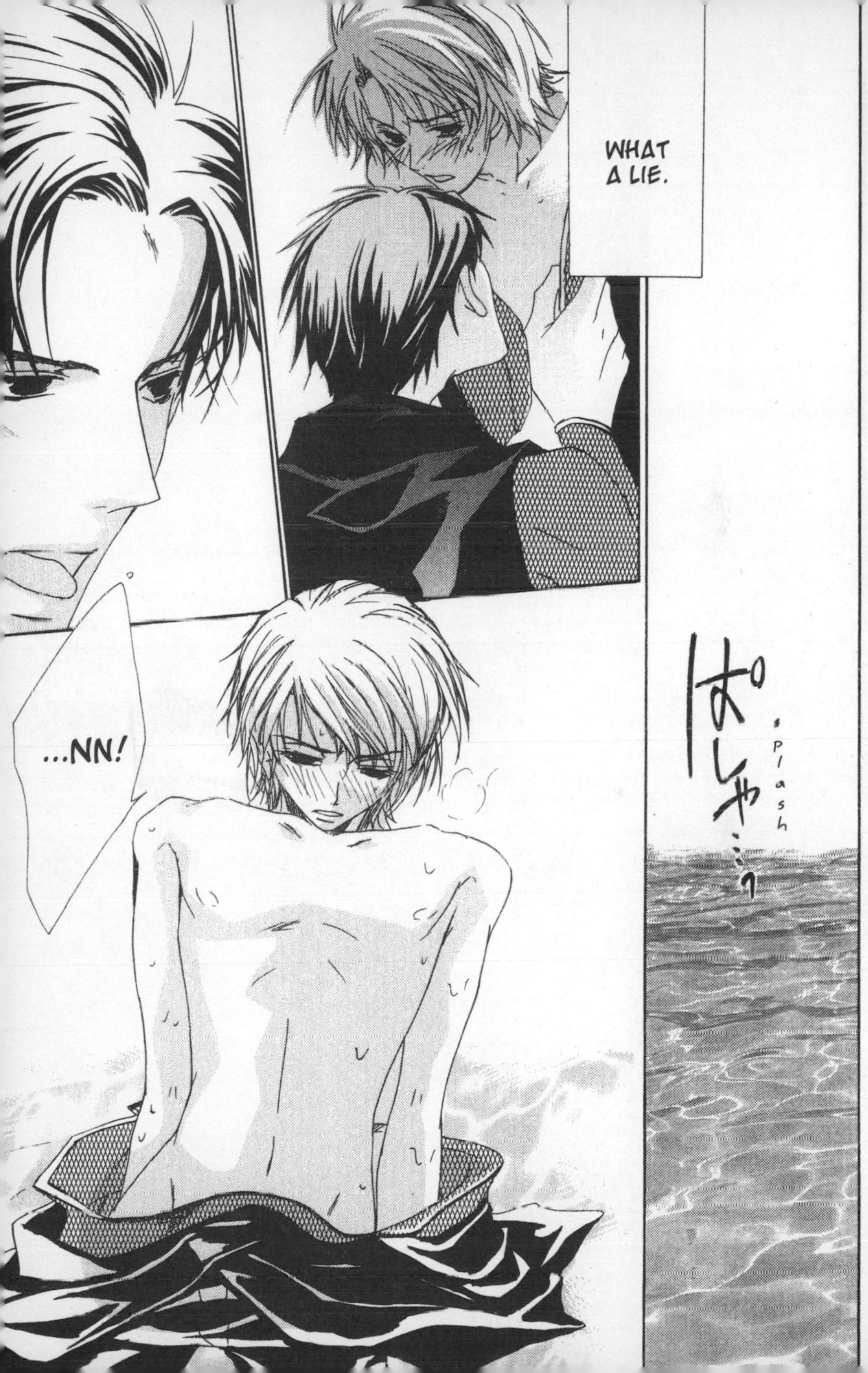
ぱしゃ…っ
splash
WHAT A LIE.
...NN!

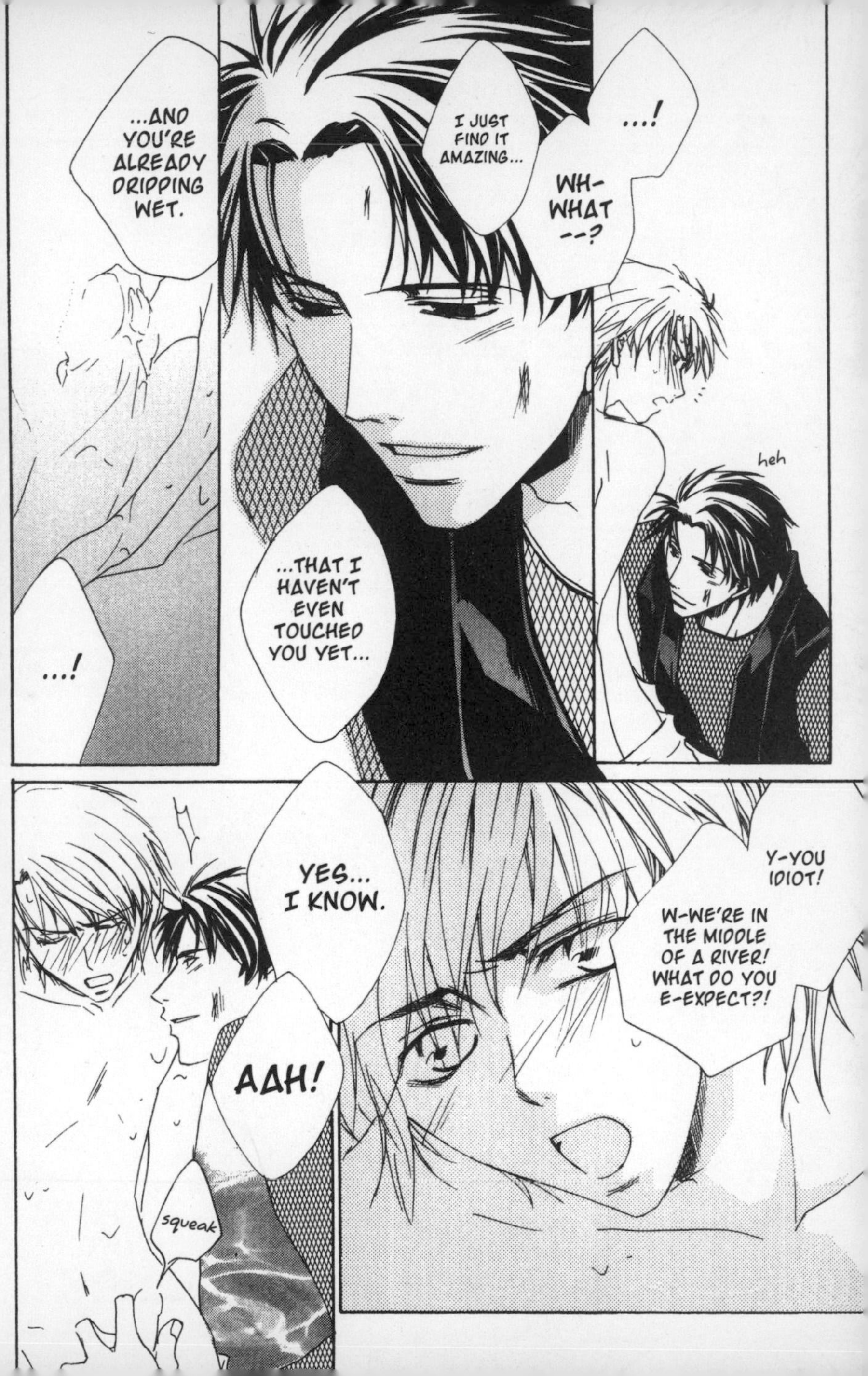
...!
WH-WHAT--?
heh
I JUST FIND IT AMAZING...
...THAT I HAVEN'T EVEN TOUCHED YOU YET...
...AND YOU'RE ALREADY DRIPPING WET.
...!
Y-YOU IDIOT!
W-WE'RE IN THE MIDDLE OF A RIVER! WHAT DO YOU E-EXPECT?!
YES... I KNOW.
AAH!
squeak

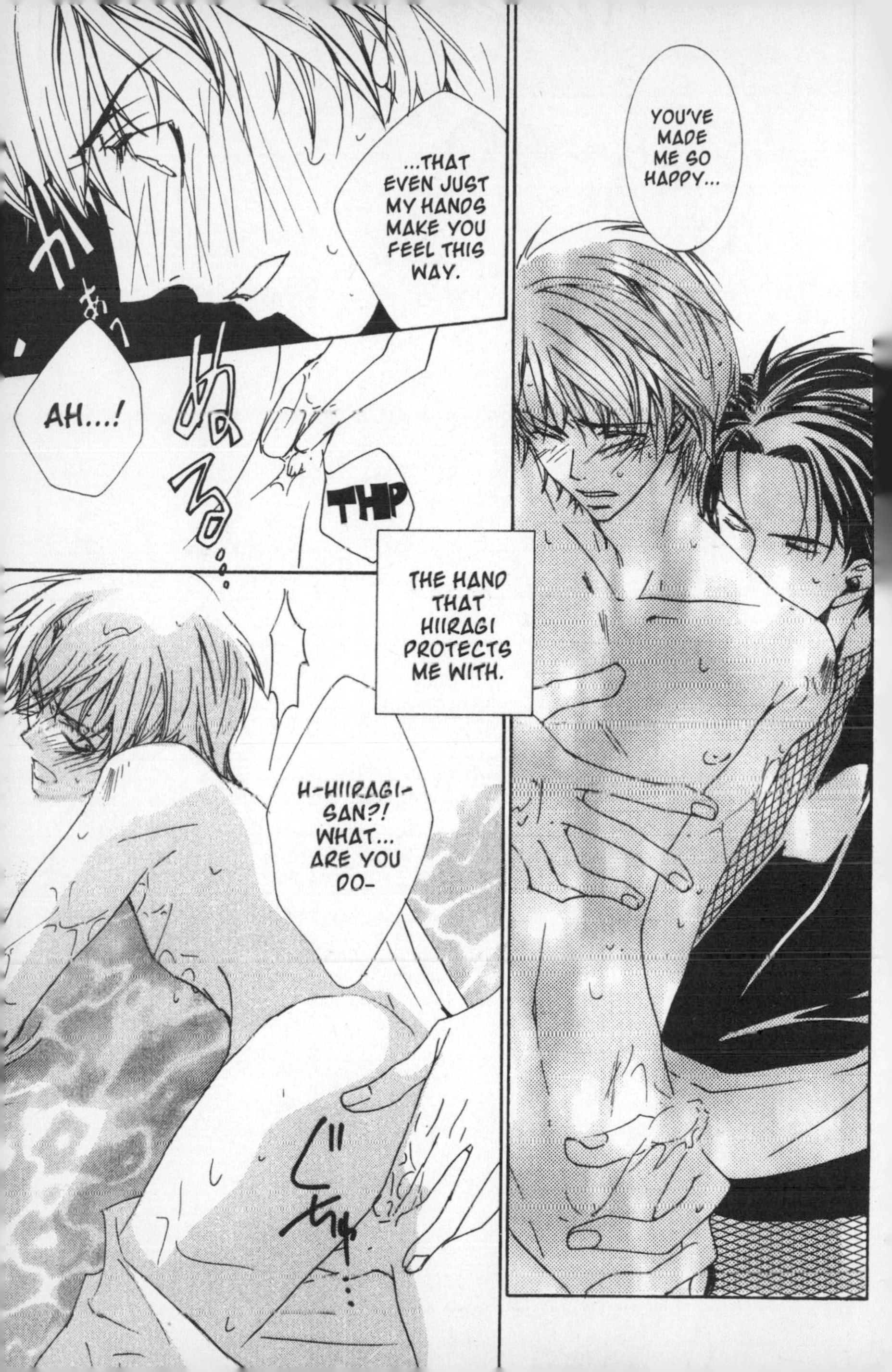
YOU'VE MADE ME SO HAPPY...
THE HAND THAT HIIRAGI PROTECTS ME WITH.
...THAT EVEN JUST MY HANDS MAKE YOU FEEL THIS WAY.
AH...!
THP
H-HIIRAGI-SAN?! WHAT... ARE YOU DO-

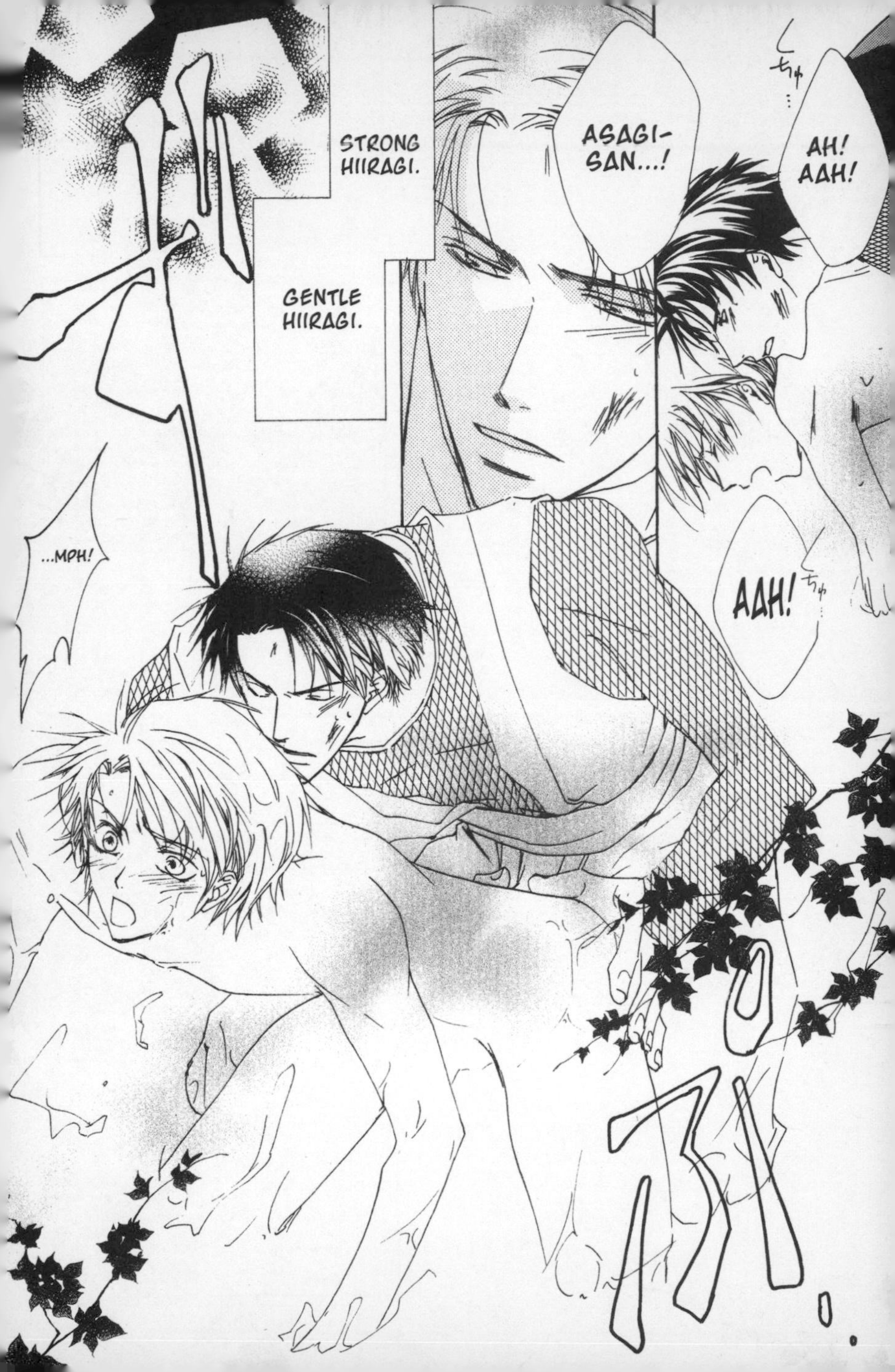
AH! AAH!
AAH!
ASAGI-SAN...!
STRONG HIIRAGI.
GENTLE HIIRAGI.
...MPH!

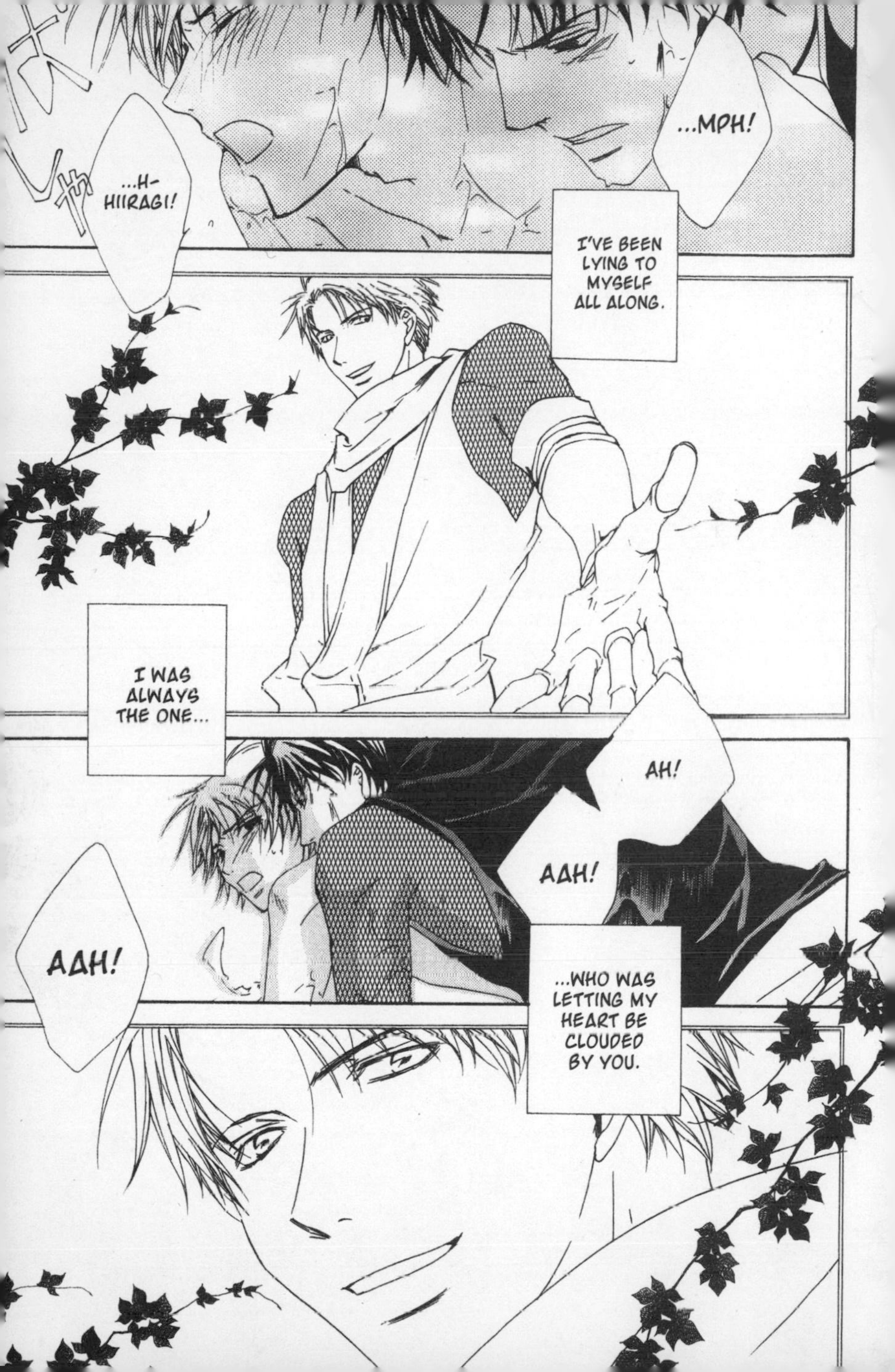
...MPH!
...H- HIIRAGI!
I'VE BEEN LYING TO MYSELF ALL ALONG.
I WAS ALWAYS THE ONE...
AH!
AAH!
AAH!
...WHO WAS LETTING MY HEART BE CLOUDED BY YOU.

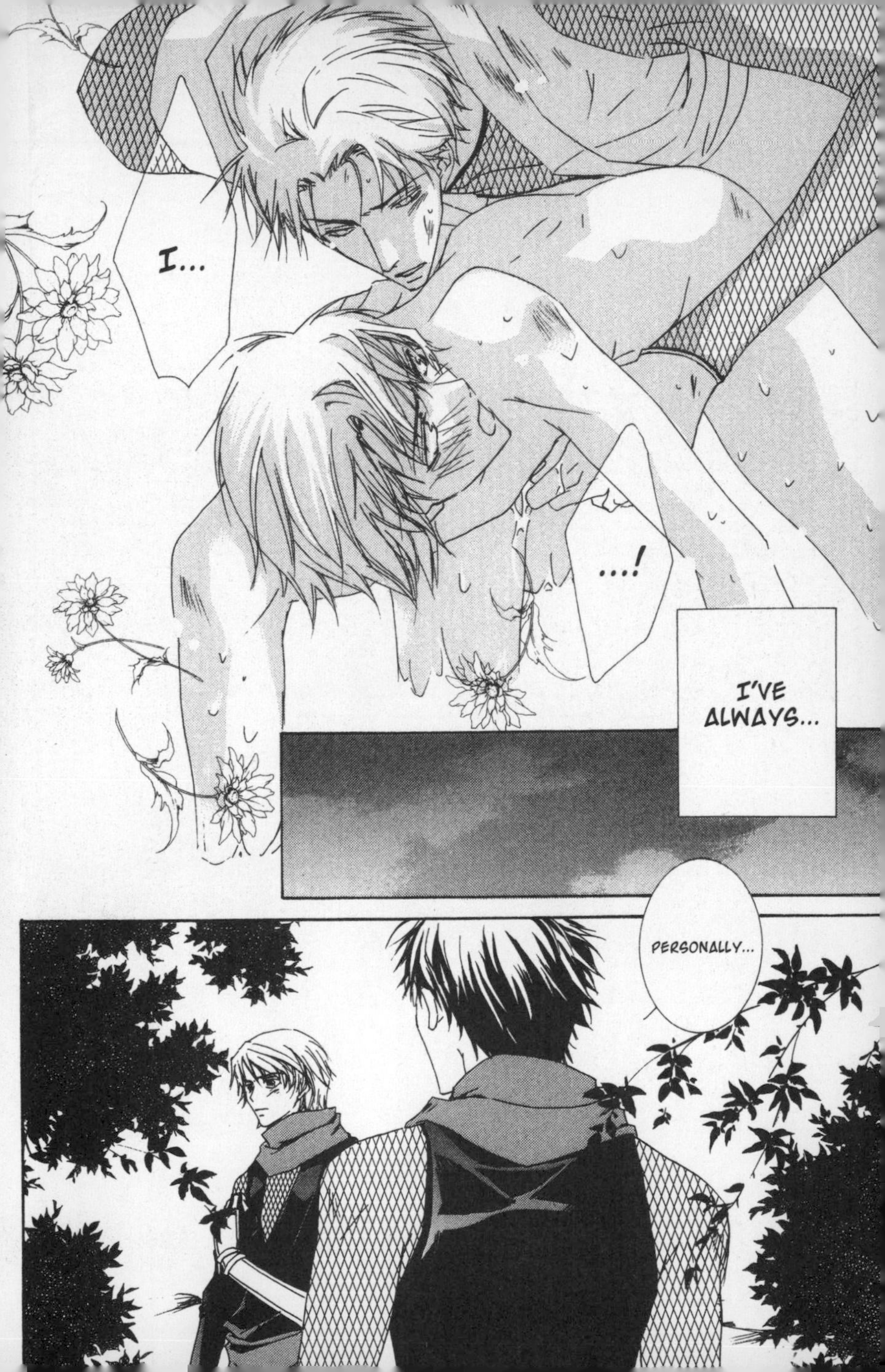
I...
...!
I'VE ALWAYS...
PERSONALLY...

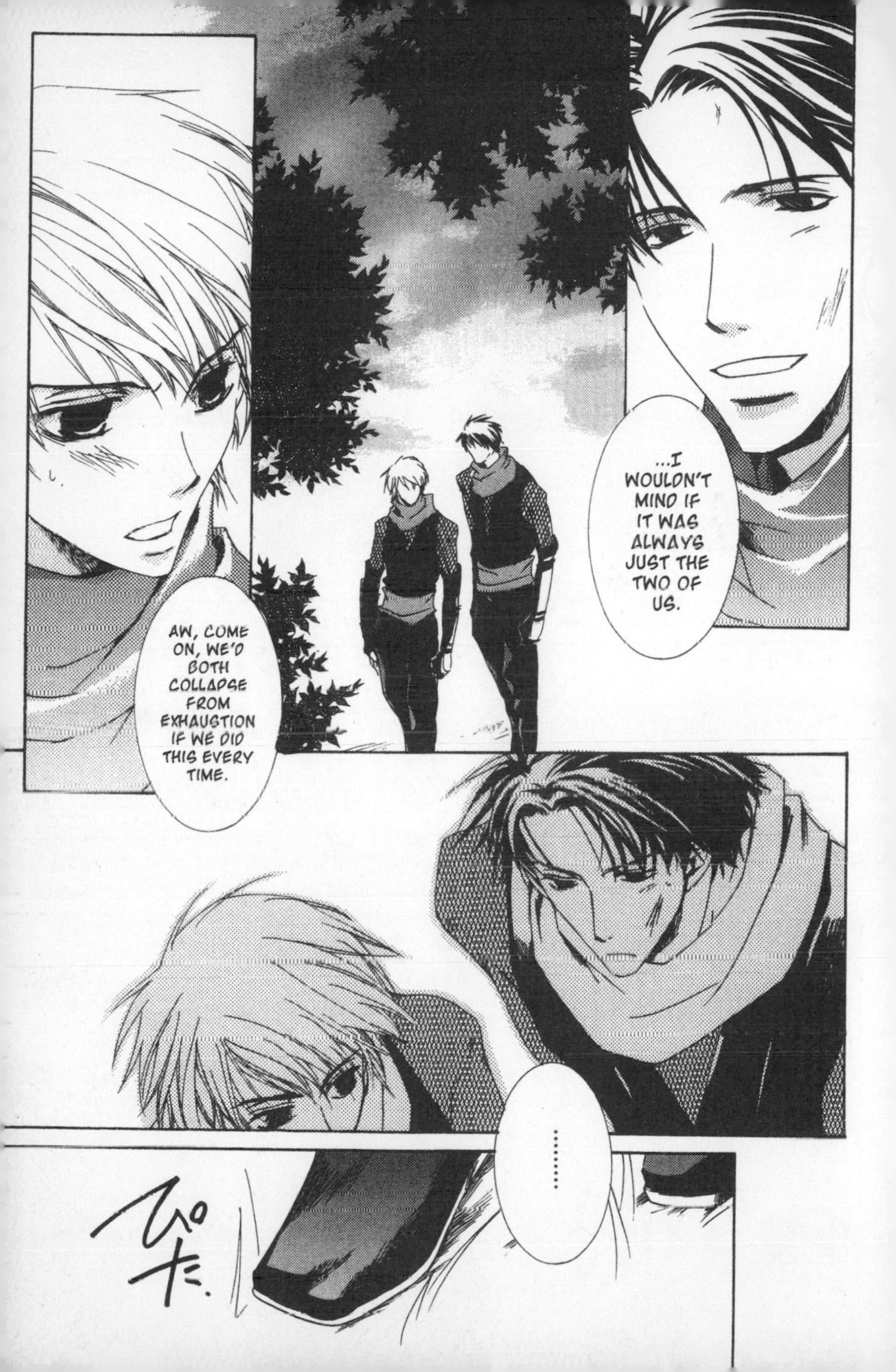
...I WOULDN'T MIND IF IT WAS ALWAYS JUST THE TWO OF US.
AW, COME ON, WE'D BOTH COLLAPSE FROM EXHAUSTION IF WE DID THIS EVERY TIME.
......
ぴた.

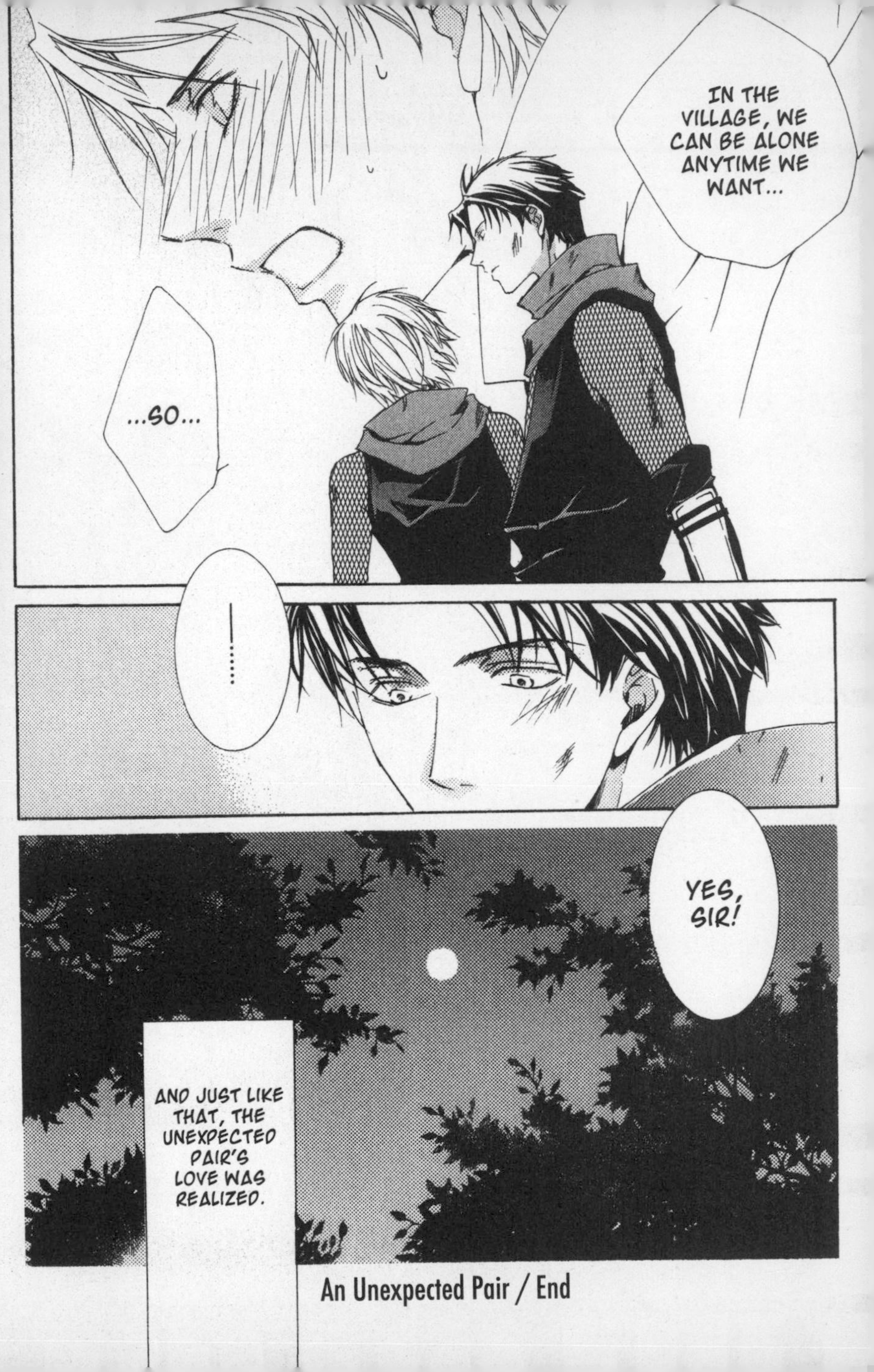
IN THE VILLAGE, WE CAN BE ALONE ANYTIME WE WANT...
...SO...
......
YES, SIR!
AND JUST LIKE THAT, THE UNEXPECTED PAIR'S LOVE WAS REALIZED.

An Unexpected Pair / End

はからずも二人

An Unexpected Pair

TEMARI MATSUMOTO

ASA G.1

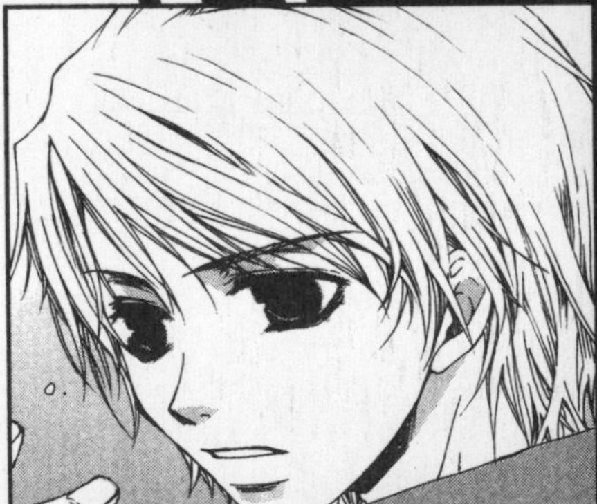

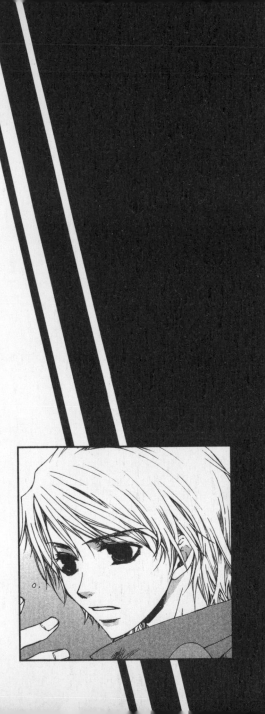

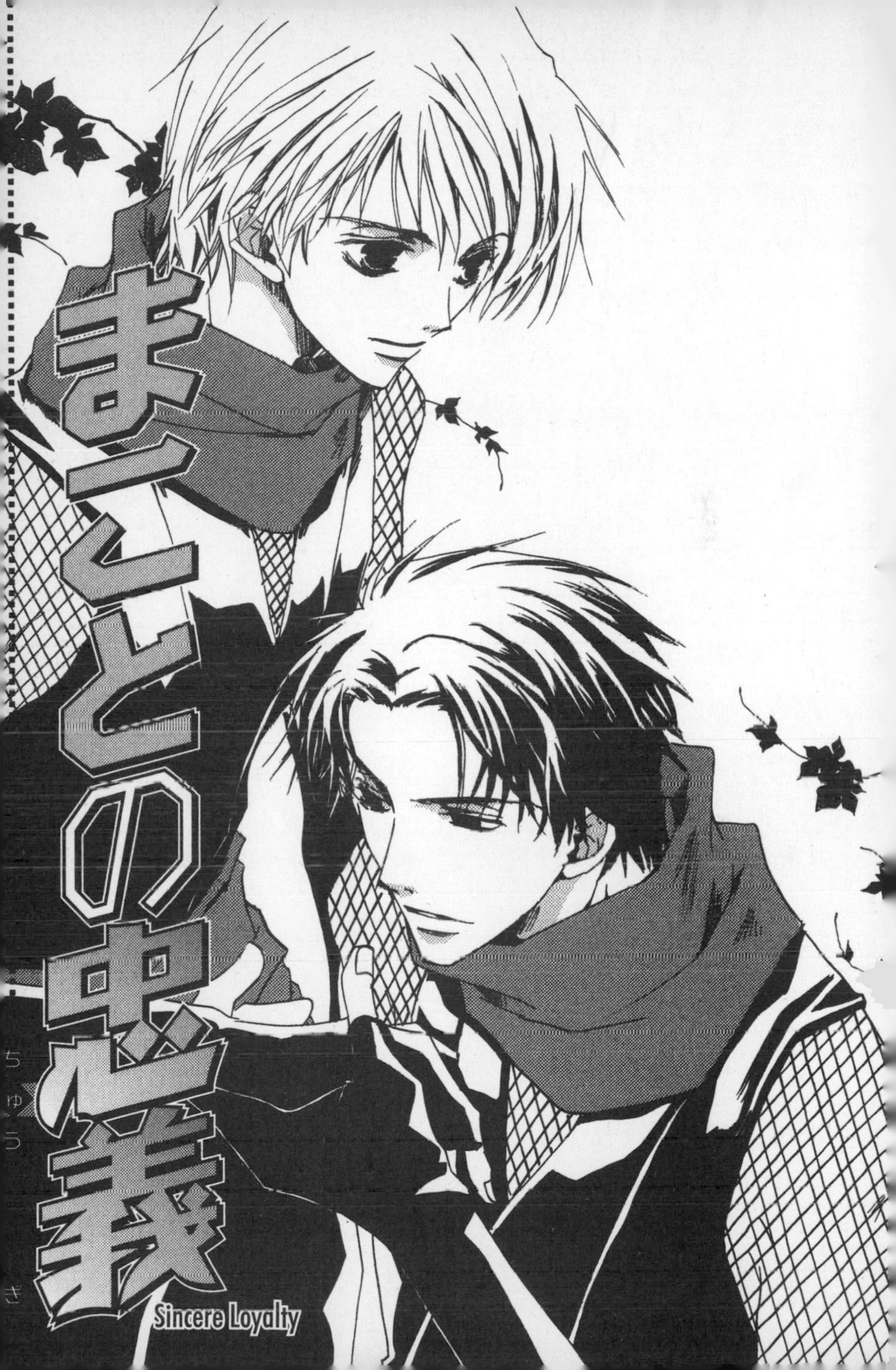
まことの忠義
ちゅうぎ
Sincere Loyalty

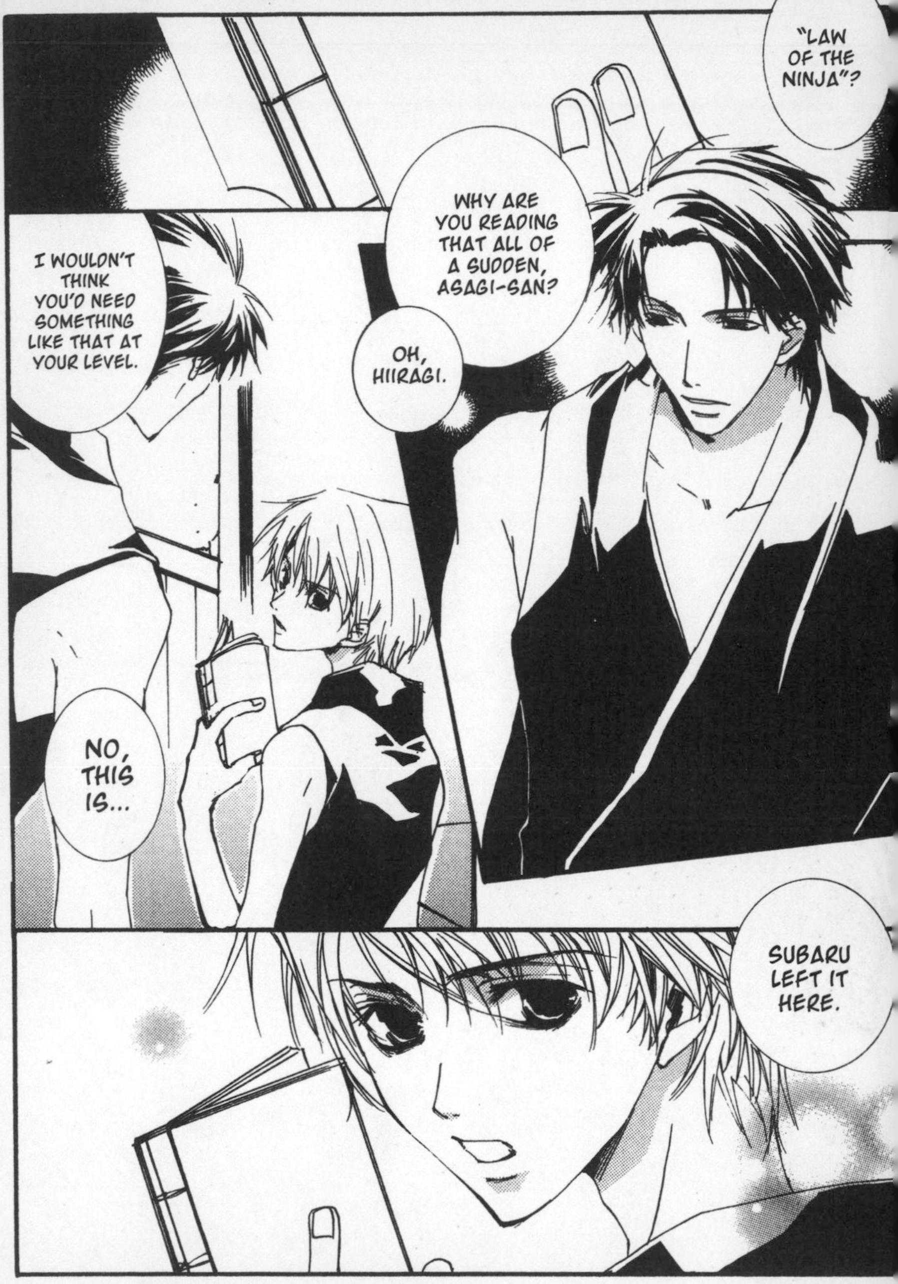
"LAW OF THE NINJA"?
WHY ARE YOU READING THAT ALL OF A SUDDEN, ASAGI-SAN?
OH, HIIRAGI.
I WOULDN'T THINK YOU'D NEED SOMETHING LIKE THAT AT YOUR LEVEL.
NO, THIS IS...
SUBARU LEFT IT HERE.

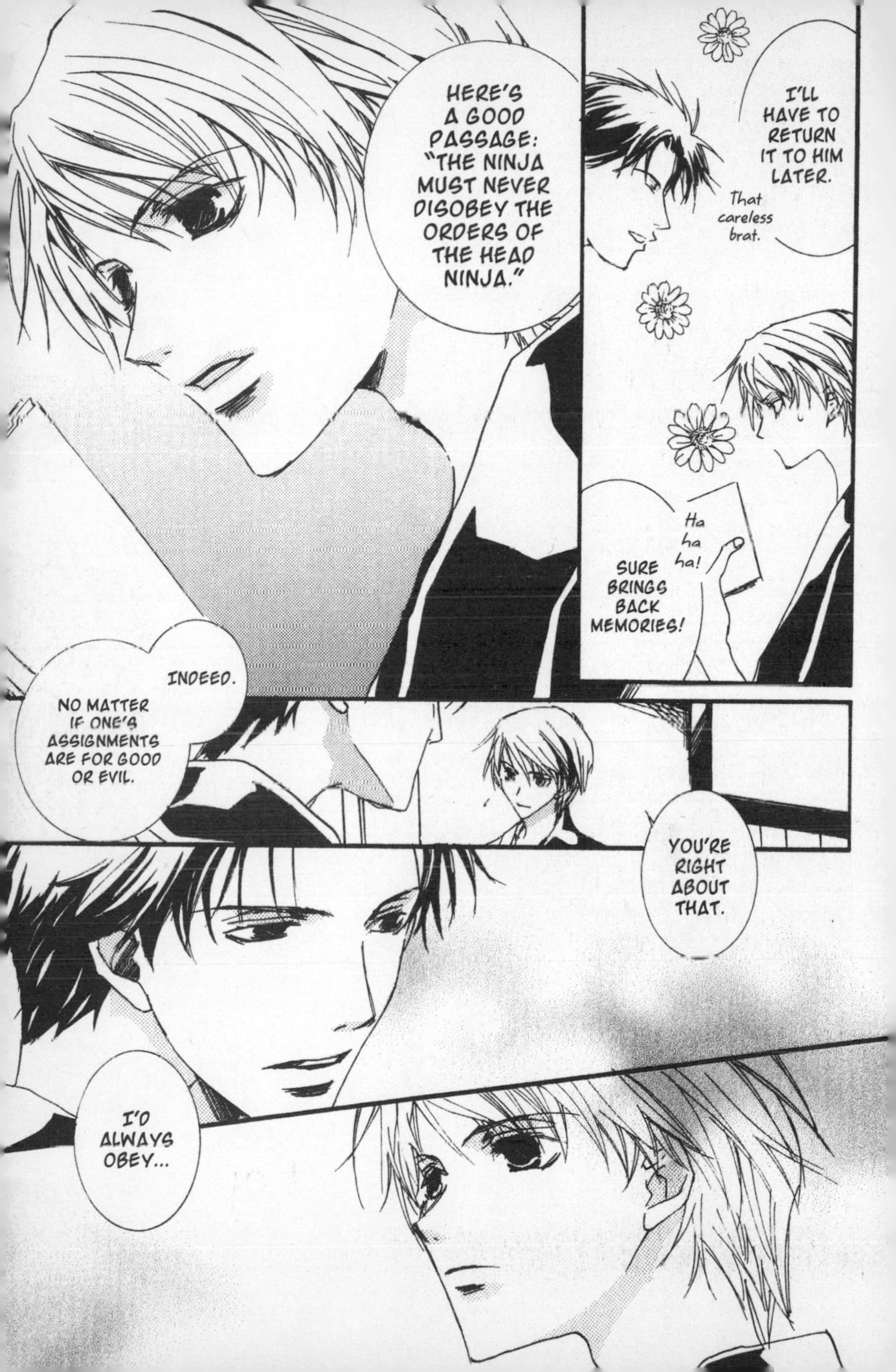
I'LL HAVE TO RETURN IT TO HIM LATER.
That careless brat.
Ha ha ha!
SURE BRINGS BACK MEMORIES!
HERE'S A GOOD PASSAGE: "THE NINJA MUST NEVER DISOBEY THE ORDERS OF THE HEAD NINJA."
INDEED.
NO MATTER IF ONE'S ASSIGNMENTS ARE FOR GOOD OR EVIL.
YOU'RE RIGHT ABOUT THAT.
I'D ALWAYS OBEY...

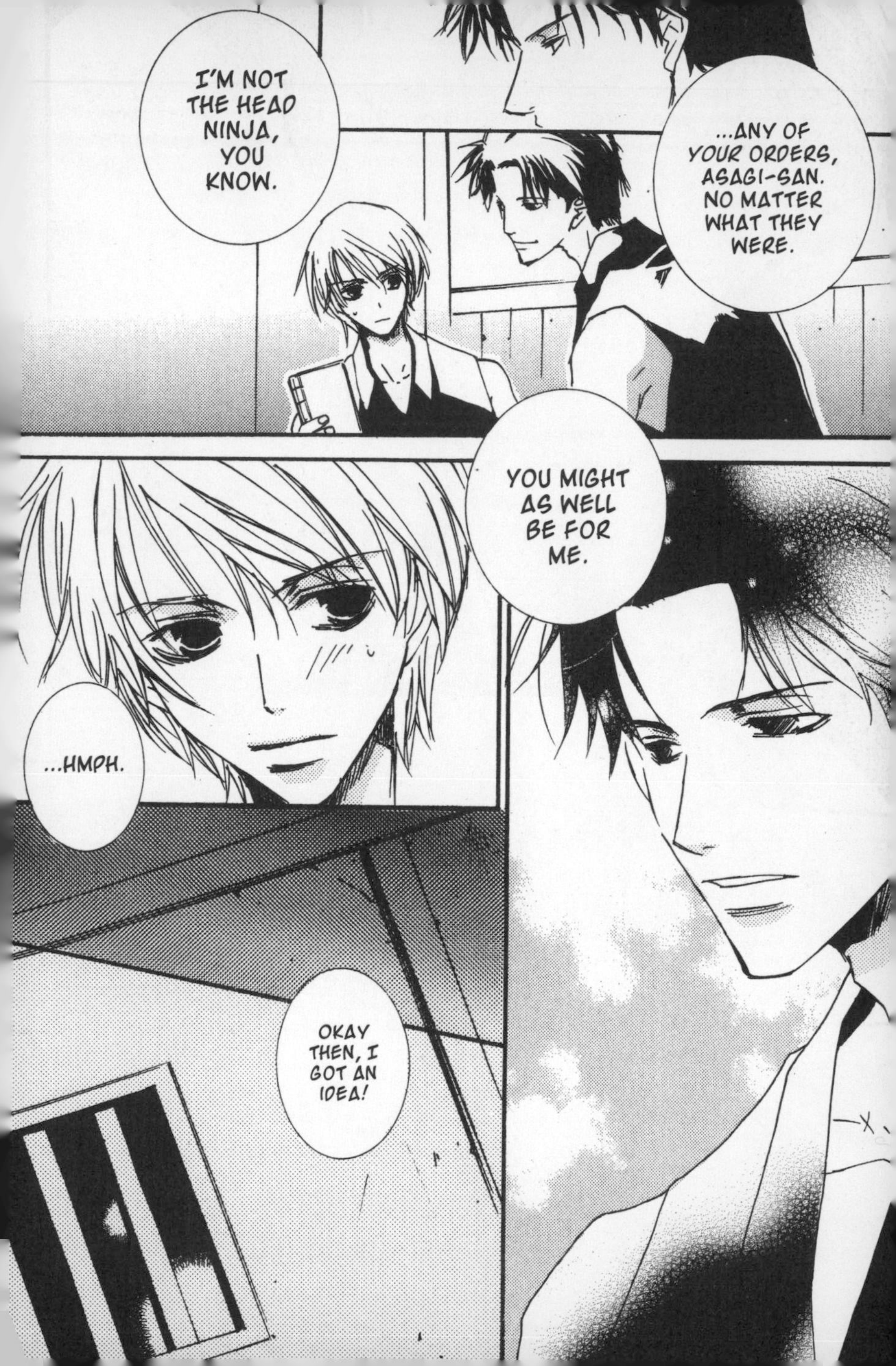
...ANY OF YOUR ORDERS, ASAGI-SAN. NO MATTER WHAT THEY WERE.
I'M NOT THE HEAD NINJA, YOU KNOW.
YOU MIGHT AS WELL BE FOR ME.
...HMPH.
OKAY THEN, I GOT AN IDEA!

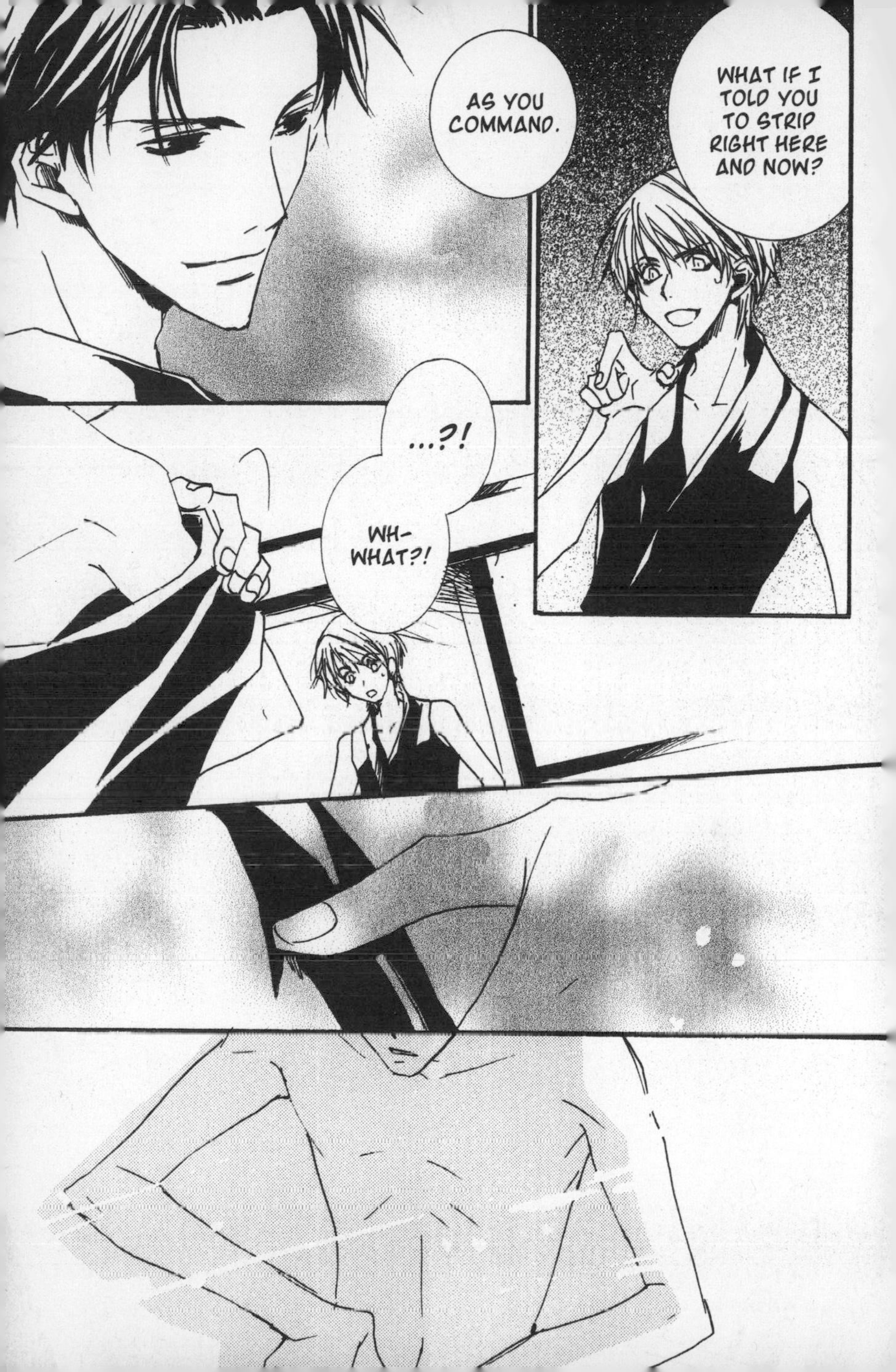
WHAT IF I TOLD YOU TO STRIP RIGHT HERE AND NOW?
AS YOU COMMAND.
...?!
WH- WHAT?!

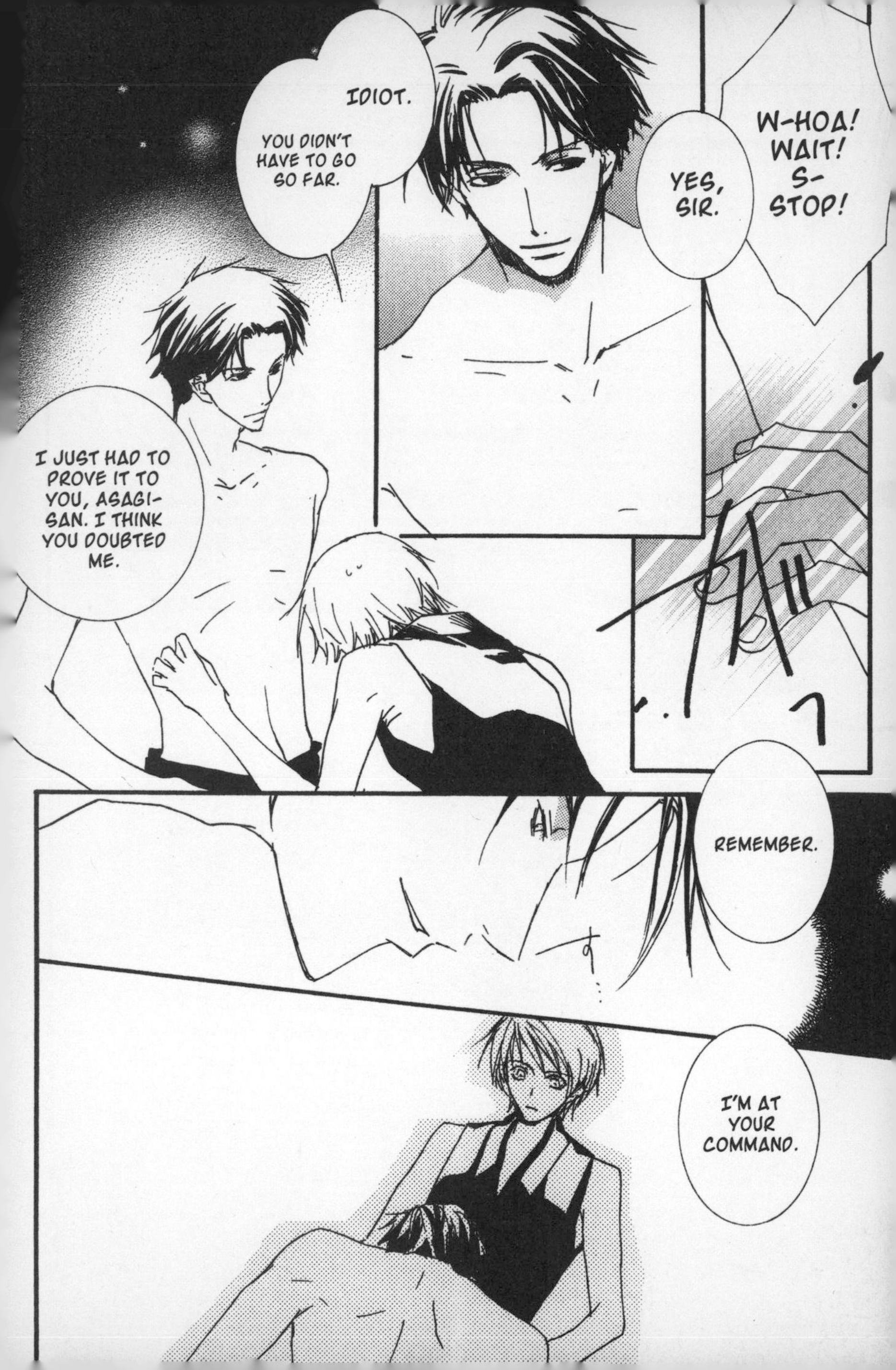
W-HOA! WAIT! S-STOP!
YES, SIR.
IDIOT.
YOU DIDN'T HAVE TO GO SO FAR.
I JUST HAD TO PROVE IT TO YOU, ASAGI-SAN. I THINK YOU DOUBTED ME.
REMEMBER.
I'M AT YOUR COMMAND.

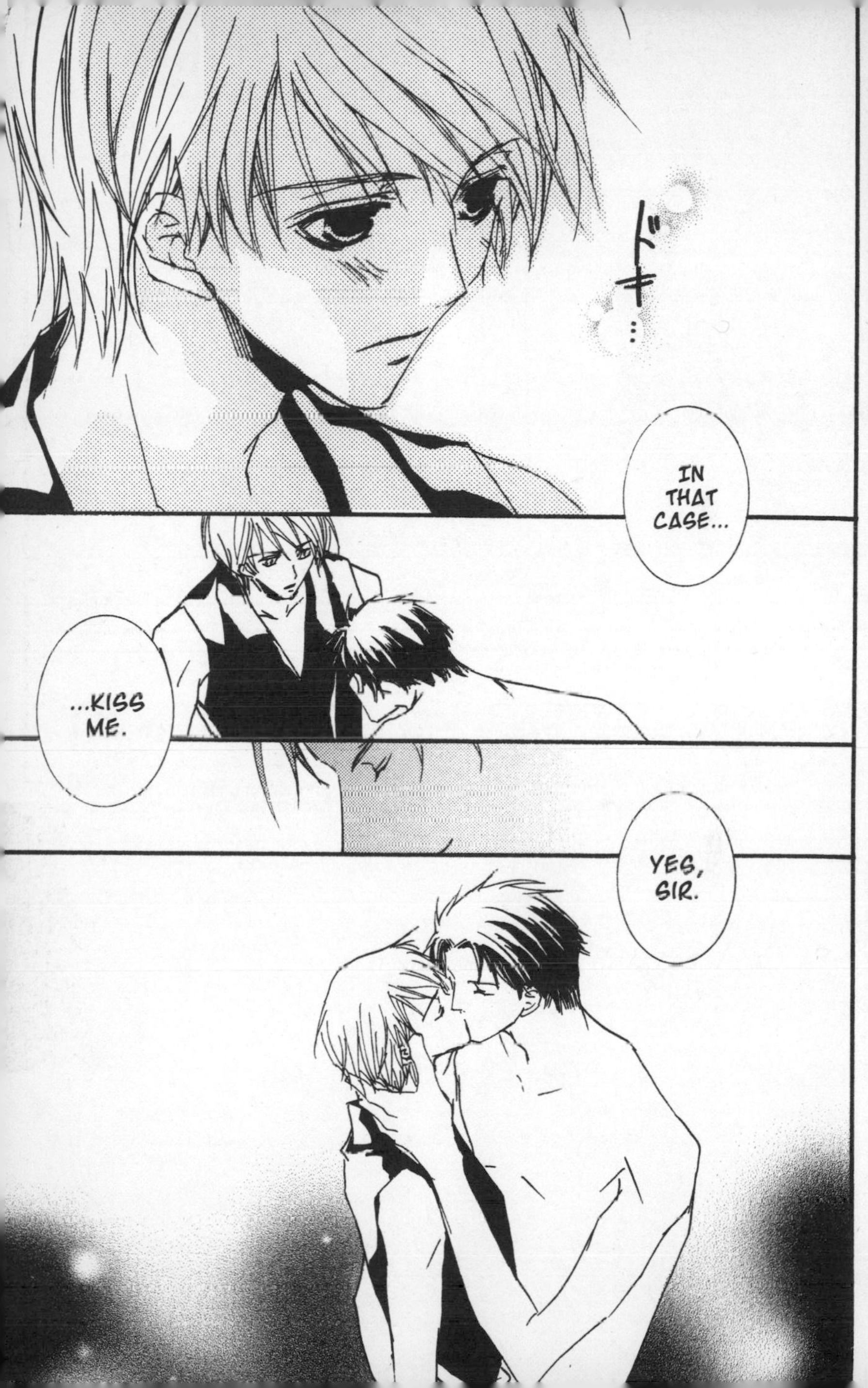
ドキ…
IN THAT CASE...
...KISS ME.
YES, SIR.

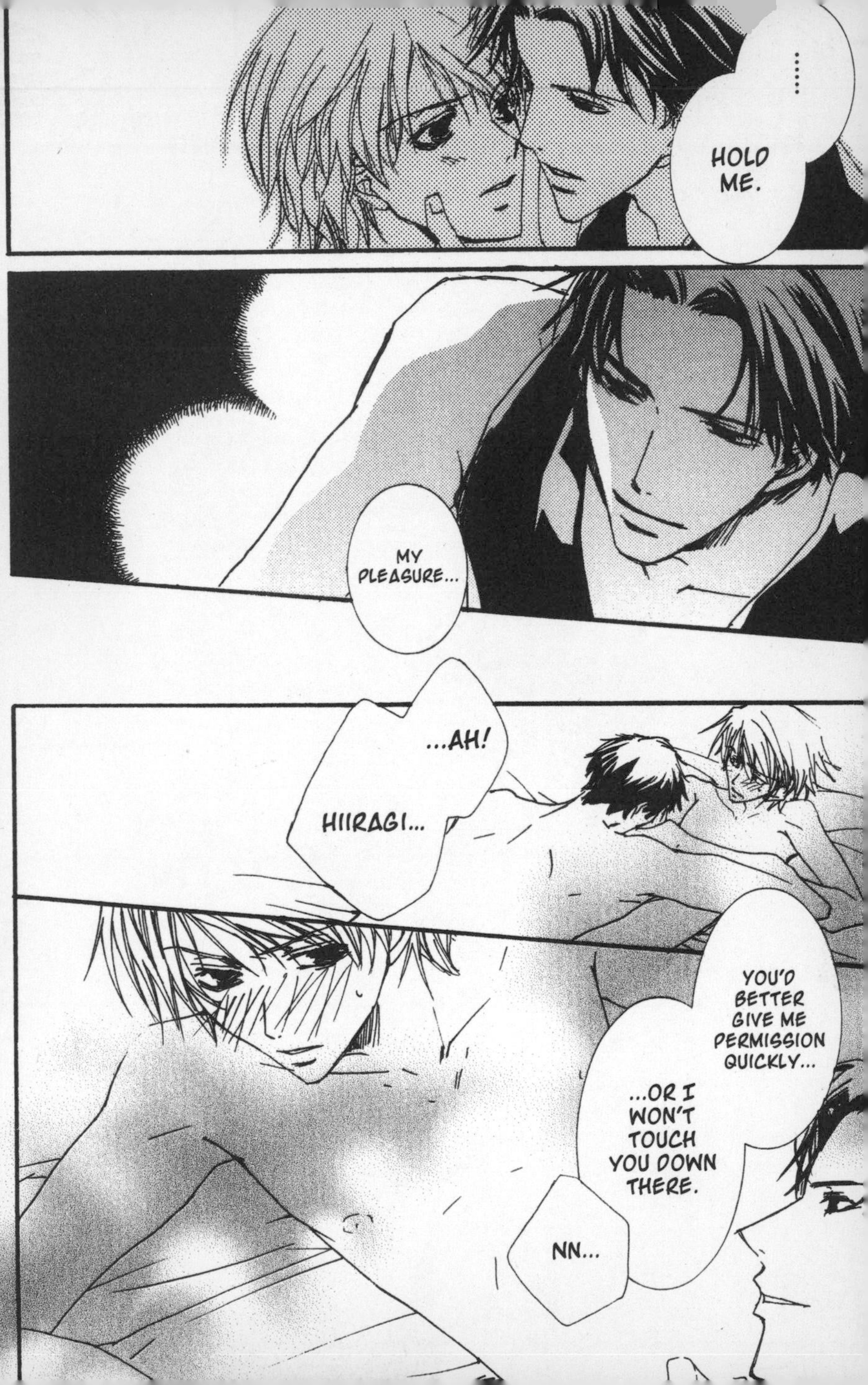
......
HOLD ME.
MY PLEASURE...
...AH!
HIIRAGI...
YOU'D BETTER GIVE ME PERMISSION QUICKLY...
...OR I WON'T TOUCH YOU DOWN THERE.
NN...

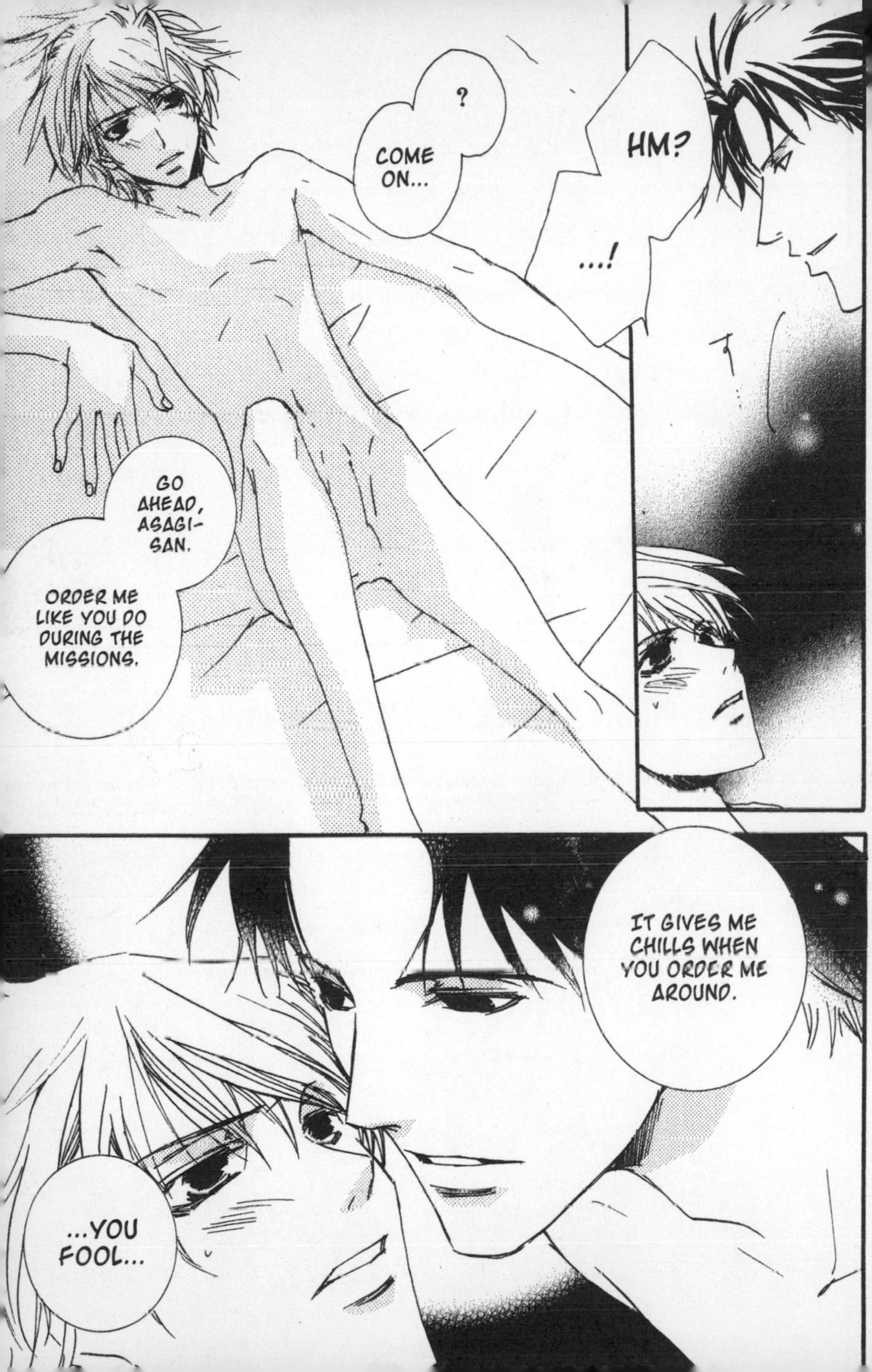
HM?
...!
?
COME ON...
GO AHEAD, ASAGI-SAN.
ORDER ME LIKE YOU DO DURING THE MISSIONS.
IT GIVES ME CHILLS WHEN YOU ORDER ME AROUND.
...YOU FOOL...

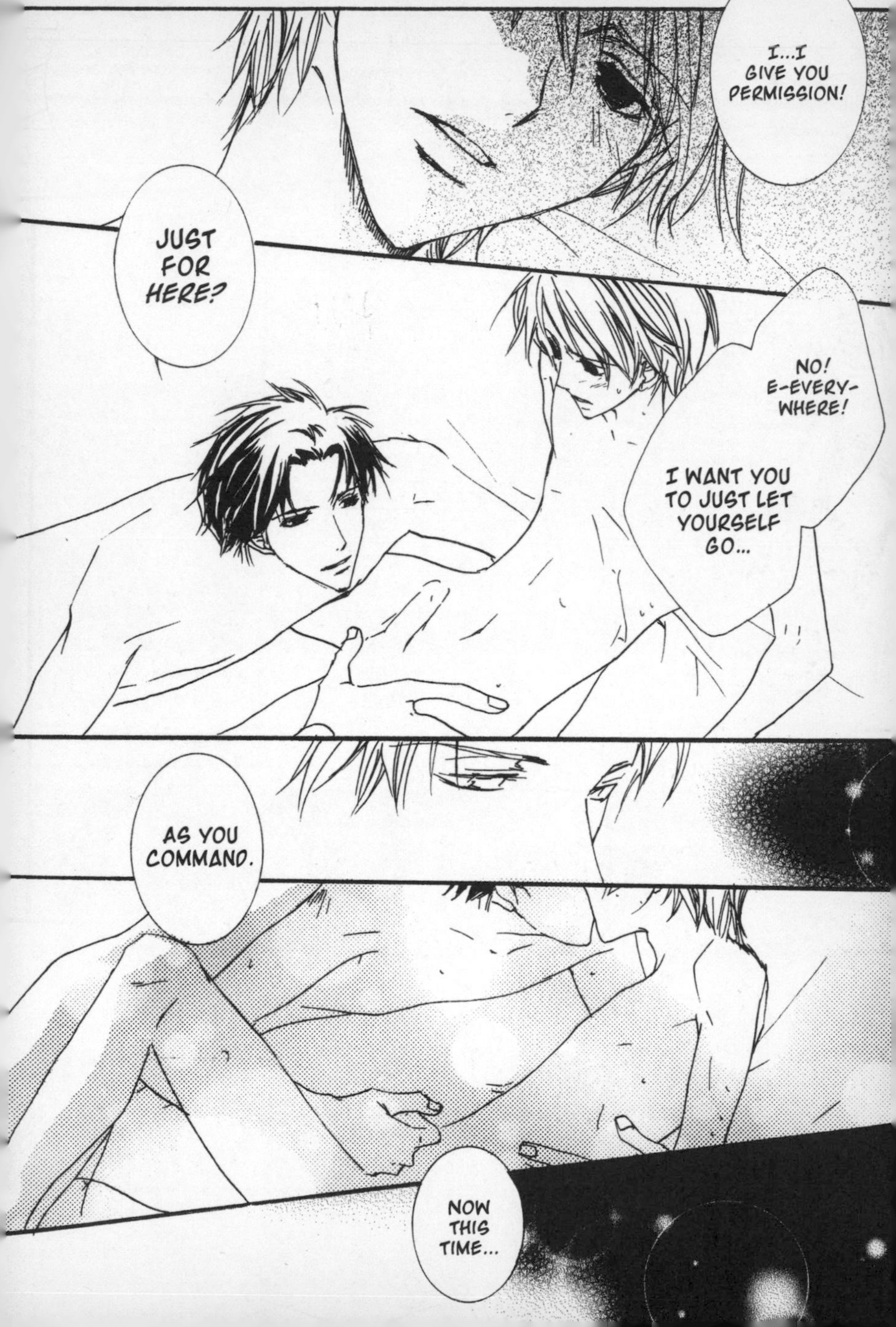
I...I GIVE YOU PERMISSION!
JUST FOR HERE?
NO! E-EVERY-WHERE!
I WANT YOU TO JUST LET YOURSELF GO...
AS YOU COMMAND.
NOW THIS TIME...

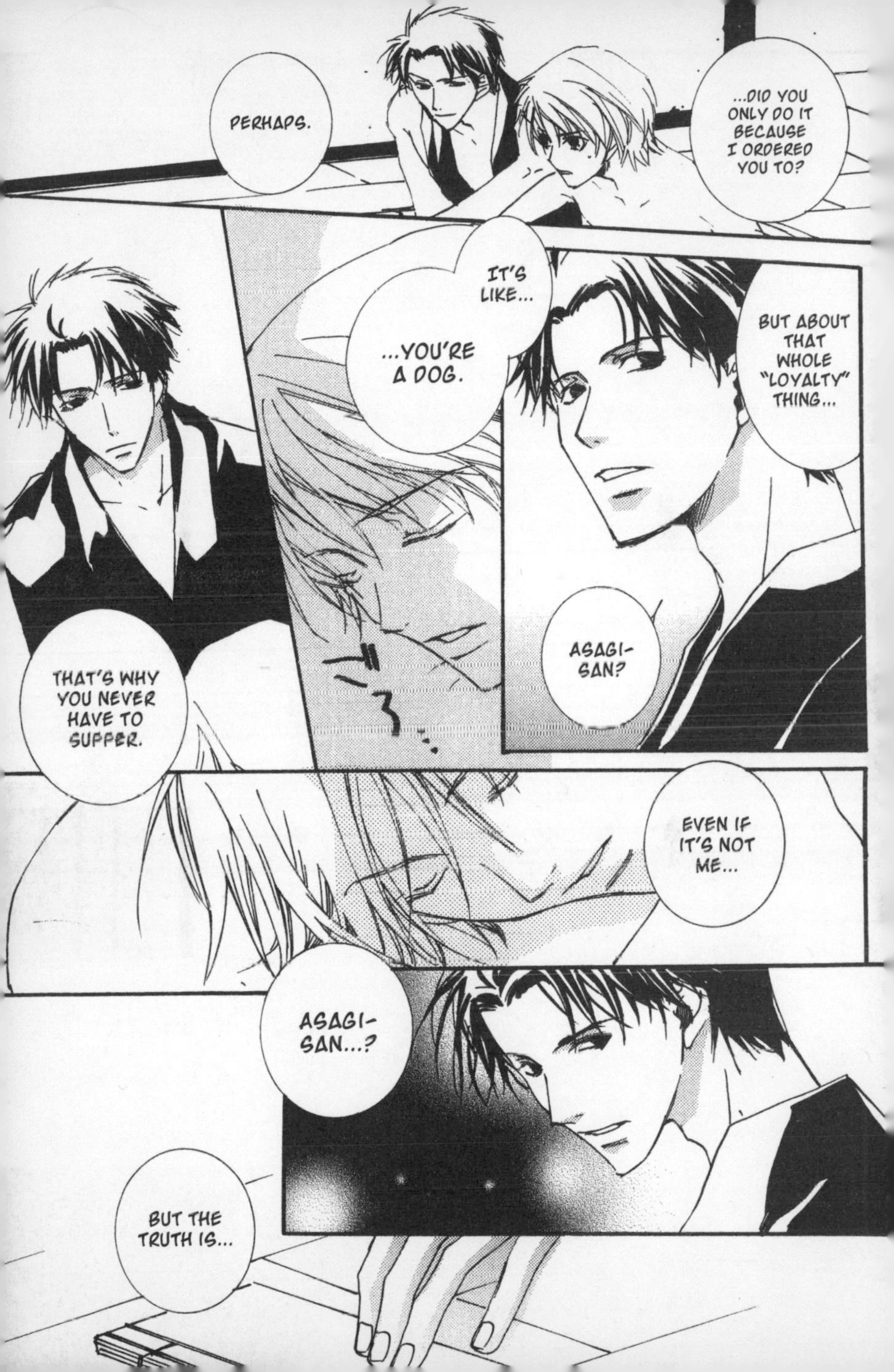
...DID YOU ONLY DO IT BECAUSE I ORDERED YOU TO?
PERHAPS.
BUT ABOUT THAT WHOLE "LOYALTY" THING...
ASAGI-SAN?
IT'S LIKE...
...YOU'RE A DOG.
THAT'S WHY YOU NEVER HAVE TO SUFFER.
EVEN IF IT'S NOT ME...
ASAGI-SAN...?
BUT THE TRUTH IS...

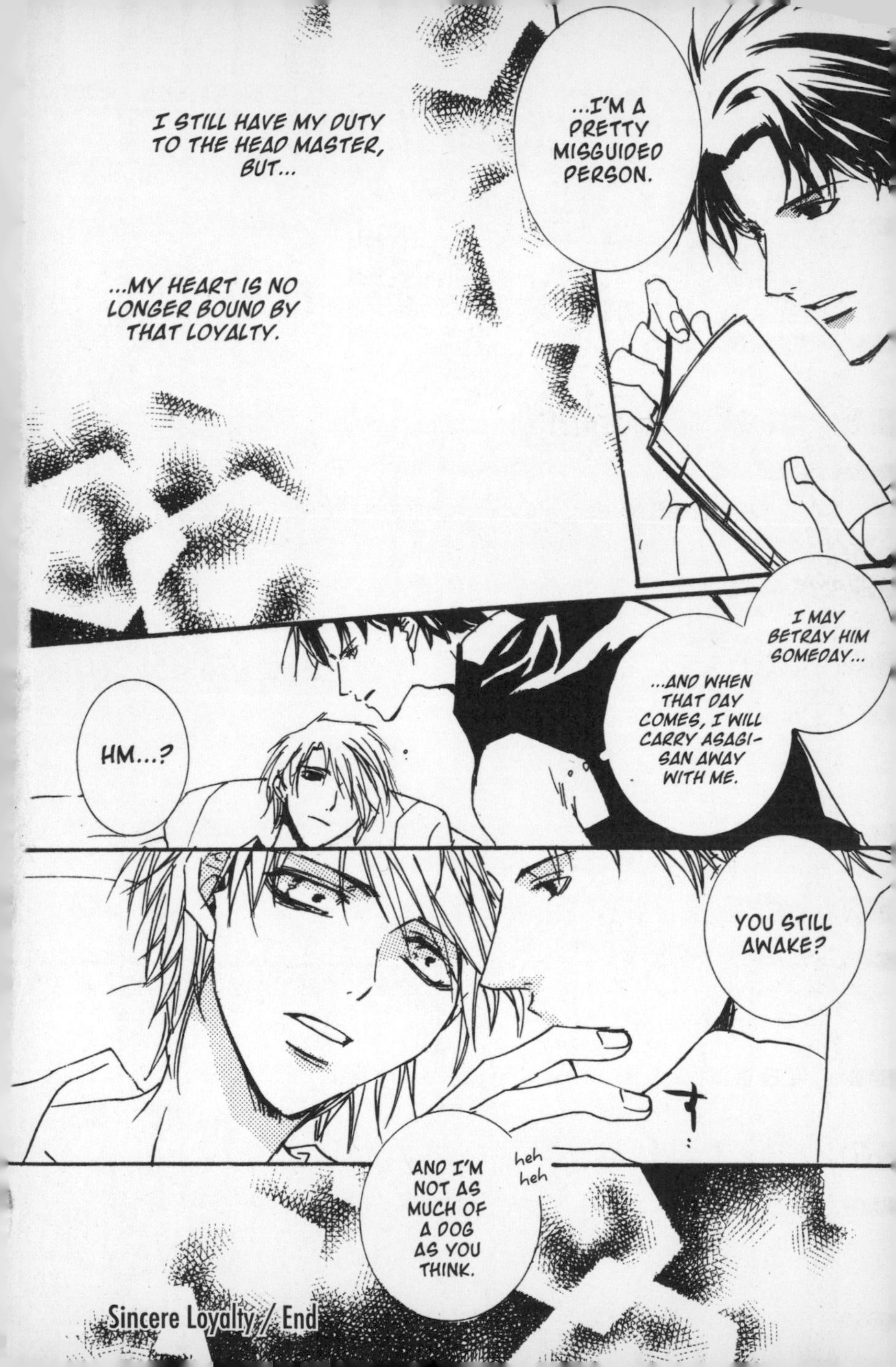
...I'M A PRETTY MISGUIDED PERSON.
I STILL HAVE MY DUTY TO THE HEAD MASTER, BUT...
...MY HEART IS NO LONGER BOUND BY THAT LOYALTY.
I MAY BETRAY HIM SOMEDAY...
...AND WHEN THAT DAY COMES, I WILL CARRY ASAGI-SAN AWAY WITH ME.
HM...?
YOU STILL AWAKE?
heh heh
AND I'M NOT AS MUCH OF A DOG AS YOU THINK.
Sincere Loyalty / End

まことの忠義

Sincere Loyalty

TEMARI
MATSUMOTO

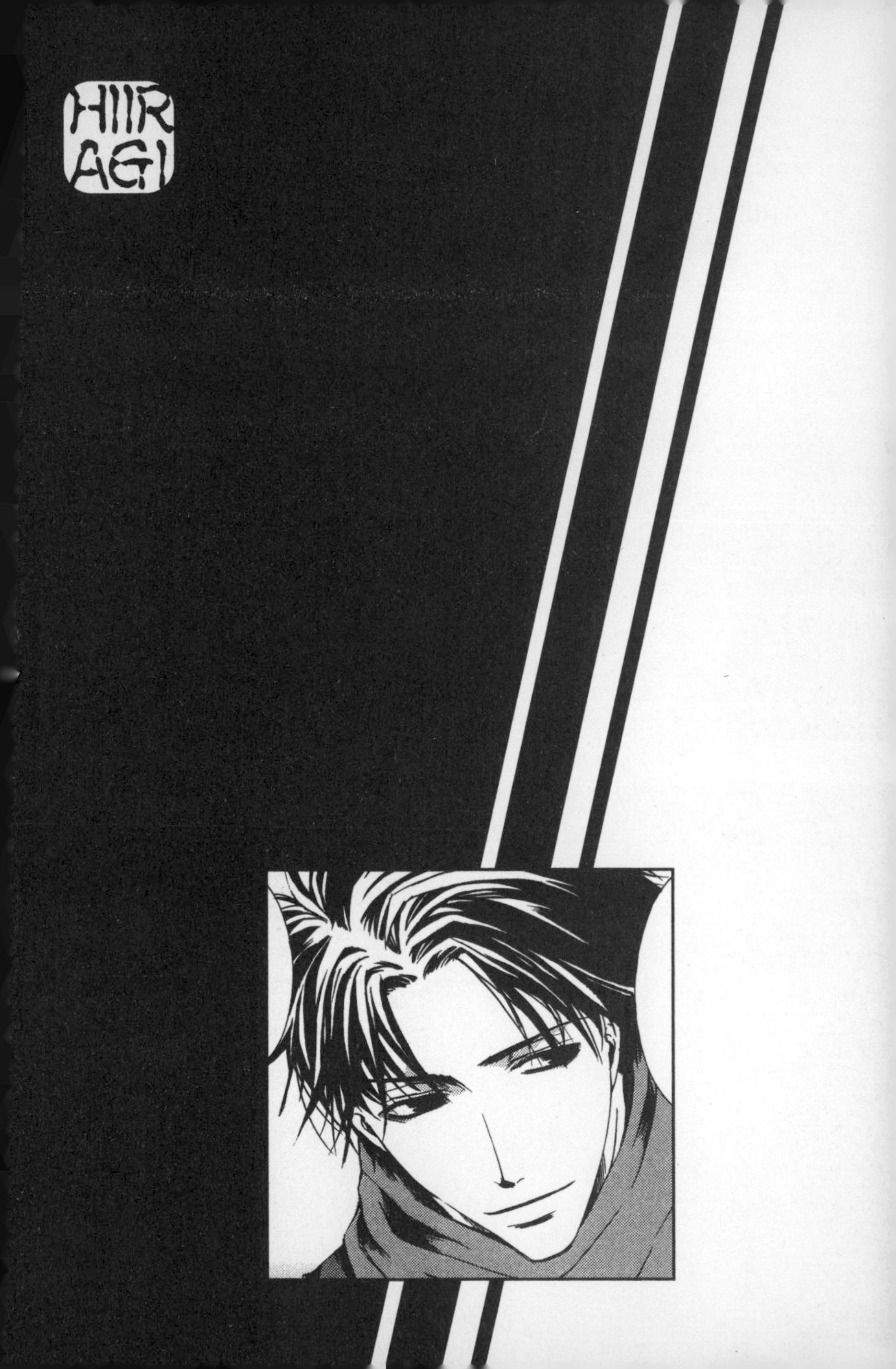
HIIR
AGI

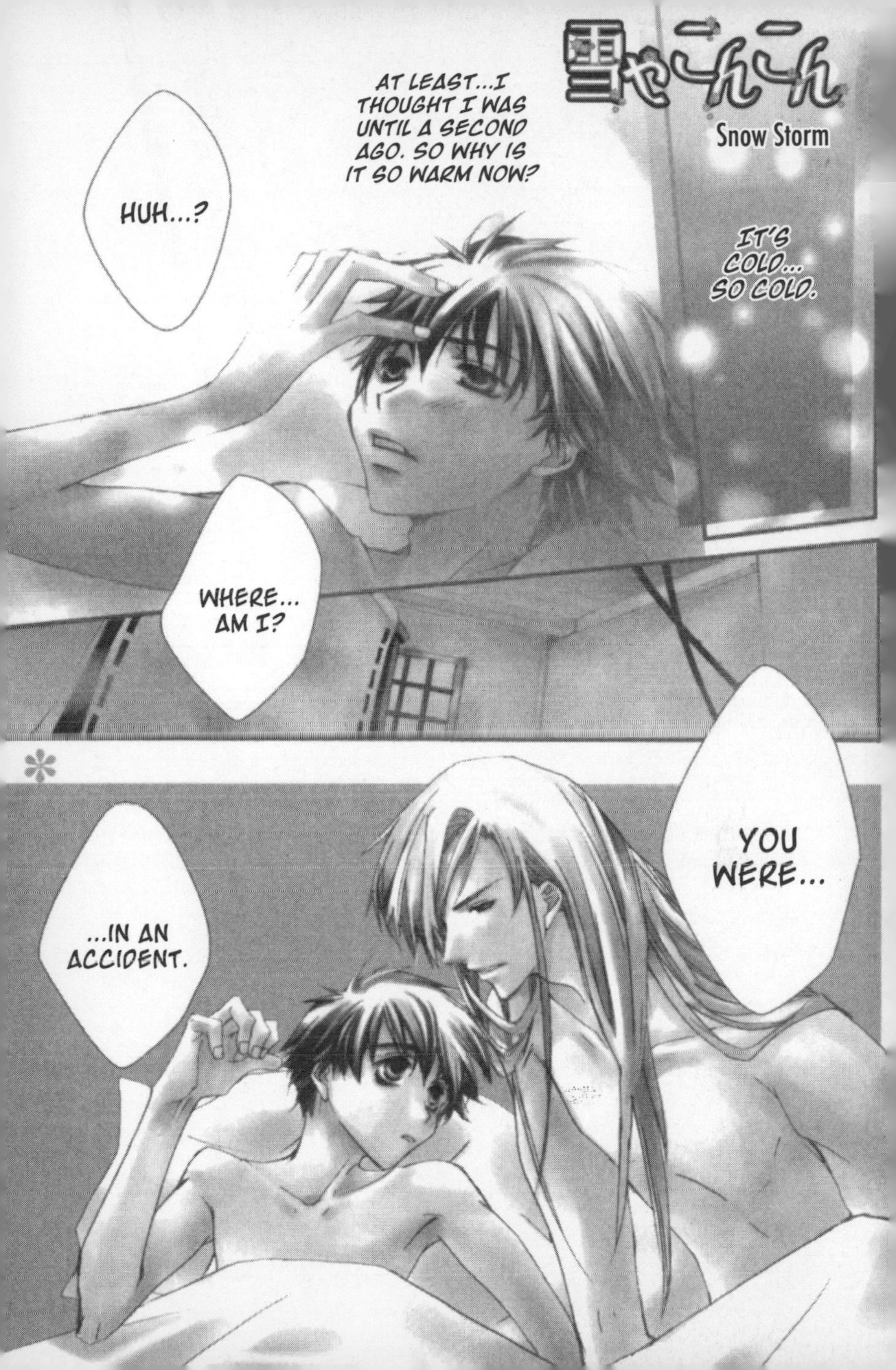
雪やこんこん
Snow Storm
IT'S COLD... SO COLD.
AT LEAST...I THOUGHT I WAS UNTIL A SECOND AGO. SO WHY IS IT SO WARM NOW?
HUH...?
WHERE... AM I?
YOU WERE...
...IN AN ACCIDENT.

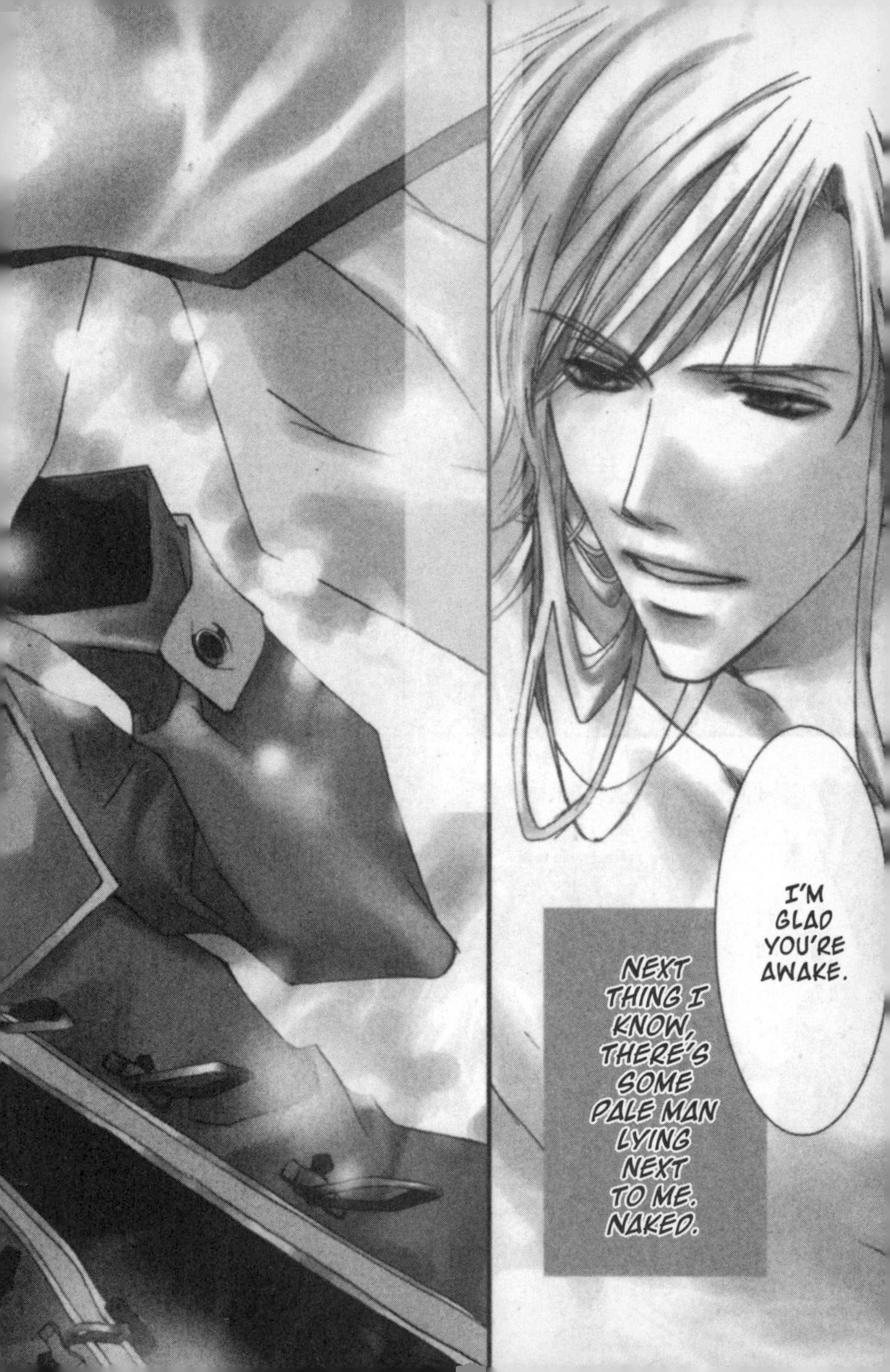
I'M GLAD YOU'RE AWAKE.
NEXT THING I KNOW, THERE'S SOME PALE MAN LYING NEXT TO ME. NAKED.

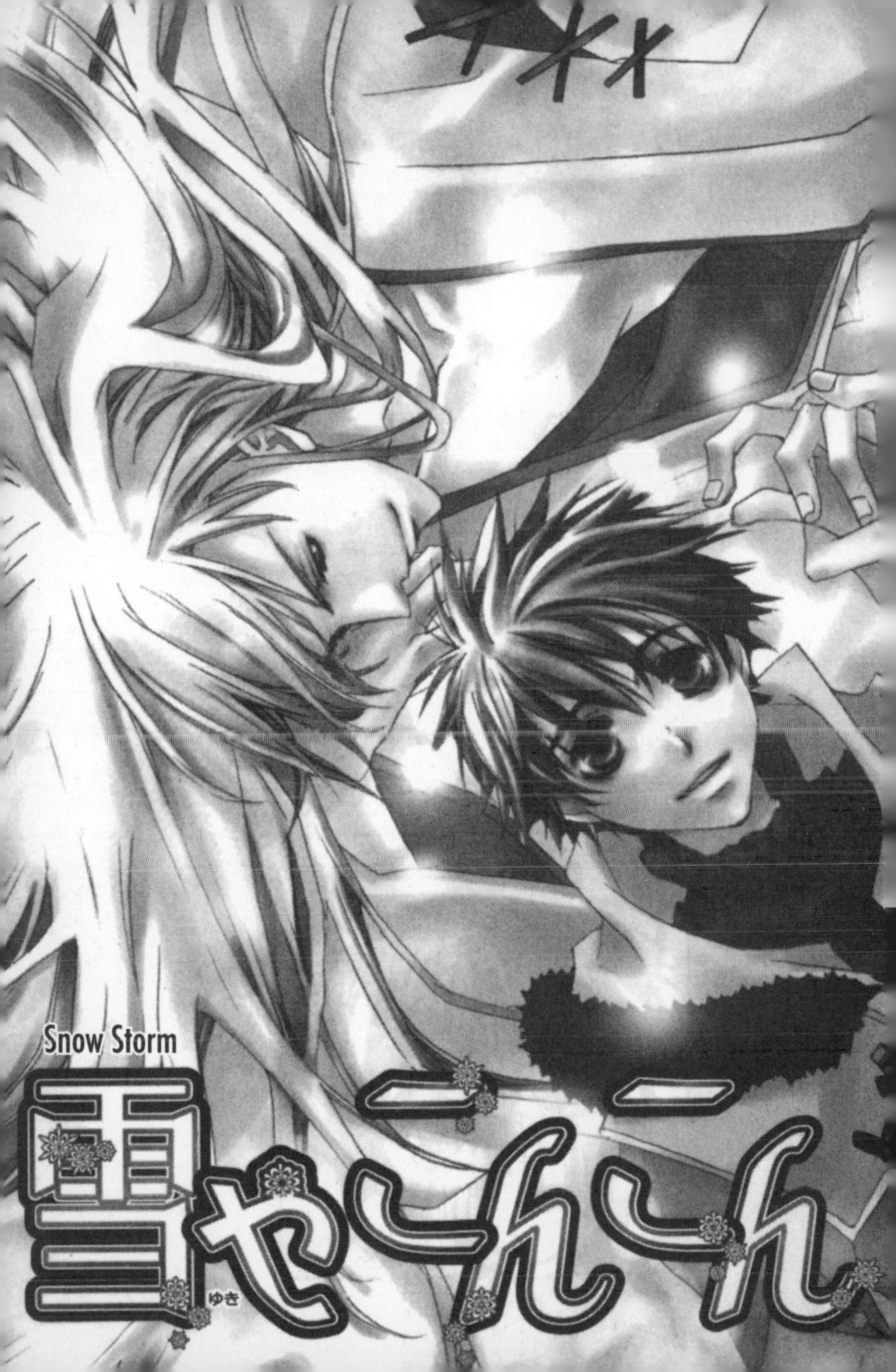
Snow Storm
雪(ゆき)やこんこん

FUTABA

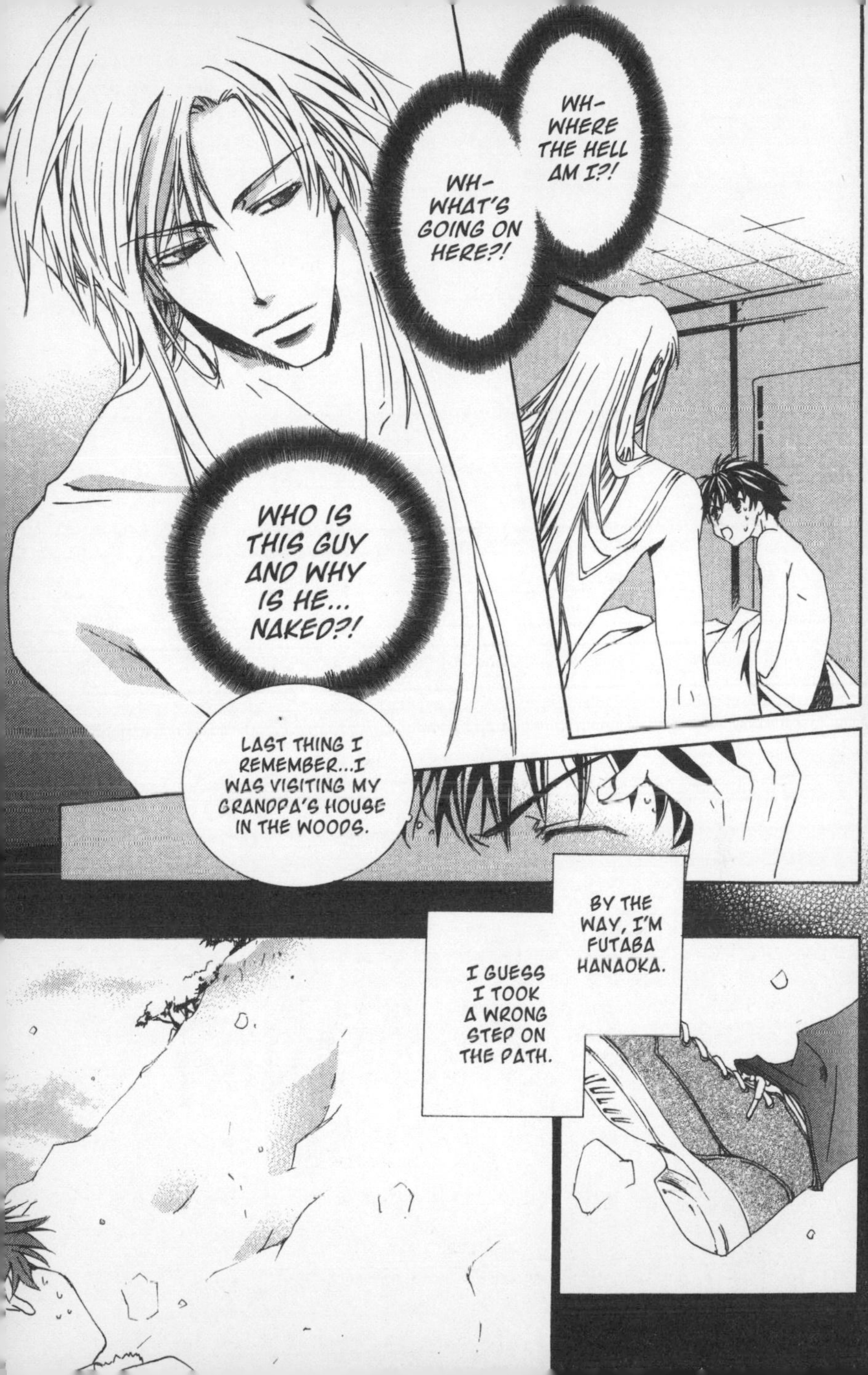
WH- WHERE THE HELL AM I?!
WH- WHAT'S GOING ON HERE?!
WHO IS THIS GUY AND WHY IS HE... NAKED?!
LAST THING I REMEMBER...I WAS VISITING MY GRANDPA'S HOUSE IN THE WOODS.
BY THE WAY, I'M FUTABA HANAOKA.
I GUESS I TOOK A WRONG STEP ON THE PATH.

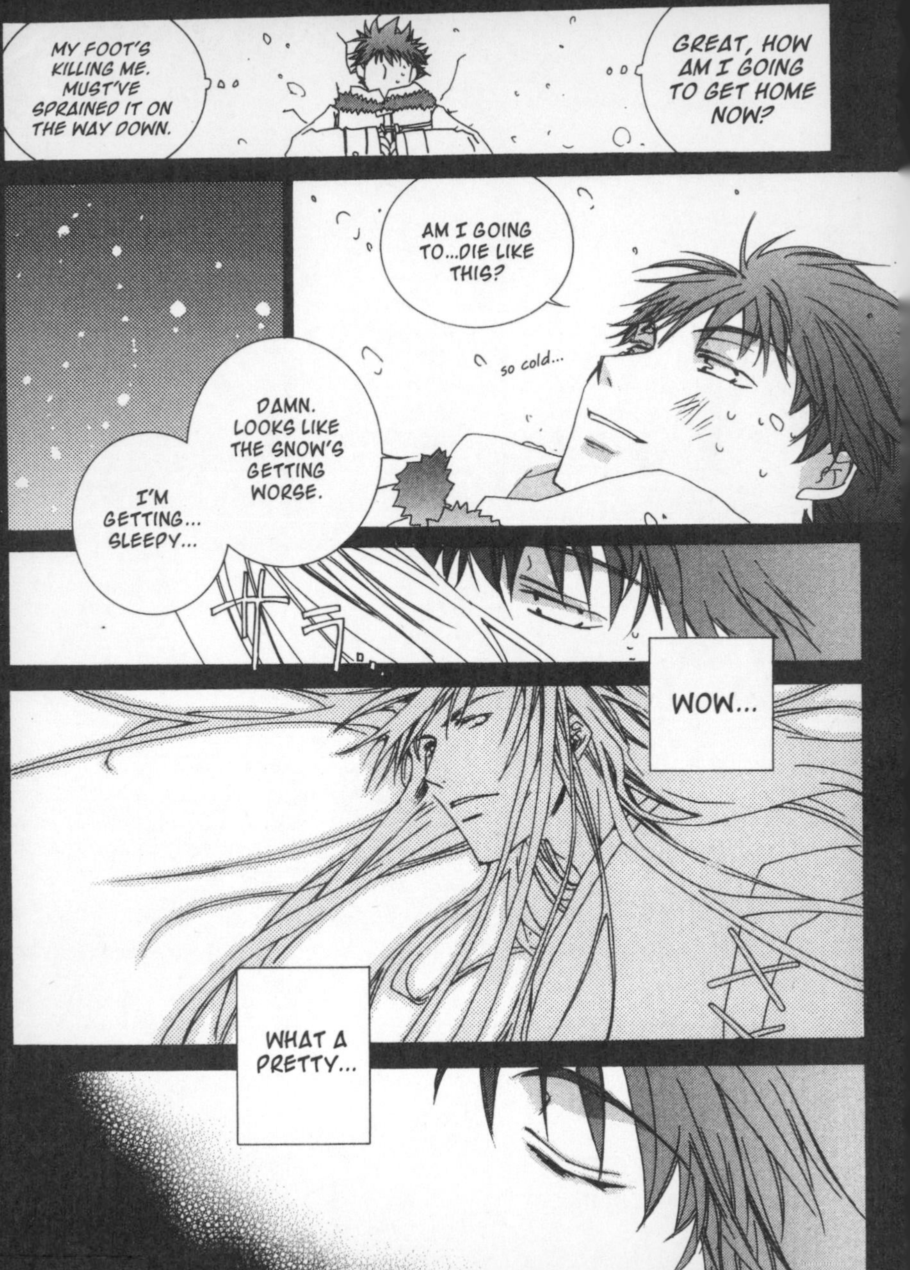
GREAT, HOW AM I GOING TO GET HOME NOW?
MY FOOT'S KILLING ME. MUST'VE SPRAINED IT ON THE WAY DOWN.
AM I GOING TO...DIE LIKE THIS?
so cold...
DAMN. LOOKS LIKE THE SNOW'S GETTING WORSE.
I'M GETTING... SLEEPY...
WOW...
WHAT A PRETTY...

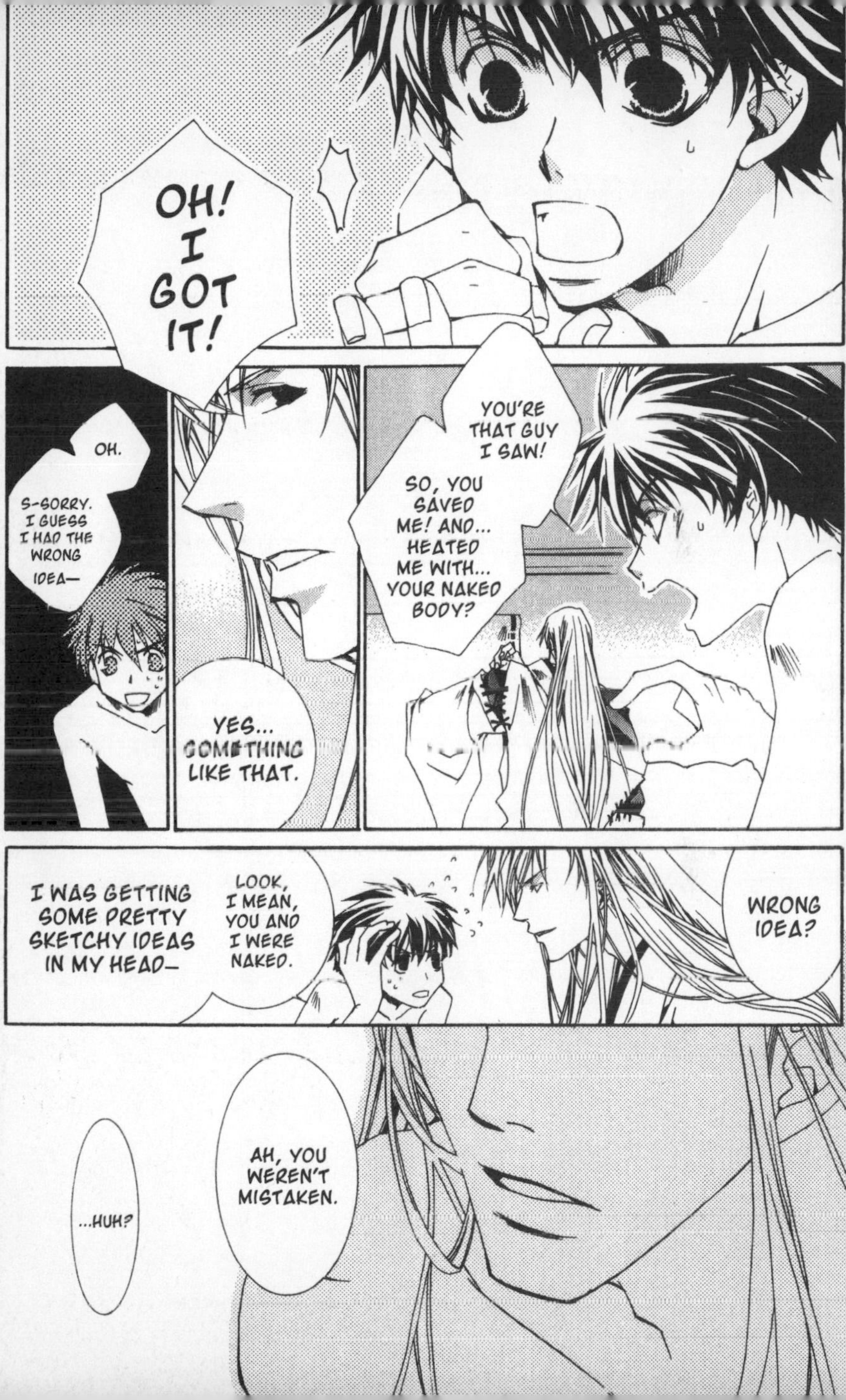
OH! I GOT IT!
YOU'RE THAT GUY I SAW!
SO, YOU SAVED ME! AND... HEATED ME WITH... YOUR NAKED BODY?
YES... SOMETHING LIKE THAT.
OH.
S-SORRY. I GUESS I HAD THE WRONG IDEA—
WRONG IDEA?
LOOK, I MEAN, YOU AND I WERE NAKED.
I WAS GETTING SOME PRETTY SKETCHY IDEAS IN MY HEAD—
AH, YOU WEREN'T MISTAKEN.
...HUH?

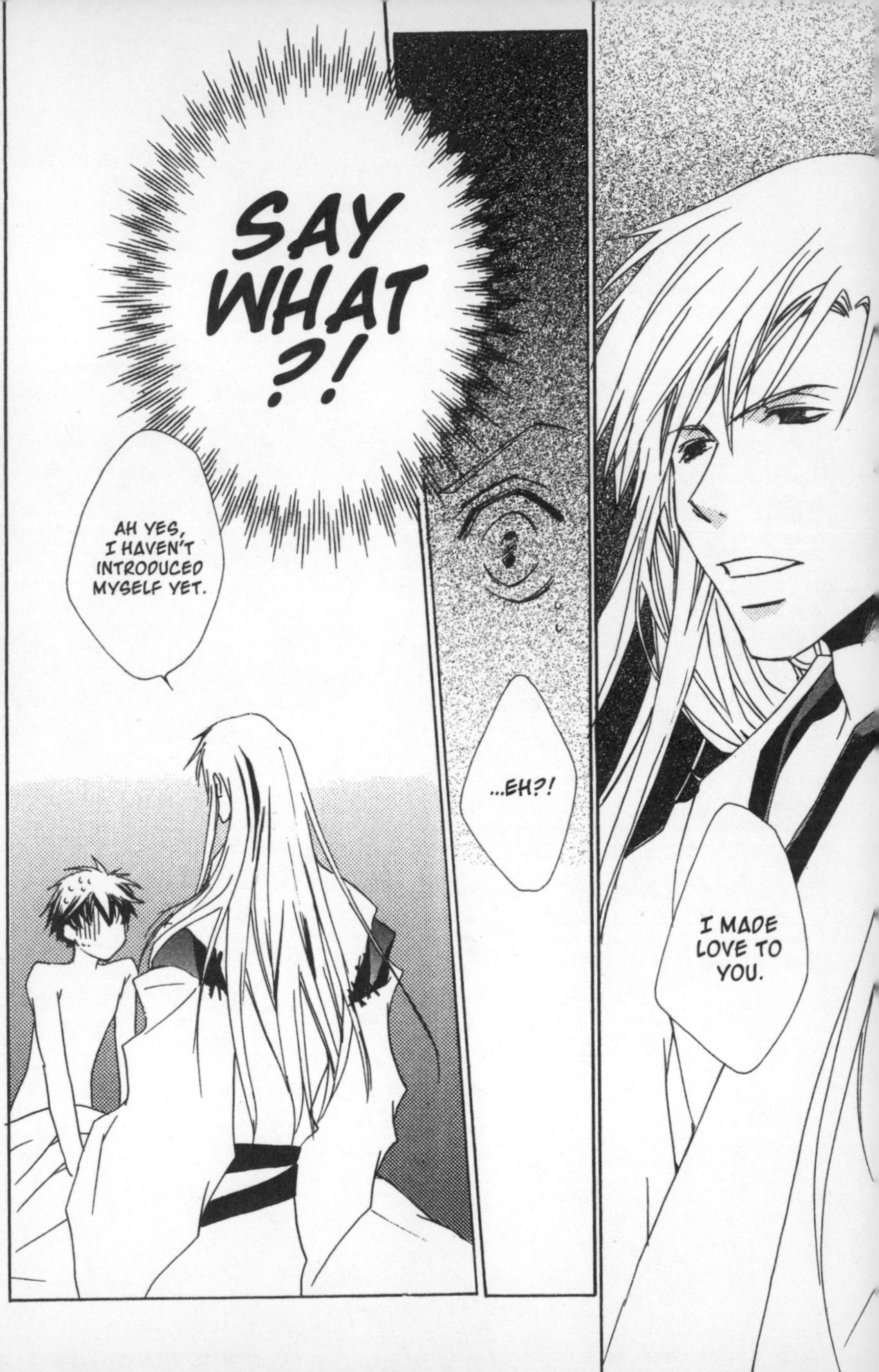
I MADE LOVE TO YOU.
...EH?!
SAY WHAT ?!
AH YES, I HAVEN'T INTRODUCED MYSELF YET.

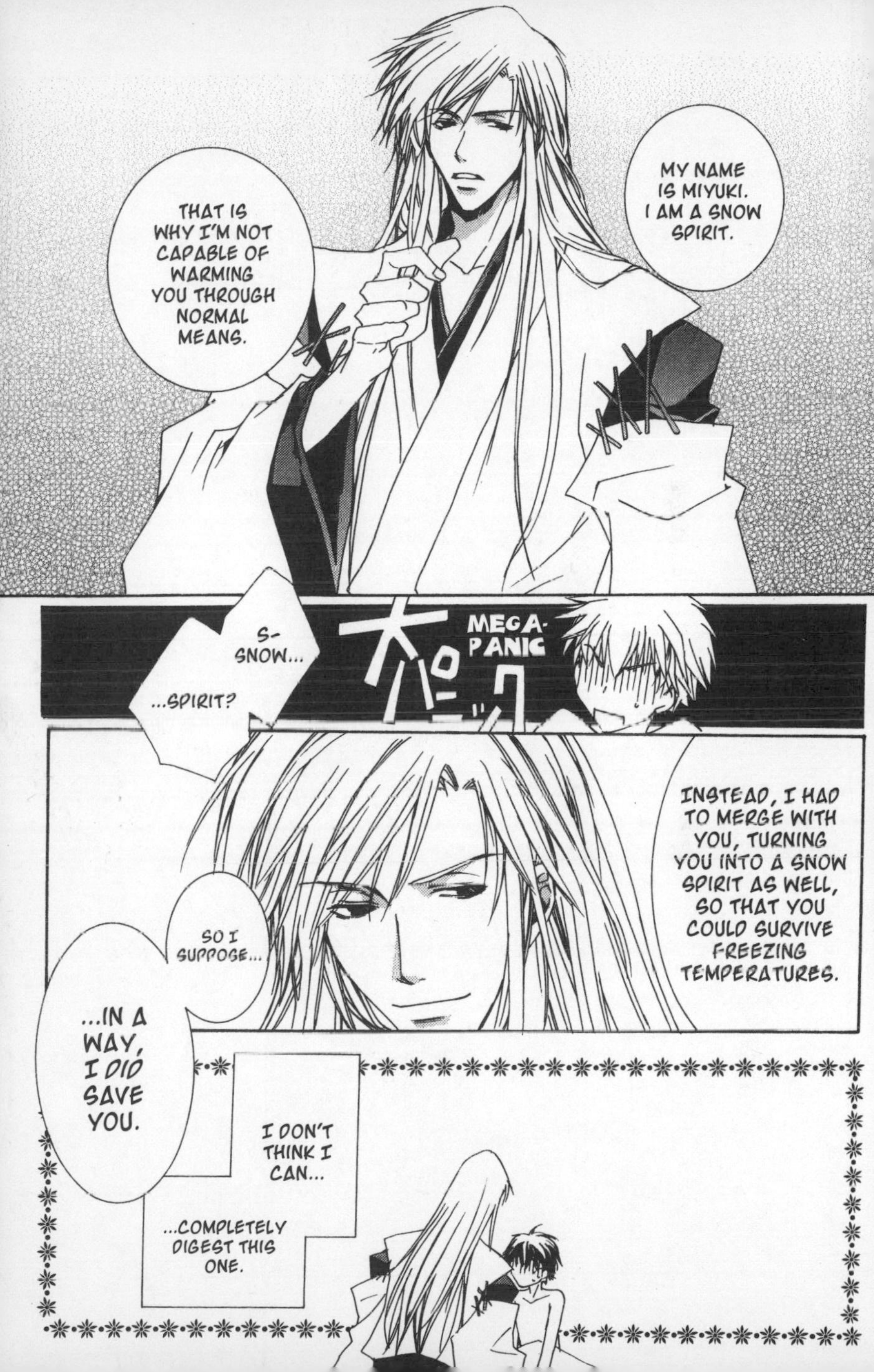
MY NAME IS MIYUKI. I AM A SNOW SPIRIT.
THAT IS WHY I'M NOT CAPABLE OF WARMING YOU THROUGH NORMAL MEANS.
MEGA-PANIC
S-SNOW...
...SPIRIT?
INSTEAD, I HAD TO MERGE WITH YOU, TURNING YOU INTO A SNOW SPIRIT AS WELL, SO THAT YOU COULD SURVIVE FREEZING TEMPERATURES.
SO I SUPPOSE...
...IN A WAY, I *DID* SAVE YOU.
I DON'T THINK I CAN...
...COMPLETELY DIGEST THIS ONE.

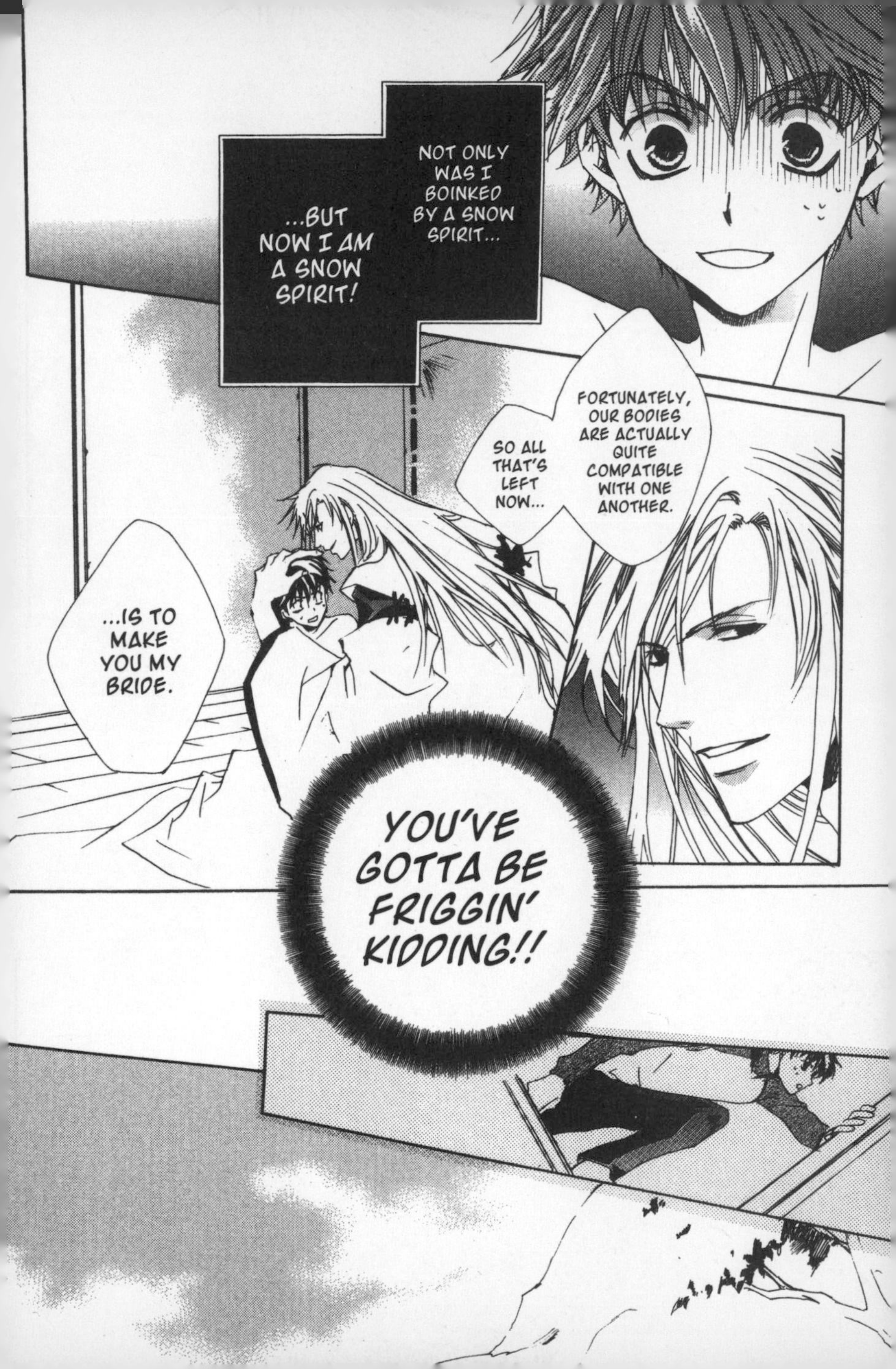
NOT ONLY WAS I BOINKED BY A SNOW SPIRIT...
...BUT NOW I AM A SNOW SPIRIT!
FORTUNATELY, OUR BODIES ARE ACTUALLY QUITE COMPATIBLE WITH ONE ANOTHER.
SO ALL THAT'S LEFT NOW...
...IS TO MAKE YOU MY BRIDE.
YOU'VE GOTTA BE FRIGGIN' KIDDING!!

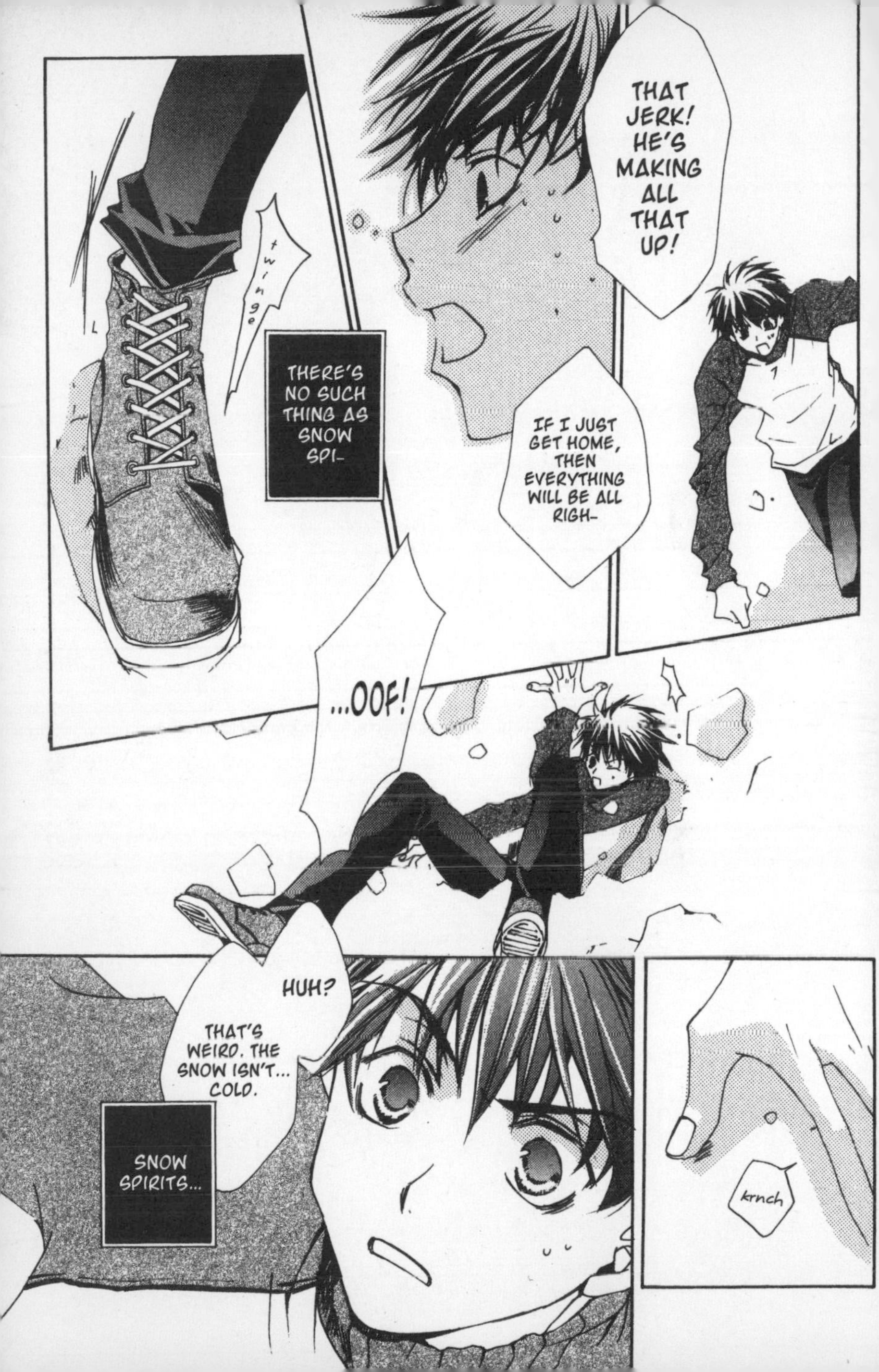
THAT JERK! HE'S MAKING ALL THAT UP!
IF I JUST GET HOME, THEN EVERYTHING WILL BE ALL RIGH-
twinge
THERE'S NO SUCH THING AS SNOW SPI-
...OOF!
krnch
HUH?
THAT'S WEIRD. THE SNOW ISN'T... COLD.
SNOW SPIRITS...

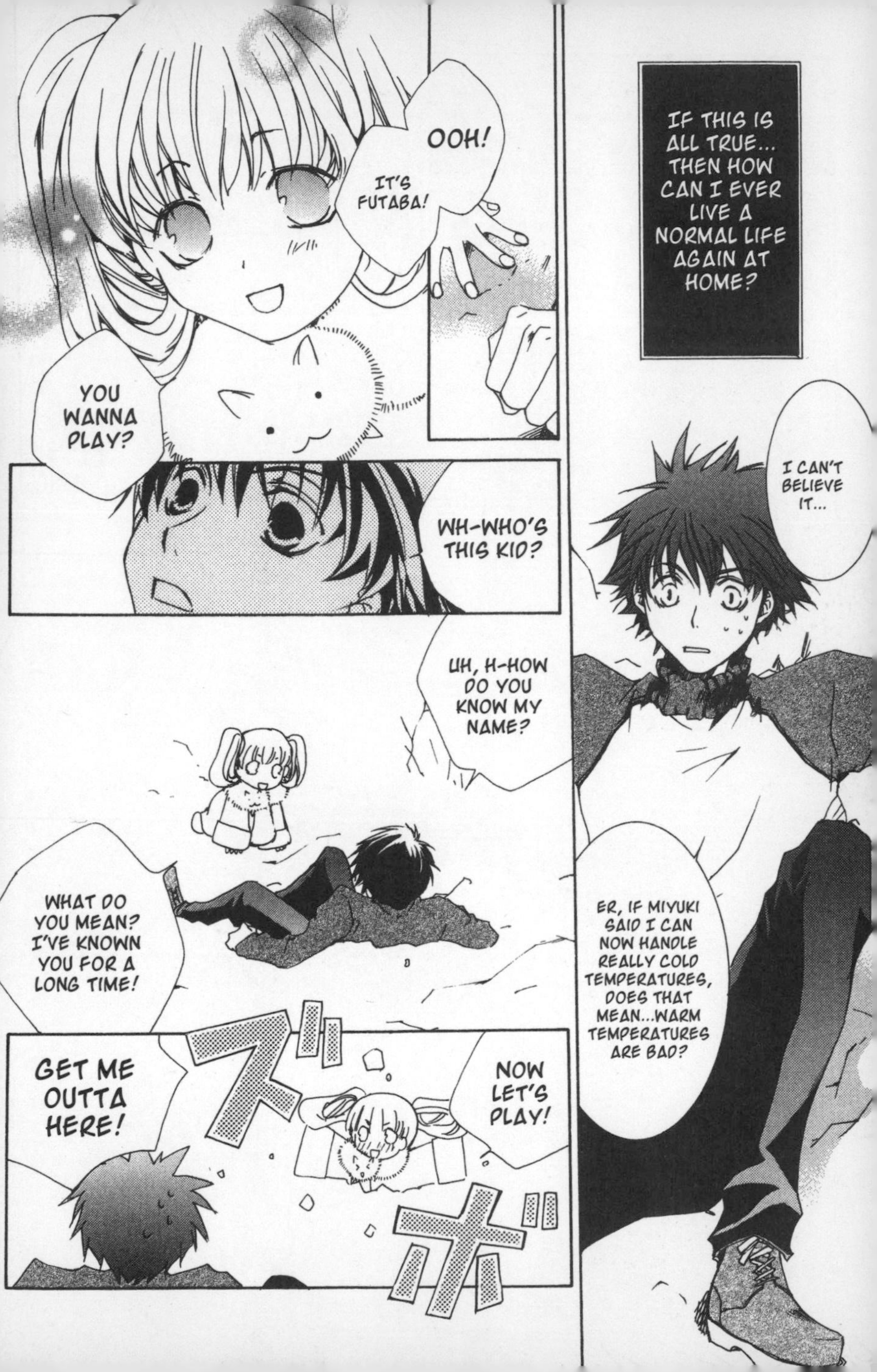
IF THIS IS ALL TRUE... THEN HOW CAN I EVER LIVE A NORMAL LIFE AGAIN AT HOME?
I CAN'T BELIEVE IT...
ER, IF MIYUKI SAID I CAN NOW HANDLE REALLY COLD TEMPERATURES, DOES THAT MEAN...WARM TEMPERATURES ARE BAD?
OOH!
IT'S FUTABA!
YOU WANNA PLAY?
WH-WHO'S THIS KID?
UH, H-HOW DO YOU KNOW MY NAME?
WHAT DO YOU MEAN? I'VE KNOWN YOU FOR A LONG TIME!
NOW LET'S PLAY!
GET ME OUTTA HERE!

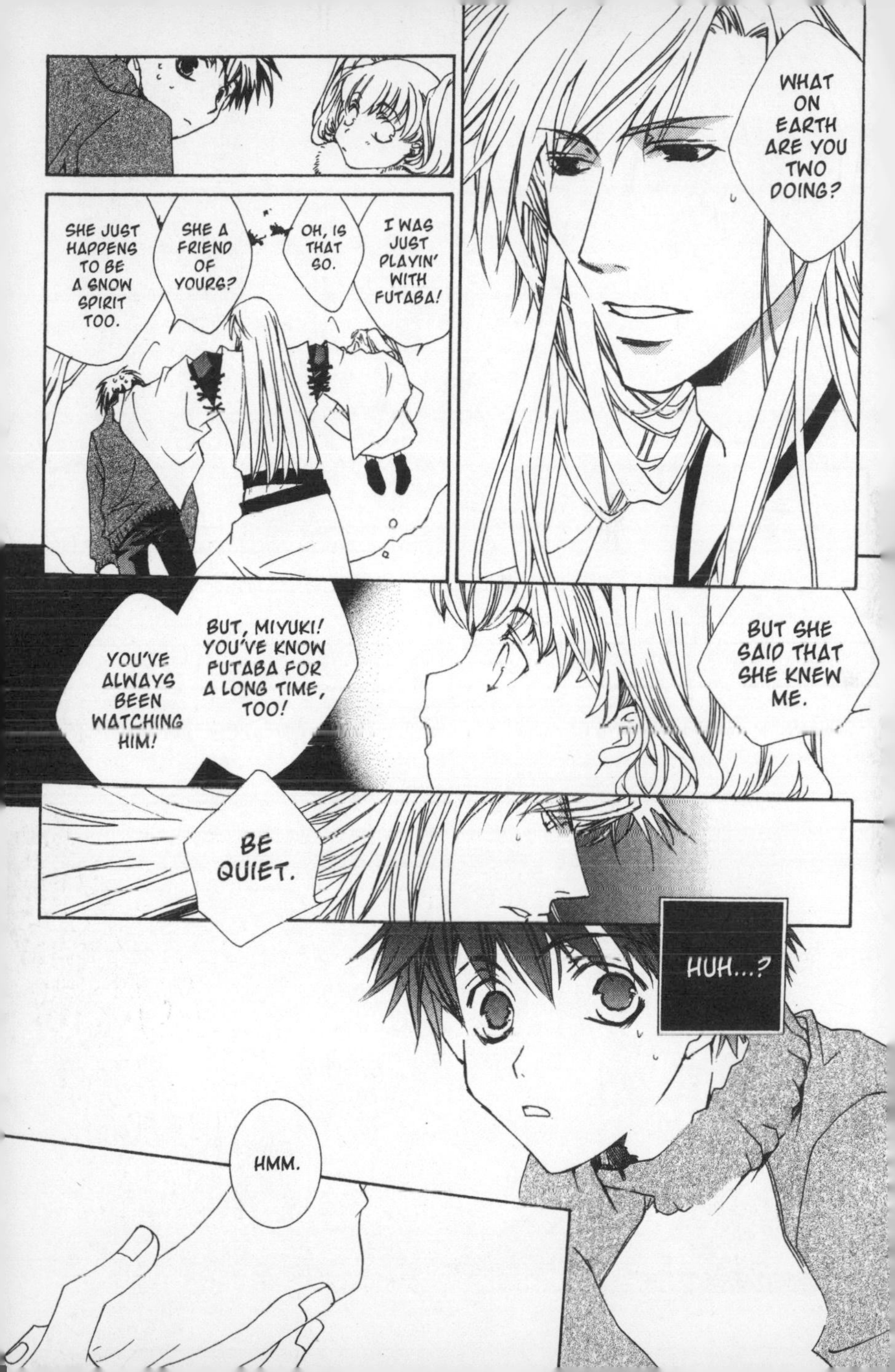

WHAT ON EARTH ARE YOU TWO DOING?
I WAS JUST PLAYIN' WITH FUTABA!
OH, IS THAT SO.
SHE A FRIEND OF YOURS?
SHE JUST HAPPENS TO BE A SNOW SPIRIT TOO.
BUT SHE SAID THAT SHE KNEW ME.
BUT, MIYUKI! YOU'VE KNOW FUTABA FOR A LONG TIME, TOO!
YOU'VE ALWAYS BEEN WATCHING HIM!
BE QUIET.
HUH...?
HMM.

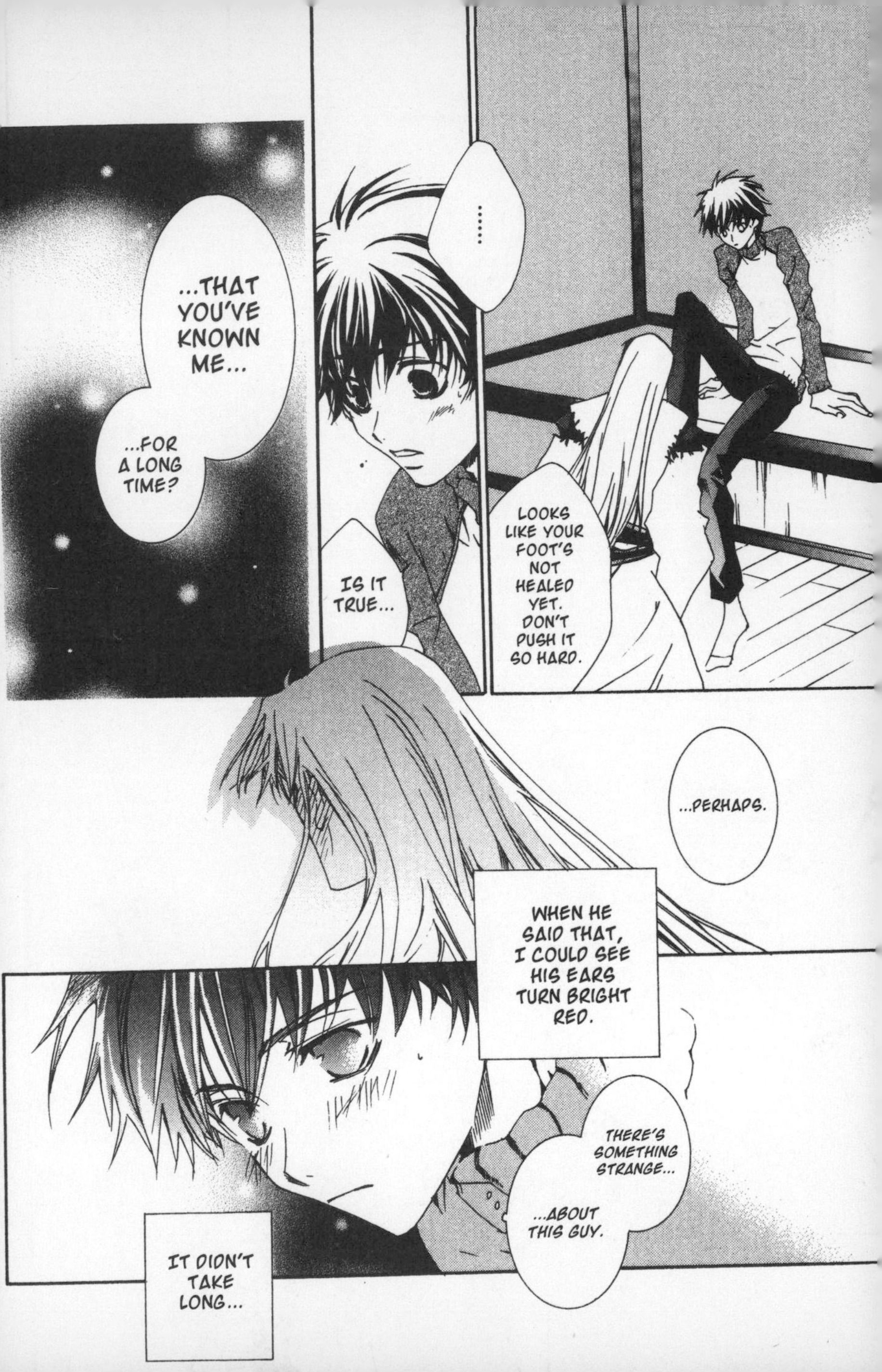
LOOKS LIKE YOUR FOOT'S NOT HEALED YET. DON'T PUSH IT SO HARD.
......
IS IT TRUE...
...THAT YOU'VE KNOWN ME...
...FOR A LONG TIME?
...PERHAPS.
WHEN HE SAID THAT, I COULD SEE HIS EARS TURN BRIGHT RED.
THERE'S SOMETHING STRANGE...
...ABOUT THIS GUY.
IT DIDN'T TAKE LONG...

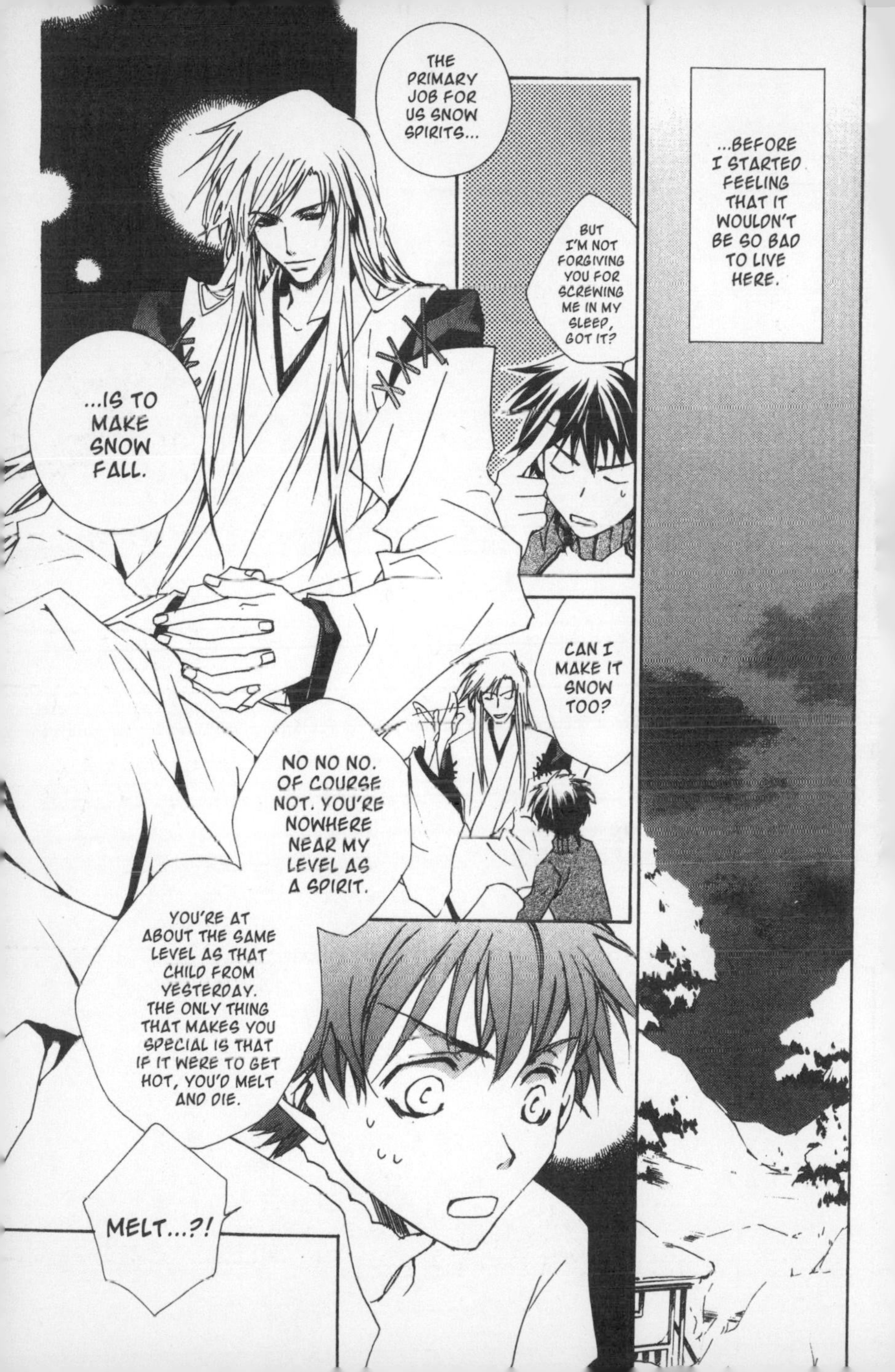
...BEFORE I STARTED FEELING THAT IT WOULDN'T BE SO BAD TO LIVE HERE.
THE PRIMARY JOB FOR US SNOW SPIRITS...
...IS TO MAKE SNOW FALL.
BUT I'M NOT FORGIVING YOU FOR SCREWING ME IN MY SLEEP, GOT IT?
CAN I MAKE IT SNOW TOO?
NO NO NO. OF COURSE NOT. YOU'RE NOWHERE NEAR MY LEVEL AS A SPIRIT.
YOU'RE AT ABOUT THE SAME LEVEL AS THAT CHILD FROM YESTERDAY. THE ONLY THING THAT MAKES YOU SPECIAL IS THAT IF IT WERE TO GET HOT, YOU'D MELT AND DIE.
MELT...?!

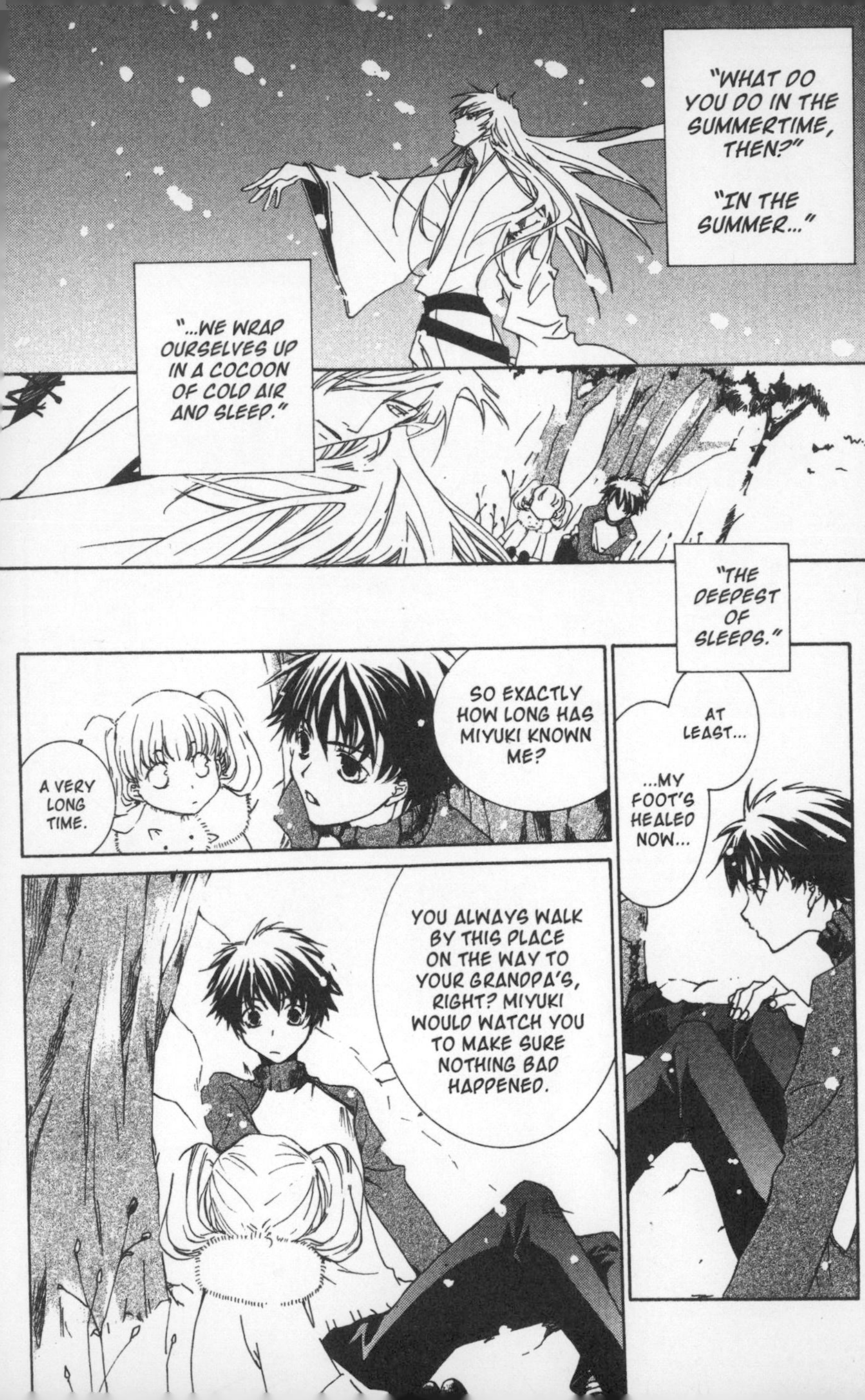
"WHAT DO YOU DO IN THE SUMMERTIME, THEN?"
"IN THE SUMMER..."
"...WE WRAP OURSELVES UP IN A COCOON OF COLD AIR AND SLEEP."
"THE DEEPEST OF SLEEPS."
AT LEAST...
...MY FOOT'S HEALED NOW...
SO EXACTLY HOW LONG HAS MIYUKI KNOWN ME?
A VERY LONG TIME.
YOU ALWAYS WALK BY THIS PLACE ON THE WAY TO YOUR GRANDPA'S, RIGHT? MIYUKI WOULD WATCH YOU TO MAKE SURE NOTHING BAD HAPPENED.

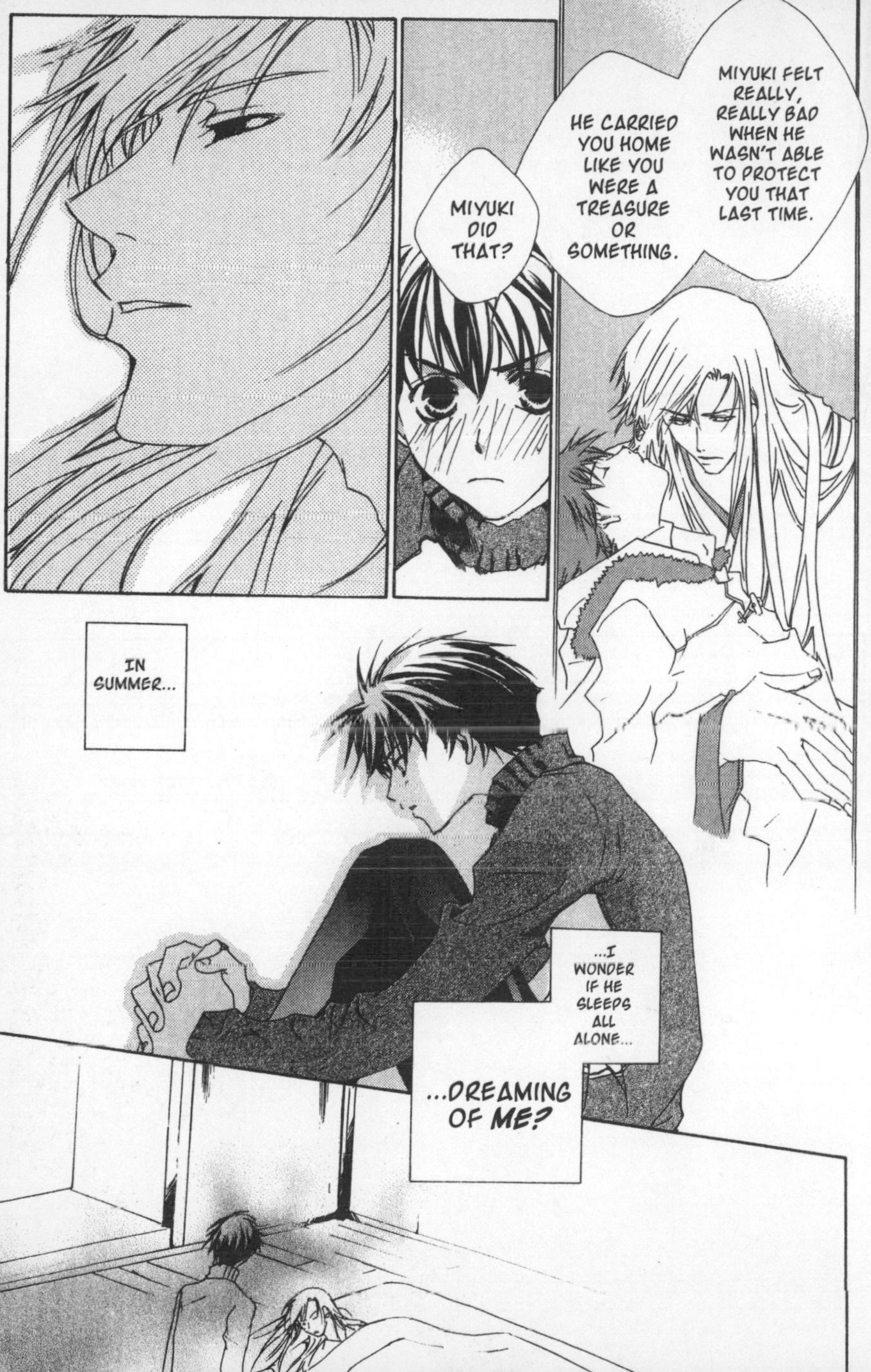
MIYUKI FELT REALLY, REALLY BAD WHEN HE WASN'T ABLE TO PROTECT YOU THAT LAST TIME.
HE CARRIED YOU HOME LIKE YOU WERE A TREASURE OR SOMETHING.
MIYUKI DID THAT?
IN SUMMER...
...I WONDER IF HE SLEEPS ALL ALONE...
...DREAMING OF ME?

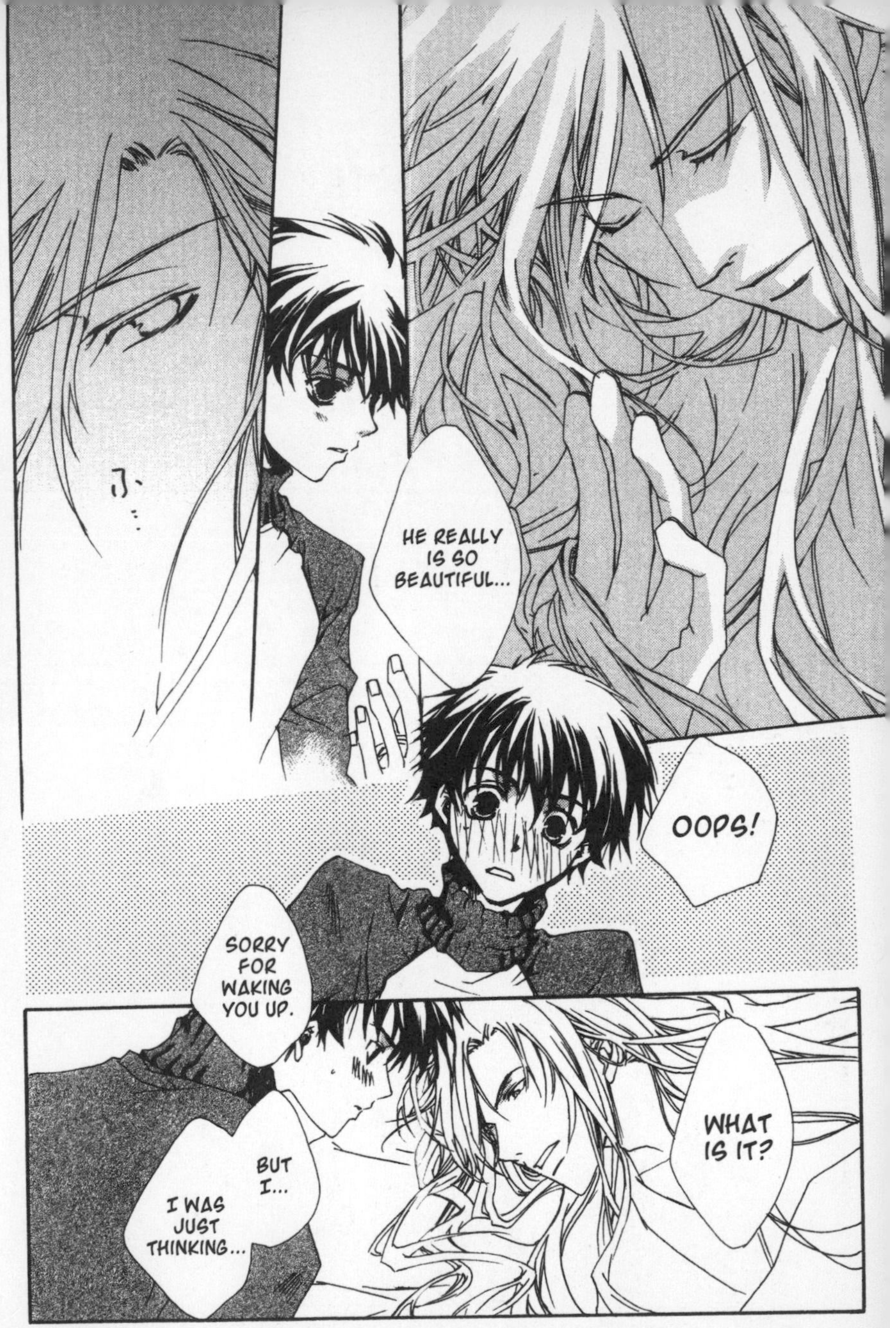
HE REALLY IS SO BEAUTIFUL...
OOPS!
SORRY FOR WAKING YOU UP.
WHAT IS IT?
BUT I...
I WAS JUST THINKING...

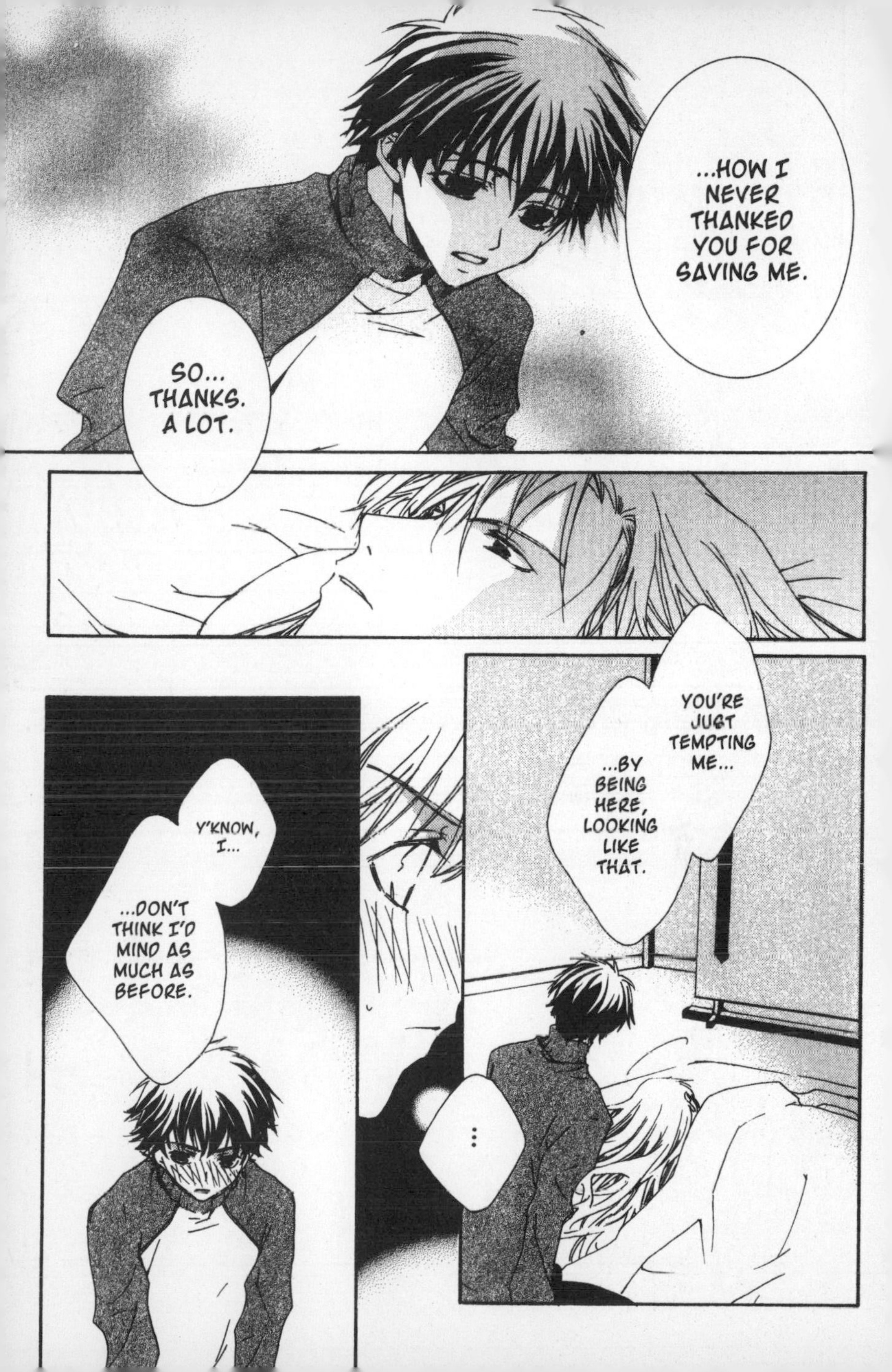
...HOW I NEVER THANKED YOU FOR SAVING ME.
SO... THANKS. A LOT.
YOU'RE JUST TEMPTING ME...
...BY BEING HERE, LOOKING LIKE THAT.
...
Y'KNOW, I...
...DON'T THINK I'D MIND AS MUCH AS BEFORE.

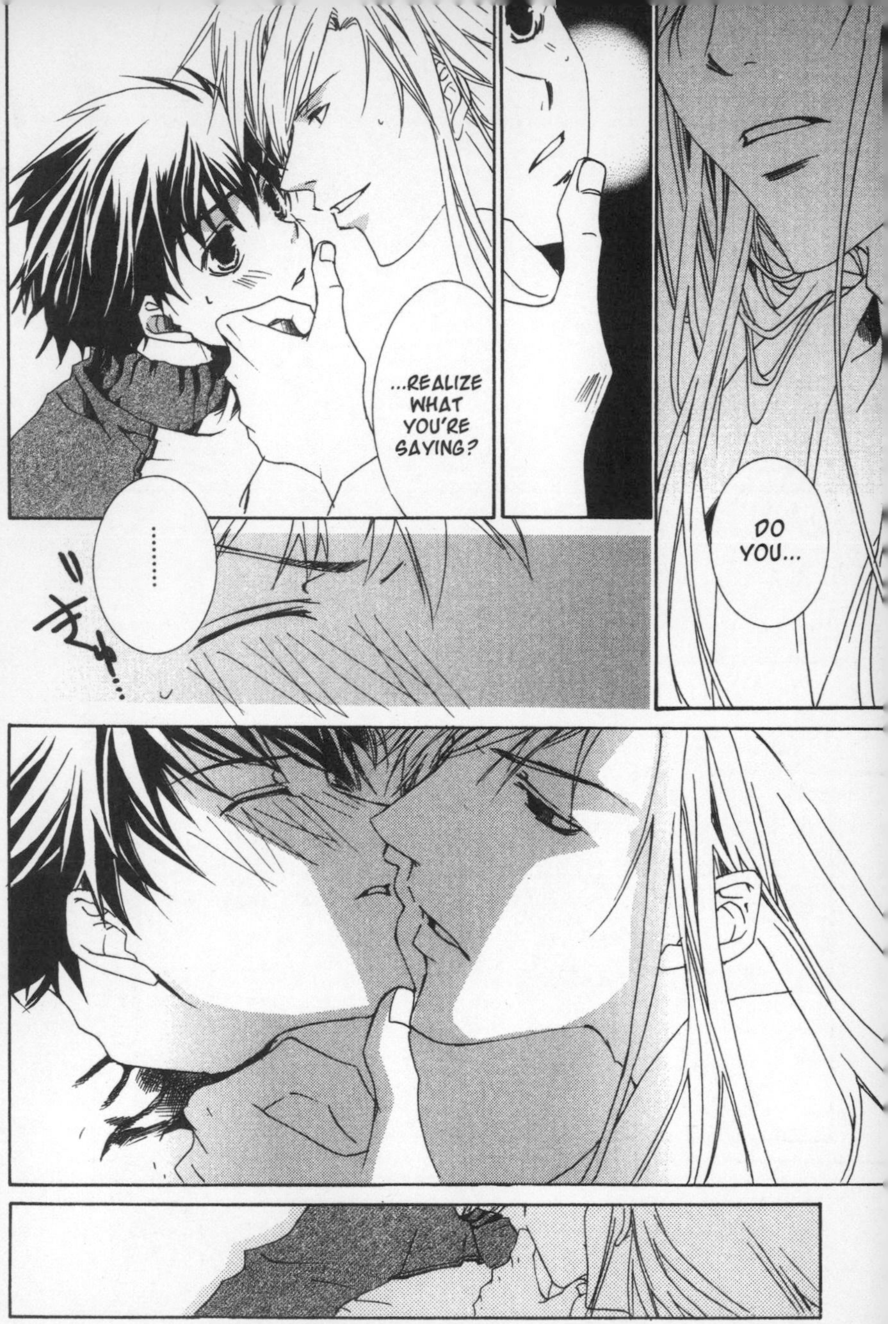
DO YOU...
...REALIZE WHAT YOU'RE SAYING?
......

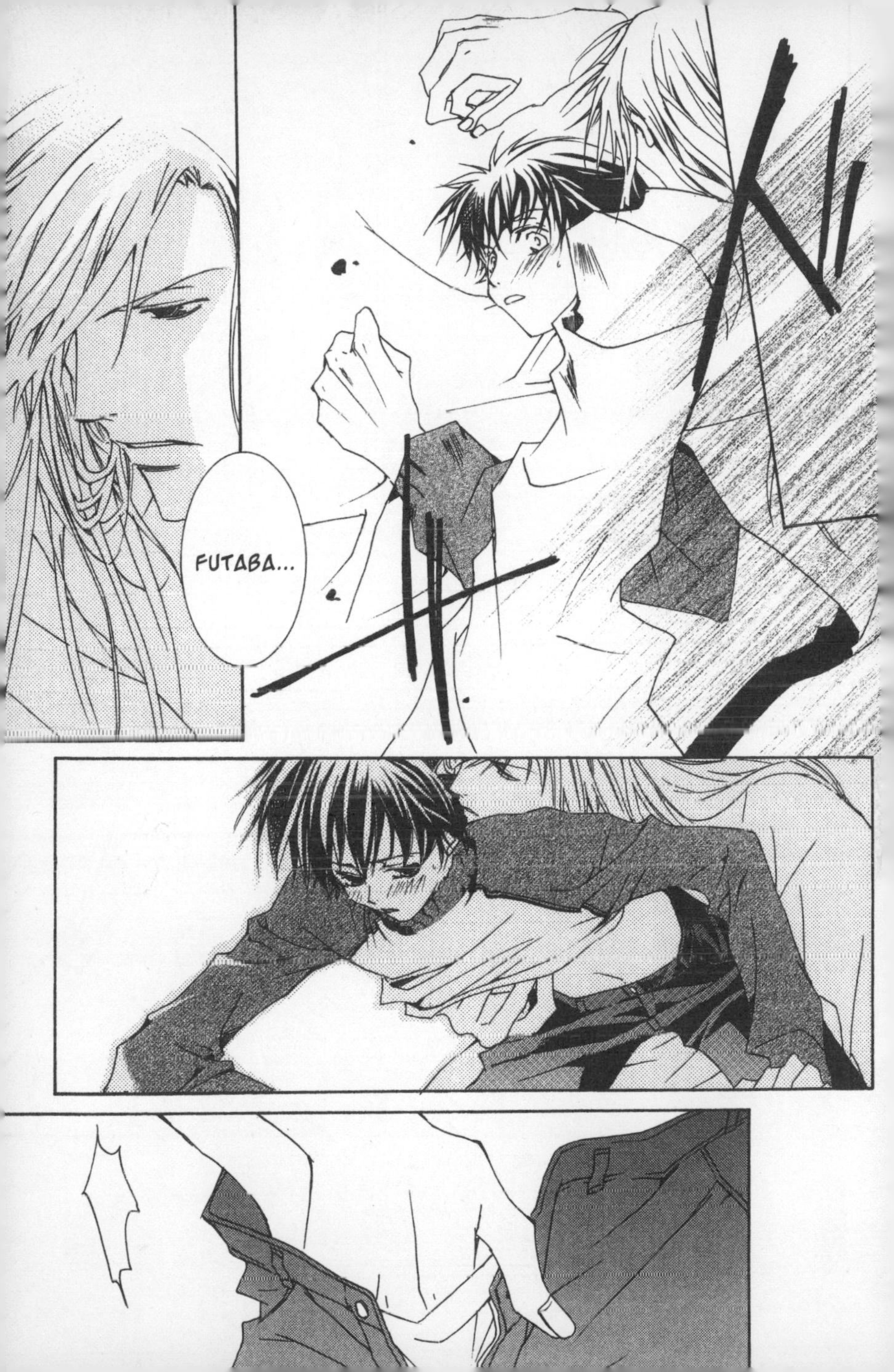
FUTABA...

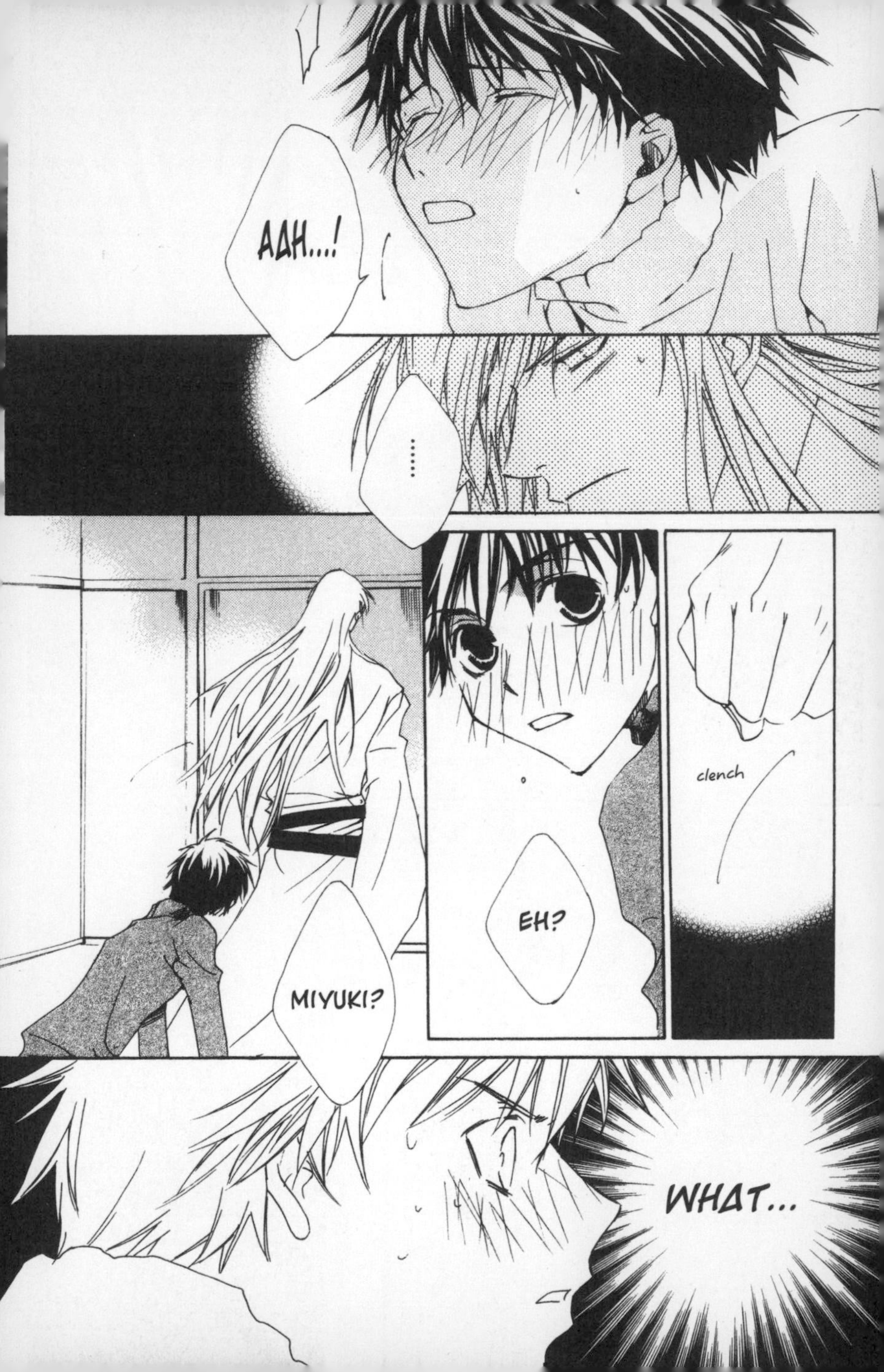
AAH...!
......
clench
EH?
MIYUKI?
WHAT...

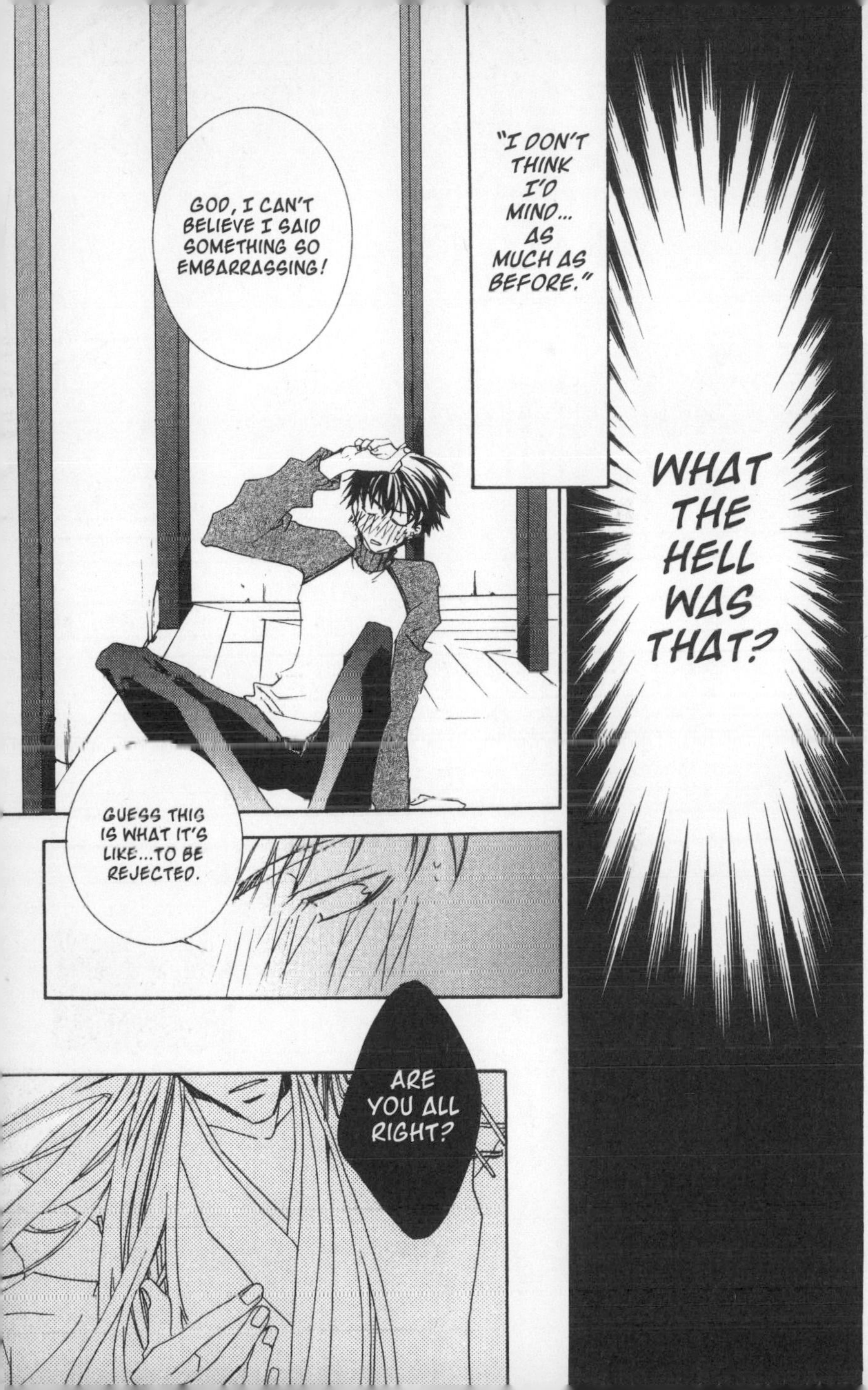
"I DON'T THINK I'D MIND... AS MUCH AS BEFORE."
WHAT THE HELL WAS THAT?
GOD, I CAN'T BELIEVE I SAID SOMETHING SO EMBARRASSING!
GUESS THIS IS WHAT IT'S LIKE...TO BE REJECTED.
ARE YOU ALL RIGHT?

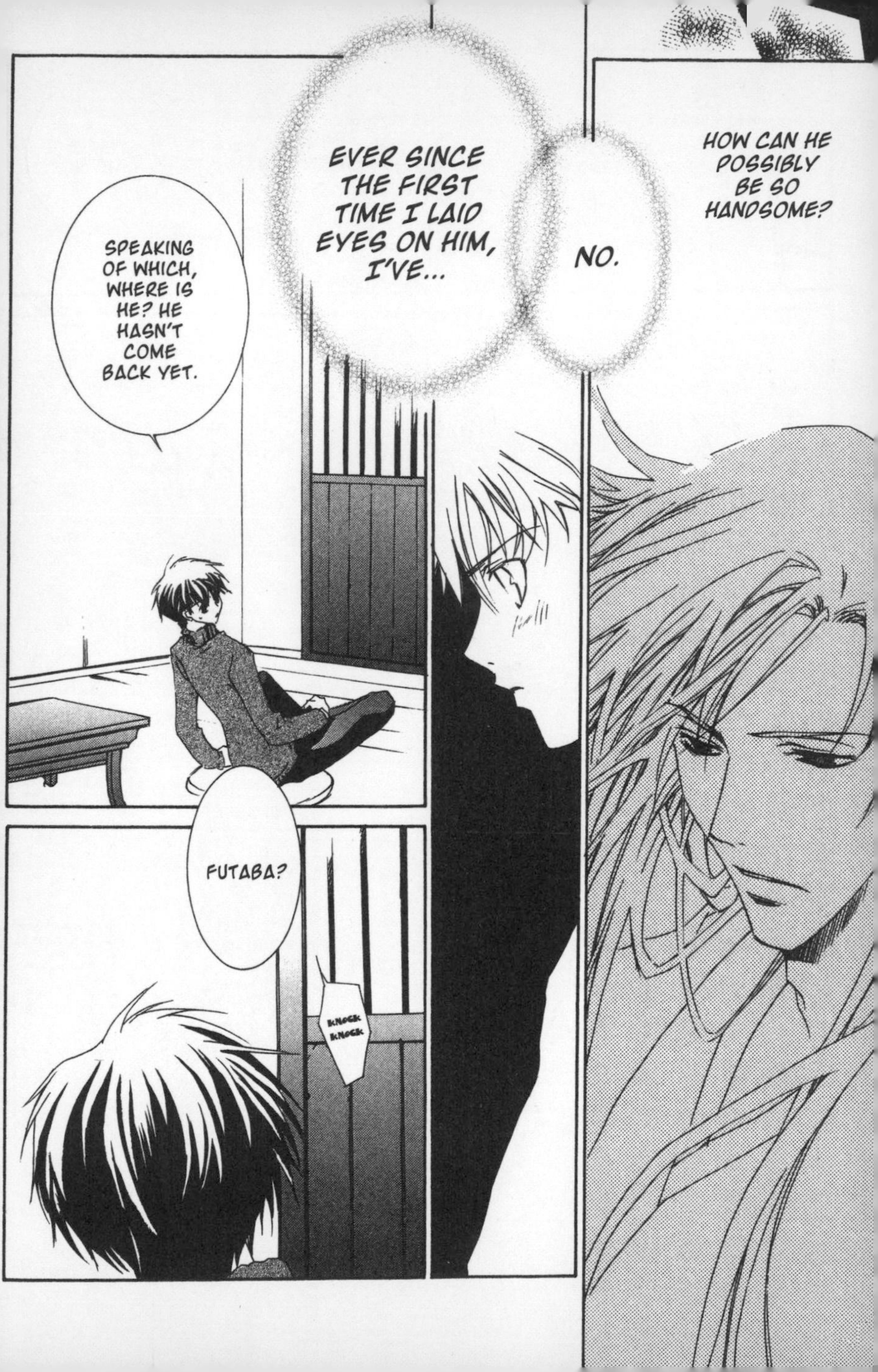
HOW CAN HE POSSIBLY BE SO HANDSOME?
NO.
EVER SINCE THE FIRST TIME I LAID EYES ON HIM, I'VE...
SPEAKING OF WHICH, WHERE IS HE? HE HASN'T COME BACK YET.
KNOCK KNOCK
FUTABA?

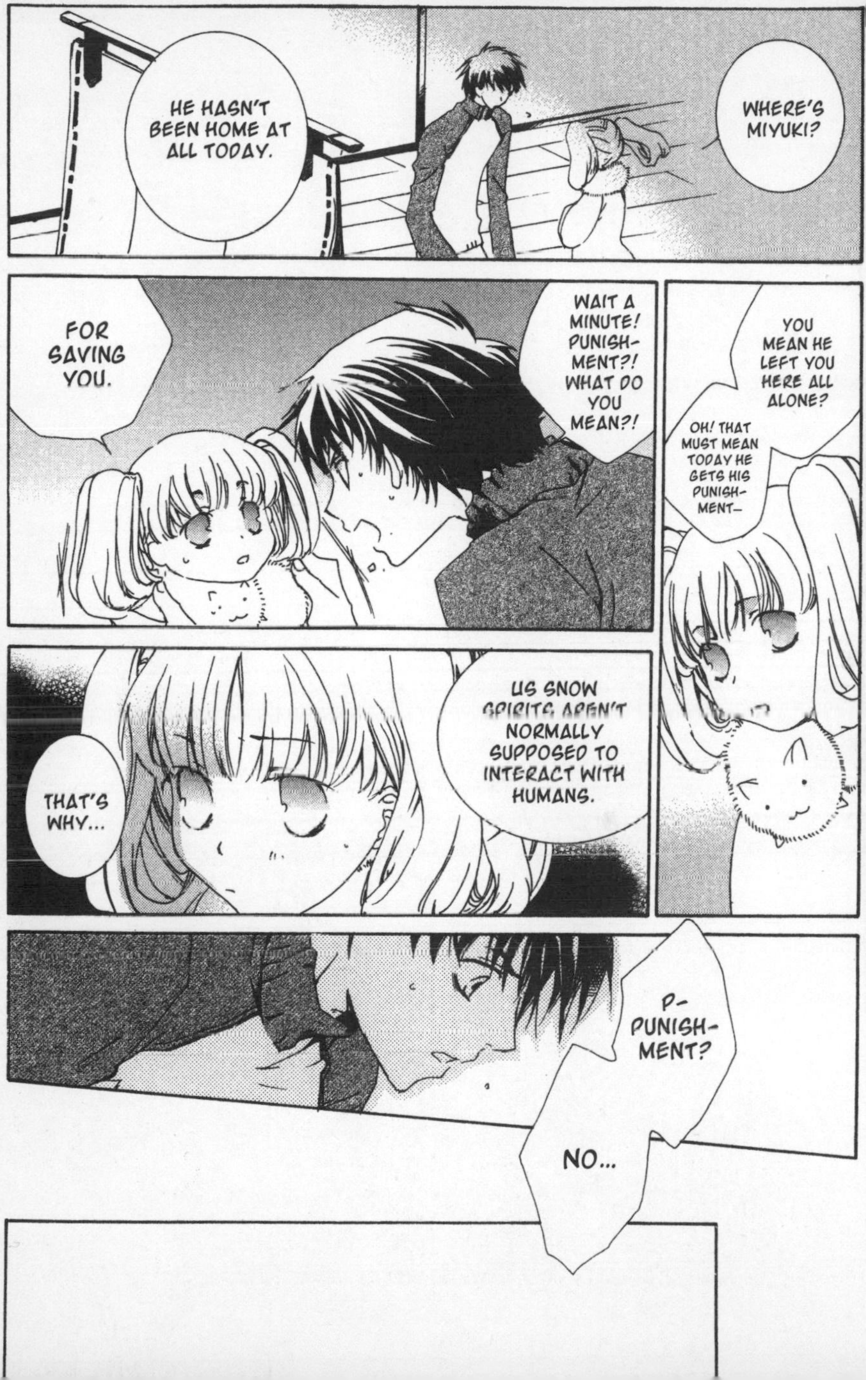
WHERE'S MIYUKI?
HE HASN'T BEEN HOME AT ALL TODAY.
YOU MEAN HE LEFT YOU HERE ALL ALONE?
OH! THAT MUST MEAN TODAY HE GETS HIS PUNISHMENT—
WAIT A MINUTE! PUNISHMENT?! WHAT DO YOU MEAN?!
FOR SAVING YOU.
US SNOW SPIRITS AREN'T NORMALLY SUPPOSED TO INTERACT WITH HUMANS.
THAT'S WHY...
P-PUNISHMENT?
NO...

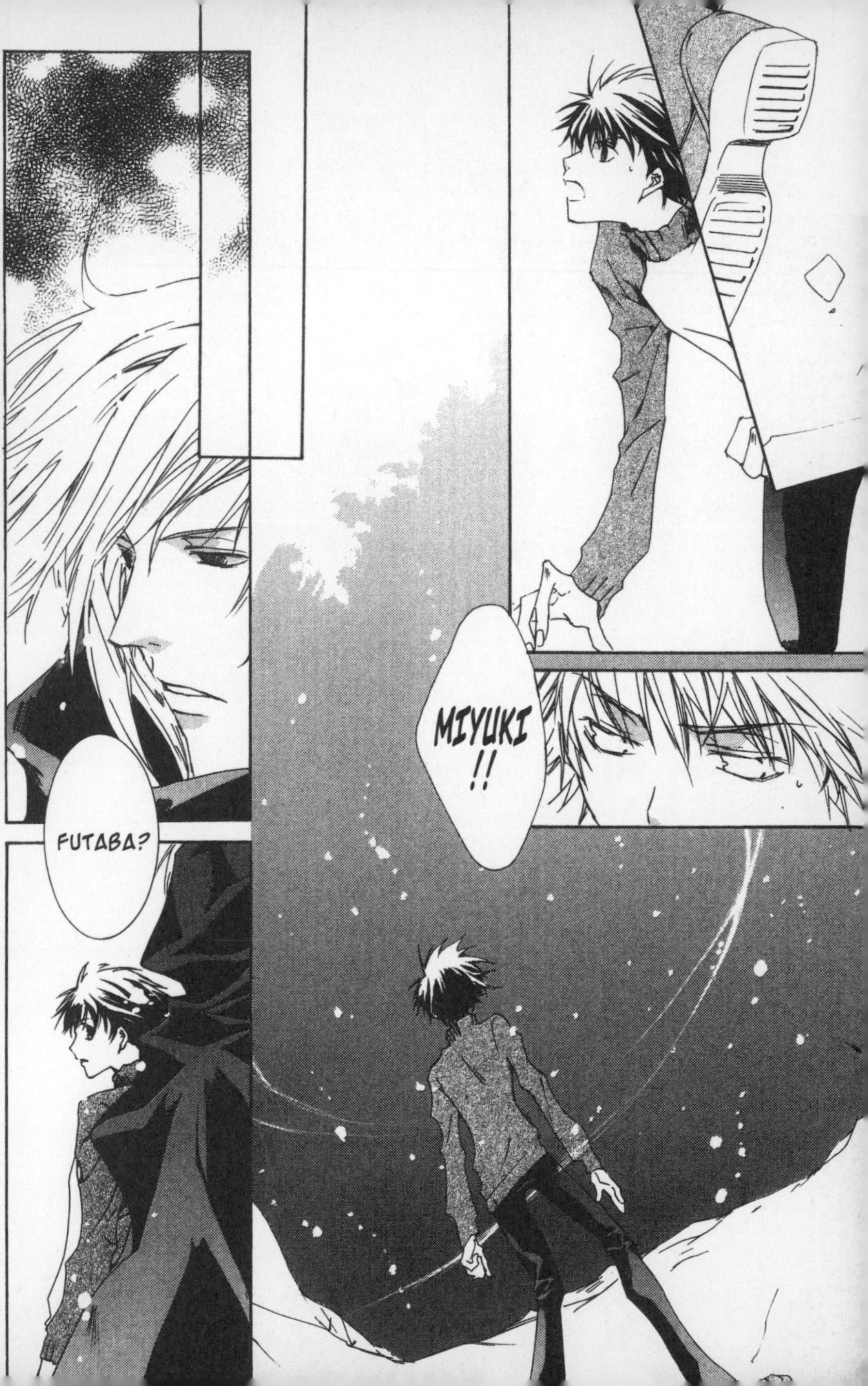
MIYUKI !!
FUTABA?

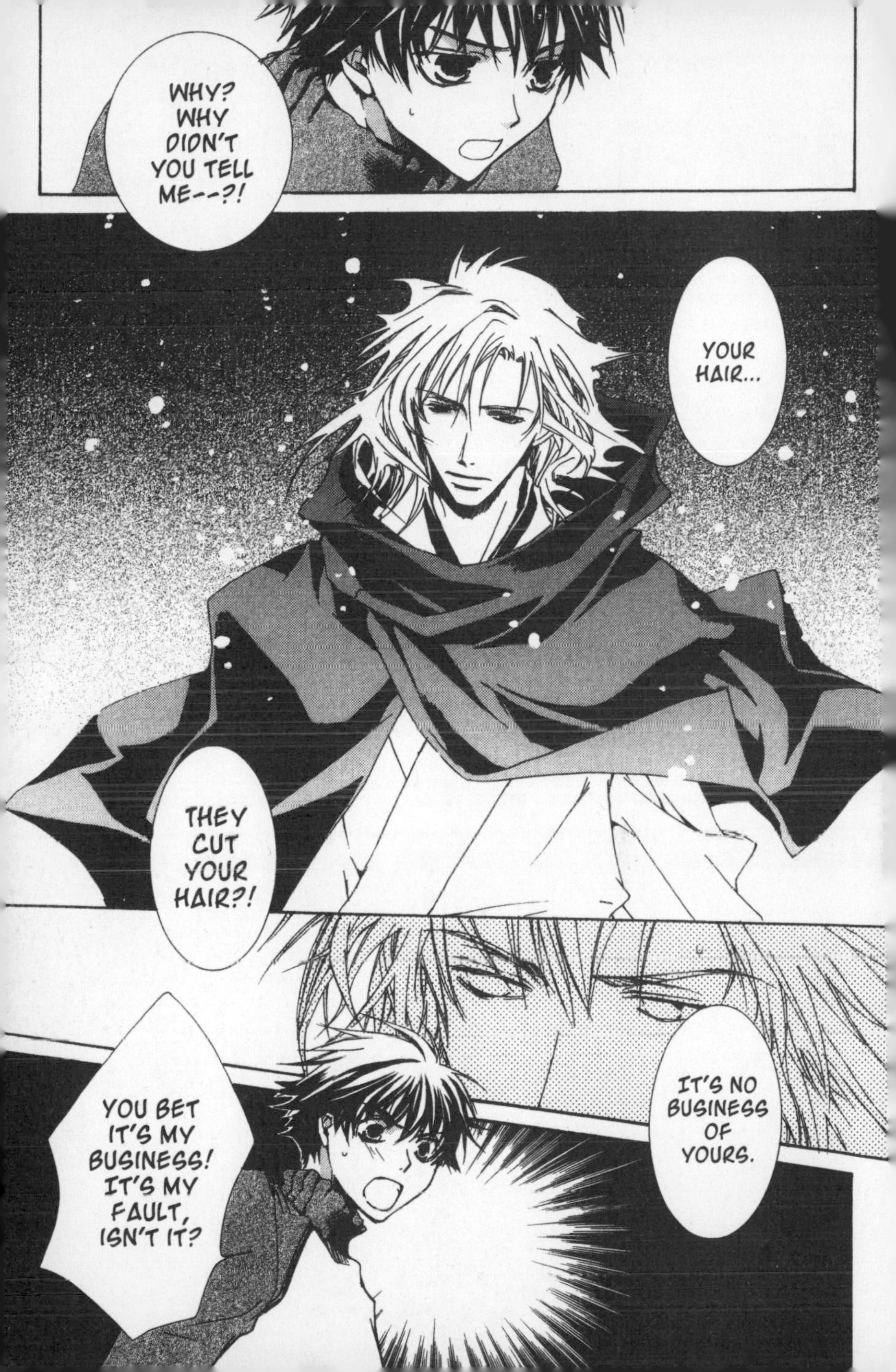
WHY? WHY DIDN'T YOU TELL ME--?!
YOUR HAIR...
THEY CUT YOUR HAIR?!
IT'S NO BUSINESS OF YOURS.
YOU BET IT'S MY BUSINESS! IT'S MY FAULT, ISN'T IT?

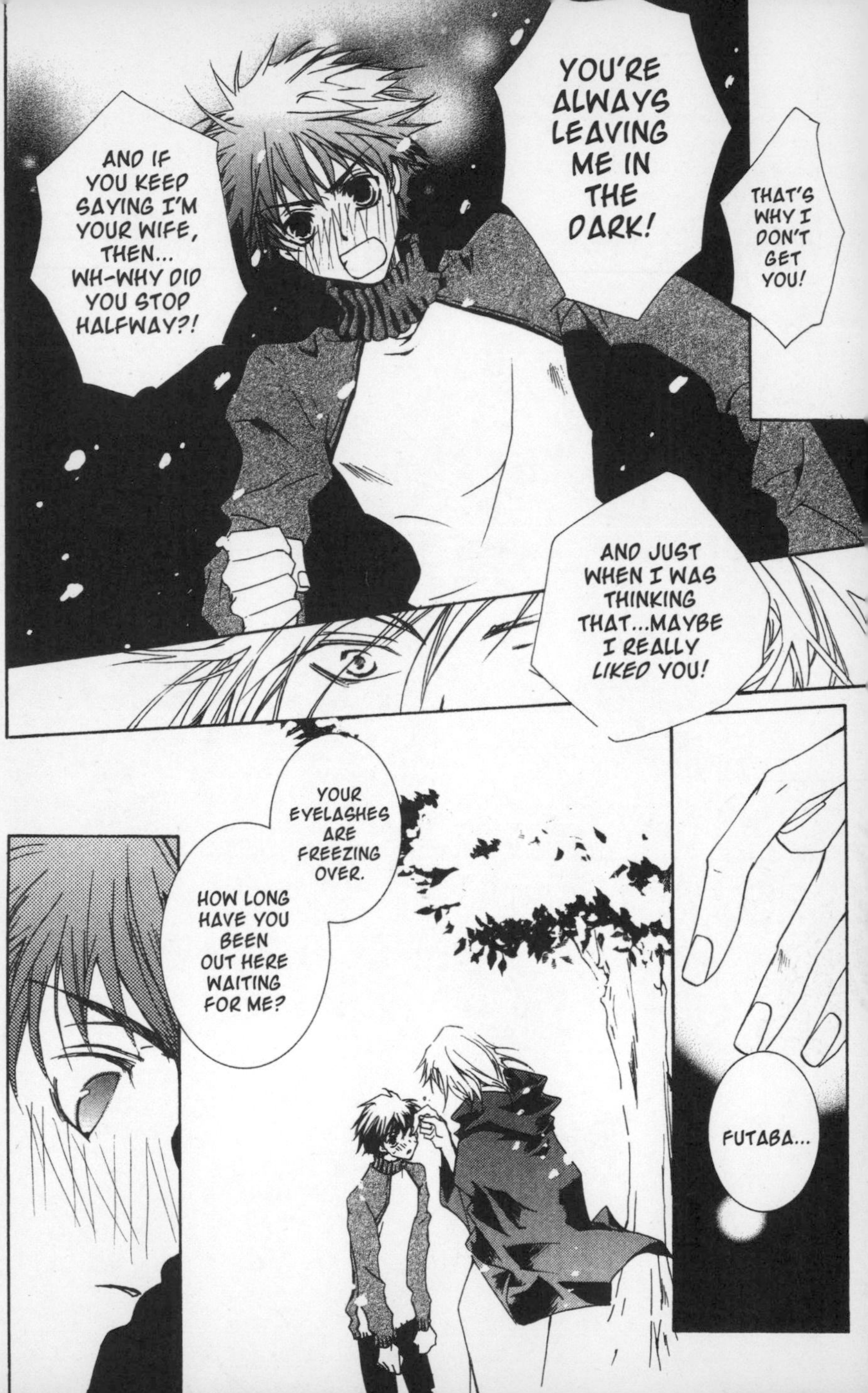
YOU'RE ALWAYS LEAVING ME IN THE DARK!
THAT'S WHY I DON'T GET YOU!
AND IF YOU KEEP SAYING I'M YOUR WIFE, THEN... WH-WHY DID YOU STOP HALFWAY?!
AND JUST WHEN I WAS THINKING THAT...MAYBE I REALLY LIKED YOU!
FUTABA...
YOUR EYELASHES ARE FREEZING OVER.
HOW LONG HAVE YOU BEEN OUT HERE WAITING FOR ME?

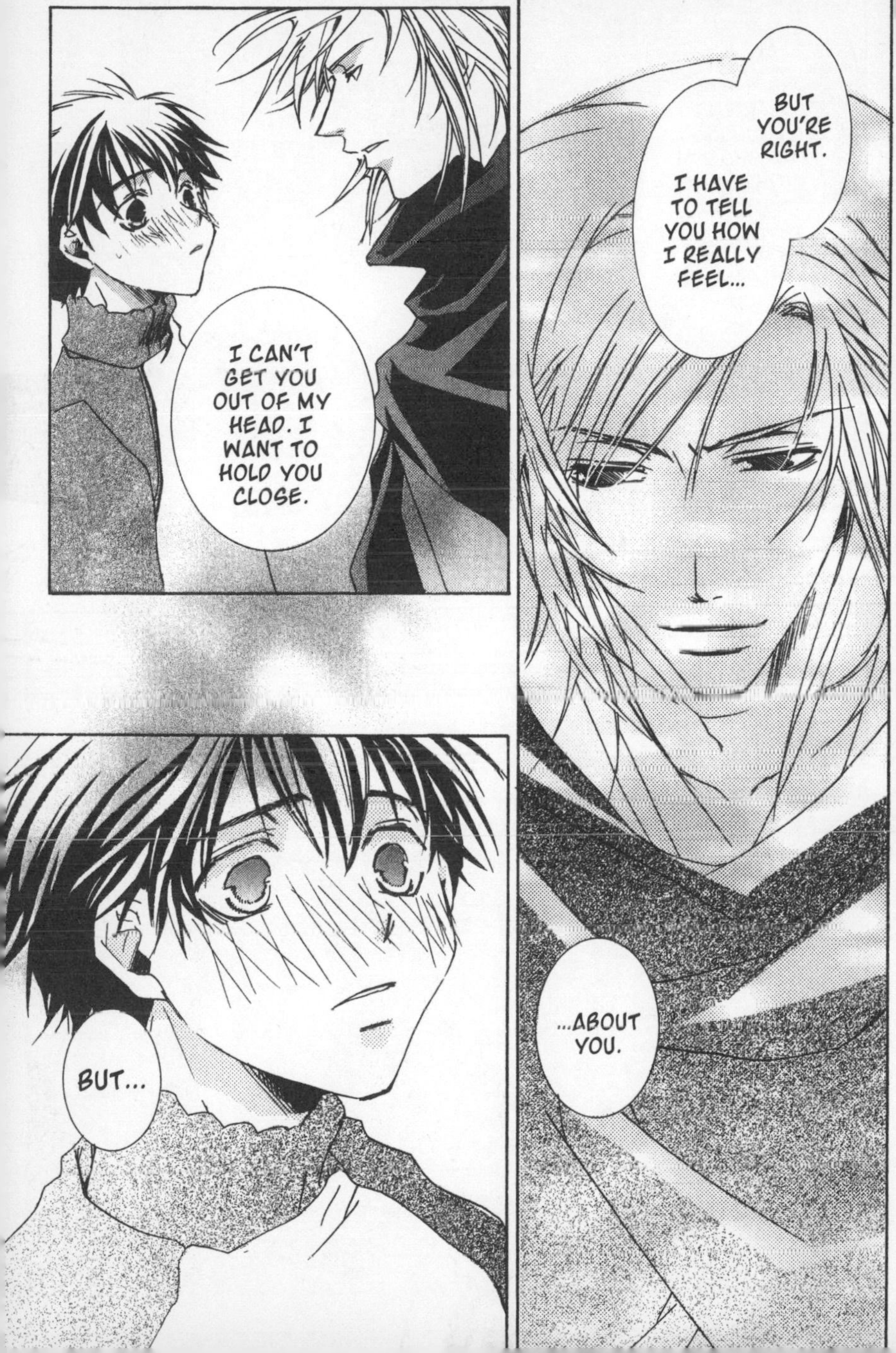
BUT YOU'RE RIGHT.
I HAVE TO TELL YOU HOW I REALLY FEEL...
...ABOUT YOU.
I CAN'T GET YOU OUT OF MY HEAD. I WANT TO HOLD YOU CLOSE.
BUT...

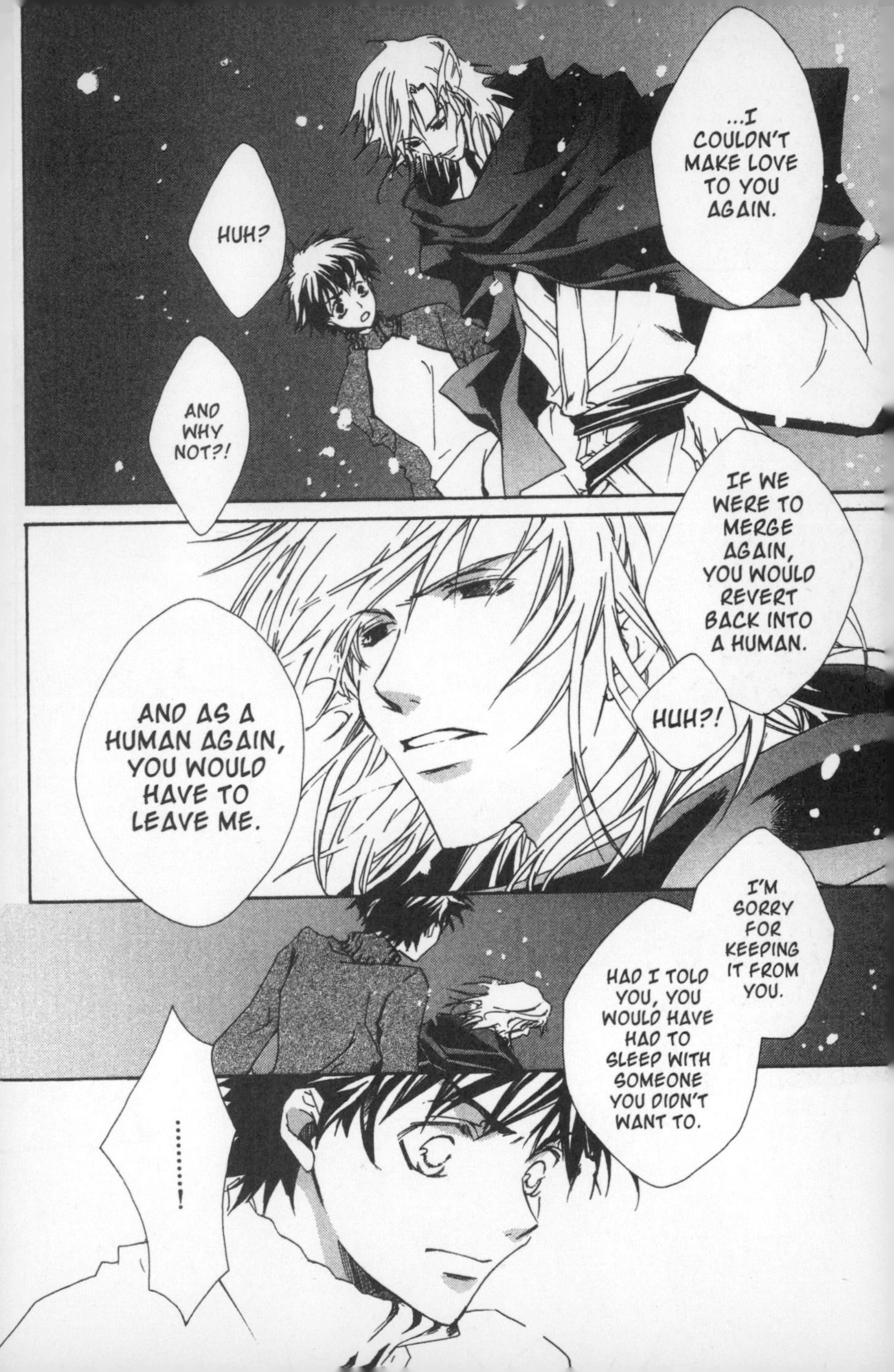
...I COULDN'T MAKE LOVE TO YOU AGAIN.
HUH?
AND WHY NOT?!
IF WE WERE TO MERGE AGAIN, YOU WOULD REVERT BACK INTO A HUMAN.
HUH?!
AND AS A HUMAN AGAIN, YOU WOULD HAVE TO LEAVE ME.
I'M SORRY FOR KEEPING IT FROM YOU.
HAD I TOLD YOU, YOU WOULD HAVE HAD TO SLEEP WITH SOMEONE YOU DIDN'T WANT TO.
......!

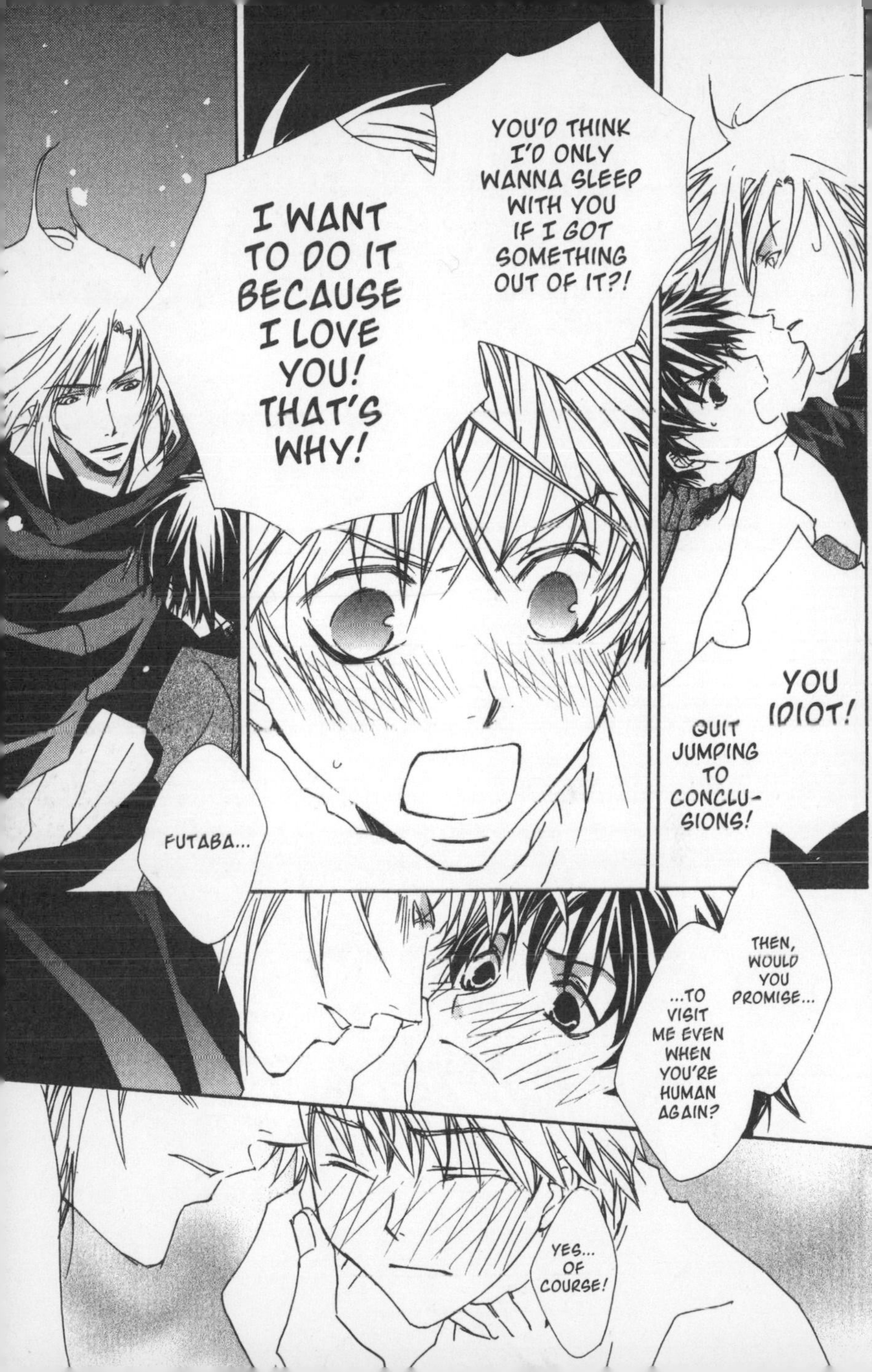
YOU IDIOT!
QUIT JUMPING TO CONCLU-SIONS!
YOU'D THINK I'D ONLY WANNA SLEEP WITH YOU IF I GOT SOMETHING OUT OF IT?!
I WANT TO DO IT BECAUSE I LOVE YOU! THAT'S WHY!
FUTABA...
THEN, WOULD YOU PROMISE...
...TO VISIT ME EVEN WHEN YOU'RE HUMAN AGAIN?
YES... OF COURSE!

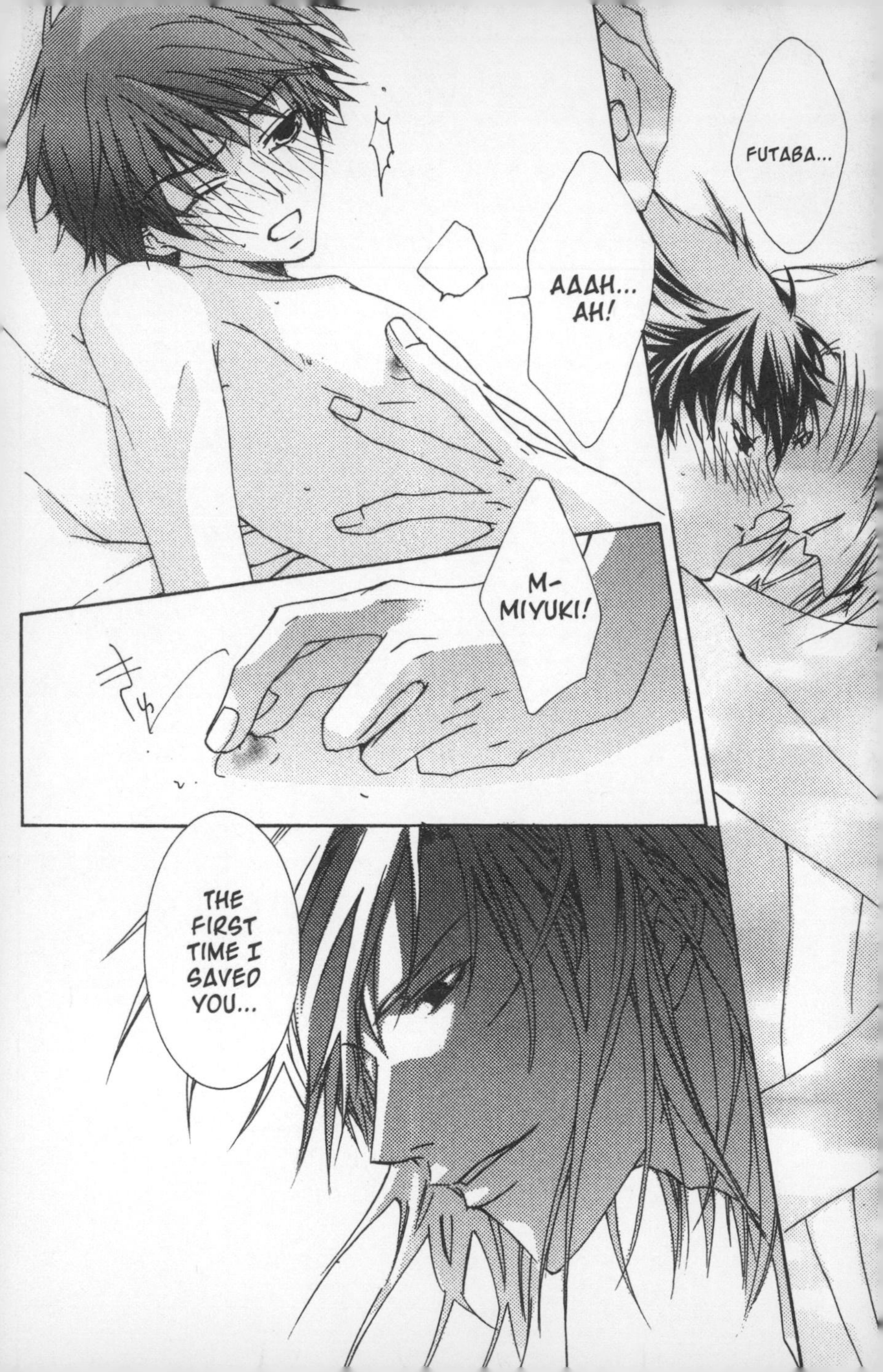
FUTABA...
AAAH... AH!
M-MIYUKI!
きゅ
THE FIRST TIME I SAVED YOU...

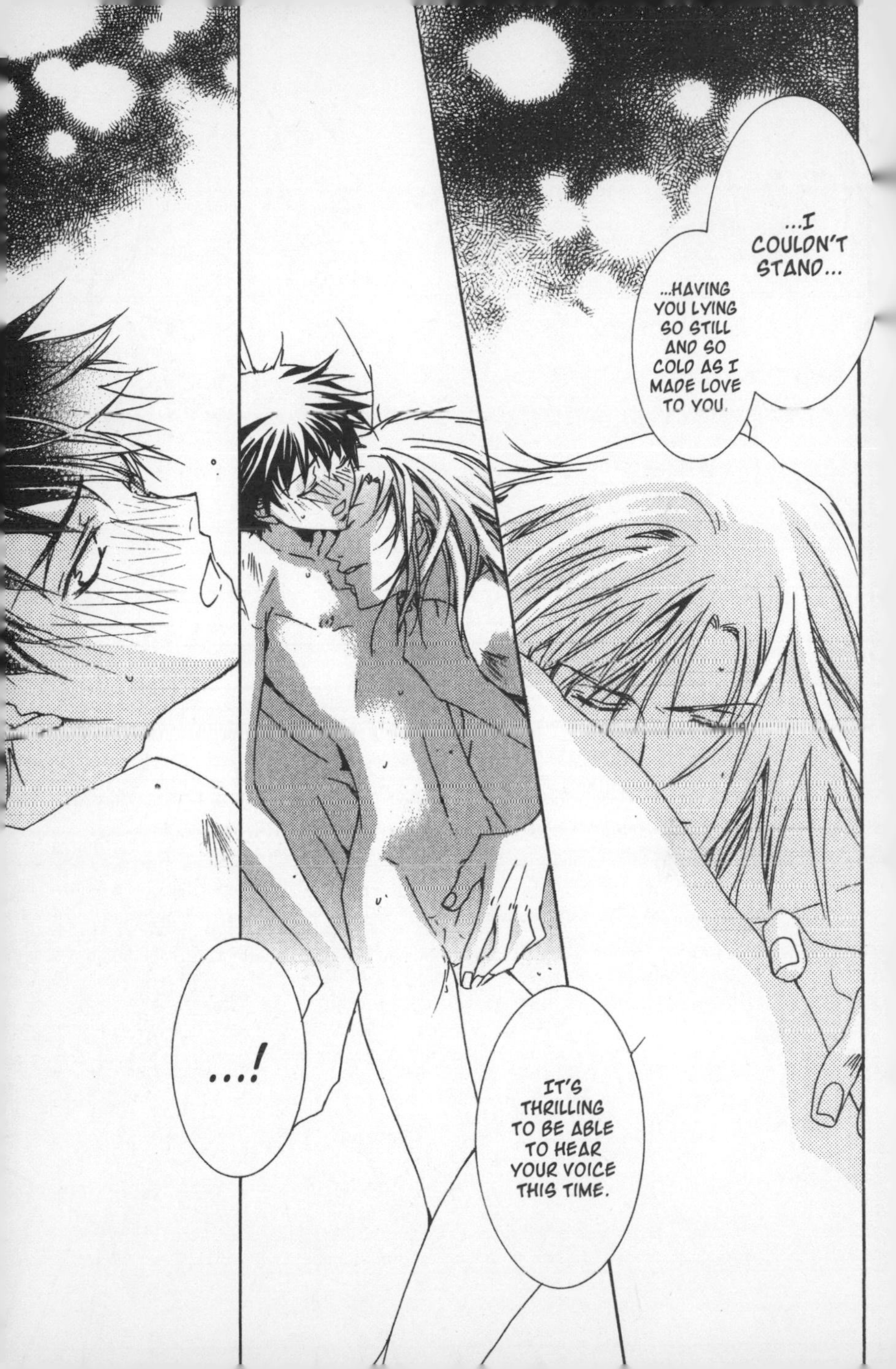
...I COULDN'T STAND...
...HAVING YOU LYING SO STILL AND SO COLD AS I MADE LOVE TO YOU.
IT'S THRILLING TO BE ABLE TO HEAR YOUR VOICE THIS TIME.
...!

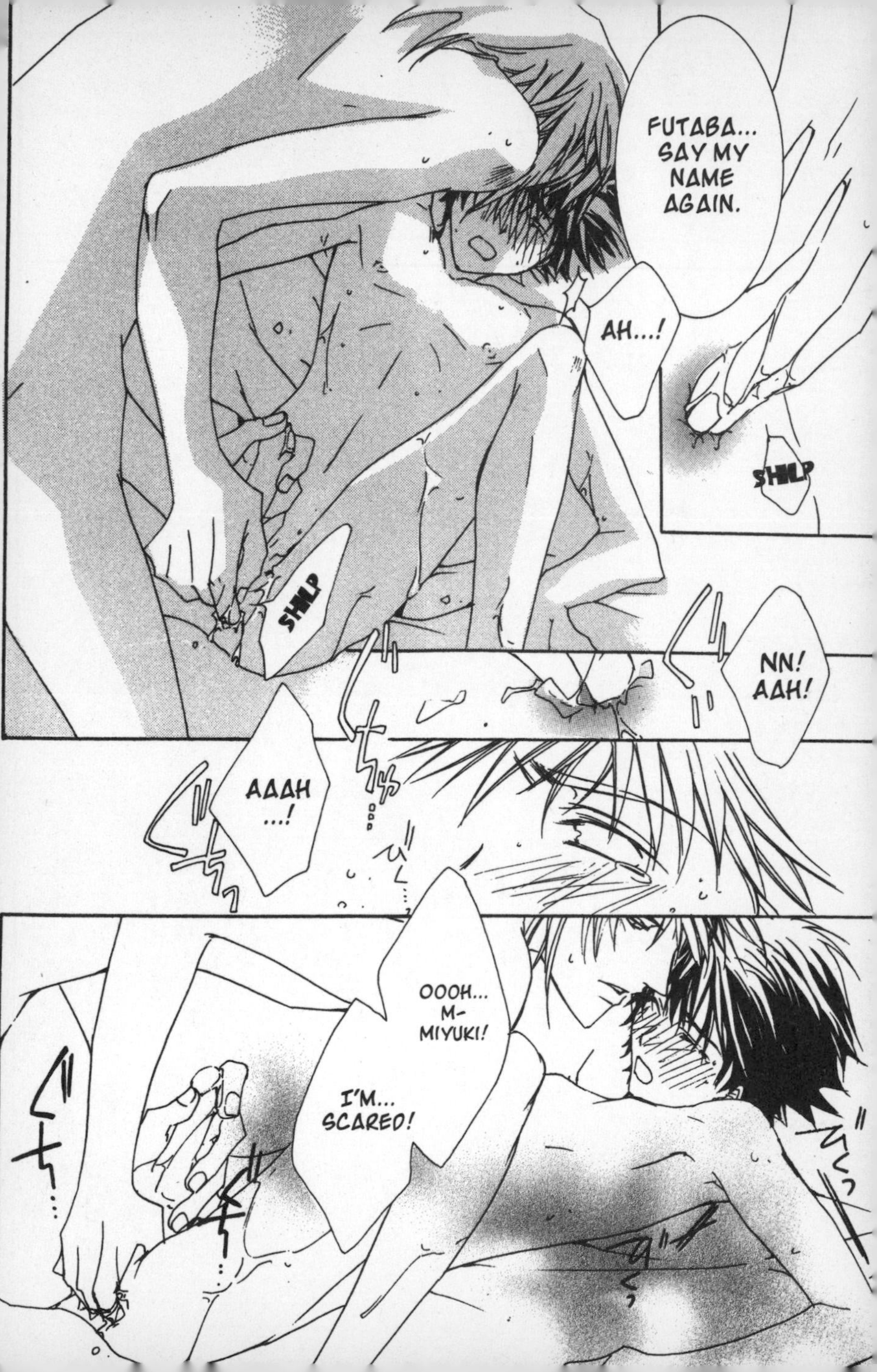
FUTABA... SAY MY NAME AGAIN.
AH...!
SHLIP
SHLIP
NN! AAH!
AAAH ...!
OOOH... M-MIYUKI!
I'M... SCARED!

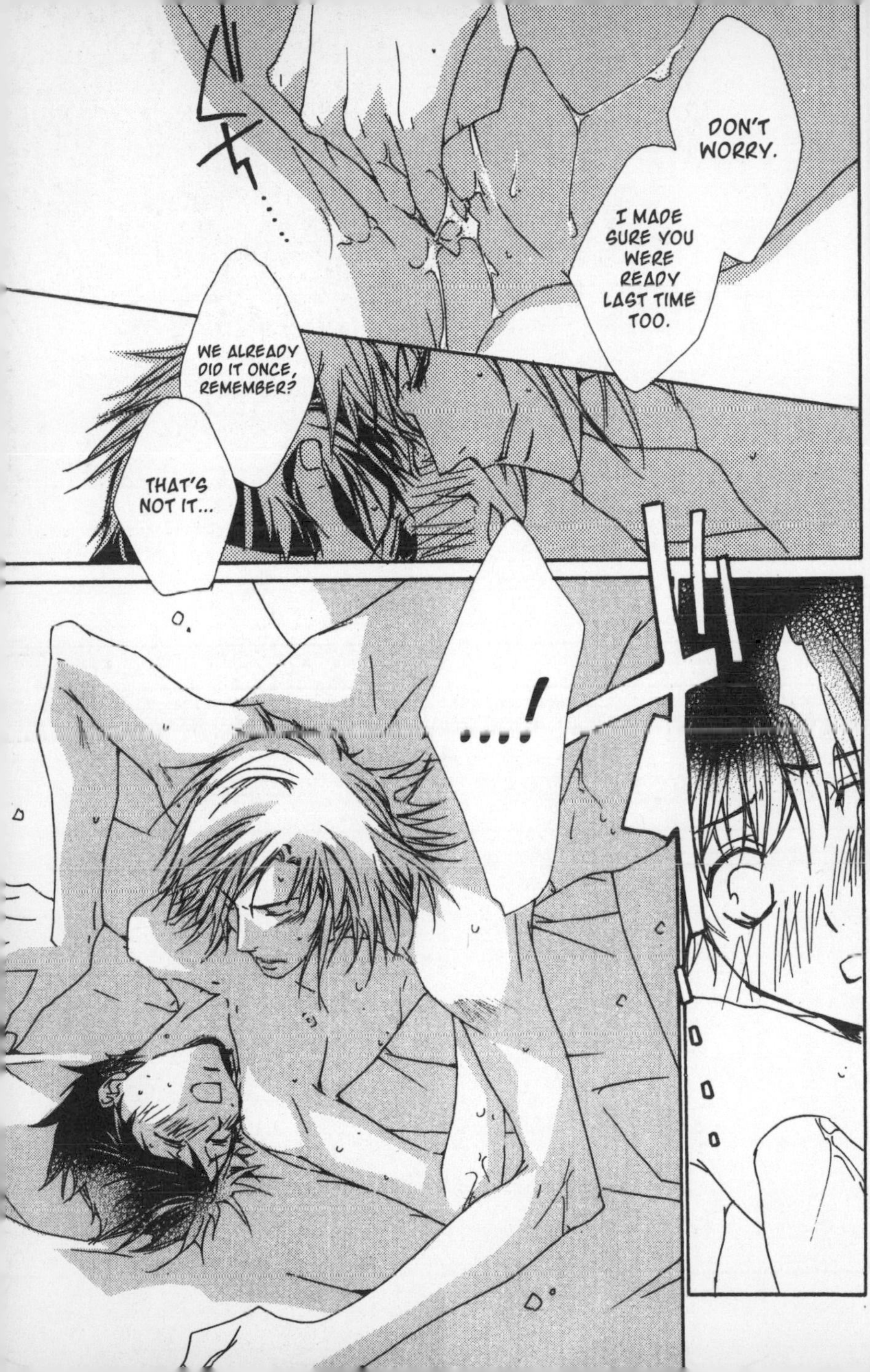
DON'T WORRY.
I MADE SURE YOU WERE READY LAST TIME TOO.
WE ALREADY DID IT ONCE, REMEMBER?
THAT'S NOT IT...
...!

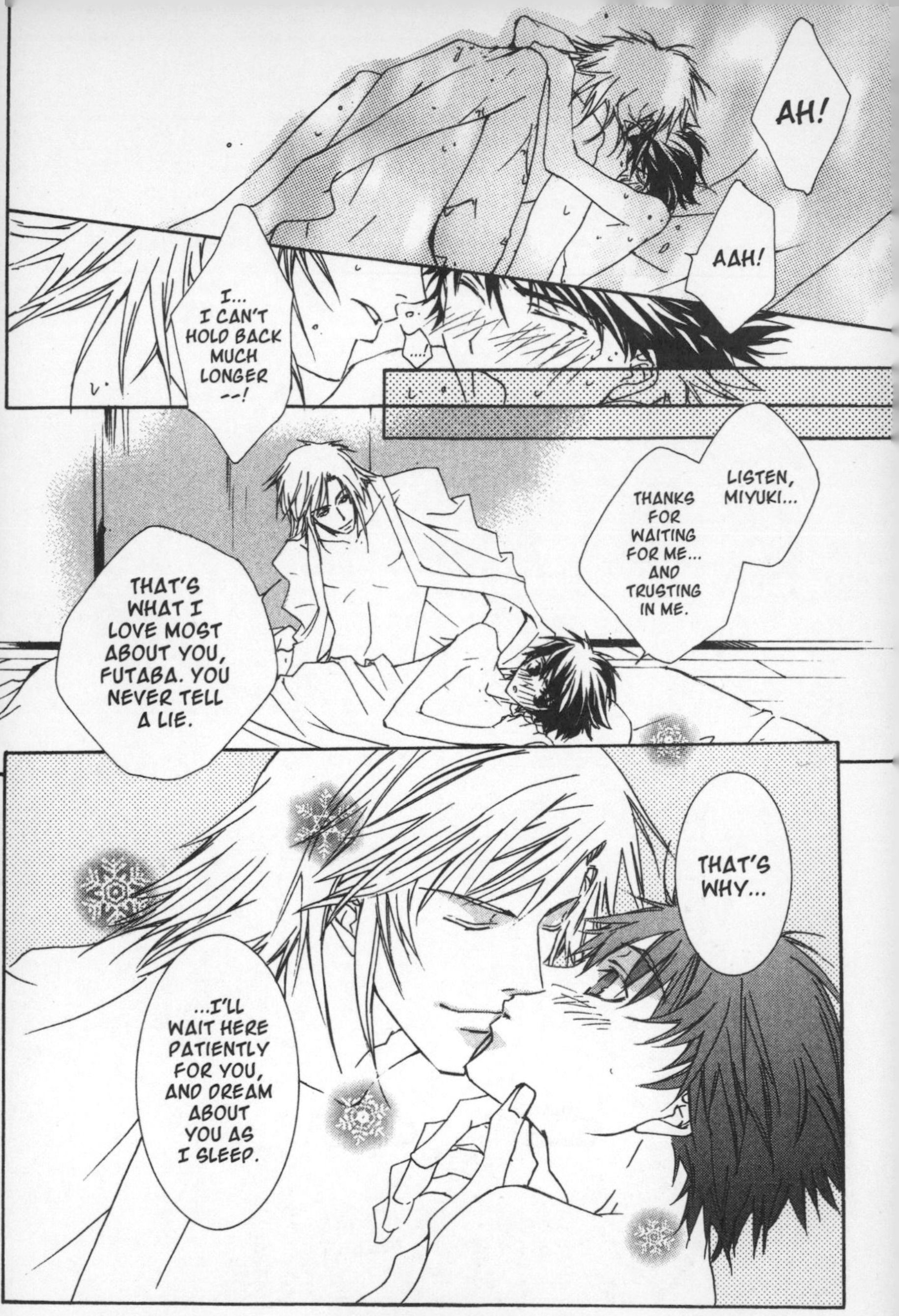
AH!
AAH!
....!
I... I CAN'T HOLD BACK MUCH LONGER --!
LISTEN, MIYUKI...
THANKS FOR WAITING FOR ME... AND TRUSTING IN ME.
THAT'S WHAT I LOVE MOST ABOUT YOU, FUTABA. YOU NEVER TELL A LIE.
THAT'S WHY...
...I'LL WAIT HERE PATIENTLY FOR YOU, AND DREAM ABOUT YOU AS I SLEEP.

Snow Storm / End

雪やこんこん

Snow Storm

MIYUKI

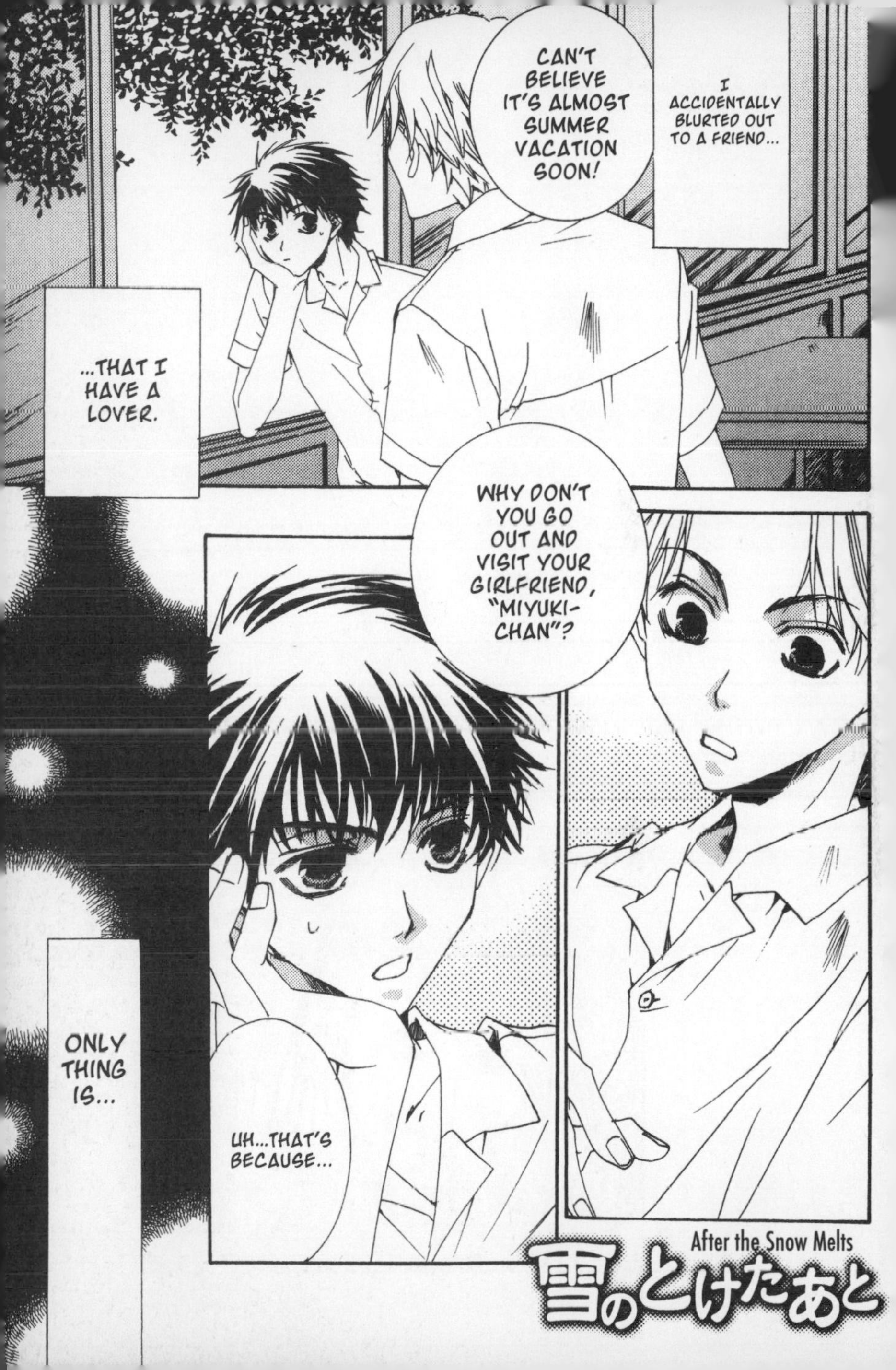
I ACCIDENTALLY BLURTED OUT TO A FRIEND...
CAN'T BELIEVE IT'S ALMOST SUMMER VACATION SOON!
...THAT I HAVE A LOVER.
WHY DON'T YOU GO OUT AND VISIT YOUR GIRLFRIEND, "MIYUKI-CHAN"?
UH...THAT'S BECAUSE...
ONLY THING IS...
After the Snow Melts
雪のとけたあと

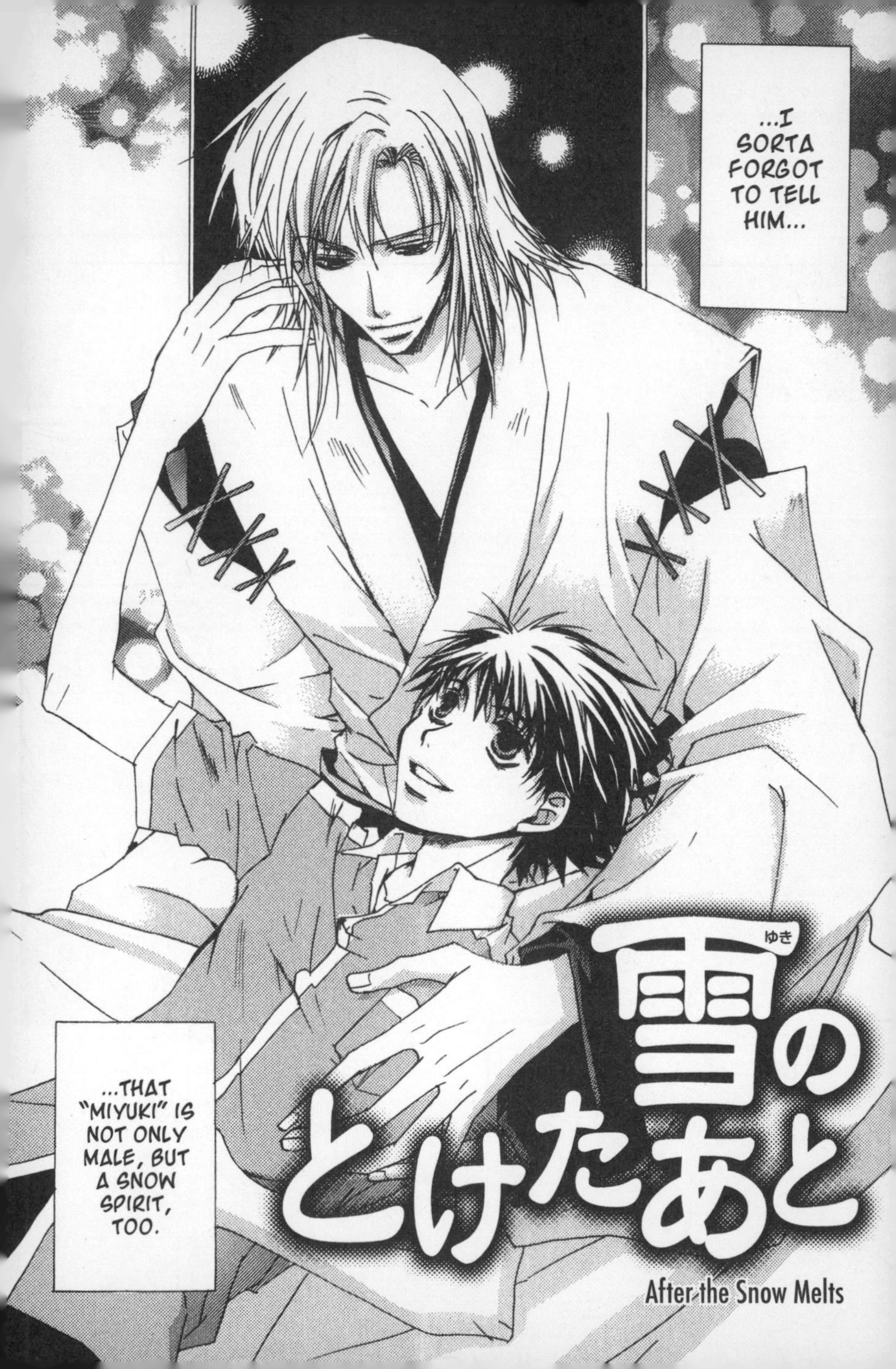
...I SORTA FORGOT TO TELL HIM...
雪(ゆき)のとけたあと
After the Snow Melts
...THAT "MIYUKI" IS NOT ONLY MALE, BUT A SNOW SPIRIT, TOO.

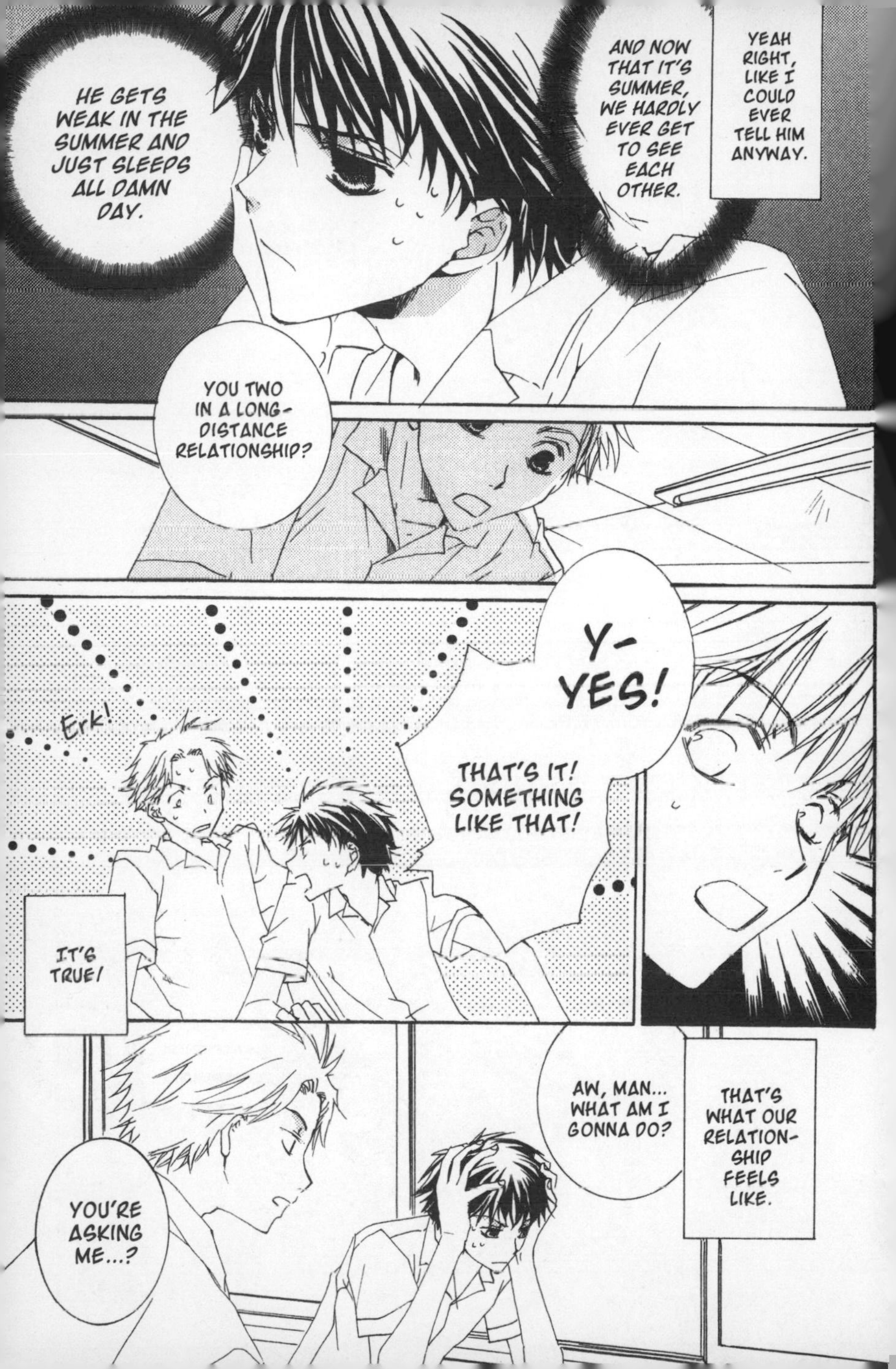
YEAH RIGHT, LIKE I COULD EVER TELL HIM ANYWAY.
AND NOW THAT IT'S SUMMER, WE HARDLY EVER GET TO SEE EACH OTHER.
HE GETS WEAK IN THE SUMMER AND JUST SLEEPS ALL DAMN DAY.
YOU TWO IN A LONG-DISTANCE RELATIONSHIP?
Y- YES!
THAT'S IT! SOMETHING LIKE THAT!
Erk!
IT'S TRUE!
THAT'S WHAT OUR RELATION-SHIP FEELS LIKE.
AW, MAN... WHAT AM I GONNA DO?
YOU'RE ASKING ME...?

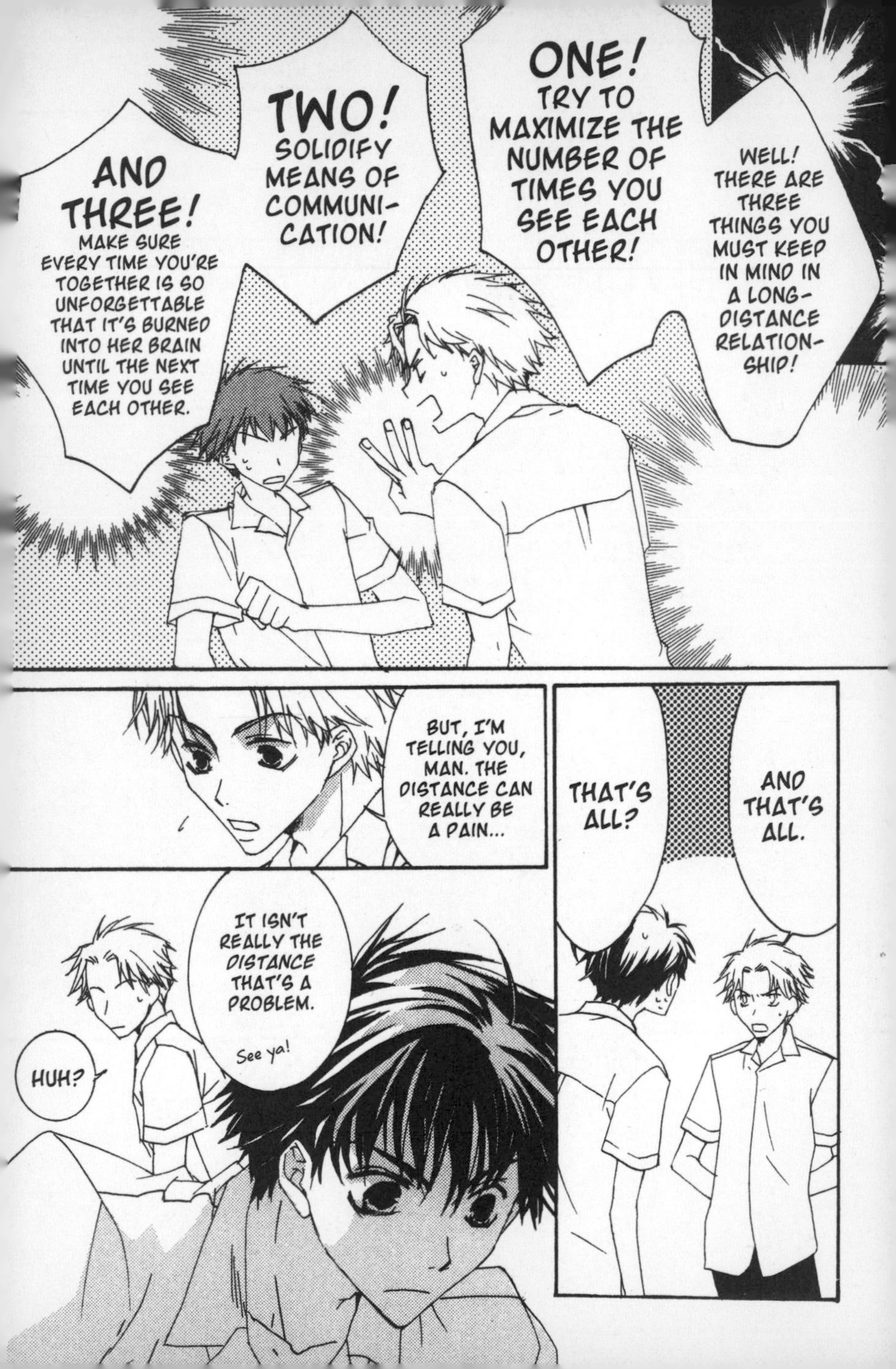

WELL! THERE ARE THREE THINGS YOU MUST KEEP IN MIND IN A LONG-DISTANCE RELATION-SHIP!
ONE! TRY TO MAXIMIZE THE NUMBER OF TIMES YOU SEE EACH OTHER!
TWO! SOLIDIFY MEANS OF COMMUNI-CATION!
AND THREE! MAKE SURE EVERY TIME YOU'RE TOGETHER IS SO UNFORGETTABLE THAT IT'S BURNED INTO HER BRAIN UNTIL THE NEXT TIME YOU SEE EACH OTHER.
AND THAT'S ALL.
THAT'S ALL?
BUT, I'M TELLING YOU, MAN. THE DISTANCE CAN REALLY BE A PAIN...
IT ISN'T REALLY THE DISTANCE THAT'S A PROBLEM.
See ya!
HUH?

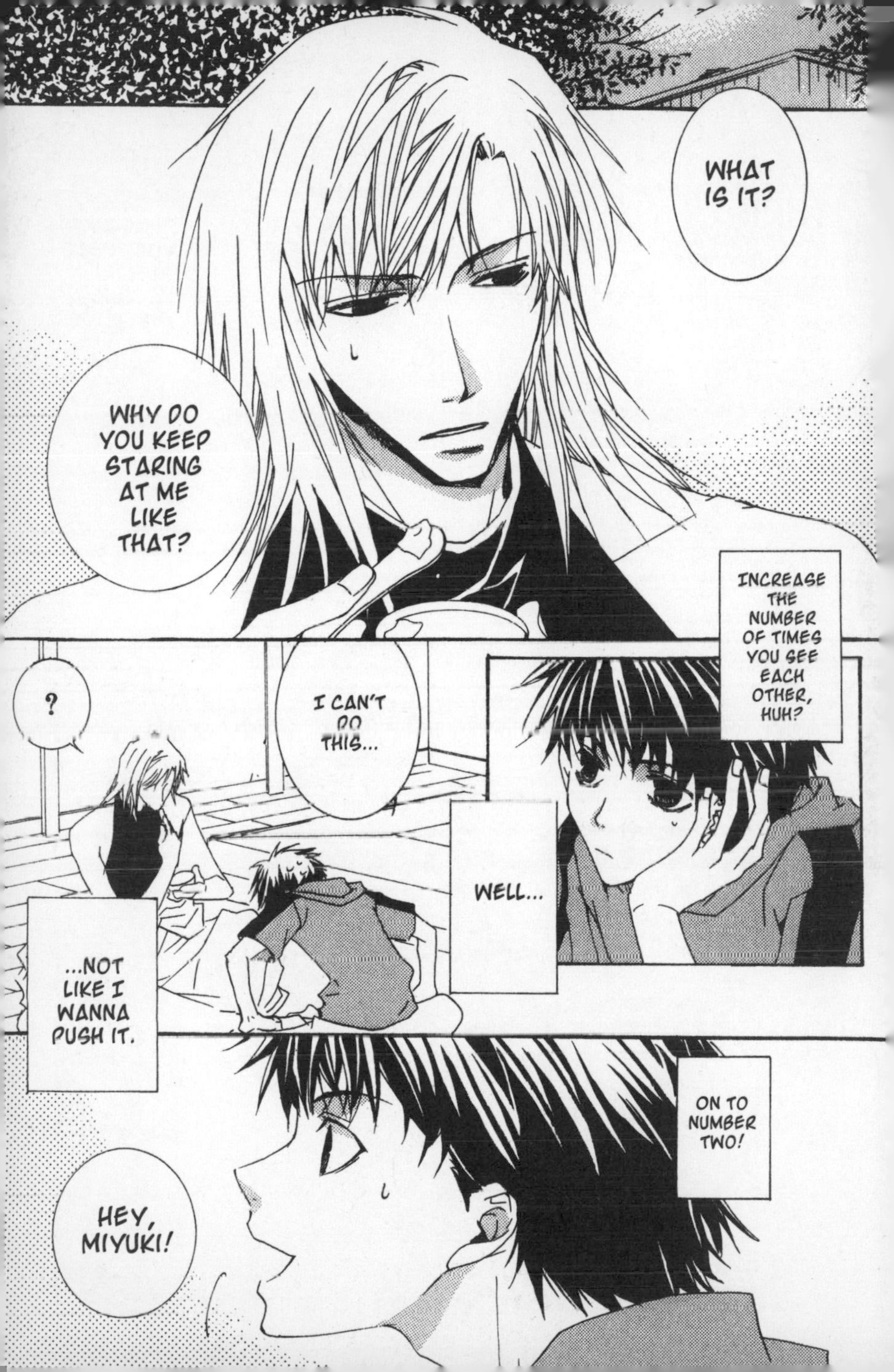
WHAT IS IT?
WHY DO YOU KEEP STARING AT ME LIKE THAT?
INCREASE THE NUMBER OF TIMES YOU SEE EACH OTHER, HUH?
WELL...
I CAN'T DO THIS...
?
...NOT LIKE I WANNA PUSH IT.
ON TO NUMBER TWO!
HEY, MIYUKI!

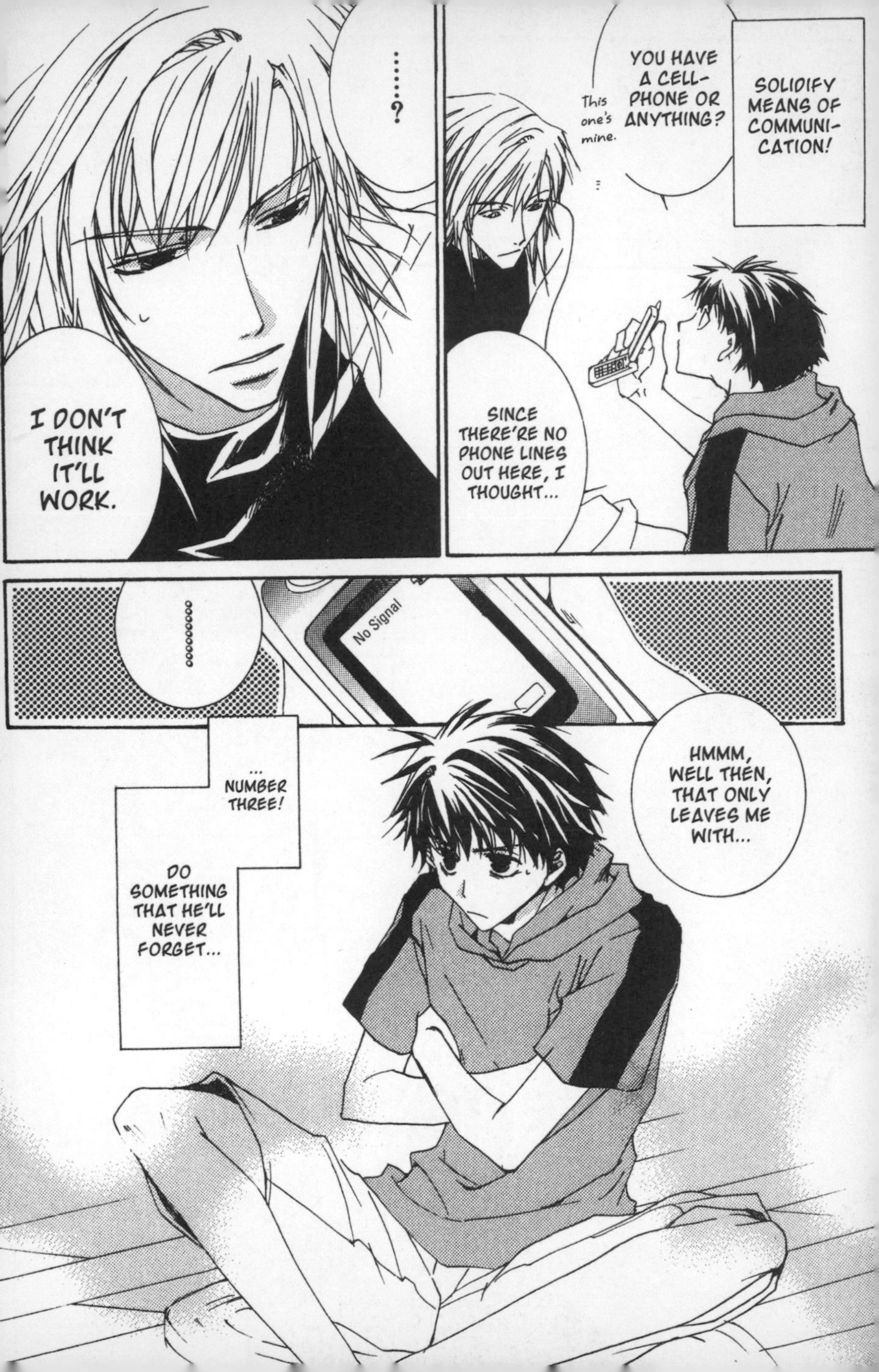
SOLIDIFY MEANS OF COMMUNI-CATION!
YOU HAVE A CELL-PHONE OR ANYTHING?
This one's mine.
...
SINCE THERE'RE NO PHONE LINES OUT HERE, I THOUGHT...
......?
I DON'T THINK IT'LL WORK.
....
No Signal
HMMM, WELL THEN, THAT ONLY LEAVES ME WITH...
...NUMBER THREE!
DO SOMETHING THAT HE'LL NEVER FORGET...

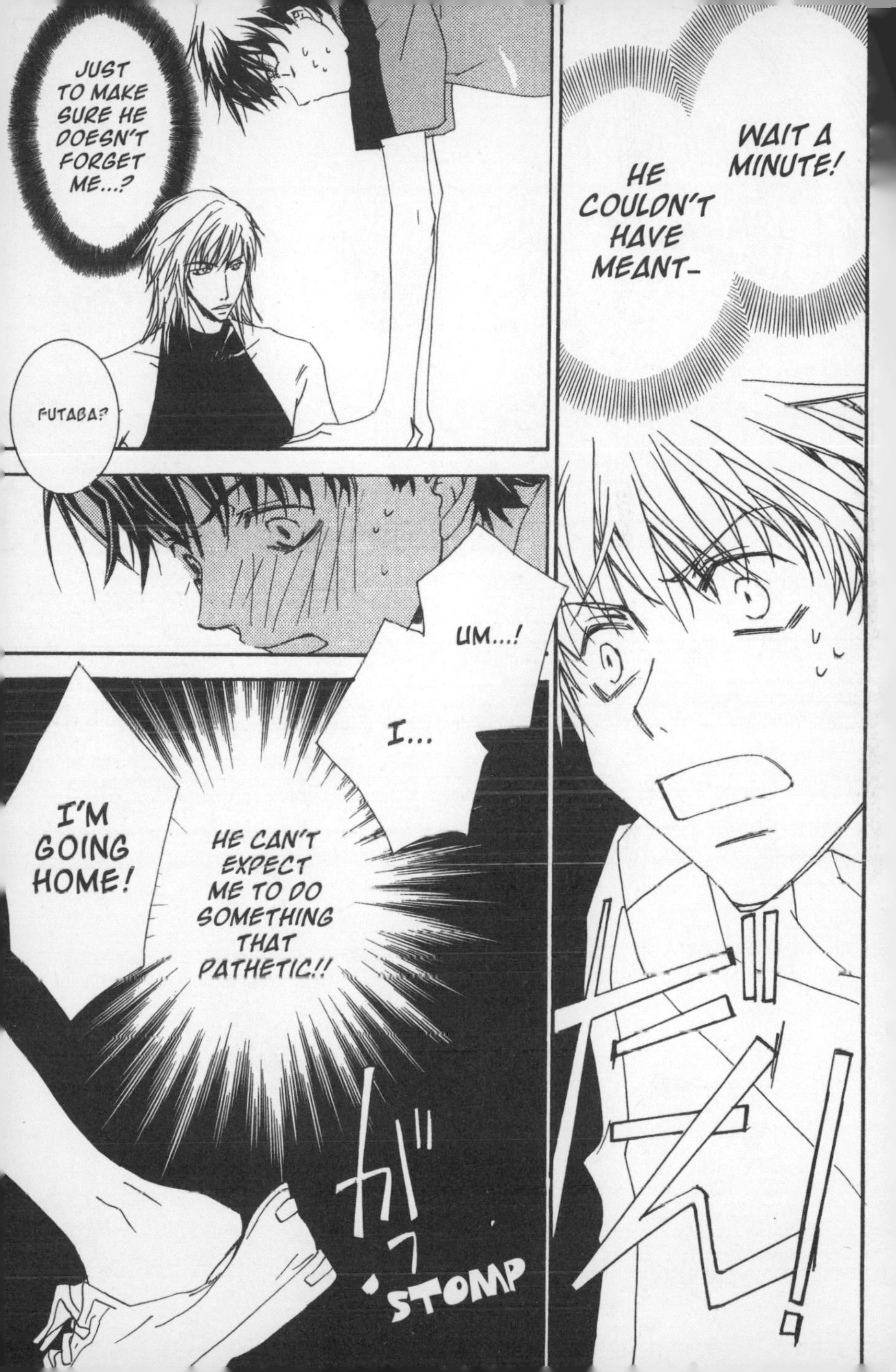
WAIT A MINUTE!
HE COULDN'T HAVE MEANT-
JUST TO MAKE SURE HE DOESN'T FORGET ME...?
FUTABA?
UM...!
I...
HE CAN'T EXPECT ME TO DO SOMETHING THAT PATHETIC!!
I'M GOING HOME!
ガッ
STOMP

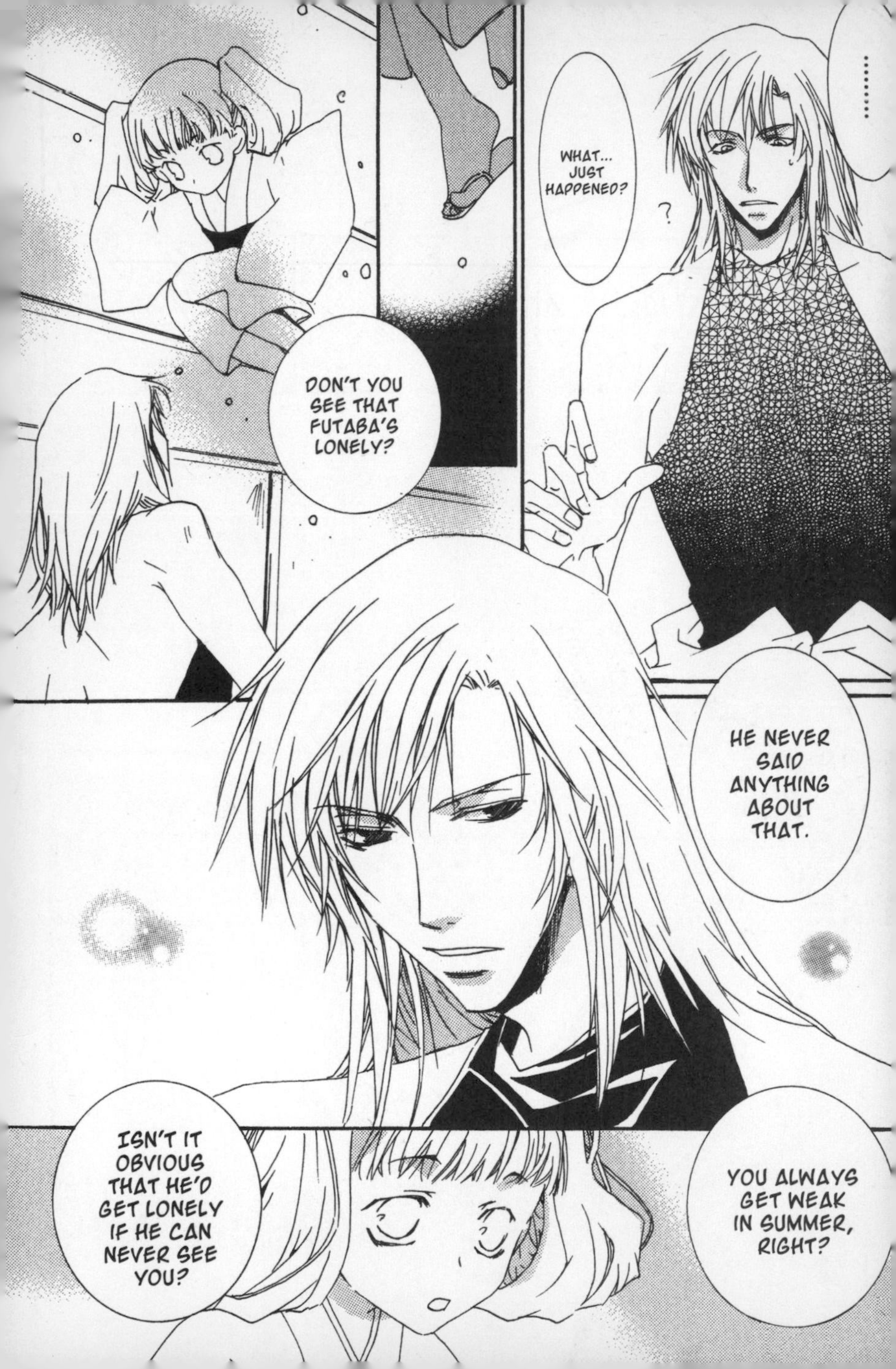

......
WHAT... JUST HAPPENED?
?
DON'T YOU SEE THAT FUTABA'S LONELY?
HE NEVER SAID ANYTHING ABOUT THAT.
YOU ALWAYS GET WEAK IN SUMMER, RIGHT?
ISN'T IT OBVIOUS THAT HE'D GET LONELY IF HE CAN NEVER SEE YOU?

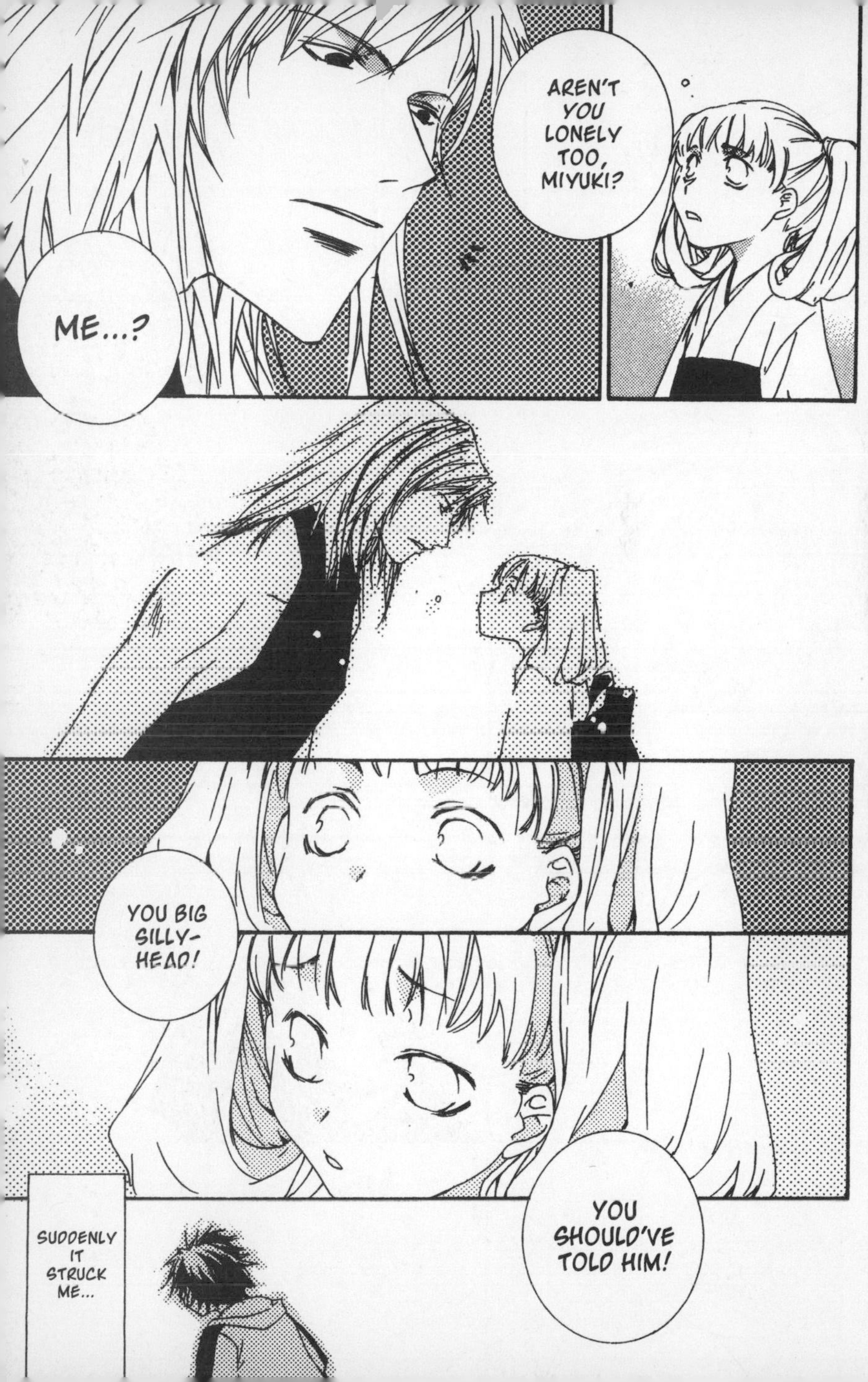
AREN'T YOU LONELY TOO, MIYUKI?
ME...?
YOU BIG SILLY-HEAD!
YOU SHOULD'VE TOLD HIM!
SUDDENLY IT STRUCK ME...

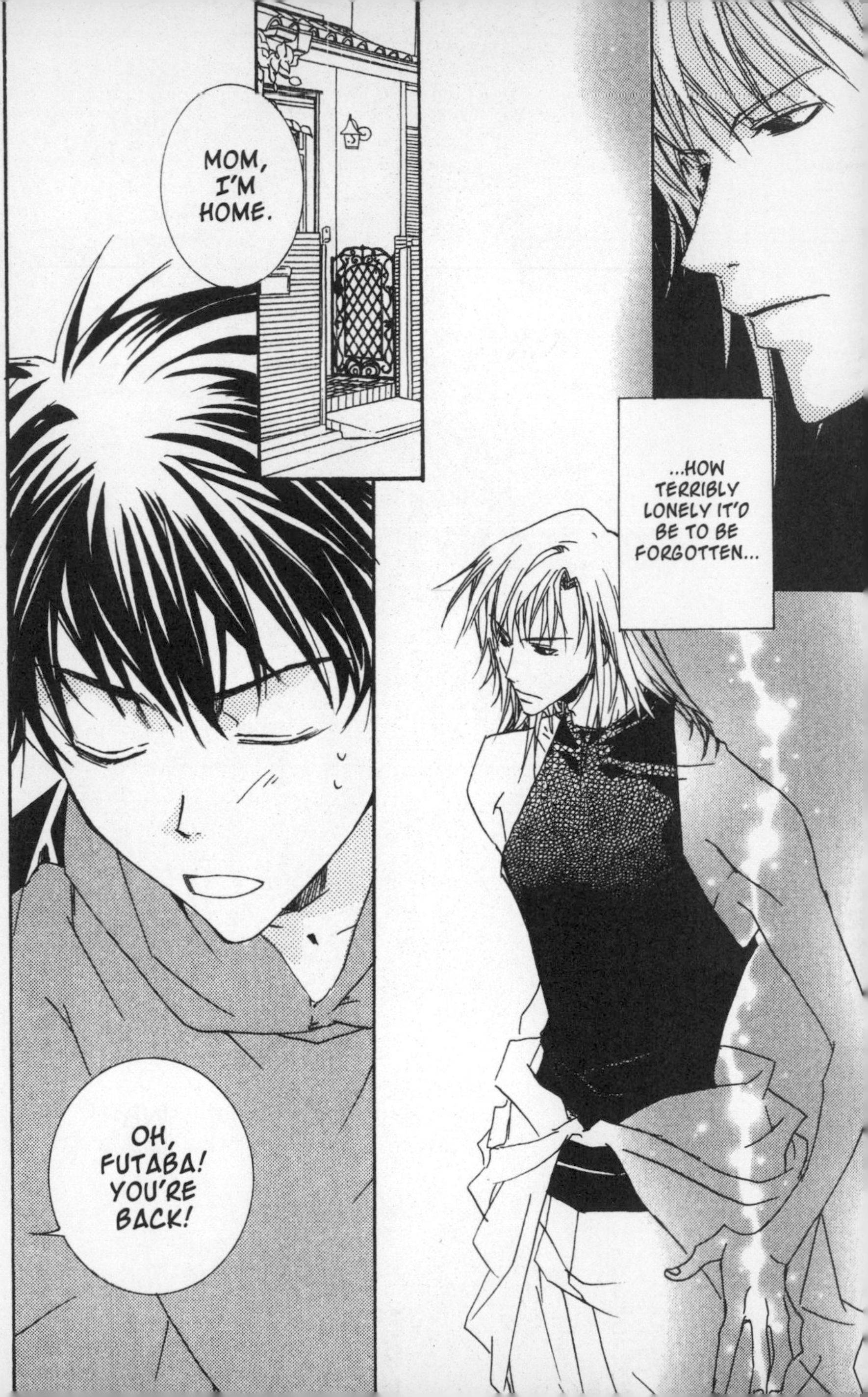
...HOW TERRIBLY LONELY IT'D BE TO BE FORGOTTEN...
MOM, I'M HOME.
OH, FUTABA! YOU'RE BACK!

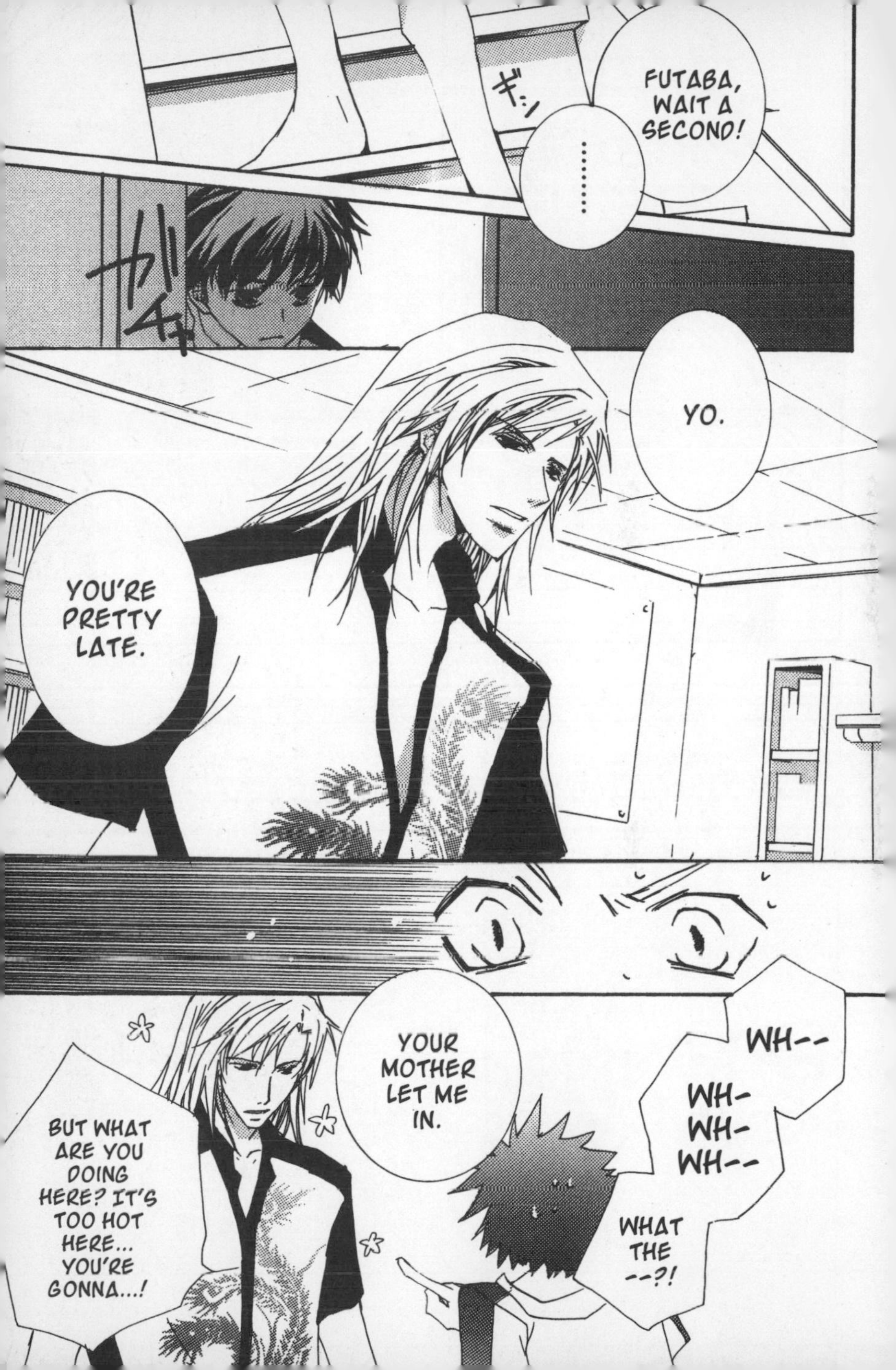
FUTABA, WAIT A SECOND!
......
YO.
YOU'RE PRETTY LATE.
WH-- WH- WH- WH--
WHAT THE --?!
YOUR MOTHER LET ME IN.
BUT WHAT ARE YOU DOING HERE? IT'S TOO HOT HERE... YOU'RE GONNA...!

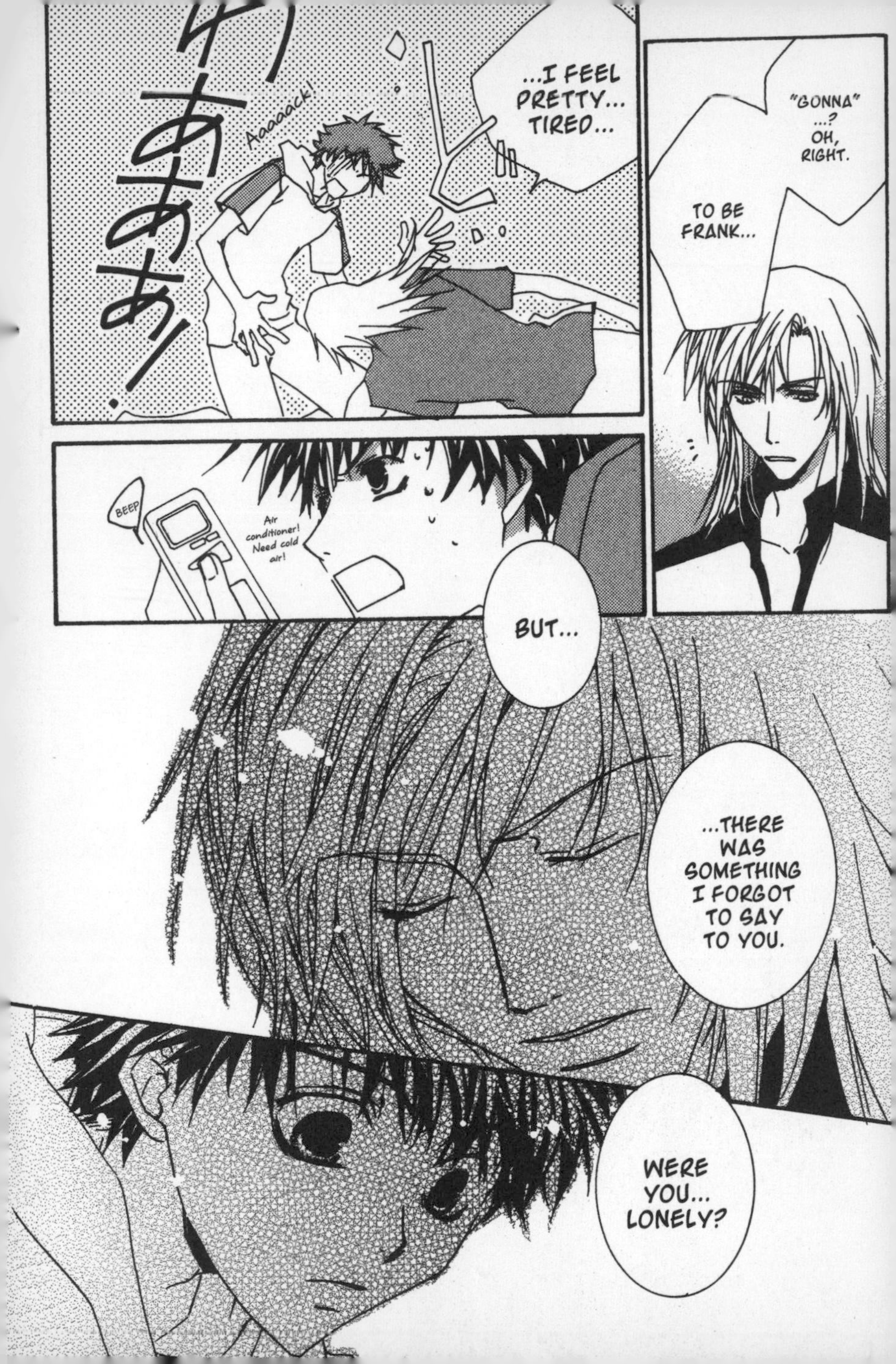
"GONNA" ...? OH, RIGHT.
TO BE FRANK...
...I FEEL PRETTY... TIRED...
Aaaaack!
BEEP
Air conditioner! Need cold air!
BUT...
...THERE WAS SOMETHING I FORGOT TO SAY TO YOU.
WERE YOU... LONELY?

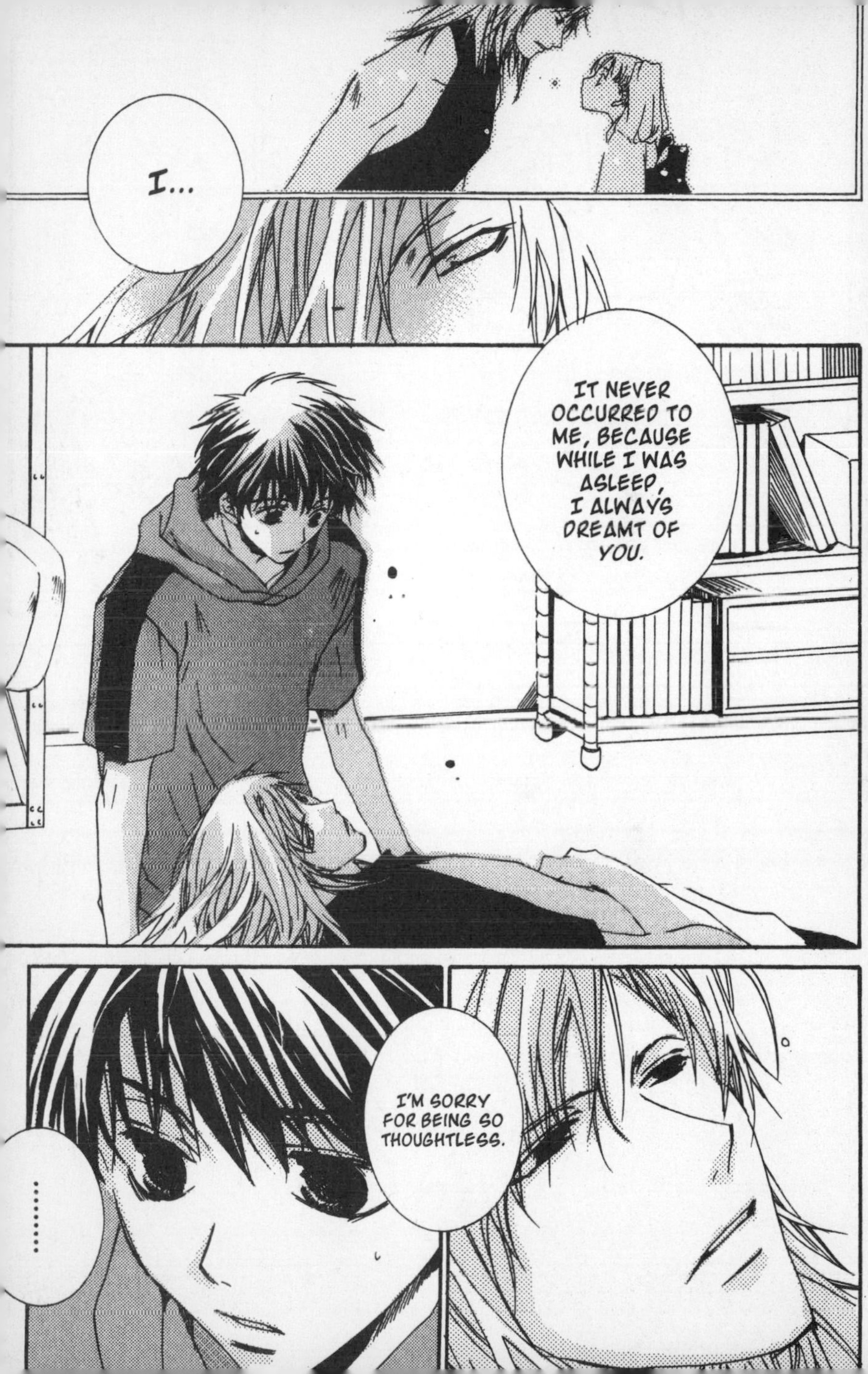
I...
IT NEVER OCCURRED TO ME, BECAUSE WHILE I WAS ASLEEP, I ALWAYS DREAMT OF YOU.
I'M SORRY FOR BEING SO THOUGHTLESS.
....

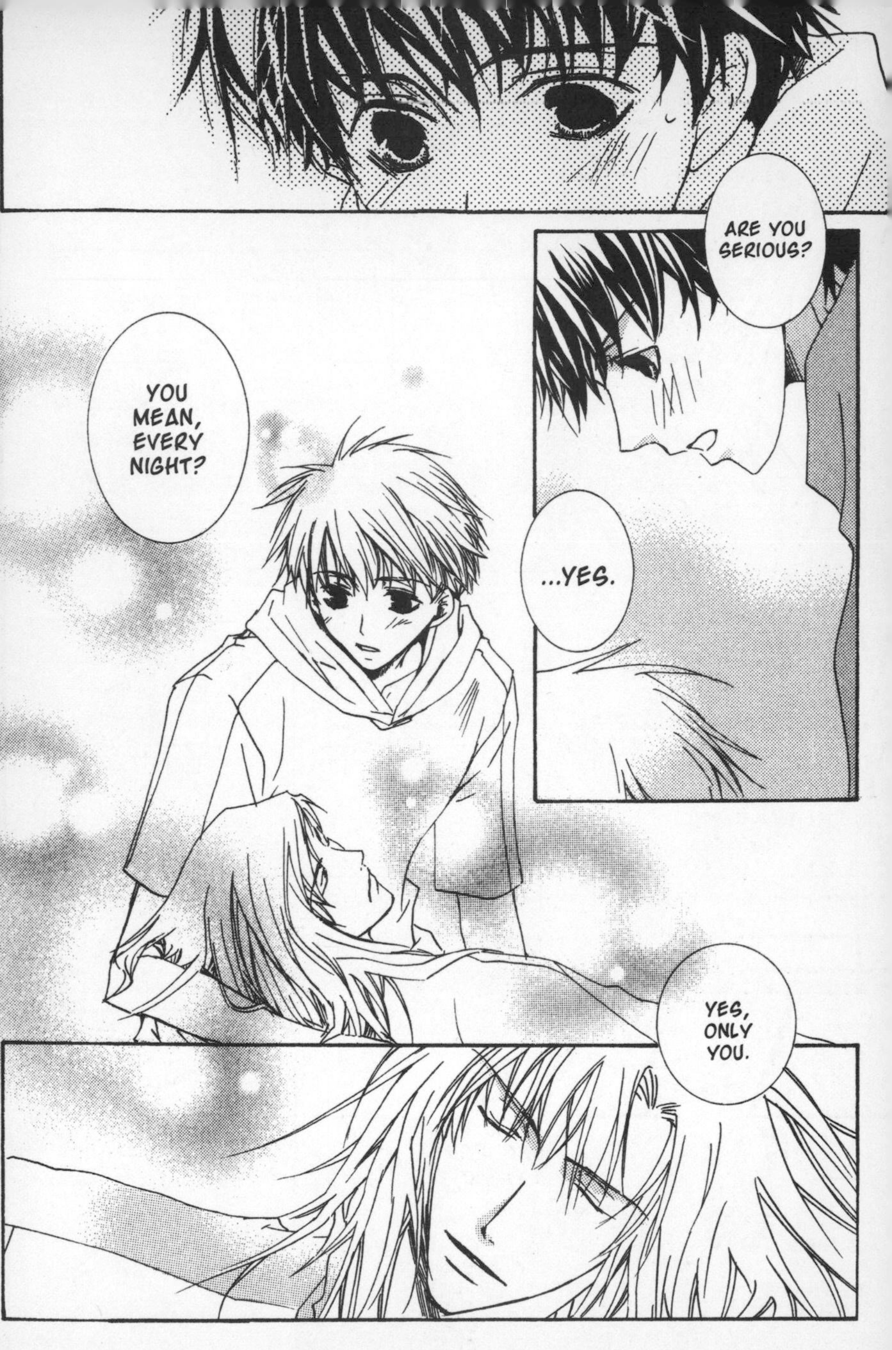
ARE YOU SERIOUS?
...YES.
YOU MEAN, EVERY NIGHT?
YES, ONLY YOU.

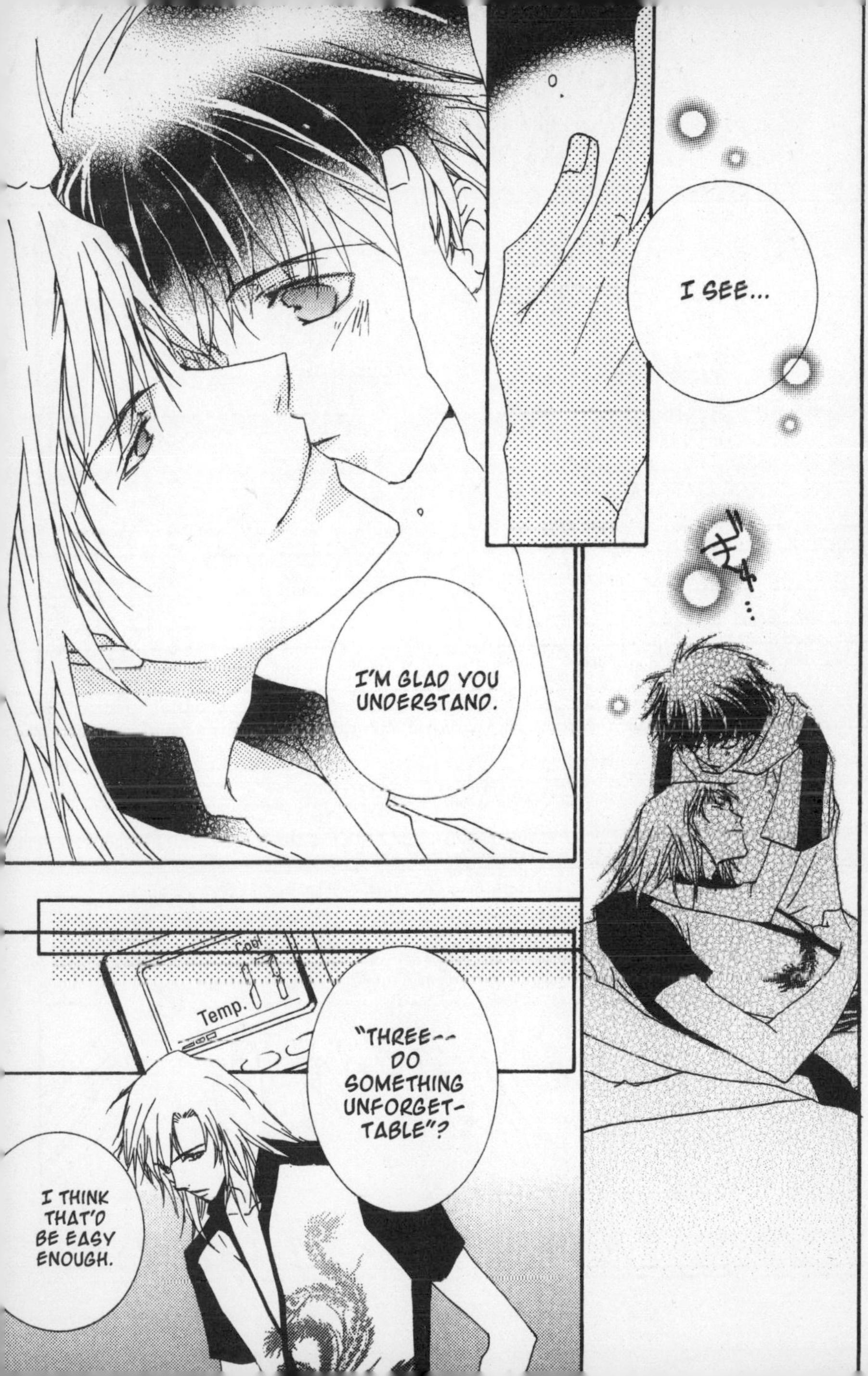
I SEE...
I'M GLAD YOU UNDERSTAND.
Temp.
"THREE--DO SOMETHING UNFORGET-TABLE"?
I THINK THAT'D BE EASY ENOUGH.

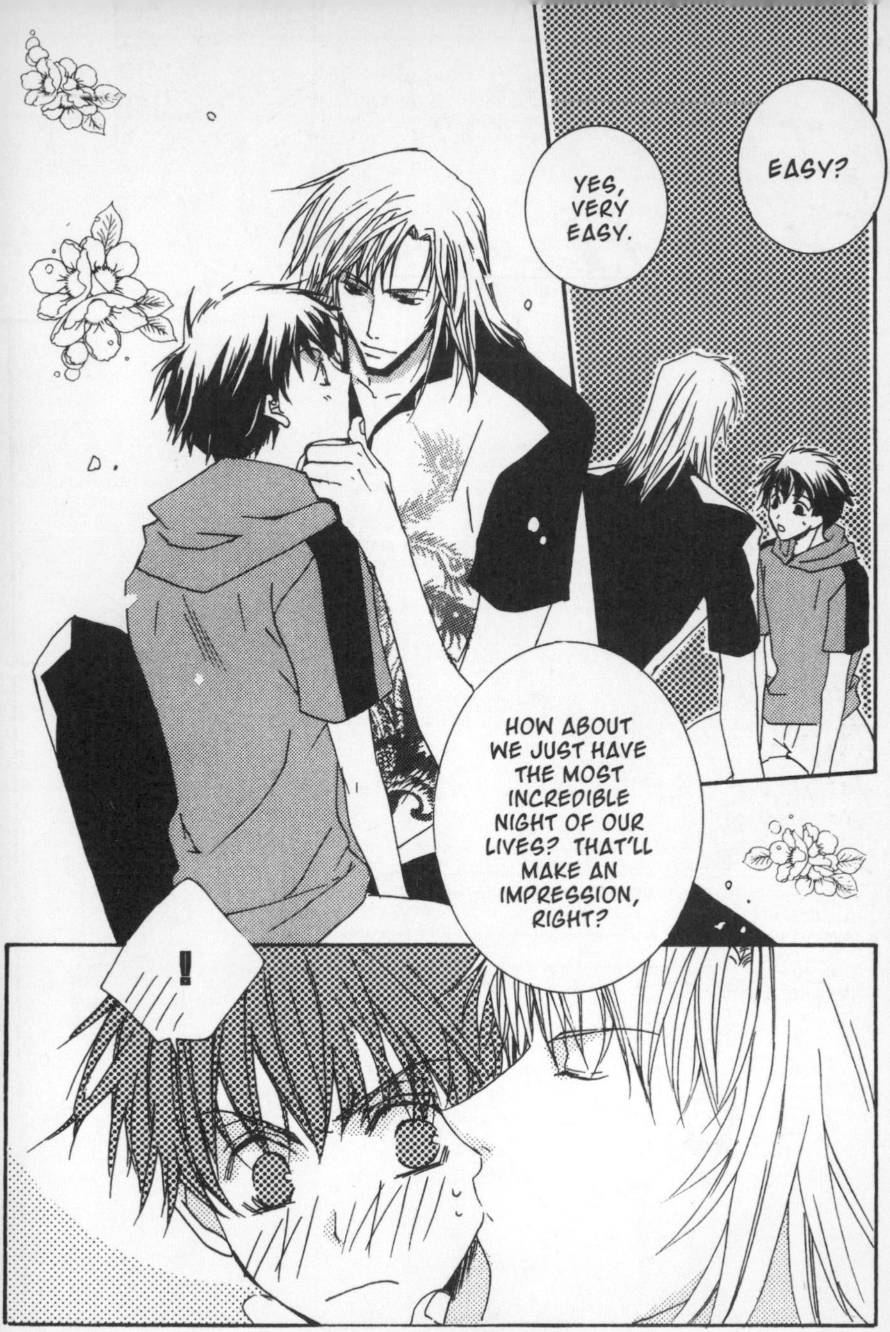
EASY?
YES, VERY EASY.
HOW ABOUT WE JUST HAVE THE MOST INCREDIBLE NIGHT OF OUR LIVES? THAT'LL MAKE AN IMPRESSION, RIGHT?
!

After the Snow Melts / End

Ninja Skills

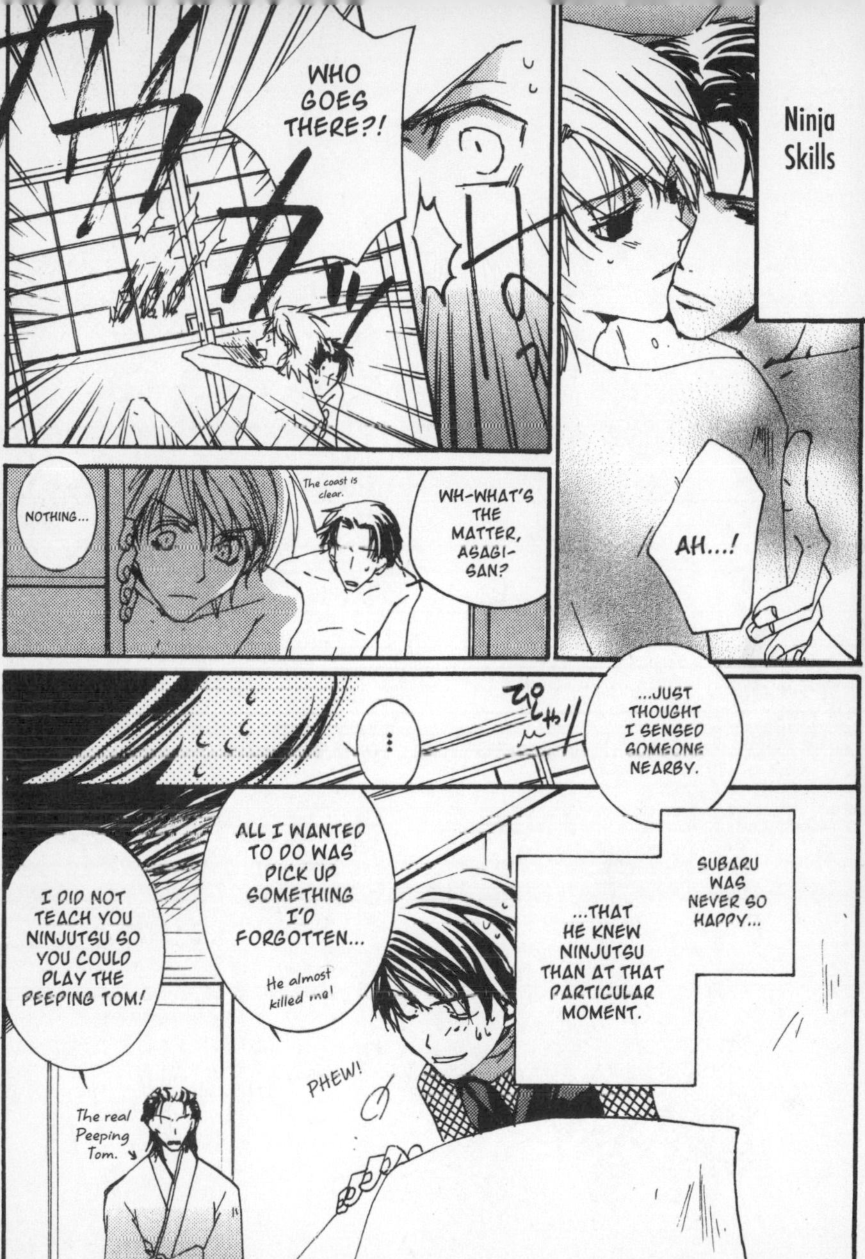

AH...!
WHO GOES THERE?!
WH-WHAT'S THE MATTER, ASAGI-SAN?
The coast is clear.
NOTHING...
...JUST THOUGHT I SENSED SOMEONE NEARBY.
...
SUBARU WAS NEVER SO HAPPY...
...THAT HE KNEW NINJUTSU THAN AT THAT PARTICULAR MOMENT.
ALL I WANTED TO DO WAS PICK UP SOMETHING I'D FORGOTTEN...
He almost killed me!
PHEW!
I DID NOT TEACH YOU NINJUTSU SO YOU COULD PLAY THE PEEPING TOM!
The real Peeping Tom.

Ninja Skills / End

Shinobu Kokoro ▪ A Ninja's Heart Is... ▪

This story is about ninja. I like ninja. This was my first time doing a book for Biblos and looking back on it, I think it flowed along pretty well. When I write master and student relationships, I usually like to make the student the "seme," but this is a rare case where I made the master take lead. [NOTE: "Seme" (and "uke") are popular words in the world of Boy's Love genre; "Uke" denoting the receiver/passive role in the relationship, and "seme" denoting the aggressor or leader in the relationship.]

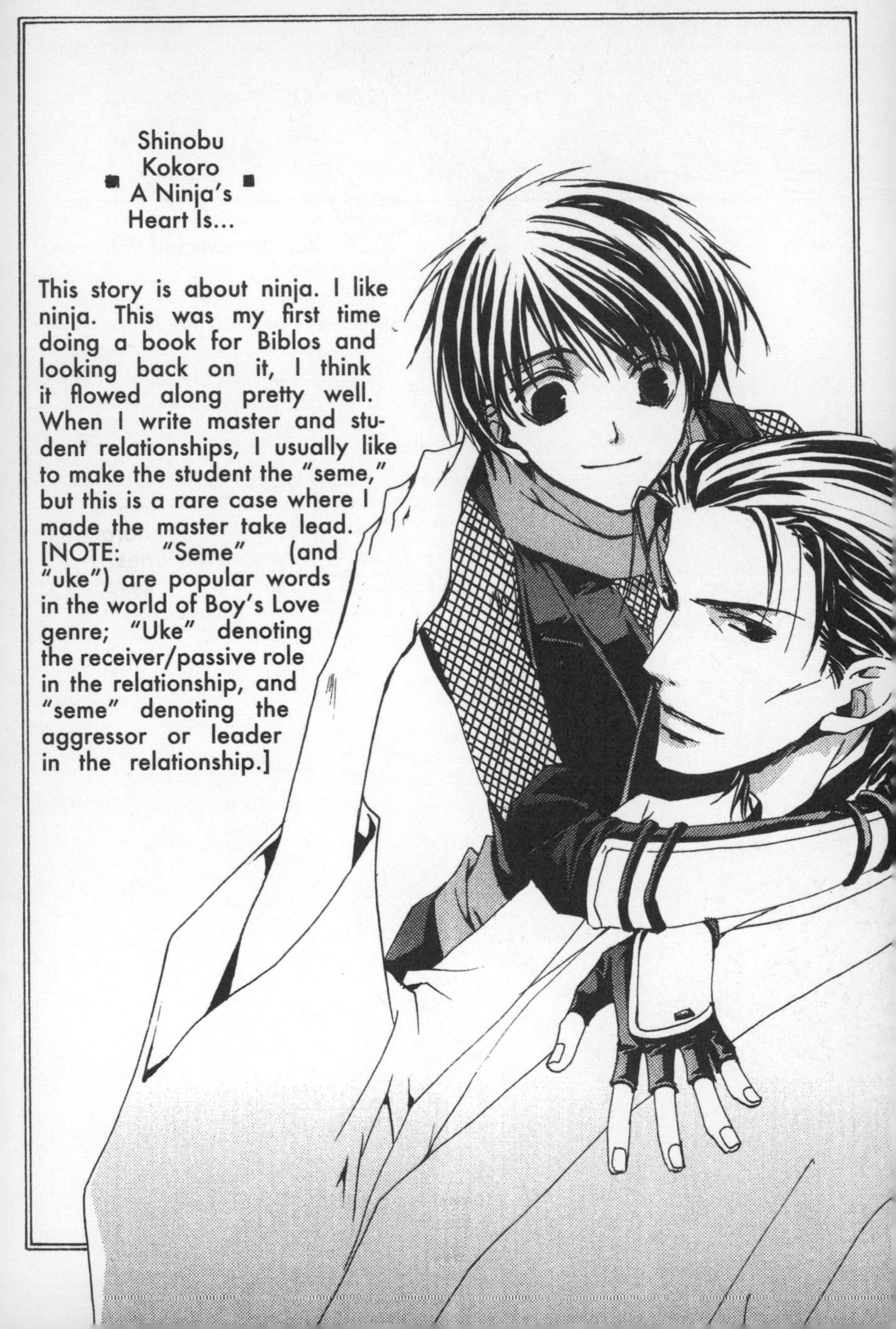

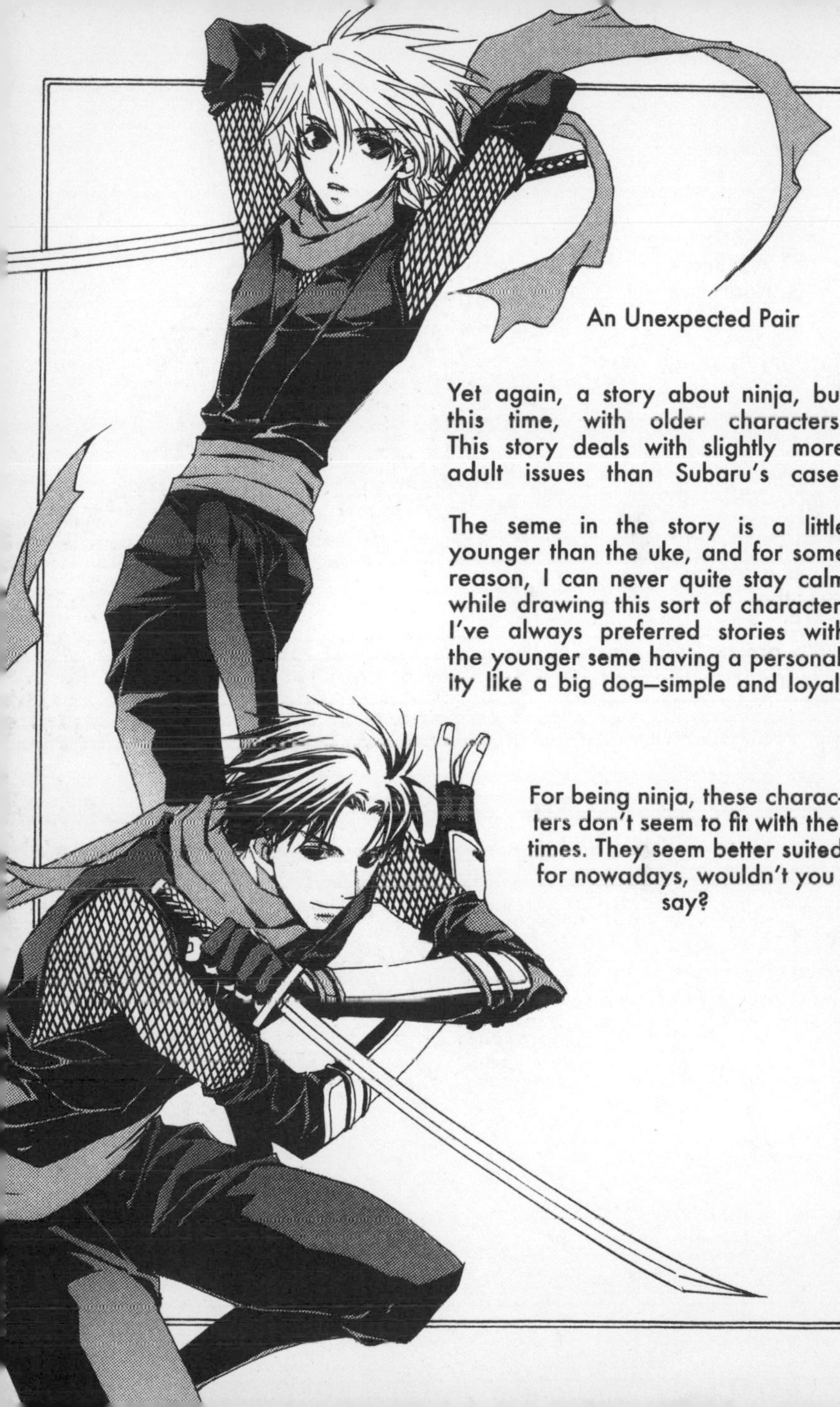

An Unexpected Pair

Yet again, a story about ninja, but this time, with older characters. This story deals with slightly more adult issues than Subaru's case.

The seme in the story is a little younger than the uke, and for some reason, I can never quite stay calm while drawing this sort of character. I've always preferred stories with the younger seme having a personality like a big dog–simple and loyal.

For being ninja, these characters don't seem to fit with the times. They seem better suited for nowadays, wouldn't you say?

■ Snow Storm ■

I just LOVE drawing long-haired sexy guys like Miyuki. It was also fun drawing a little girl for once. The countryside of Nagano can sure be chilly.

I know my works are all lacking and I cannot even raise my head for making so much trouble for my editors...

And here's a full-fledged thank you to all of us who picked up this book and read through it. Well then, until next time!

2004. 松本テマリ

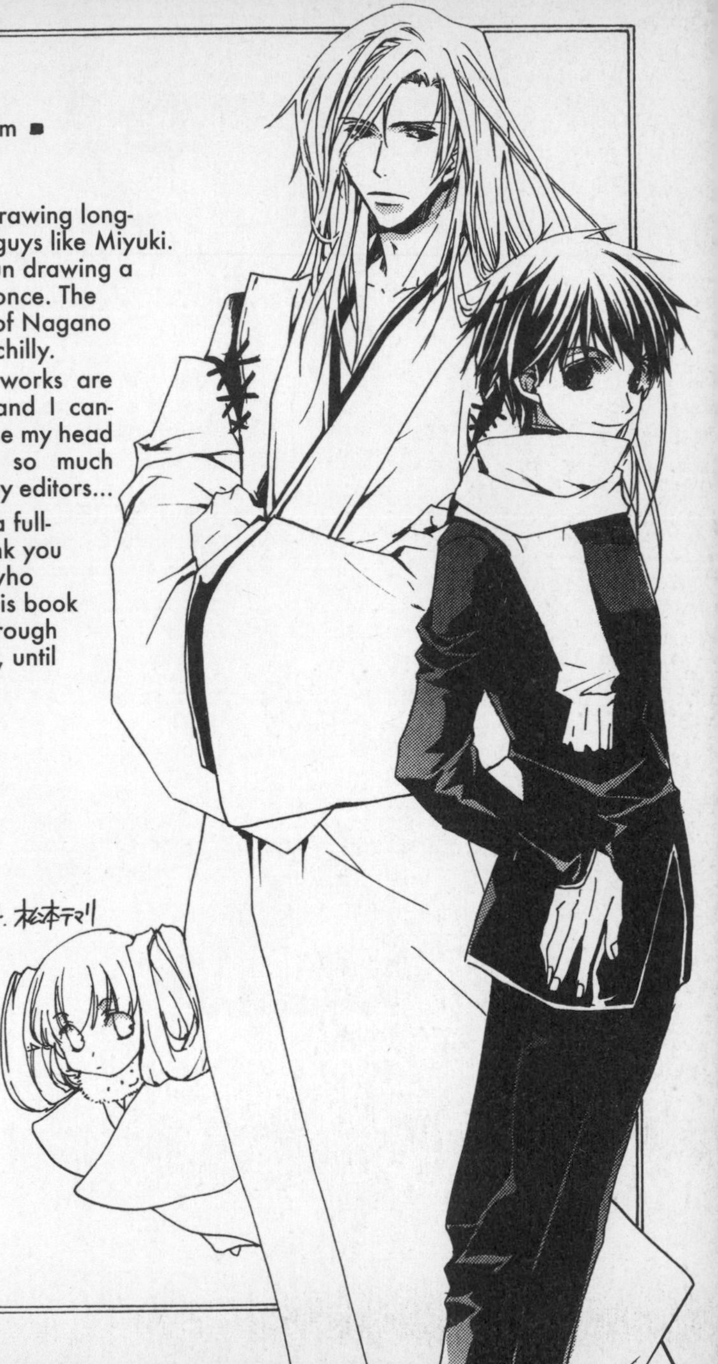

SHINOBU KOKORO: HIDDEN HEART
Created by Temari Matsumoto

ISBN: 1-59816-021-4

First Printing: November 2005
10 9 8 7 6 5 4 3 2 1
Printed in Canada

青BLU

BOYS' LOV

Earthian Vol. 1

Angels walk among us—they are scattered across the globe helping humans in crisis. Chihaya and Kagetsuya travel tirelessly, dealing with an array of characters and their hopeless problems. But when a growing legion of angels is plagued by the Black Cancer, it's up to Chihaya and Kagetsuya to find the fallen Lord Seraphim, who may have the key to the salvation of their celestial kind.

Wild Rock Vol. 1

BLU hits boys' love fans with a hot, one-shot volume from fan-favorite creator Kazusa Takashima. Meet Emba and Yuuen, two very different heirs to warring clans, who meet and fall in love. Two side stories feature the respective clan leaders as tempestuous youth, and introduce Yuuen and Emba's niece, the adorable little Nava.

Shinobu Kokoro: Hidden Heart

Follow the sizzling sessions with a young ninja-in-training as his master teaches him the secrets of the clan with a little hands-on instruction! Meanwhile, two shinobi take their relationship to new heights when a tragic separation leaves one of them caught between a rock and a hard place.

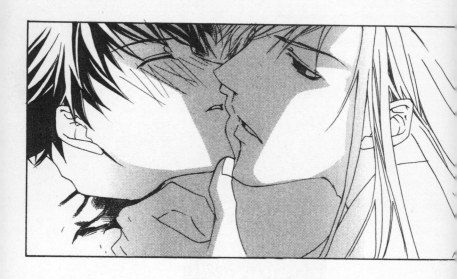

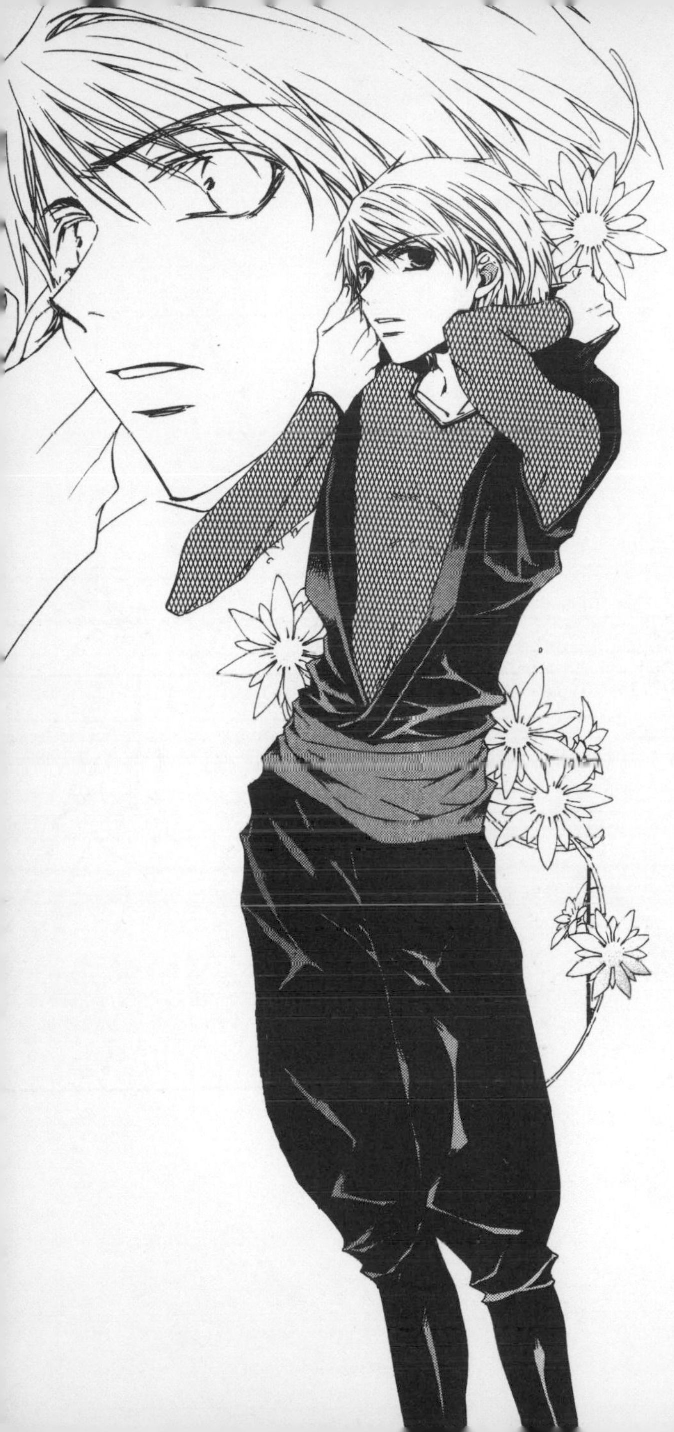

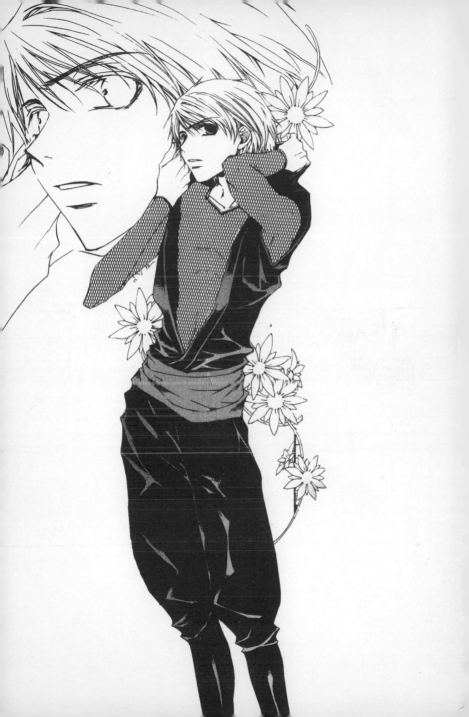

stop

blu manga are published in the original japanese format

go to the other side and begin reading